THE BATTLE

THE BATTLE

A NEW HISTORY OF
WATERLOO

ALESSANDRO BARBERO

Translated from the Italian by John Cullen

Walker & Company
New York

First published in the United States of America in 2005 by
Walker Publishing Company, Inc.; published simultaneously in
Great Britain by Atlantic Books, an imprint of Grove Atlantic Ltd.
Originally published in Italy in 2003 by
Gius. Laterza & Figli as *La battaglia, Storia di Waterloo*.

Distributed to the trade by Holtzbrunck Publishers

For information about permission to reproduce selections from this book,
write to Permissions, Walker & Company, 104 Fifth Avenue,
New York, New York 10011.

Library of Congress Cataloging-in-Publications Data available upon request
ISBN 0-8027-1453-6
ISBN-13 978-0-8027-1453-4

Visit Walker & Company's Web site at www.walkerbooks.com

Printed in the United States of America

10 9 8 7 6 5 4 3 2 1

The history of a battle is not unlike the history of a ball! Some individuals may recollect all the little events of which the great result is the battle won or lost; but no individual can recollect the order in which, or the exact moment at which, they occurred, which makes all the difference as to their value or importance.

— *Wellington*

———✦———

I object to all the propositions to write what is called a history of the battle of Waterloo. . . . But if a true history is written, what will become of the reputation of half of those who have acquired reputation, and who deserve it for their gallantry, but who, if their mistakes and casual misconduct were made public, would NOT be so well thought of?

— *Wellington*

———✦———

Leave the battle of Waterloo as it is.

— *Wellington*

CONTENTS

PART THREE – "A Stand-up Fight Between Two Pugilists"

ILLUSTRATIONS

Marshal Grouchy. Engraving. (*The Art Archive/Musee Carnavelet Paris/Dagli Orti*)

The battle around the farmhouse and stables at La Haye Sainte. Painting by R. Knotel. (*Mary Evans*)

Count d'Erlon holding his marshal's baton. Engraving by Collier after Larivière. (*Collection Viollet*)

"That old rogue," Sir Thomas Picton. (*Mary Evans*)

The charge of the Scots Grays. Painting by Lady Butler. (*Mary Evans*)

Marshal Ney. (*Mary Evans*)

French cuirassiers charging a Highlanders' square. Painting by Félix Philippoteaux, 1874. (*The Art Archive/Victoria & Albert Museum/Eileen Tweedy*)

Colonel von Ompteda. (*National Army Museum*)

Nassauers defending their position at La Belle Alliance. Painting by R. Knotel. (*Mary Evans*)

Blücher orders his men to attack Plancenoit. Painting by Adolf Northern. (*Bridgeman*)

An officer of the mounted chasseurs of the Imperial Guard. Painting by Gericault. (*Mary Evans*)

Napoleon, viewing the attack on his Imperial Guards through a spyglass. Painting by James Atkinson. (*The Art Archive*)

Colonel Hew Halkett captures the French general Cambronne. Painting by R. Knotel. (*Mary Evans*)

Wellington signaling the general British advance on Waterloo. Painting by James Atkinson. (*The Art Archive/The British Museum*)

The Earl of Uxbridge, commander of the Allied cavalry. Painting by Peter Edward Stroehling, *c.* 1816. (*National Army Museum*)

The surgeon's saw used to amputate Lord Uxbridge's leg. (*National Army Museum*)

The famous meeting between Wellington and Blücher, depicted here in front of the inn at La Belle Alliance. (*Mary Evans*)

General von Gneisenau. (*Victoria & Albert Museum*)

Napoleon among his men as he faces defeat. His carriage awaits his flight. Painting by Ernest Crofts. (*Mary Evans*)

Napoleon Bonaparte burning the eagles and standards of his Imperial Guard after the battle. (*The Art Archive*)

A burial party at work near La Belle Alliance, seven days after the battle. Engraving by E. Walsh, drawn on the spot. (*Mary Evans*)

British soldiers removing French cannons, July 1815. (*Collections Viollet/Bibliothéque Nationale*)

Detail of a Ferris & Capitaine map of 1797, as used by
Napoleon and on which Wellington's own map was based.

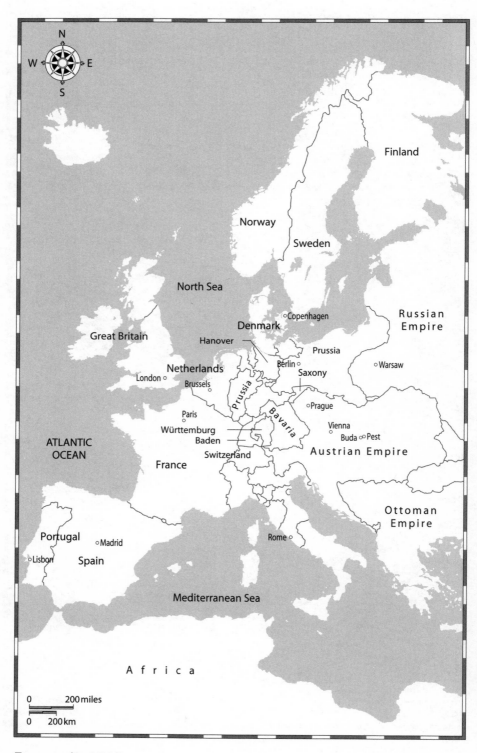

Europe in 1815

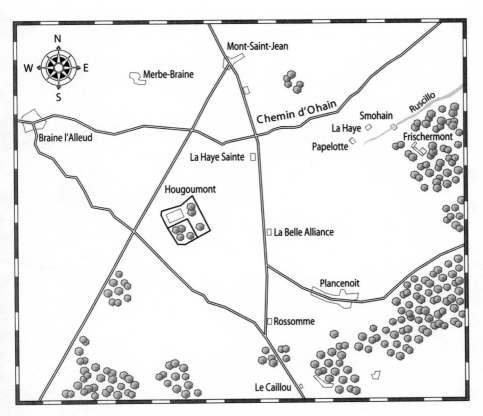

Overview of the Battle Area

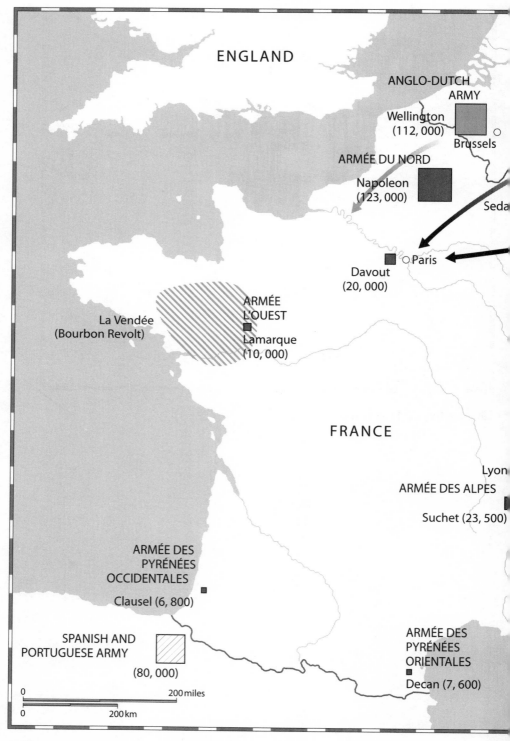

Allied Advances in June/July 1815

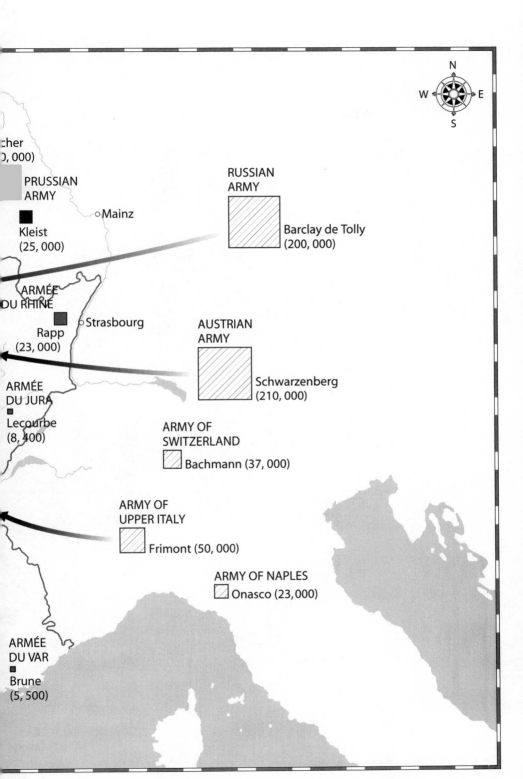

cher
), 000)

PRUSSIAN
ARMY

Kleist
(25, 000)

○Mainz

RUSSIAN
ARMY

Barclay de Tolly
(200, 000)

ARMÉE
DU RHINE

Rapp
(23, 000)

○Strasbourg

AUSTRIAN
ARMY

Schwarzenberg
(210, 000)

ARMÉE
DU JURA

Lecourbe
(8, 400)

ARMY OF
SWITZERLAND

Bachmann (37, 000)

ARMY OF
UPPER ITALY

Frimont (50, 000)

ARMY OF NAPLES

Onasco (23, 000)

ARMÉE
DU VAR

Brune
(5, 500)

N
W   E
S

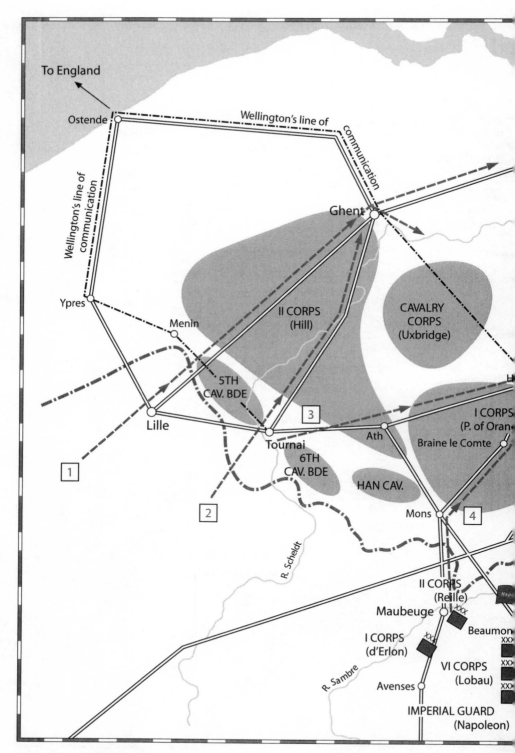

Deployment of French troops

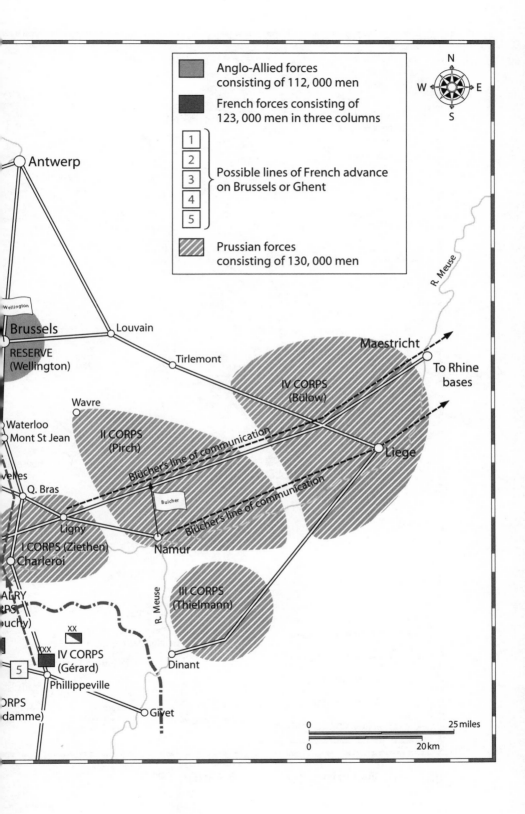

Legend

- **Anglo-Allied forces** consisting of 112, 000 men
- **French forces** consisting of 123, 000 men in three columns
- 1
- 2
- 3
- 4
- 5

  Possible lines of French advance on Brussels or Ghent
- **Prussian forces** consisting of 130, 000 men

N
W E
S

Antwerp

Wellington

Brussels

Louvain

RESERVE (Wellington)

Tirlemont

Wavre

Waterloo

Mont St Jean

II CORPS (Pirch)

IV CORPS (Bülow)

Maestricht

R. Meuse

To Rhine bases

Blücher's line of communication

velles

Q. Bras

Buicher

Ligny

Blücher's line of communication

Liege

I CORPS (Ziethen)

Charleroi

Namur

ALRY
RS
uchy)

R. Meuse

III CORPS (Thielmann)

XX

XXX

5

IV CORPS (Gérard)

Phillippeville

Dinant

ORPS
damme)

Givet

0   25 miles
0   20 km

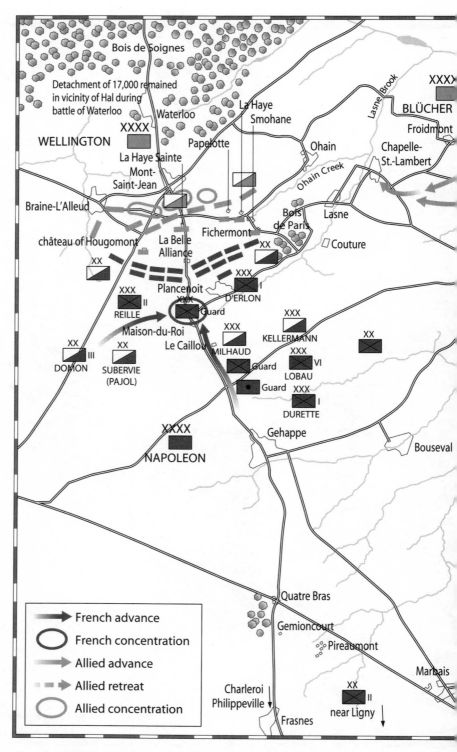

Bois de Soignes

Detachment of 17,000 remained
in vicinity of Hal during
battle of Waterloo

Waterloo

La Haye
Smohane

XXXX
BLÜCHER

Froidmont

XXXX
WELLINGTON

Papelotte

Ohain

Chapelle-
St.-Lambert

La Haye Sainte

Mont-
Saint-Jean

Ohain Creek

Braine-L'Alleud

Bois
de Paris

Lasne

Fichermont

Couture

château of Hougomont

La Belle
Alliance

XX

XX

Plancenoit

XXX
D'ERLON

I

XXX
II
REILLE

XXX
Guard

XXX
KELLERMANN

XX

Maison-du-Roi

Le Caillou

XXX
MILHAUD

XX
III
DOMON

XX
SUBERVIE
(PAJOL)

Guard

XXX
VI
LOBAU

Guard

XXX
I
DURETTE

XXXX
NAPOLEON

Gehappe

Bouseval

Quatre Bras

Gemioncourt

Pireaumont

Marbais

Charleroi
Philippeville

near Ligny

XX
II

Frasnes

| French advance |
| French concentration |
| Allied advance |
| Allied retreat |
| Allied concentration |

Battle of Waterloo, 10.00hrs, 18 June 1815

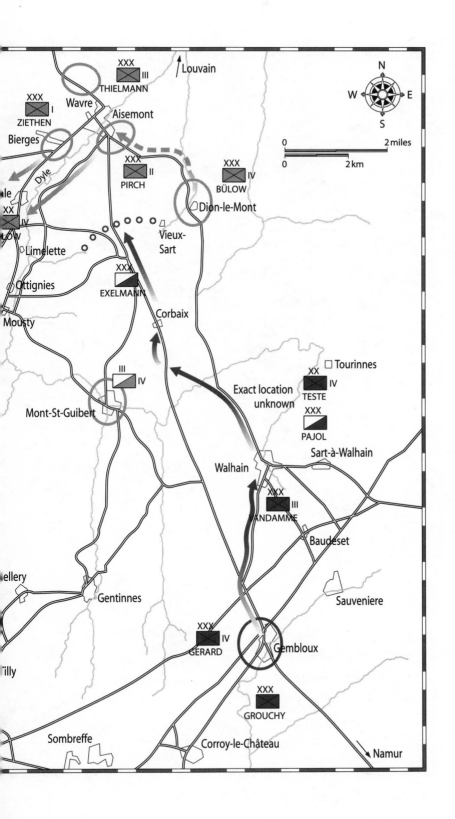

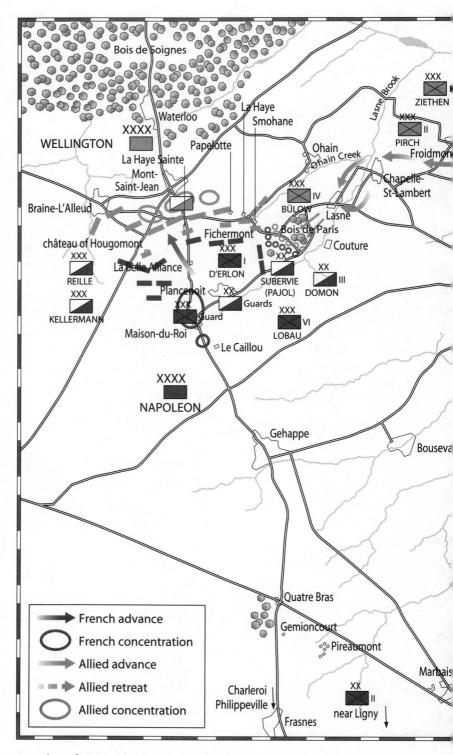

Battle of Waterloo, 16.00hrs, 18 June 1815

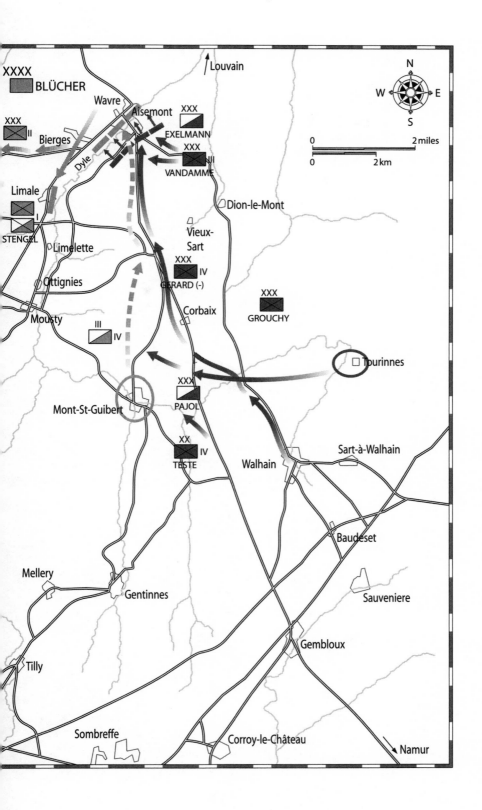

THE BATTLE

PROLOGUE

I n the afternoon of March 1, 1815, a fleet consisting of one warship and six smaller vessels dropped anchor off Golfe-Juan on the southeastern coast of France, in view of what are today the most luxurious vacation spots on the Côte d'Azur but were then miserable fishing villages clinging to the edge of an inhospitable landscape. As soon as they were anchored, the ships lowered their small boats. Shortly thereafter squads of soldiers began to disembark on the shore, despite the protests of the flabbergasted customs official who had rushed to the scene to contest this highly irregular landing. The first troops to reach solid ground went to knock on the gates of the nearby French fort at Antibes and were immediately placed under arrest; but the small boats kept bringing ashore other soldiers, and soon more than a thousand grenadiers had been disembarked, along with two cannon and an entire squadron of lancers who spoke Polish among themselves. Finally, toward evening, the leader of this host came ashore in person, walking over an improvised gangway, which his men, standing in water to their waists, held up for him; and an officer was sent to notify the commandant of the fort that the emperor Napoleon, after ten months of exile on the island of Elba, had returned to France to reclaim his throne.

Even in an age without the benefit of mass media, the news of Napoleon's return was so astonishing that it traveled throughout the continent in a few days, arousing consternation or enthusiasm everywhere. Europe had really believed that the Napoleonic Wars were over, and with them the French Revolution, which together had inflamed the world for twenty-five years. Kings had regained possession of their thrones, armies had been demobilized, and a cosmopolitan, self-satisfied political class was preparing for the tranquil task of managing a long period of peace. The fact that Napoleon was still alive, exiled to an island somewhere in the Mediterranean Sea, was certainly irritating, but people tried hard not to think about it. When the Duke of Wellington announced to the Congress of Vienna—where, since Napoleon's abdication, representatives of the European powers were leisurely redrawing the political map of Europe—that the exile had escaped from Elba and landed in France, the delegates burst into laughter, believing that the announcement was some sort of joke. A few days sufficed to change their minds: On March 13, the Congress published a resolution, couched in the diplomatic French of the period, in which Napoleon was proclaimed an outlaw, subject to "*vindicte publique*," whereupon the English Parliament and half the chancelleries of Europe began discussions to decide whether this formula meant that anyone could kill him with impunity, or whether it would first be necessary to arrest him and put him on trial.

Meanwhile, on March 20, the emperor made a triumphant entry into Paris, while King Louis XVIII and the whole Bourbon family fled hurriedly to Belgium. From there he sent personal letters to all the sovereigns of Europe, assuring them in the most modest tones that he desired only peace and that he renounced all claims whatsoever to any of the territories that previously, at the apogee of his empire, had belonged to France. But the European chancelleries did not deign to respond to these missives; in London, the prime minister would not even permit the prince regent to open the letter and had it returned with its seal intact. One year earlier, four great powers—England, Austria, Russia, and Prussia—had combined to defeat Napoleon; now, on March 25, 1815, the same four countries signed a treaty in which each of them pledged to put an army of 150,000 men into the field as soon as possible, with the set purpose of invading France from all sides. England, then the dominant economic power in the world, agreed to finance the mobilization of the Allies, and the Rothschild bank began gathering quantities of cash, eventually furnishing His Majesty's government with the immense sum of 6 million pounds sterling, which corresponded to the estimated total cost of the undertaking.

In these circumstances, Napoleon's only recourse was to rearm, and he did so with all his extraordinary talent for organization, a talent that the passage of time had not diminished. The army he inherited from the Bourbons was brought back up to full strength, the previous year's conscripts were recalled, the National Guard was mobilized, the mass production of muskets began, and all available horses were either bought or confiscated; as a result, French treasury reserves were consumed in a few weeks' time, and financing had to be extorted from reluctant banks. Even with their help, however, the emperor could not hope to be successful in opposing the four armies that were about to invade France; he had tried to accomplish such a feat a year before, when his resources were decidedly more extensive, and things had not turned out well for him. His only hope was to beat his opponents to the punch.

2

Even though the training period for new conscripts could be reduced, in times of emergency, to a few weeks, the armies of the day still required several months to equip their forces properly and put themselves on a war footing. As spring drew to an end, only two of the four invading armies had assembled on the borders of France. The one commanded by the Duke of Wellington included, along with its British contingent, troops from the Low Countries and from various German principalities; the other army was Prussian, commanded by the elderly field marshal Gebhard Leberecht von Blücher. Considered alone, each of these two armies was weaker than the Armée du Nord, which Napoleon had assigned to defend his northern border. If the emperor could manage to attack them separately, therefore, he had a good chance of defeating them.

A quartered army awaiting the start of military operations occupied a vast amount of territory. Soldiers were lodged with civilians, who were legally obligated to provide the troops with room and board, and it was indispensable to spread out such a great number of men and horses if they were to obtain proper food and shelter. In early June, Wellington's and Blücher's armies were quartered over nearly all of Belgium, one in the northwest and one in the southeast. Calculating that each of these generals would need at least two or three days to concentrate his forces and give battle under optimum conditions, the emperor planned to make a surprise advance between the two armies and destroy the first one he came upon before the other could intervene. Obviously, secrecy was indispensable to the success of Napoleon's plan: In the first days of June, he closed the borders and ordered that not one man, not one carriage, not one letter should exit France. Then, very swiftly, he concentrated the Armée du Nord close to the Belgian border, and at dawn on June 15 the first cavalry patrols crossed over into enemy territory, followed at once by long columns of infantry. Thus began the Waterloo campaign, which survivors from both sides—all equally convinced of having striven in a just cause—would later consider, in the words of an English officer, "a terrible fight fought for a terrible stake: freedom or slavery to Europe."

PART ONE

———⋙◈⋘———

"We'll See Tomorrow"

ONE

———◆•◆•◆———

THE NIGHT BEFORE

The rain had started falling in the early afternoon of June 17, 1815, soaking the Brabant hills and turning them into a sea of mud. Only the cobblestone road, the big main highway that led from the French-Belgian border to Brussels, was still practicable—though with difficulty—and this road was crowded with Napoleon's soldiers, horses, and guns, all in pursuit of Wellington's retreating army. Under normal conditions, the mid-June daylight should have lasted until well past nine o'clock, but on this day, after a series of cloudbursts had displaced the warm morning sunshine, the horizon had grown steadily darker, as though night were falling early. All the soldiers in both armies, right down to the lowliest Dutch or German farm boy recruited into the militia a few weeks earlier and completely ignorant of war, understood that there was no more chance of fighting a battle that day.

Riding on horseback in the torrential rain, Napoleon arrived at an inn and farmhouse called La Belle Alliance, which stood, and stands today, on a panoramic spot near the main road, in the commune of Plancenoit. From there one could see the road descending in dips and rises across a broad area of cultivated fields, which the rain had reduced to bogs, and then climbing toward a long ridge, parallel to the line of the horizon and marked, in those days, by a large, solitary elm tree. There the Brussels road intersected another, smaller road, a lane, sunken in some places and known locally as the chemin d'Ohain, which ran the entire length of the ridge. Past this crossroads, the main road, no longer visible from the farmhouse, descended to another farm and a small cluster of houses, barely a village; both farm and village were called Mont-Saint-Jean. A man on foot needs a good quarter of an hour to cover the distance between La Belle Alliance and the crossroads, which still exists today, though to be sure the surfaces are all paved, and a little group of hotels and restaurants has replaced the elm.

Extending the telescope that one of his aides had hastened to offer him, Napoleon studied the horizon. A dark column of enemy infantry was crossing the shallow valley at a brisk pace and preparing to march up the opposite slope, under the protection of the British cavalry standing in line along the ridge and ready to charge, as it had already done several times during the course of that arduous day, to cover the retreat of these last foot soldiers. The vanguard troops of the French cavalry had ridden into the valley as well, and they were maintaining but little distance between themselves and the enemy's rear guard, wishing to make the retreating soldiers feel the hot breath of their pursuit. The rain came down in torrents, and it was impossible to see anything else in the gloomy gray light. The bulk of Wellington's hastily assembled army—whose English, German, Belgian, and Dutch troops spoke in four different languages— had already disappeared behind the ridge of Mont-Saint-Jean.

The emperor dismounted from his horse and entered the inn. While he was removing his rain-drenched hat and overcoat, he ordered his map to be spread out on a table. This map, which Napoleon always carried in a special compartment of his traveling carriage, together with all the books and documents that might prove useful to him during the course of a campaign, had been drawn by Ferraris for the Austrian government in 1777 and printed in Paris by Capitaine in 1795. On it the emperor could see that the road to Brussels, after it crested the ridge and passed the village of Mont-Saint-Jean, ran past a few more isolated farms and some windmills before coming to another, larger village: Waterloo. Beyond Waterloo stood a vast woodland, the forest of Soignes; the road passed through the village and advanced resolutely into the trees. Continuing to follow the road with his finger on the map, the emperor could easily calculate that an infantry column, marching on the *pavé*—the cobblestones—could traverse the forest in a few hours; and when the troops broke into the open, they would be within sight of the bell towers of Brussels.

For Napoleon, the situation was clear. If Wellington intended to defend Brussels, he would have to turn and give battle before reaching Waterloo, and so his army must have halted behind the long, low ridge that hid the duke's forces from the emperor's telescope. In a time when a general and his officers could rely only on the sight of their persons and the sound of their voices to maneuver an army and maintain its cohesion, one did not give battle in a forest. As for the possibility that the duke and his entire army might take refuge in the city and passively await the course of events, perhaps generals of another generation would have done so; but, after the lessons that Napoleon had taught the world, no commander would be so mad as to place his forces in such a trap voluntarily, particularly when his opponent was the emperor himself. Therefore, if Wellington wished to defend Brussels and spare his ally, the king of the

Netherlands (which at that time included Belgium), the shame of losing one of his two capital cities in the very first days of the war, he would spend the night at Mont-Saint-Jean, and tomorrow he would give battle.

If, on the other hand, the enemy columns were continuing their gloomy retreat through the pouring rain, that would mean the vanguard had already entered the forest of Soignes and the duke had abandoned the defense of Brussels. But this hypothesis, despite its favorable appearance, could have brought no joy to the emperor's heart. Among the same gently rolling hills, somewhere to the east but not too far away, another army was on the march in the rain. The Prussian army, which Napoleon had defeated at Ligny the previous day, was retreating, although Napoleon could not yet know on what roads and in what direction. If Wellington accepted the loss of Brussels and continued to withdraw, he would still be able to join forces with the Prussians; in that case, the capture of the city would cease to have any significance. The purpose of Napoleon's invasion of Belgium and his surprise advance against the two enemy armies massing along the border with France had been to face and defeat them separately; to allow the English to escape and link up with the Prussians would be equivalent to watching the objective of his campaign go up in smoke.

For this reason, the emperor preferred that Wellington should not march his exhausted men any farther into the nocturnal darkness, but rather that he should halt and prepare to accept battle on the Mont-Saint-Jean ridge. Napoleon felt confident of winning that battle, and then the forest of Soignes would be transformed into a fatal trap for the defeated army. It was imperative, therefore, to discover Wellington's purpose; because if his troops were continuing their retreat on the other side of the hill, the emperor's forces would have to push forward at once and pursue the enemy without giving him a chance to breathe. But if the enemy army was preparing to bivouac just beyond the ridge, then the similarly exhausted French units, as they reached La Belle Alliance, could also be ordered into bivouac, there to prepare for battle the next day by cooking their soup and trying to get a few hours' sleep in the rain.

Together with the vanguard of the French cavalry, two batteries of horse artillery—a total of twelve 6-pounder cannon—had arrived at La Belle Alliance. The emperor ordered the gunners to unlimber the guns, get them into position, and open fire on the opposing ridge, where the waiting enemy cavalry could still be glimpsed through a veil of rain. At that distance, and in the steady downpour, the guns could do little damage, but if the English riders were simply carrying out a covering operation, they would abandon their positions and join the retreat, the infantry being safe. Before much time had passed, however, the enemy artillery opened fire in response, and not with just a few pieces, but with a large number of batteries dispersed along the whole length of the ridge. The columns of French infantry that were approaching La Belle Alliance on the main road found themselves under fire and suffered some casualties before their officers could succeed in withdrawing them to a more secure position, and some cannonballs struck the inn of La Belle Alliance. After a little while, Napoleon judged that he had learned enough and ordered the artillery to stop firing. Wellington had decided to accept battle with his back to the forest, and in Napoleon's view his army was doomed.

As long as a little light remained in the gathering dusk, the emperor continued to peer through his telescope, examining the terrain that would become a battlefield. The ridge of Mont-Saint-Jean was the principal defensive position, and doubtless the enemy army would await his attack under cover of that rising ground, which would shelter the Allied troops from artillery bombardment. According to the emperor's generals, whom Wellington had defeated one after another during the long, ferocious war in Spain, this had always been the duke's favorite tactic. Furthermore, there were a few positions ahead of the ridge that could impede the French offensive, and Napoleon had no doubt that his enemy would fortify them. In the center of the battlefield, right beside the Brussels road, stood the farmhouse of La Haye Sainte, a stone building surrounded by stout walls and half hidden in a fold of the earth. Before the French could break through the center of the enemy position, they would have to take La Haye Sainte. Away on the left, the emperor's telescope revealed a thickly planted wood. His eye could see only trees, but the map indicated that they concealed a complex of buildings: the château of Hougoumont. Should he decide to turn the enemy's right flank, Napoleon knew he would have to take possession of that wood, which extended toward him from the château. Hougoumont and its grounds lay at the bottom of the shallow valley, halfway between the two ridges of La Belle Alliance and Mont-Saint-Jean. Finally, at the opposite end of the terrain, far on the emperor's right, barely visible in the midst of sparse clumps of trees, were some small communities, indicated on the map with the names of Papelotte, La Haye, and Smouhen (or Smohain, as it is written today), which if defended would protect Wellington's left flank.

While Napoleon was surveying the position, his corps commanders reported to him and received instructions for the bivouac of their troops: on the ridge of La Belle Alliance, or farther to the rear, or—in the case of those units that were still too far from the front—along the road. Aside from the bivouac orders, the emperor gave his generals no further commands. Before mounting his horse to ride to the farm of Le Caillou, a few kilometers to the rear, where his numerous imperial staff were already preparing his dinner and his camp bed, Napoleon spoke to d'Erlon, the commander of the I Corps: "We'll see tomorrow," he said. And in truth, the emperor knew too little about the enemy positions on the other side of the ridge to be able to determine in advance what would happen. Besides, he himself had repeatedly declared that battles could not be blocked out and directed as though they were plays in a theater; one had to know how to improvise: "*On s'engage, et puis on voit.*" Provided that the enemy remained where he was, there would be plenty of time to force him to reveal his positions, and only then would the emperor see where to deliver the decisive attack.

Napoleon dined alone, in a room in the farmhouse of Le Caillou. In an adjoining room, another table had been set for his aides-de-camp and several high-ranking officers, among them Colonel Combes-Brassard, the VI Corps chief of staff. In the course of the officers' dinner, one of them spoke in a loud voice about the battle awaiting them on the morrow, and the emperor heard him. Napoleon burst into the room and took a few paces with his hands behind his back; then, without turning around, addressing no one in particular, he exclaimed: "A battle! Gentlemen! Are you sure you know what a battle is? Between a battle won and a battle lost, there are empires, kingdoms, the world— or nothing." Saying no more, he returned to his chamber. A few days after the battle, Colonel Combes-Brassard wrote that in that moment he had seemed to hear the sentence of Fate.

TWO

"WHO WILL ATTACK THE FIRST TOMORROW?"

The Duke of Wellington never had any intention of abandoning Brussels without a fight. Two days previously, when he received the appalling news that Napoleon had invaded Belgium—catching the duke, whose spies had given him no warning, by surprise—Wellington had sought to concentrate his army between Brussels and the Belgian-French border so that he might intercept the enemy advance as soon as possible. Meanwhile, farther to the east, the duke's Prussian colleague, Field Marshal Blücher, began gathering his forces. On June 16, all this activity had resulted in two simultaneous battles, one at Quatre Bras and the other at Ligny. At Quatre Bras, Wellington had barely managed to halt the advancing French columns led by Napoleon's second-in-command, Marshal Ney, while not far away at Ligny, the emperor, commanding the bulk of his army, had defeated the Prussians. The following morning, perceiving that the Prussian rout had made his position at Quatre Bras indefensible, Wellington had ordered his troops to retreat. "Old Blücher has had a damned good licking and gone back to Wavre, eighteen miles. As he has gone back, we must go too." Nevertheless, the duke was determined to try his luck again and fight Napoleon on this side of Brussels. If he abandoned the capital of Belgium without a fight, he realized, the bloody encounter at Quatre Bras would look like a defeat, and the English press would eat him alive. Wellington was a prudent general, but he was also an ambitious politician with an image to maintain, and his only choice was to face another battle.

Given the situation, there was but one place where he could do so: in front of the village of Waterloo, the last inhabited spot before the great forest. An episode that supposedly took place in the Duke of Richmond's house in Brussels on the evening of June 15 has passed into legend. Having first expressed his irritation at the way things were going ("Napoleon has *humbugged* me, by God!"), Wellington is said to have pointed at two spots on the map spread out before him: Quatre Bras ("but we shall not stop him there") and Waterloo ("and if so, I must fight him *here*"). In reality, no superhuman clairvoyance was required for this perception; along all the nearly thirty-five kilometers of road that stretched between Quatre Bras and Brussels, the series of parallel ridges and shallow valleys south of Waterloo presented the most suitable terrain for a defensive battle. On an inspection tour the previous year, Wellington had observed the position, surveying it with the eye of a professional accustomed to evaluating the lay of the land wherever he found himself and filing away a mental note that might prove useful in the future.

Recently, moreover, after it had become clear that Napoleon was preparing to strike, the duke had returned to Waterloo and asserted to more than one officer that, should he ever find himself compelled to defend Brussels, this was the place where he intended to make his stand. At dawn on June 15, very shortly after the Allied troops had been put on alert, word was already circulating among the British officers that the army was going to have to march to a place called Waterloo, a name that meant nothing to most of them. That morning, the commander of the Allied horse artillery, Sir Augustus Frazer, after a conversation with his superior officer, Sir George Wood, sat down and wrote a letter to his wife: "I have just learned that the Duke moves in half an hour. Wood thinks to Waterloo, which we cannot find on the map: this is the old story over again." The following day, as the retreat from Quatre Bras was getting under way, Wellington sent his quartermaster general, Colonel De Lancey, back to Waterloo, with orders to reconnoiter the ground and identify precisely the position that the Allied army would defend. Sir William De Lancey first considered the ridge of La Belle Alliance, but he decided that there the defensive line would be too long, and in the end he opted for the next ridge, on Mont-Saint-Jean.

In that late afternoon of June 17, therefore, the Duke of Wellington did not order his troops on to Brussels; they marched up the slope of Mont-Saint-Jean and down the other side, disappearing from the enemy's sight, and as the units reached him, the duke sent them into bivouac, one after another, along the entire length of the ridge, where they would be in position to receive the French attack the next day. A small road ran along the ridge, crossing as it did so the main road to Brussels. This secondary road, the chemin d'Ohain, was actually a deeply sunken lane, bordered for most of its length by willow trees and thorny bushes. The Allied troops took up their positions beyond the lane; the artillerymen ranged their guns in batteries and prepared to bivouac under the ammunition wagons, while the exhausted infantry soldiers, who were without even so poor a shelter as this, lay down in the fields to sleep as they could. Only the innumerable carts loaded with severely wounded troops from the Quatre Bras battle and their escort—the throng of those less seriously hurt and still able to plod along on their own two feet—continued the dismal march on the cobblestones, bound for the hospitals of Brussels.

When the French appeared in force on the high ground of La Belle Alliance and their artillery began firing, the Allied gunners up and down Wellington's line, acting either on orders from the nearest generals or on the initiative of the battery commanders themselves, returned to their weapons and set up an answering fire. "We opened our fire upon the French Infantry who had followed us up rather too close, and [were] disposed to continue," one of the officers remembered. "The range we had was La Belle Alliance, or just where the road widens into a quarry or open space." The Duke of Wellington, who had given no such order, was distinctly irritated by the indiscriminate bombardment, which revealed his positions to the enemy, and he took steps to silence the guns. Some time passed, however, before the cease-fire order could reach the farthest batteries.

Captain Cavalié Mercer, commander of a troop of horse artillery, was enthusiastically participating in the cannonade when a civilian appeared in the midst of his guns and started chatting with him. The stranger wore a threadbare greatcoat and a round hat that had seen better days. Convinced that the man was an English tourist who had come from Brussels to see the battle, Mercer spoke to him rather brusquely, and only after his visitor finally went away was the captain told that he was Sir Thomas Picton, one of the most famous generals in the British army, respected for his courage and feared for his irascible temperament. (To the men who had known him in Spain, he was simply "that old rogue Picton.") Meanwhile, the darkness gathered, and the guns started falling silent all along the line. One of Mercer's officers waved his hand in the direction of the French and shouted, "*Bonsoir, à demain!*"

In the village of Waterloo, the officers in charge requisitioned the peasants' houses, scribbling in chalk on the doors the names of the generals who would spend the night there. Before retiring, the Earl of Uxbridge, commander of the Allied cavalry, decided to inquire into the duke's plans for the following day. Lord Uxbridge, one of the many officers at Waterloo who had never fought under Wellington's command, had been forced on him by the minister of war, a state of affairs that elicited from the duke a variety of nasty comments. The presence of Uxbridge was all the more disagreeable to Wellington in that six years previously the earl, who was one of the prince regent's favorites and a companion of his revels, had run off with Lady Charlotte Wellesley, the duke's brother's wife and the mother of four children. Although he himself had a wife and eight children, Uxbridge had eventually married Lady Charlotte, after a year and a half of hesitation and gossip, a double divorce, a duel, and the birth of an illegitimate daughter. The Victorian Age was still to come, and the Duke of Wellington was certainly not a man to be scandalized by so small a matter; nevertheless, it seems he was less than overjoyed to find Uxbridge again in his path, this time in Belgium. The earl's appointment was equally unpopular with his officers. Shakespear, of the Tenth Hussars, spent the eve of the battle reflecting on the errors His Lordship had committed up to that point and on those he would very probably commit the next day; according to Tomkinson, of the Sixteenth Light Dragoons, Uxbridge was "too young a soldier to be much relied on with a separate command." Apparently, the earl's brash style—he continued to wear the uniform of his old regiment, the Seventh Hussars—did a pretty effective job of hiding his forty-seven years.

Lord Uxbridge made his way to the Waterloo inn, where the door bore the chalked legend "His Grace the Duke of Wellington," went inside, and asked the duke to tell him his plans for the next day. His Grace responded with a question of his own: "Who will attack the first tomorrow—I or Buonaparte?"

"Buonaparte," the general replied.

"Well," said the duke, "Buonaparte has not given me any idea of his projects; and as my plans will depend upon his, how can you expect me to tell you what mine are?"

At this point, however, Wellington realized he was going too far and tried to smooth things over. "There is one thing certain, Uxbridge, that is, that whatever happens, you and I will do our duty."

THREE

"THE DECISIVE MOMENT OF THE CENTURY"

Like Napoleon and Wellington, Prince Blücher, the commander of the Prussian army, had ridden on horseback through downpours the entire day, with the difference that he was not forty-six years old, as were both his colleagues in arms, but seventy-two. The night before, at the end of the battle of Ligny, the old man had nearly been killed while commanding a cavalry charge and had escaped capture only by a miracle: An aide had covered him with his coat while French cuirassiers galloped past them a short distance away. But on June 17, after having his contusions massaged with a mixture of garlic and schnapps and fortifying his stomach with a magnum of champagne, Blücher was back in the saddle. When he met the English liaison officer, Sir Henry Hardinge, the prince felt obliged to excuse himself. "*Ich stinke etwas*," he said—"I stink a bit"—though it seems likely Sir Henry's thoughts were elsewhere, given that his arm, shattered by a cannonball, had just been amputated. The old man remained in the saddle until nightfall, riding through the rain in the midst of his soldiers as they retreated northward toward the road junction at Wavre.

In the chaos following the battle of Ligny, the small town of Wavre had been chosen as a rendezvous point for all the retreating Prussian troops, chiefly because it was readily identifiable on maps. Early on June 17, when Baron von Müffling, the Prussian liaison officer at Wellington's headquarters, found Wavre on the map, he was shocked to see how far to the rear it was. "*Ma foi, c'est fort loin!*" he said.[1] Only then did Wellington, who until that moment had been convinced that Blücher would hold out at Ligny, perceive the necessity of abandoning his lines at Quatre Bras and withdrawing equally far to the north, in order to avoid being flanked.

But the map also showed that Blücher's troops, once arrived in Wavre, could easily interrupt their northward retreat, turn west, and march toward Waterloo.

By deciding to retire on Wavre, instead of heading farther east to Namur or Liège, the Prussian generals had kept open the possibility of remaining in contact with their ally; rarely has a strategic decision, made in a few minutes by candlelight, under a driving rain, and in the midst of the chaos that attends a disintegrating army, proved more unerring. It was, Wellington later remarked, "the decisive moment of the century."[2]

After having decided to retreat from Quatre Bras early on June 16, the duke sent a letter to Blücher, informing him that he would give battle at Mont-Saint-Jean the next day, provided that the field marshal would send at least one army corps to his aid. That evening, in the midst of their troops' immense bivouac in the fields around Wavre, the Prussian generals discussed at length what course of action they should take. The decisive voice in this council was that of the chief of staff, General von Gneisenau; for although Blücher was the commander in chief, a national hero, and a military leader capable of exercising an extraordinary moral ascendancy over his soldiers, Gneisenau, for all practical purposes, planned the army's movements. As Müffling maliciously observed, "In Europe it was no secret that old Prince Blücher, having passed his seventieth birthday, understood absolutely nothing about conducting a war; indeed, when his staff submitted a plan to him, he was incapable of forming a clear idea of it or of judging whether it was good or bad. This state of affairs made it necessary to place at his side someone in whom he would have absolute faith, someone who possessed inclinations and abilities that would be employed in the general interest." However, this system of dual command—which imperial Germany would reinstate a century later with another famous pair, Hindenburg and Ludendorff—wasn't simply a matter of coupling a politician and a military technician; in this particular case, the "technician," Gneisenau, had his own ideas, which didn't always coincide with those of his superior officer.

For example, Gneisenau had little faith in Wellington, with whom he had quarreled during the preparations for the campaign. When Gneisenau sent Müffling to the English, he recommended that the baron "remain very much on guard" in his dealings with the duke, "because his relations with India, and his experience in negotiating with the shrewd nabobs, have so accustomed this distinguished general to deceit that he has become a master of the art, surpassing in duplicity the nabobs themselves." During the catastrophic night that followed the Prussian defeat at Ligny, Gneisenau had bitterly recalled the promises made by Wellington in the course of the previous days and repeated on the very morning of the battle, when the duke had again guaranteed that his army would come to the Prussians' aid. Today we know that Wellington was himself under severe pressure from the French at Quatre Bras and unable to fulfill his promise, but in those anxious hours, Gneisenau could not know these facts, nor did he wish to know them; and so he remained convinced that his ally could not be trusted.

Understandably, therefore, the idea of exposing his army to great risk by rushing to assist Wellington displeased Gneisenau greatly, and all the more so because on the night of June 17 the Prussian command was still without news of a large part of its munitions train, with which contact had been lost during the retreat. But Blücher was determined to adhere to the terms of the Allies' treaty, and in the end he succeeded in winning over his reluctant chief of staff. At eleven o'clock that night, Blücher gave the good news to Sir Henry Hardinge ("Gneisenau has given in. We are to march to join Wellington") and immediately dictated a letter to Wellington, in which he guaranteed that General von Bülow's IV Corps—the only one of the four corps in the Prussian army that had not yet been in combat, and therefore the freshest—would begin marching toward Waterloo at dawn, while the II Corps, commanded by General von Pirch, would be ready to follow it. On paper, these two corps were nearly equivalent to Wellington's entire army; their arrival would dramatically shift the balance of power against Napoleon.

FOUR

———◆◇◆———

THE NATURE OF THE ARMIES

In general, the quality of the troops that were about to confront one another between La Belle Alliance and Mont-Saint-Jean was relatively homogeneous. By 1815, Europe had been at war for more than twenty years, and this practical experience had raised the professional competence of all European armies to the highest level, so that basically they all resembled one another. The tactical differences between the most advanced armies, as the French army was in 1815, and the most conservative, the British, were much smaller than they had been at the beginning of the French Revolutionary Wars. French troops were still capable of marching more rapidly and performing maneuvers more smoothly than any other, but the discrepancies were no longer great enough to decide the outcome of a battle.

Nevertheless, there were still some identifiable differences in quality between the armies in the field that had little to do with national character. Such an assertion would have surprised the combatants' contemporaries, who put great faith in clichés about the racial qualities of various peoples; indeed, many generalizations of this kind were considered to have indisputable scientific value. In fact, however, the comportment of troops on the battlefield at Waterloo was substantially the same whatever their nationality. Even in Wellington's composite, heterogeneous army, the gap between British troops and "foreign" troops—a gap that British officers and soldiers, with their ingrained chauvinism, considered unbridgeable—did not prove significant under fire. Only 35 percent of the duke's soldiers were in British units; the Dutch-Belgian army contributed 26 percent, Hanover 16 percent, and Brunswick 9 percent, while another 9 percent belonged to the so-called King's German Legion, and a contingent from the duchy of Nassau made up 5 percent. So heterogeneous an army certainly had its disadvantages from an organizational point of view, but on a tactical level, contrary to what some historians have maintained, the fighting quality of battalions and squadrons in Wellington's army was substantially the same irrespective of their nationality.

On the other hand, there were important differences in the methods used to recruit the troops, and the decisions made in this area were essentially political. The armies of 1815 found themselves in the middle of the transition from professional or "mercenary" recruitment to the compulsory military service that was to characterize the national armies of the future. Revolutionary France had been the first to adopt the principle of universal conscription, according to which all young men of draft age were subject to being called up; in fact, however, a system of drawing names was in place, and as a result, only a minority of those eligible were enrolled every year. Generally speaking, under the empire one hundred thousand conscripts were called up annually, which meant that about one name in seven was drawn. The last conscripts to join their units en masse were those of 1814, whose call-up had been advanced to the preceding year. The majority of the army that Napoleon rebuilt after returning from Elba, therefore, was composed of soldiers who had at least one campaign behind them, although in the eyes of veterans of Egypt or Austerlitz, the recruits of 1814 (nicknamed the "Marie Louises" from the name of Napoleon's empress) still seemed like little boys.

Apart from France, the only nation that practiced conscription was Prussia, where the national reawakening that sparked the 1813–14 wars of liberation had allowed the government to institute the revolutionary policy of universal, compulsory military service. Since the available human resources were less abundant than in France, every year one Prussian conscript out of five was called to serve. But precisely because conscription had been adopted so recently, Prussian subjects who were more than twenty years old had never performed any compulsory service, and the king could not allow himself to disregard such a resource. Therefore, alongside the regular army, Prussia had organized a territorial militia, the *Landwehr*, composed of civilians chosen by lot from each province. These troops were required to undergo periodic training under the command of officers on loan from the regular army or recalled from retirement to serve in this capacity.

By contrast, the different national contingents that made up Wellington's heterogeneous army reflected governments which, for political reasons, could not permit themselves to adopt universal conscription. In the armies of England, the Netherlands, Hanover, Brunswick, and Nassau, the infantry units were manned by paid soldiers who signed up to serve for several years or, more frequently, for life. They were enrolled by recruiting officers who scoured the country for volunteers, luring them with offers of cash premiums. The British army's recruitment pool encompassed the British Isles, so the vast majority of volunteers were subjects of the king, and the army retained a distinctly national connotation. By contrast, the kings of the Netherlands and Hanover and the minor German princes, who had barely regained possession of their territories after the long hiatus of French occupation, had all formed their armies by enlisting professional soldiers, many of them recently discharged from the French army or from that of the Napoleonic Kingdom of Westphalia, without much concern for the nationality of those who signed up.

Thus all these sovereigns spared their subjects the burden of compulsory military service. Even in these countries, however, the thirst for manpower provoked by the Napoleonic Wars was so great that the regular army had to be backed up with a territorial militia, formed from the civilians that every province was obligated to provide in proportion to the number of its inhabitants. In general, the drawing of lots for the militias was carried out according to criteria designed to reduce its social impact and to avoid any confusion with the hated policy of conscription. In the Kingdom of the Netherlands, for example, the militia was recruited on the basis of one man for every hundred inhabitants, with broad exemptions for only sons and orphans with sisters to support, in order to render the measure more politically tolerable. By this means, it was possible to make use of the human potential available in the country without arousing the kind of opposition that would have greeted universal conscription. In Wellington's army, therefore, the Dutch-Belgian, Hanoverian, and Nassauer contingents consisted in part of regular army regiments and in part of militia regiments; only the British contingent was entirely composed of regular soldiers, because in Great Britain constitutional guarantees blocked the use of the militia outside the kingdom.

The difference between troops of the line and militia presented, in terms of effectiveness, the greatest discrepancy on the battlefield at Waterloo. Cobbled together and improperly trained, militia units, even though commanded by both professional and noncommissioned officers, inevitably possessed a level of preparation and moral cohesion inferior to that of regular troops. This discrepancy was perhaps less marked among the Prussians, owing to the strong national spirit that animated a large part of their *Landwehr*, but it was particularly evident in the other continental armies; and it was one of the reasons why the Duke of Wellington, assessing the army that had been placed under his orders, had judged it "an infamous army, very weak and ill equipped." The quality of his troops explains why Wellington had been obliged to establish and defend his line, while Napoleon, with the more professional army, had pursued him defiantly the day before and would attack him relentlessly on the eighteenth.

FIVE

THE BRITISH ARMY:
"THE SCUM OF THE EARTH"

The fact that the British army was composed entirely of professional military men carries none of the elite implications that the expression may suggest to the modern reader. The soldierly profession, badly paid and subject to the harshest discipline, was not greatly appreciated in the United Kingdom—was, in fact, a decidedly proletarian vocation. It was no accident that a high percentage of those who enlisted were Irish, since Ireland, overpopulated as it was with a deeply impoverished peasantry, had always been the major provider of cannon fodder to His Majesty's armies; except for a few Scots regiments whose recruiting had been notably regional, Irish soldiers generally made up between 20 percent and 40 percent of the infantry battalions that Wellington marshaled at Waterloo.

Furthermore, in the course of the Napoleonic Wars, the British army, desperately short of men, had been obliged to avail itself of the reservoir of recruits constituted by the militia: Men chosen by lot in local drawings to join the territorial regiments were strongly pressured to sign up for the regular army after completing their training; hence, in many regiments at Waterloo, more than half of the men had enlisted after some experience in the militia. These recruits likely produced a statistical rise in the average level of education and social class among the troops, which by then included some decently educated, lower-middle-class young men whose ineluctable fate it was to become noncommissioned officers; to such men we owe the relatively few letters or diaries written by enlisted men, as opposed to officers, in Wellington's army.

The vast majority of soldiers still came from the ranks of the otherwise unemployed, men who had not found another way to earn a living. The few available statistics show that around half of the troops had been farm laborers and

22

the rest textile workers or apprentice tradesmen. In such a class-conscious society as England's, the proletarian origins of the troops opened a chasm between them and their officers; one day the Duke of Wellington, a man devoid of democratic feelings and little given to mincing his words, said that the English army was recruited from among "the scum of the earth."

His enemies shared this uncharitable judgment. Years later, when French veterans recalled the Angluches, they were still surprised by the rigid class lines that divided the men from their officers. According to the French, English soldiers obeyed blindly; if they commited a fault, they were punished with the whip; and when off duty, they got fabulously, unconscionably drunk. The noncommissioned officers were excellent; "they never rise higher in rank; the concept of class is so ingrained in them that they take this to be the natural order of things." As for the officers, "they are, for the most part, quite courageous, but fairly ignorant of their trade, for the English education is not directed toward the profession of arms; moreover, all their manners are those of aristocrats: haughty and disagreeable." The impression that the British and their army made on the French was a reflection of undeniable social realities. As one of Napoleon's veterans remembered, "The officers were all upper-class, all nobles or gentlemen, and the soldiers, who were all from the working class, obeyed them without question."

A more modern attitude, the notion that troops should be treated more humanely, was just beginning to manifest itself in English society; but Great Britain was still the country where a person could be sentenced to death for any one of more than sixty different crimes, and where women or half-grown children were hanged every day for the theft of a piece of fruit. Unsurprisingly in such a society, army officers, particularly those of the old school, maintained a rigid, pitiless discipline. Even for minor infractions, a soldier could be condemned to hundreds of lashes, which grew to one or two thousand in the most serious cases. Lashes were administered with a cat-o'-nine-tails until the victim fainted. In the weeks that preceded Waterloo, several sentences of this type were carried out in public, to the disgust of the Belgian citizenry and the dismay of the local authorities, who appeared before the British high command and requested them to put a stop to these barbaric displays.

Not all officers, however, were members of the aristocracy. Among the lower-ranking officers in the British regiments, many were the sons of clerks or shopkeepers, members of the hardworking urban middle class that was creating England's wealth. Still, such officers were unlikely to receive much advancement; lacking the money to buy a higher rank, they grew old as lieutenants or captains. Indeed, the customary way to obtain promotion in the army was to purchase a "commission," which was both a rank and an appointment to a command. There was a comparable practice in all the old monarchies, where all public offices were for sale to the highest bidder. In every respect, the acquisition of a rank was an investment; if an officer grew tired of military life, he could always sell his commission. The War Ministry limited itself to ratifying the transaction and to making sure that no one skipped one or more grades, for an officer on his way up in the army was required to occupy all the ranks, one after the other. The rich were still able to advance quickly, buying a commission to the next-higher rank as soon as one was offered in any regiment whatsoever. Before he became the Duke of Wellington, Arthur Wellesley had been an ensign at the age of eighteen and a lieutenant colonel at twenty-four; in six years, he had received five promotions, all of them in return for payment, and he had passed through seven different regiments, without having served a single day in battle.

Nonetheless, promotion based on merit was not totally unknown in His Majesty's army, and there were several astonishing cases of men who started at the bottom and came up through the ranks. Sir John Elley, a colonel in the Royal Horse Guards, wounded at Waterloo while serving on Wellington's staff, was a porter's son who had enlisted in the army as a simple soldier. The criterion the ministry followed was to grant promotions on merit only in order to replace officers fallen in battle, since in such cases the positions came open of themselves and there was no need to reimburse anyone. Accordingly, one can understand why the officers of Sir John Lambert's brigade, sailing from America to England in spring 1815, exulted when they learned that Napoleon had escaped from Elba. Major Harry Smith, the brigade adjutant, upon hearing the great news from a merchantman encountered in the English Channel, threw his hat into the air: "Such a hurrah as I set up, tossing my hat over my head! 'I will be a Lieutenant-Colonel yet before the year's out!'" Troops of the Fortieth Regiment on board another ship learned the news from an English frigate, and "the young officers, who were looking ravenously forward to promotion, were so rejoiced at the news that they treated all the men to an extra glass of grog, to make everybody as lively as themselves."[3]

By 1815 the British army had been fighting without interruption for many years, and the battles of the Peninsular War had exacted an enormous toll in blood; it seems legitimate, therefore, to assume that the percentage of officers who had been promoted on merit was much higher at Waterloo than it had been a few years before or would be a few years later. All in all, Wellington's army was more middle-class and more meritocratic than one might suppose, yet this alone did not make it more professional. Wellington complained that nobody in the British army ever read a regulation or an order except as one might read an amusing novel, and the conduct of many British officers at Waterloo corroborated his observation. The worth of a good officer was determined by the physical courage with which he led his men, and by nothing else. His bravery was the result of the rigid sense of honor that all gentlemen shared.

The process by which officers were assigned to command a brigade, division, or corps was quite deliberate. Such assignments could not be purchased; rather, they were temporary appointments, granted for the duration of a campaign. In this matter—the selection of the army's highest commanders—the government proceeded with great care, as befitted one of the old monarchies. The average age of the corps and division commanders in the British army at Waterloo was forty-four and a half. An exception was the Prince of Orange, the son of the king of the Netherlands, to whom the command of a corps had been entrusted—for obvious political reasons—even though he was only twenty-three years old, in conformity with another custom that was widespread in the old monarchies.

On the whole, the harsh judgments on the British army pronounced by the Duke of Wellington and the French veterans had nothing to do with its military efficiency. However proletarian and semiliterate he may have been, the English soldier, well nourished with meat and beer, stimulated with gin, and convinced of his own racial superiority to the foreign rabble he had to face, was a magnificent combatant, as anyone who has ever seen hooligans in action at a soccer match can readily imagine. This analogy is not disrespectful, given that Wellington himself admitted the frequency and the enormity of the crimes committed by his soldiers against the civilian population, adding that he could not explain it except with the fact that many soldiers in the army, lured by the temptation of a few guineas to finance their binges, had left their families to starve.

On this subject, the French general Foy, basing his remarks on his experiences in Spain, wrote that "the English soldier is stupid and intemperate," but that this was an advantage: "An iron discipline exploits some of these faults and blunts the others." All in all, Foy wrote, the British army's "main strength lies in the fact that its masses of ignorant men allow themselves to be led blindly by men who are more enlightened than they are." The Duke of Wellington would certainly have agreed with Foy's judgment. The full version of the duke's scathing comment about his troops reveals that he was actually pronouncing a kind of ambiguous tribute to the British soldier: "Our friends—I may say it in this room—are the very scum of the earth. People talk of their enlisting from their fine military feelings—all stuff—no such thing. Some of our men enlist from having got bastard children—some for minor offences—many more for drink; but you can hardly conceive such a set brought together, and it really is wonderful that we should have made them the fine fellows they are."

SIX

THE FRENCH ARMY:
"ALL MUST MARCH"

The French army, recruited on the basis of compulsory military service, presented a different aspect. Even though entering the draft lottery was theoretically required of all male citizens, multifarious exemptions, favors, and bribes—together with every man's perfectly legal right to buy a replacement if he could afford one—guaranteed that the burden of conscription fell principally upon the rural working class. Nevertheless, the army considered itself, and wished to be considered, as representative of the entire society, in a way that would have been inconceivable to the English. Wellington himself remarked on this significant difference between the composition of a French army and that of a British one: "The conscription calls out a share of every class—no matter whether your son or my son—all must march."

In 1815 the army's upper echelons were composed of officers in the regiments the Bourbon monarchy had maintained on active duty (though with reduced personnel) during the brief period of the First Restoration; these were joined by a certain number of officers, noncommissioned officers, and ordinary soldiers who had been discharged in 1814 but responded to Napoleon's appeal by returning to arms under his banners. The egalitarian ideas of the French Revolution had remained alive in the army; perfectly compatible with the cult of the emperor, they were particularly reflected in the officers, most of whom were former enlisted men or noncommissioned officers who had been promoted on merit: some three-quarters of the officers who served under Napoleon had come up through the ranks. In comparison, the equivalent percentage in the British army fluctuated between 5 and 10 percent.

26

At the highest levels, Napoleon's army also included a large number of career officers, who had served under the *ancien régime* and whose families belonged to the old aristocracy. But the emperor made no distinctions between them and those of equal military rank who had started at the bottom and who, in former times, would probably have been the lackeys or attendants of the wellborn officers. Count d'Erlon, the commander of the I Corps, had been an ordinary soldier under the monarchy; at the outbreak of the revolution, he was promoted to the rank of corporal. Among his four division commanders, Marcognet, the son of a true count, came from the rural nobility of the Vendée and was already an officer when the revolution began, and Durutte, likewise an officer before the revolution, had even been condemned to death as a monarchist during the Reign of Terror. But the third commander, Donzelot, had begun his career as an ordinary soldier of the king and received a promotion to officer during Robespierre's time, and the fourth, Quiot, had enlisted as a sixteen-year-old volunteer in 1791, at the height of the revolution.

Napoleon's officer corps at Waterloo encompassed all social classes and was formed in great part by men of humble origin, but it was no longer as young as it used to be. Especially in the highest ranks, the average age was little different from that in much more conservative armies, among them the British. The twenty-six corps and division commanders who fought at Waterloo had an average age of forty-four and a half, exactly the same as their British counterparts, and as in the Anglo-Allied army, the youngest French commander was a prince of the blood, Jérome Bonaparte, the emperor's brother, who had been given command of a division even though he was only thirty-one years old. Considered this way, the imperial army seems to bear more of a resemblance to the armies of the old monarchies than to the revolutionary army that engendered it. One veteran, Captain Blaze, addressed this subject: "After every battle, a swarm of officers sent from Paris descended on our regiments to secure the best vacant posts for themselves. The new nobility was just as greedy as the old; all nobilities are the same. Had the Empire lasted ten more years, the fact that a plebeian had reached the rank of colonel would have been cited as something remarkable."

Students of the battle have advanced contradictory opinions concerning the overall quality of the troops Napoleon led at Waterloo. According to some, this army, all of whose soldiers were French, was the best outfit the emperor had commanded in many years. Moreover, since the conscripts of 1815 had not been able to join their units in time, every one of Napoleon's men must have been a veteran of at least one campaign; yet several eyewitnesses stated that many regiments included a high percentage of young soldiers who had never been under fire. In what is probably the most convincing judgment in this matter, the nineteenth-century French historian Henry Houssaye, after analyzing an enormous mass of documents and eyewitness accounts, drew the following conclusion: "Volatile, always ready to argue, undisciplined, suspicious of its leaders, undermined by fear and betrayal and therefore perhaps susceptible to panic, but also battle-tested, war-loving, thirsty for revenge, capable of heroic efforts and furious élan, and more spirited, more passionate, more fanatical than any other French army, whether Republican or Imperial: such was the army of 1815. Napoleon had never held in his hand an instrument of war so fearful, nor one so fragile."

Contemporary opinions are mostly negative, but the fact that they were written under the shock of the catastrophe undermines their accuracy. One commentator, Captain Duthilt, observed that too many regiments had been formed by throwing together men who had fought many battles, but on different fronts, so that they didn't know one another and couldn't have complete faith in their officers. Furthermore, he thought, the soldiers who had suffered the defeats of the emperor's recent years and then served under the Bourbon monarchy—and to a greater extent the returned prisoners of war from England or Russia—had lost a great deal of their enthusiasm. Desales, the I Corps artillery commander, wrote of his men: "I had a rather considerable force; with the exception of the officers, none was very educated or very combat-hardened. There was a prodigious gap between them and our old soldiers from the Camp de Boulogne." But all these writers found that French soldiers were more than sufficiently combat-hardened when they engaged the enemy. As an English officer replied when asked whether he had faced the Old Guard at Waterloo, "We regret, exceedingly, that we are not informed as to the name or quality of our opponents. They might have been the Old Guard—Young Guard—or no Guard at all; but certain it is, that there they were, looking fierce enough, and ugly enough to be anything."

SEVEN

———•◆•———

THE PRUSSIAN ARMY

The army of the Kingdom of Prussia, considered the first in Europe under Frederick the Great (1712–86), had been destroyed by Napoleon in 1806. Subsequently, during the course of the Napoleonic Wars, it had undergone a drastic reorganization. In the 1813–14 wars of liberation, when Prussia shook off the yoke of French domination and reversed the alliance Napoleon had forced upon it, the new army, although smaller than its predecessor, had performed at a fairly high level of effectiveness. Prussia not only adopted but also modernized the French system of compulsory military service, introducing the practice by which conscripts who had finished their military service remained on the rolls; in case of war, these veterans were called up again and formed into reserve regiments. Although less efficient than line units, such regiments, led by professional officers and noncommissioned officers, were on the whole equally reliable. The German and Polish peasants who made up the bulk of the Prussian army's recruits, although suddenly transformed from subjects to citizens in the flurry of reforms that attended the wars of liberation, continued to be excellent soldiers, just as they had been in former days.

The officers who commanded them were still drawn exclusively from the landowning aristocracy and preserved a strong link with Frederick the Great's old army. At Waterloo, almost all the Prussian officers from the rank of captain up had begun their military service before 1806, yet the average age of the corps and division commanders in Blücher's army—forty-five—was the same as in Napoleon's and Wellington's—one more confirmation of the parity that characterized the armies of the period. Here, too, the only general officer who was truly young was a royal scion, Prince Wilhelm of Prussia, the king's eighteen-year-old son, who commanded the cavalry of the IV Corps; he would live long enough to become emperor of the new German empire in 1871.

On the eve of Waterloo, the Prussian army was afflicted by what we may call a crisis of growth. The Congress of Vienna in 1814 had elevated the Kingdom of Prussia to the rank of a great European power, thus considerably expanding its borders and the recruitment pool at the service of its military. The human resources in the new territories, however, were thought to be less reliable than those in the old provinces of the kingdom. At the same time, the Prussian government had decided to incorporate into the regular army the reserve regiments, the various volunteer contingents (*Freikorps*) established during the wars of liberation, and several German units that had passed from Napoleon's service to Prussia's. This multitude of formations, with their differing levels of efficiency and their widely divergent uniforms, were transformed on paper into Prussian line regiments, but their reorganization had barely begun when Napoleon's return compelled Prussia to concentrate its army in Belgium.

Of the thirty-one infantry regiments that then constituted the army of Prussia, fully twenty-five were under Blücher's orders in June 1815. But of those twenty-five, only seven were traditional regiments that had already existed prior to 1815, with stable troop strength and regular uniforms. Another ten were reserve regiments, recently renumbered as regiments of line infantry but still heterogeneously dressed: Some wore old uniforms donated by England, while others had French uniforms seized in earlier wars. Two regiments, formerly comprising the infantry of the Grand Duchy of Berg, had been incorporated just as they were, with their white uniforms cut in the French style. Another two regiments came from the Russo-German Legion, which the Russians had assembled in 1812 from prisoners of war representing a wide variety of nationalities; they still wore their old dark-green Russian uniforms. Finally, there were three regiments that had been formed by combining *Freikorps* veterans, the remaining troops from the Napoleonic Kingdom of Westphalia, and replacements recruited in Prussia's newly acquired Rhineland provinces.

While most of these troops behaved properly on the battlefield, they were not comparable to the old Prussian regiments in terms of cohesiveness, level of training, and patriotism. The number of soldiers already trained and discharged proved insufficient to reach the new, ambitious troop levels, so that even the line regiments had to incorporate a certain number of inadequately prepared troops into their ranks. As Peter Hofschröer, the most recent historian of Prussian and German participation in the Battle of Waterloo, wrote, "The armed forces fielded by the Kingdom of Prussia in 1815 were, in terms of quality of manpower, equipment and coherence of organisation, probably the worst Prussia employed in the entire Revolutionary and Napoleonic Wars."

As for the Prussian militia, the *Landwehr*, which in 1815 furnished a grand total of eighteen infantry regiments and seventeen cavalry regiments to the army in Belgium, it fielded many veterans of the wars of liberation and was better on the battlefield than the militias of other countries. Comparing militia cavalries is harder, since other countries judiciously avoided organizing them as cavalry troops needed much more intensive training before they could be profitably used in battle. But for the Prussian generals, and perhaps especially for the Prussian politicians, quantity counted much more than quality in the late spring of 1815.

EIGHT

THE MINOR ARMIES

The minor armies on the Allied side—those of the Dutch-Belgian kingdom of the Netherlands, the electorate of Hanover, and the two duchies of Brunswick and Nassau—provided nearly two thirds of the troops under Wellington's command and shared one characteristic: They had all been constituted—or reconstituted—very recently. Belgium and Holland, annexed to France by Napoleon, had regained their independence only in 1814; later that year, the Congress of Vienna amalgamated them into a single kingdom. Its new army could count on a fairly extensive recruitment pool, because the Low Countries had furnished Napoleon with the obligatory annual conscript levies, and a great many Dutch and Belgian officers had made their careers in the armies of the revolution and the empire. By absorbing these veterans, the army of the Netherlands secured for itself a cadre of excellent officers; however, they had fought under Napoleon's orders for too long not to arouse some suspicions about their current loyalties. Indeed, fears of this sort are understandable when one considers such biographies as that of Jean-Baptiste van Merlen, who commanded an Allied cavalry brigade at Waterloo: At the age of fifteen, he volunteered to join the Belgian revolutionaries in their struggle against Austrian domination; after fleeing to France, he enlisted in the French army, becoming a second lieutenant at nineteen; he was a veteran of the Peninsular War in Spain, where he gained distinction—fighting against the British, no less—as a cavalry commander; and in 1812 he was promoted to general and named a baron of the empire. Like many other Belgian and Dutch officers at Waterloo, Major General van Merlen found himself going into battle for the first time against the army in which he had served all his life.

The armies of Hanover and Brunswick had been reconstituted in 1813, after the two principalities regained their independence from France. Each consisted of recruits commanded by professional soldiers who had fought under the British in Spain and by officers and noncommissioned officers from the former Napoleonic Kingdom of Westphalia, which had been dissolved in 1813. At the time of Napoleon's return from Elba, Hanover was still in the process of organizing a *Landwehr* militia alongside its regular troops; three months later, the task had been rushed to completion. The troops fielded by both the Hanoverians and the Brunswickers in 1815 were rather young and short on experience. The Brunswickers in particular, despite their menacing black uniforms and the death's heads that adorned their shakos, struck the English officers as excessively young. ("They were all perfect children," Captain Cavalié Mercer observed.) The average age of the company commanders in the army of Brunswick was twenty-eight, and their battalion commanders averaged thirty, both very youthful by the standards of the age. Moreover, because of grave losses suffered at Quatre Bras, several Brunswick battalions were commanded by captains, and one of the brigades by a major, on the day of the battle.

The mercenary King's German Legion (KGL) was quite different, however. In 1803, after the French invaded Hanover, many soldiers and officers of the Hanoverian army fled to England, where King George caused them to be formed into a unit and maintained in his personal service. In the course of the following years, the KGL had fought under Wellington in Spain and attained such a high degree of professionalism that it was considered equal in every way to the best British units. Yet the effort to assimilate the KGL into His Majesty's army had not been completely successful: Its troops wore English uniforms and were trained, at least in part, according to the British manual of arms, but orders continued to be given in German. Assimilation was more advanced at the officers' level: In 1815 many junior officers were English, while some German officers originally attached to the KGL held command positions in the British army. Karl von Alten ("Sir Charles Alten" to the English), for example, commanded a division at Waterloo.

The experience of the Nassau troops was similar to that of the KGL, but it had been gained on the other side. For years, Napoleon had maintained two infantry regiments recruited from this Rhineland duchy. Incorporated into the French army of Spain, the Nassauers acquitted themselves well. In December 1813, after Wellington invaded southern France, one of these regiments—the Second Nassau, commanded by Colonel von Kruse—deserted to the British; a year and a half later, it was still part of the Allied army in Belgium. The French disarmed and interned the other regiment, the First Nassau, in Spain, but in the course of 1814, the men of this regiment returned home. Kruse had reconstituted the regiment around a nucleus of these veterans, recruiting army volunteers as well as a militia battalion. A third regiment, called the Orange-Nassau, had been recruited by the Prince of Orange, whose principality bordered the duchy of Nassau. Like the

Second Nassau, this unit was also built around officers who had served Napoleon in Spain.

All told, these regiments accounted for more than seven thousand men—more than a tenth of Wellington's army—but they by no means constituted a discrete, coherent entity. For example, after the Congress of Vienna gave the Prince of Orange-Nassau the new Kingdom of the Netherlands, the Orange-Nassau Regiment was incorporated into the Netherlands army and wore its uniform. The Second Nassau, though continuing to wear the green uniform of the duchy, also entered into the service of the Netherlands. Therefore these two regiments were united into a single brigade (officially part of the army of the Netherlands, even though the brigade's troops were actually German) and placed under the command of Prince Bernhard of Saxe-Weimar. By contrast, the First Nassau, which was mostly composed of barely trained recruits, had joined the army only a few days before the beginning of the campaign and constituted an independent force under the command of Kruse, who in the meantime had been promoted to general. Thus the organizational complexity of Wellington's army precisely reflected the heterogeneity of the political coalition from which it had sprung.

NINE

———◆•◆———

"AS BAD A NIGHT AS I EVER WITNESSED"

Like all his comrades, Sergeant William Wheeler, of the Fifty-first Light Infantry, was soaked through, "as wet as if we had been plunged over head in a river." His regiment had camped for the night in a rye field on the extreme right of the Allied line, behind the château of Hougoumont, in a no-man's-land where there was always the possibility that an enemy patrol might suddenly appear out of the darkness. The officers, therefore, had forbidden their men to light fires and wrap themselves up in blankets, and so the soldiers remained seated on their knapsacks under the cold rain all night long, smoking incessantly in an attempt to keep warm and stay awake. Wheeler later wrote to his family, "You often blamed me for smoking when I was at home last year but I must tell you if I had not had a good stock of tobacco this night I must have given up the Ghost."

Other factors helped the men of the Fifty-first make it through the night. The previous evening, a man from the nearest village had come to their bivouac, selling bread, cheese, and the local juniper brandy. As it happened, during the march one of the soldiers in Wheeler's squad had picked up a moneybag dropped by a Belgian light cavalryman and had seen fit not to return it. Well aware that such opportunities were not infrequent in wartime, Wheeler's veterans had already agreed to share whatever booty should come their way, and so that night they were able to buy themselves a variety of comforts. Despite this abundance, however, the incessant rain eventually put all of them in a bad humor. Those who had fought in Spain remembered that many great battles had been preceded by storms and thunder and lightning, and all such struggles had been victories; but not even this provided much consolation to men soaked with rainwater and shivering from cold. The only real satisfaction was the knowledge that the enemy was suffering the same misery.

Wheeler and his men had already been drinking and smoking for a while when Sergeant Mauduit of Napoleon's Imperial Guard, also drenched and exhausted, finally arrived at his bivouac. The Guard's march that day had been turbulent and undisciplined. The men had broken into houses, looking for food, and had stopped and plundered supply wagons, laughing in the faces of the outnumbered gendarmes assigned to maintain order along the road: General Radet, commander of the military police, was so disturbed by this behavior that he tendered his resignation that very evening. When night fell, the troops were still on the march and far from the villages where they were supposed to be billeted. In the darkness and the driving rain, some units lost their commanders and no longer knew what direction to march in. The road was so muddy that many men tried to take shortcuts through the fields, only to get lost and wander all night long in search of their units. The veterans of the Guard cursed their commanders, accusing them of not knowing what they were doing; more than one soldier, suspecting the top brass of sympathizing with the Bourbon monarchy, muttered "Treason!" At midnight, Sergeant Mauduit's regiment arrived at a farmyard and received the welcome order to stop there for the night after a heavy day of marching. The men's trousers and overcoats were encrusted with mud. Many had even lost their shoes and were marching barefoot.

In the fields behind the château of Hougoumont, Captain Cavalié Mercer was trying to sleep in the field tent he shared with the four other officers in his battery. When he realized that closing his eyes was impossible because the rainwater was dripping through the saturated tent, he and his lieutenant left their comrades and found a hedge that offered a little more shelter. Mercer's companion had an umbrella with him, brought from his home. This piece of equipment had caused him to be the object of merciless ragging, but now it turned out that he'd been right after all; sheltered by the umbrella, the two managed to make a fire and sat down to smoke a tranquil cigar. After a while a German soldier, a straggler or a deserter, passed by and lit his pipe at their fire. The two officers persuaded him to let them have a hen that he'd stolen from some barnyard and immediately put their prize in a cooking pot. Quite soon, however, the other officers exited the tent and claimed their portions, and the meal, shared among so many, turned out to be distinctly frugal.

Captain Duthilt, an aide-de-camp to one of the brigade commanders in Count d'Erlon's corps, watched the troops making camp for the night along the main road, on the heights above the village of Plancenoit. Men and horses were entirely covered with black, oily sludge, which the captain thought could be explained by the nearby coal mines and the fact that the road was used to transport the mineral. Bread was distributed, and in the village—which had been abandoned by its inhabitants—the men cooked their rice as best they could; but there wasn't enough to go around, and as for wine and brandy, the soldiers had to do without them. The day before, in fact, I Corps's supply train had been seized by a sudden panic; many drivers had fled, and many wagons had been plundered. In the midst of a surreal landscape of burst baggage and opened trunks, Captain Duthilt had found his valise, ripped open with a knife and completely empty; he had lost his gear, his papers, and the little money he possessed, and his general and the other aide found themselves in the same situation.

Captain Cotter of the Sixty-ninth Regiment, camped on the ridge behind La Haye Sainte, had given up trying to sleep. The night was too cold—a steady, frigid wind whipped the ridge—and the rain had so flooded the marshy ground that one sank ankle-deep in mud with every step; it seemed to Cotter that lying down in such a bog was out of the question. In his efforts to keep warm, the captain walked back and forth all night, examining the sky for the first signs of dawn, which with all its uncertainties would at least put an end to this particular torture. Inevitably, there came into his mind (and into the minds of who knows how many other British officers that night) the famous scene in Shakespeare's *Henry V* in which the two encamped armies, the night before the Battle of Agincourt, await the morning light; Captain Cotter found himself repeating, more and more nervously, the dauphin's words: "Will it never be day?"

The Second Light Battalion of the King's German Legion, stationed around La Haye Sainte farm, had a somewhat easier time of it than their comrades who were camped out in the open. The rifleman Friedrich Lindau, nonetheless, was mightily displeased with his company's assignment to the orchard, where there was nary a dry spot to be found: "It kept on raining, the orchard was full of mud, and no one was comfortable. Some leaned against a tree or part of the wall, while others sat on their knapsacks; lying down was impossible." Having heard that there was wine in the farmhouse cellar, he went down to see for himself and found a half-full bottle. He filled his canteen with its contents and went out in search of his two brothers, who were serving in other units. As soon as he reappeared, however, his comrades surrounded him and drank all his wine, and Lindau, though he descended into the cellar and refilled his canteen several times, never succeeded in his plan to share a little drink with his brothers. In compensation, all his comrades drank their fill in his company, and the wine helped them bear the night in the muddy orchard.

Not far away, the men of the Seventh Hussars were on their feet next to their horses and passing "as bad a night as I ever witnessed," as Sergeant Cotton later recalled. "We cloaked, throwing a part over the saddle, holding by the stirrup leather, to steady us if sleepy; to lie down with water running in streams under us, was not desirable, and to lie amongst the horses not altogether safe." Finally, one of the Hussars—a comrade of Cotton's, Robert Fisher, a tailor by trade—

proposed that they go in search of something they could lie on. Sergeant Cotton went off and returned a little later with a bundle of leaves and stalks obtained from Mont-Saint-Jean farm. The Hussars strewed the cuttings on the ground and lay down on their improvised bed. "The poor tailor," Cotton reported, "had his thread of life snapped short on the following day."

Major Trefcon, chief of staff in a division of the French II Corps, spent a large part of the night sheltered from the rain in an abandoned barn while working with his commander, General Bachelu. The two men received reports from their colonels and brigade commanders, calculated the number of available troops, and took all the measures necessary for going into battle the following day. Then they ate something, divided a bale of straw, and flung themselves down to sleep. During the night, one of the division's two brigadiers, unable to find other lodgings, sought shelter in the barn, and Trefcon had to share his straw with the newcomer. "The soldiers were no less exhausted than we were," the major observed. "They lay down wherever they could. Most of them simply went to sleep in the mud." The difference between recruits and veterans showed in their ability to arrange for a modicum of comfort, even in those exceptional conditions. Almost all the troops in bivouac that night, of whatever nationality, had a blanket to wrap themselves in (although the Scots of the Forty-second Regiment, the Black Watch, had secretly sold the blankets distributed to them after they disembarked in Flanders), but only a resourceful few, veterans who knew all the tricks, smeared their blankets with mud and slept as though covered by some impermeable fabric.

TEN

ON THE BRUSSELS ROAD

The men who had the most trouble sleeping were those in the regiments camped near the main road, because the *pavé* was crowded with traffic all night long. Corporal Dickson of the Scots Grays was kept awake by an incessant rumbling that reminded him of the sound of wind in a chimney; it was the French army wagons, arriving continuously at La Belle Alliance. The traffic was still heavier on the Allied side, because the military convoy had to make its way through a throng of wounded soldiers and fleeing civilians. The Fortieth Regiment had taken shelter from the rain in the stables, barns, and piggeries in the surroundings of Waterloo; but according to Sergeant Lawrence, a veteran who at twenty-four had already seen six years of war in Spain and North America, "All that night was one continued clamour, for thousands of camp-followers were on their retreat to Brussels, fearful of sticking to the army after the Quatre Bras affair. It was indeed a sight, for owing to the rain and continued traffic the roads were almost impassable, and the people were sometimes completely stuck in the mud; and besides these a continual stream of baggage-wagons was kept up through the night."

Sergeant Costello, of the Ninety-fifth Rifles, had suffered a shattered right hand at Quatre Bras, but the cries of the seriously wounded men who were being transported to Brussels in wagons prevented him from sleeping even more than his own suffering did. Searching for a familiar face, a number of people, mostly women, crowded around each vehicle as it passed with its load of wounded. Costello, with his arm in a sling, thought he heard an outburst of Homeric laughter, approached the wagon it seemed to have come from, and asked the men inside to tell their tale. One of them—whom Costello recognized—explained that he had seen a woman he knew well, the wife of a comrade, as she was drawing near the wagon, and had mimicked her husband's voice so well that she mistook him in the darkness. Believing he was her husband, she handed him a bottle of liquor and kept walking anxiously alongside the wagon, trying to get a good look at his face. Finally, the man gave the empty bottle back to her, accompanying it with a wish that her husband might not be wounded at all. The woman's disappointment and anger had been greeted with loud laughter by all the soldiers present, and Costello did not fail to join in their merriment, complimenting his friend on his spirit of initiative.

Soldiers at Waterloo were not infrequently accompanied by their wives, and just about everything imaginable was part of an army's train. When Major Harry Smith landed in Belgium, he was accompanied by his Spanish wife, Juana, a brother who was with him as an army volunteer, two servants, one chambermaid, six horses, and two mules. A certain number of rank-and-file soldiers also had permission to bring with them, and to maintain at the army's expense, their wives and children, who otherwise would have ended up on the street. When the Forty-second—the Black Watch—embarked in Ireland for the voyage to Ostend, every company was allowed to bring along four women, each of whom was entitled to half rations. Having arrived in Flanders, the regiment had to board barges to continue the voyage on the canal, and orders came down limiting each company to only two women. Without much ceremony, the others were returned weeping to a barracks, but they all managed to escape and quickly rejoined their husbands. If the proportions were the same in every regiment, many thousands of women must have followed Wellington's army to Belgium, and many more joined them after the troops disembarked. Jack Parsons, a grenadier in the Seventy-third Regiment, collected a Flemish girl and brought her with him all the way to Waterloo; at dawn on the day of battle, waking from a bad dream and afflicted by dire premonitions, he asked his captain to help him make a will in which he left the girl his back pay, all that he possessed in the world.

In the first days of the campaign, women and children had stayed close to their respective husbands and fathers, sometimes running the same risks as they did. During the retreat from Quatre Bras, some riflemen from the Ninety-fifth found a woman lying dead with a musket ball in her head and a living child in her arms; they gathered up the little boy and carried him along until they found his father and turned his son over to him. But the night before the Battle of Waterloo, the duke ordered all noncombatants sent back behind the lines so as not to interfere with the army's operations. Not everyone obeyed. Elizabeth Watkins, a five-year-old child, claimed to have remained on the field, together with her mother, throughout the battle, helping her tear cloth into strips for bandages; she was still alive, and she still remembered, in 1903. Most of the women and children, however—like most of the other civilians, servants, workmen, and peddlers—thronged the high road in the darkness, headed for the relative safety of Brussels.

In order to be rid of anything that might encumber his army's mobility the following day, Wellington also ordered that all baggage, whether conveyed in wagon trains for the regimental rank and file or privately transported for officers, was to be sent back to Brussels and from there directed to Antwerp. This multitude of vehicles and beasts of burden joined the crowd of refugees who were already packing the road, fleeing from the imminent devastation of what had been, until a few days ago, a tranquil stretch of countryside. Terrified by the soldiers' destructiveness, all the country people in the region had left their homes and hastened into the forest of Soignes, with their pitiful household goods piled on carts and whatever animals had escaped requisitioning. Numerous wagons loaded with bread, victuals, and rum for the troops tried to make their way to the front against the tide of refugees but had to be abandoned in the middle of the road; the horses pulling these wagons had been requisitioned by Wellington's officials from the local peasantry, and in the general confusion the owners of the beasts had managed to reclaim them and run off into the forest. This seems to have been the coup de grâce as far as the road was concerned. Soon it was transformed into an immense jam, a mass in which it was almost impossible to move. That night, the men of Sir John Lambert's brigade, on the march from Brussels to Waterloo, had to clear a path for themselves by roughly dumping abandoned or stuck vehicles into the nearest ditches, thus preserving from total strangulation the only line of retreat available to Wellington's army.

ELEVEN

————•◦•————

LETTERS IN THE NIGHT

T he fear that the enemy might resume his march and slip away in the night prevented Napoleon from sleeping. The emperor's servants had prepared a camp bed for him in one of the rooms in the farmhouse of Le Caillou, and a fire was burning in the chimney. Shortly after dinner, the emperor lay down to rest, but before one o'clock he was awake again. Unable to fall back asleep, he went out, accompanied by a single aide-de-camp, reached the bivouac area on foot, and walked along his entire line, examining the horizon. In the intervals between one downpour and the next, the soldiers of both armies had managed to light fires, and thousands of glimmering beacons distinctly marked out their positions in the darkness. Sometime later, Napoleon seemed to recall the scene: "The forest of Soignes looked as though it were in flames; the horizon was aglow with the fires of the bivouacs. The most profound silence reigned." About two-thirty in the morning, when he reached the woods around Hougoumont, the emperor heard the sounds of a column on the march and grew worried; should the enemy withdraw, Napoleon had decided, he would awaken his troops immediately and take up the pursuit in the darkness. But the sounds faded away almost immediately, and the rain started up again, harder than ever.

At least, that was the story the emperor told in his memoirs. Unfortunately, there is no trace of this thrilling nocturnal reconnaissance in the accounts left by his servants, all of whom agree that the emperor did indeed sleep very little, because the traffic along the road was quite noisy and officers were continually arriving at Le Caillou to give reports or request instructions, but nonetheless he remained in the house until morning. Marchand, his valet, saw him walking around undressed, absently trimming his fingernails with a pair of scissors and looking out the window at the rain that continued to thrash the countryside. Around three in the morning, the emperor actually did decide that a reconnaissance was necessary, but he sent one of his orderly officers, General Gourgaud, and he was under the covers again when the general returned to report that the roads were in terrible condition and the ground impracticable because of the rain, so there would be no hurrying to get an early start.

At three in the morning, in his room in the Waterloo inn, the Duke of Wellington was awake, too. He had gotten out of bed a little while before, ordered candles brought to his table, and begun writing many letters. Their tone proves that the duke was well aware of the risks he was running by accepting battle at Waterloo, and that he hadn't yet received the reassuring note in which Blücher promised to join him in force the next day. Wellington wrote a long letter in French to the Duc de Berry, brother of King Louis XVIII, who was still in exile in Ghent. The duke advised his correspondent that the French court would do well to go to Antwerp and take refuge in the citadel; that way, should the Allied army be forced to evacuate Belgium, the royal party would be able to board an English ship. Wellington wrote to the governor of Antwerp, ordering him to prepare his fortress for a state of siege and to deny access to everyone but the Bourbons and civilians fleeing from the enemy. He wrote to Sir Charles Stuart, the British ambassador in Brussels, recommending that he see to the maintenance of calm among the numerous English who were in the city: "Let them all prepare to move, but neither in a hurry nor a fright, as all will yet turn out well." Finally, the duke wrote a note to Lady Frances Webster, a young woman in whose intimate company he had spent time during the preceding weeks in Brussels.

Exactly how far their intimacy went has remained a matter of debate ever since. Lady Frances was a charming twenty-two-year-old, married to an officer in the Hussars who publicly betrayed her, and she had quickly learned to avenge herself for her husband's infidelities; on the other hand, she was in the eighth month of a pregnancy, a fact that the duke's biographers have found sufficient to clear him of all suspicion. However, their Victorian zeal seems excessive when one considers that the preceding year, in Paris, Wellington had conducted one love affair with Giuseppina Grassini, a singer at the Opéra, and another with Mademoiselle Georges, the most famous actress at the Comédie Française, both of whom had already passed through Napoleon's bed.

Whether or not they formed a liaison, the addressee of the last letter Wellington wrote before he called for his horse and set off to rejoin his troops in the pouring rain was Lady Frances Webster: "As I am sending a messenger to Bruxelles, I write to you one line to tell you that I think you ought to make preparations, as should Lord Mountnorris,[4] to remove from Bruxelles. We fought a desperate battle on Friday, in which I was successful, though I had but few troops. The Prussians were very roughly handled, and retired in the night, which obliged me to do the same to this place yesterday. The course of the operations may oblige me to uncover Bruxelles for a moment, and may expose that town to the enemy; for which reason I recommend that you and your family should be prepared to move to Antwerp at a moment's notice." It is not at all clear from this letter whether the duke had really made a final, definite decision to give battle, or whether an inner voice was warning him that he would do better to get his army out of there before it was too late.

The sky began to lighten around four o'clock. Napoleon was still at Le Caillou, his fear that the enemy would evacuate his position under cover of night unfounded; several officers sent to reconnoiter, as well as a few spies who had got close to the enemy's bivouacs, confirmed that the English had not moved. The emperor's chief concern was that the bad weather might continue, thus preventing him from pressing his advantage and destroying the army that had been so incautious as to stop and wait for him. But when he saw, low on the horizon, the red disk of the sun beginning to peek through the clouds between one squall and the next, the emperor grew calm, convinced that this dawn heralded a great day. "Tonight," he said, "we shall sleep in Brussels."

Among the dispatches that arrived during the night was one written at ten the previous evening, from Marshal Grouchy. He had been charged with pursuing the defeated Prussians and had taken with him most of the troops that had fought at Ligny. The emperor's instincts told him that the Prussians were retreating eastward after their rout, intent on sheltering in the fortresses of Liège and Namur, and that for at least a couple of days they would not be heard from again. But Grouchy's dispatch forced Napoleon to consider a problem he had already decided not to waste time on, for the marshal informed the emperor of his cavalry's reports that at least one of the two Prussian columns had headed north, in the direction of Wavre. To the southeast, however, on the road to Namur, Grouchy's cavalry had also surprised some retreating Prussians and captured wagons and guns. So the marshal was, for the moment, unable to say in what direction the bulk of the Prussian army was marching, but he had no doubt that this information would soon be his. In any case, should it turn out that the forces marching toward Wavre were of any considerable size, Grouchy pledged himself to follow hard on their heels and prevent them from joining Wellington.

The dispatch was dated from Gembloux, a small town northeast of Ligny. In itself, the fact of the marshal's presence there was not at all strange, given that Napoleon himself had ordered him to pursue the Prussians in that direction. Nevertheless, it is unclear how Grouchy thought he could start from Gembloux and be able to stop enemy columns that were marching in the direction of Wavre, since they were necessarily closer than he was to the battlefield at Waterloo. Had Napoleon accorded any importance to those columns and studied the situation on his map, he would have felt some uneasiness. But the emperor was convinced that Blücher, after his defeat at Ligny, would be careful not to risk his already battered army a second time, and he believed that the mere appearance of Grouchy's vanguard in pursuit of the Prussians on the road to Wavre would cause them to accelerate their retreat. Napoleon therefore concluded that there was no need to worry on that score and, serenely confident, did not even bother to send Grouchy a reply.

In the dawning light, Napoleon began to feel weary; too many hours on horseback the previous day, followed by a bad night, were taking their toll. One of his staff officers, Colonel Pétiet, had already noticed that the emperor was unable to spend as much time in the saddle as he used to in the past: "As soon as he dismounted from his horse to study maps or listen to reports or send messages, his staff people would set up a crude little wooden table, accompanied by a chair in the same style, and he would remain seated there for long periods of time." It's impossible to know with certainty if at Waterloo Napoleon was suffering from bladder pains, or perhaps from hemorrhoids, as many have hypothesized; but the emperor's physical movements had been a source of alarm to Pétiet from the moment he saw him after his return from Elba: "His corpulence, his dull, pallid complexion, and his stiff gait made him seem quite different from the General Bonaparte I had known at the beginning of my career." While day was breaking outside, Napoleon warmed himself by the crackling fire in his room, called for the latest ministerial dispatches from Paris, and grew absorbed in reading them, almost as if by doing so he might drive away all thoughts of the work awaiting him.

The Duke of Wellington had just mounted his horse and was riding out of the village of Waterloo with his entourage when a Prussian officer approached him with a message from Blücher. Wellington asked Baron von Müffling to assist him, and together they deciphered the dispatch, in which Blücher promised to come to the duke's aid with twice as many troops as he had requested. The previous collaboration of the two commands had left much to be desired, and Wellington was inclined to blame the Prussians' slowness for the late warning he'd received of Napoleon's advance. "Blücher picked the fattest man in his army to ride with an express to me, and he took thirty hours to go thirty miles," Wellington remarked. With the latest dispatch, however, the duke had written confirmation that his allies had no intention of abandoning him. Had he doubts about the advisability of giving battle at Waterloo, they must have fallen away at that moment; nevertheless, it remained to be seen whether Blücher would manage to keep his promise, and to keep it within a reasonable amount of time, because the arrival of his reinforcements would mean the difference between victory and defeat.

PART TWO

———◆———

"It Will Be as Easy as Having Breakfast"

TWELVE

———◆———

"VERY FEW OF US WILL LIVE TO SEE THE CLOSE OF THIS DAY"

The day was just beginning to dawn. Inside a radius of a few kilometers, almost 150,000 men—blue with cold, bristling with several days' growth of beard, dressed in wet uniforms whose colors were already starting to fade, and encrusted with mud from head to foot—were bustling around the remains of their bonfires, trying to revive the embers doused by the rain. All the wood, straw, and water that could be found in the area, in the villages and at the farms, had already been conveyed to the bivouacs; fences had been torn down, doors and windows burned, stables and haylofts emptied. Slowly, blood began to flow back into extremities, and even men who had awakened stiff with cold and unable to move gradually got back on their feet. The men dried and cleaned the barrels and flintlocks of their muskets, then fired them to be certain they were back in working order; the rattle of isolated gunfire that rang out everywhere reminded the more seasoned warriors of a skirmish between outposts. Hygienic conditions must have been frightful, and yet we know that many soldiers—perhaps more than would be the case today—took the opportunity of those first hours of light to shave and perhaps even to put on a fresh shirt, "because soldiers," as a French officer said, "don't like to fight when they're dirty."

Captain Verner of the Seventh Hussars had spent the whole night in the saddle, as had all the members of his squadron, sitting astride their horses in a field of rye so tall they almost disappeared in it; from this advanced position, the captain and his comrades were charged with covering the right wing of the Allied army. This order had mightily displeased the captain when he received it the previous evening, because his men had been severely engaged during the retreat from Quatre Bras. Naturally, however, he'd obeyed without a word and followed the regiment's sergeant major in the pitch dark to the place where the picket would take up its position. After having remained there all night, on horses sinking up to their knees in mud and with rainwater running into their boots, the Hussars were glad of the dawn, but then it revealed to them that their position was, in fact, only a few meters from their own front line and so their all-night vigil had been perfectly useless. Verner declared that he had never seen his men so weary and depressed, not even during the hardest moments of the war in Spain.

In the center of Wellington's deployment, the regiments of Sir Colin Halkett's brigade were trying to shake off their nocturnal torpor. The men of the Thirtieth Regiment had eaten no warm food for three days. The day before, they had started to cook their rations during a halt in the retreat, but almost at once the march began again in great haste, and they had poured out the soup and meat in the fields. Since then, no supply wagon had caught up with them, and so they had been compelled to face the night without anything to eat, except for whatever remained of the three and a third pounds of bread issued to each of them two days before. In the morning, the regiment's officers realized that their men—most of whom had been under fire for the first time at Quatre Bras—were "almost petrified with cold, many could not stand, and some were quite stupefied."

Farther left, the men of Sir Denis Pack's brigade—also known as the Scottish Brigade—were no better off. "Men and officers, with their dirty clothes, and chins unshorn, had rather a disconsolate look in the morning," reported one. Many officers who had been wounded two days before at Quatre Bras but had refused to abandon their men "were unable to hold out any longer, and were persuaded to go to Brussels about eight o'clock in the morning." In case they should not survive the battle, those who remained wrote their last wills in pencil on slips of paper and entrusted them to their wounded comrades. "Kempt's and Pack's brigades had got such a mauling on the 16th, that they thought it as well to have all straight. The wounded officers shook hands, and departed for Brussels."

General Desales, the I Corps artillery commander, had yielded his lodgings to his superior officer, Count d'Erlon, and had therefore spent the night in bivouac drenched to the skin. Eager to change his clothes and put on dry linen, the general wandered among the artillery wagons until he found an open, abandoned coach, climbed in immediately, disrobed, and put on whatever dry items he could find in his bags. Desales was famous for having constructed bridges over the Danube in record time during Napoleon's Wagram campaign. As a result of his service, he was raised to the rank of baron and granted an estate worth four thousand francs a year. Like many other French officers, Desales had adapted fairly well to the return of the Bourbons in 1814; he had, after all, been born at

Versailles, the son of a former servant of the royal family. ("I sucked in love for the Bourbons with my mother's milk, and besides, when I was a child, I saw them every day.") Napoleon's unexpected return and Louis XVIII's precipitous flight had convinced Desales that he should present himself to the emperor and ask to reenter his service on condition that he be allowed to keep the general's rank to which he had been promoted after the emperor's abdication. Napoleon, who very much needed technical experts, recognized Desales's rank, and the general commanded the forty-six guns of I Corps's artillery.

On the ridge behind the Papelotte farm at the extreme left of the Allied line, the three Hussar regiments of Sir Hussey Vivian's brigade were laboriously getting themselves back in order after a disastrous night, during which their horses, frightened by the thunderclaps and the lightning, had prevented everyone from catching as much as a wink of sleep. The officers of the Tenth Hussars took refuge in a small farmhouse, lit a fire in the chimney, and stood about naked as their uniforms dried. The prince regent was the honorary colonel of this cavalry regiment, which was at the time quite fashionable and known to London gossips as "the Prince's Dolls"; its select company included the Duke of Rutland's son, the Earl of Carlisle's son, and the grandsons of four other lords. But all the officers were new to the regiment, and so they hardly knew one another. The previous year, Colonel George Quentin, commander of the Tenth, had appeared before a court-martial, accused of cowardice in the face of the enemy. All the officers in the regiment at the time backed up this accusation; nevertheless, Quentin was acquitted, and afterward the officers were transferred en masse. But the colonel wasn't exactly popular among his new officers, either. When they were putting their clothes back on, one of them, Captain Wood, noticed with satisfaction that "Old Quentin" had burned the soles of his boots and was having great trouble getting them on his feet again.

At the château of Hougoumont, abandoned the previous day by proprietor and peasant alike, Private Matthew Clay of the Third Foot Guards began searching through the empty buildings, looking for something to eat. He found a piece of stale bread and a boiling-pot with a pig's head in it, but the meat wasn't completely cooked, and Clay found it too revolting even to taste. After consuming the bread, he decided to adjust his clothing. Like all his comrades, he was soaking wet, but the previous day he'd come across the corpse of a German soldier and had had the foresight to remove the dead man's underwear, so now he could at least put on something dry. He changed his undershirt and underpants, slipped back into his still-damp red coat, and went looking for a bit of dry straw to sit on while he waited for his orders.

The men of the Eighty-fifth Ligne[5] had spent the night in the mud, with no shelter from the rain. Because it had been formed in the Normandy port towns of

Granville and Cherbourg, the Eighty-fifth included a great many former prisoners of war, men who had been captured in Spain and subsequently released from the hellish pontoons, the prison-barges where the British segregated enemy captives. In the opinion of Captain Chapuis, none of these veterans could wait to come to grips with the Inglisman and pay them back for the mistreatment suffered at their hands; the men of the 85th Ligne, Chapuis thought, would sooner die than be taken prisoner a second time. As he looked around that morning, however, the captain could discern little of the combative spirit that had animated the troops when they set out for the war. At roll call, the gloomy silence in the ranks was a sign that the miserable night had left the men exhausted and that they would need a few hours of genuine rest before they could march against the enemy.

Sir Augustus Frazer, commander of the Allied horse artillery, slept under a roof in the village of Waterloo and arose feeling fairly well rested. At the first light of dawn, he sat down and wrote a long letter to his wife, in which he gave her an account of what had happened at Quatre Bras and tried to imagine what would take place later that day. Occasionally, his distress at the losses recently suffered by his troops broke through his confiding, serene tone: "Our own wounded we brought off on cavalry horses, except such as could not be found in the standing corn, poor fellows! In these scenes, not in the actual rencontre, one sees the miseries of war. I saw Henry Macleod last night, free from fever and pain, and doing well. He has three pike stabs in the side, a graze in the head, and a contusion on the shoulder. Poor Cameron I hear is dead, but I am unwilling to believe it.—Adieu. In all these strange scenes, my mind is with you, but it is tranquil and composed, nor is there reason why it should be otherwise. All will be very well. God bless you."

In Captain Mercer's troop, a corporal sent in search of ammunition returned instead with a cart full of food and drink. After distributing and consuming the rum on the spot, the gunners put some oatmeal on the boil and improvised a porridge they called "stirabout." When Mercer saw that the cart contained meat as well, he refused to eat the gunners' pap and gave orders to prepare a soup. As Mercer's officers waited for their meal, they too speculated about what would happen that morning. No one could exclude the possibility that the Allied troops would continue their retreat in a little while, heading north along the main road to Brussels just as they had done the previous day, with the French hard on their heels. Since he had nothing to do, Mercer took a walk around the cavalry bivouacs, listening to the soldiers' chatter: "Some thought the French were afraid to attack us, others that they would do so soon, others that the Duke would not wait for it, others that he would, as he certainly would not allow them to go to Brussels." After a while, the captain returned to his battery, hoping that the soup would be ready, only to learn that the order to stand to arms had been given and the soldiers had thrown everything away.

A little to the rear of Mercer's position were the fusiliers of the Second Battalion of the Ninety-fifth Regiment. Having received permission to plunder the surrounding farms, they broke up whatever wood they found and built a fire that would serve to dry their clothes and cook the few farm animals the peasants had left behind. Upon entering a farmyard, a group of fusiliers found the body of one of their comrades and immediately concluded that he had been poisoned, although it is much more probable that he had simply drunk himself to death. Beside themselves with rage, the fusiliers began systematically to destroy everything on the farm. They went down into the cellar, broke open the casks, and filled their canteens with wine. Then, since the dead man belonged to a company just arrived from England and fitted out with new uniforms, while their company had been in Flanders for more than a year and their uniforms were reduced to tatters, the soldiers agreed to strip the corpse and divide the deceased's clothing.

In the fields near La Belle Alliance, the soldiers of the Twenty-eighth Ligne, having disassembled, dried, and oiled their muskets and changed their flintlocks, were preparing a meal. The previous evening, as they scoured the area, they had seized a sheep, which they prudently decided to keep in reserve for the following day. A corporal who had been an apprentice butcher before enlisting slaughtered the animal, skinned it, and chopped it into pieces. Then the meat was put on the boil, together with a certain amount of flour, which another corporal, Canler, had found who knows where. Barely eighteen years old, Canler had known no other life except the army: The son of a soldier, he had lived with his father in the field, and at fourteen he had signed up as a drummer boy. Although a survivor of many bad soups, Canler noted that this one was particularly disgusting, because there was no salt and the cook had had the bright idea of adding a handful of gunpowder for flavor. Nevertheless, the men were so hungry that they all ate their soup, including the company captain and lieutenant, who came up and claimed their rightful portions.

A commissariat wagon loaded with gin stopped behind the Seventy-third Regiment's position, and two men from each company went to draw the gin ration for their unit. Private Tom Morris was one of them, and while he was waiting his turn someone pointed out to him a gigantic cavalry soldier, from the Second Life Guard, who was commanding a lot of space and guzzling vast quantities of strong drink. Morris observed him admiringly, for this was the famous Shaw, one of the best prizefighters in England. When Morris returned to his company, he discovered that the gin ration had been calculated to supply all the men whose names were on the rolls, without subtracting those whom the carnage at Quatre Bras had killed or put in the hospital. As a result, after the gin rations were distributed, the private was left with a goodly amount of liquor. Morris, who was not yet twenty years old, and Sergeant Burton, who was over fifty, took advantage of their opportunity and prepared themselves a double ration of grog. Then Burton ordered his comrade to put a little gin aside for after the battle; Morris, however, considered this idea not worth the trouble. "Very few of us will live to see the close of this day," he objected. But the old sergeant had a presentiment of good fortune: "Tom, I'll tell you what it is: there is no shot made yet for either you or me."

Not far from La Haye Sainte, the Earl of Uxbridge observed the remains of a cottage that the men of the First Battalion of the Ninety-fifth Rifles had started to tear down the previous evening, using the lumber and the straw from the roof to feed their fire; but the battalion commander, Sir Andrew Barnard, had stopped them from demolishing the structure completely, for the very good reason that he intended to spend the night in it.[6] A wisp of smoke rose from the cottage roof, of which there now remained only the beams of the frame, and Lord Uxbridge, deducing the presence of something warm in the ruined hovel, stepped inside. There he found Sir Andrew and his officers making tea, and Uxbridge took a cup with them. Such condescension on the part of such a great personage profoundly impressed the younger officers. That tea remained impressed in the minds of many, including Captain Kincaid, the adjutant of the battalion. Upon arising that morning, Kincaid had discovered that his mare had gone missing, and he had been obliged to spend an hour slogging through mud before finding her among the artillery horses. He recalled with gratitude the camp kettle full of tea, to which abundant quantities of milk and sugar had been added, bubbling over the fire when he returned, and he remembered that "all the big-wigs of the army" passed near there in those first hours of the day. Kincaid believed that "almost every one of them, from the Duke downwards, claimed a cupful."

By seven o'clock in the morning Major von Bornstedt, commander of a battalion of the First Kurmark[7] Landwehr, arrived with his exhausted men at the bivouacs prepared for them on the banks of the River Dyle, near the town of Wavre. The men, who belonged to General von Thielemann's III Army Corps, had marched not only all the previous day but also all the previous night, engaging in various skirmishes with the more advanced enemy patrols, for Bornstedt's battalion constituted the rear guard of the entire Prussian army. While they marched, the rain drenched them as it did everyone else, and they had never had time to stop and eat. The troops were ready to collapse on the wet ground and finally snatch a few hours of sleep, but the major ordered them first to clean and dry their weapons, because they might be attacked at any moment. The soldiers grumbled, but they knew he was right.

Major von Witowsky had been sent out before dawn with a patrol from the Sixth Hussars to reconnoiter the roads that Bülow's corps would have to take that morning in order to reach Waterloo. They were not roads so much as tracks, full of mud from the previous days' rains, and the intervening watercourses, the Rivers Dyle and Lasne, were swollen and turbid. Fording them would be treacherous, so they would have to be crossed by means of the few available bridges. But this bad news was largely counterbalanced by the astonishing absence of the enemy. If the French cavalry was looking for the Prussians, it wasn't looking for them there. When the Silesians and Poles who made up Witowsky's patrol came into contact with an enemy patrol for the first time, they were already in view of the bell tower of Maransart, practically at the back of the unwitting French right wing. At about the same time, other Prussian officers sent out on similar missions were arriving at identical conclusions; soon their reports would start to reach the vanguard of Bülow's columns with the vital information that their way lay open.

THIRTEEN

———◆◈◆———

THE EMPEROR'S BREAKFAST

Several hours after daylight, an officer from one of the outposts arrived at Le Caillou and reported to Napoleon that the enemy, according to all appearances, was falling back. Electrified, the emperor stopped dealing with his Parisian correspondence and dictated a hasty note to the commander of the I Corps, ordering him to begin the pursuit of the enemy immediately. Then Napoleon called for the horses to be saddled and rode off to observe in person what was happening along the bivouac line. But when he reached d'Erlon, he learned that the troops of the I Corps had not moved; according to the general, the enemy in his front wasn't withdrawing at all, and the only visible movements were those of units on the march to their battle positions. Napoleon, unconvinced, wanted to see with his own eyes. He and d'Erlon rode forward to the outposts, dismounted so as not to offer too conspicuous a target to some enemy sentry, and peered through a telescope at what was happening on the ridge of Mont-Saint-Jean. The emperor quickly persuaded himself that his general was right, and that Wellington's army was taking up defensive positions in anticipation of an attack. "Order the troops to cook their soup and put their weapons in order," Napoleon ordained. "And around noon, we'll see."

Noon may seem quite late, but the emperor had his reasons for taking time. A good half of his army had been compelled to bivouac well to the rear of the French positions at La Belle Alliance, and those men would need several hours to get themselves in line of battle: II Corps's vanguard wouldn't reach Le Caillou until after nine. Furthermore, the muddy terrain would not allow cavalry to maneuver and was even more inhospitable to artillery, which always moved laboriously through fields. Napoleon knew the sun would dry the ground in a few hours. He invited d'Erlon to breakfast with him and returned to Le Caillou.

Breakfast *à la fourchette* was served on the massive imperial silver, a small meal of cold meat and wine. While the troops who were already in line were cleaning their weapons and cooking their soup and those who had bivouacked in the rear were plodding through the muddy fields to their assigned positions, Napoleon was lingering at the table with his generals. It was a numerous company: Along with the army chief of staff, Marshal Soult, there were Drouot, the commander of the Imperial Guard, and d'Erlon, accompanied by his four division commanders. After the meal was consumed, Napoleon had his map spread out on a table. He studied it for a while, and then he announced to his generals, "The enemy's army outnumbers ours, but we have ninety chances on our side and not even ten against us." As he later declared in exile on St. Helena, none of his battles had ever seemed to him a surer thing than this one.

At that moment, Marshal Ney entered the inn. The bravest, if not the most intelligent, of Napoleon's generals, he had joined the army barely five days previously, but that had been long enough for him to make a poor impression, for he had led the attack at Quatre Bras without much success. Ney, too, had heard that Wellington's army was withdrawing, and he was coming in great haste to warn the emperor. Napoleon complacently informed him that he was mistaken; the enemy army, even if it wanted to retreat, could no longer do so without risking catastrophe. He concluded, "Wellington has rolled the dice, and they are in our favor." Soult, who had fought without success against Wellington in Spain, suggested that Grouchy could be ordered to join them with part of his force, but Napoleon interrupted him: "Because you've all been defeated by Wellington, you consider him a great general. But I tell you that he's a bad general, and it will be as easy as having breakfast."

The emperor himself may not have completely believed what he was saying, but he always made it a practice to speak ill of the enemy in public, by way of reinforcing troop morale: "And in war, morale is everything." In any case, his only direct experience of Wellington had come in the past few days, and it had certainly done nothing to justify the high opinion that his generals seemed to have of the enemy commander. For starters, hadn't Wellington let himself be caught by the invasion unprepared, and now wasn't he pinned with his back against the forest, without any possibility of retreat, in front of an army stronger than his own? In all probability, Napoleon was genuinely convinced that the duke had been overestimated.[8]

Other generals joined the emperor's table: Reille, commander of the II Corps, which was finally reaching its positions in front of Hougoumont, and two of his division commanders, one of whom was Jérome Bonaparte, Napoleon's brother. Reille, too, had fought in Spain, and when he was asked for his opinion, he observed that the English infantry was excellent, and that when it was in a good defensive position, its steadiness of character and its superior firepower made dislodging it almost impossible. But the British army was also the last of the old-style armies, impervious to revolutionary changes, accustomed to marching prudently and never straying too far from its supply base: "It's less agile, less flexible, less skillful in maneuver than ours. If we can't beat them with a frontal attack, we can beat them by maneuvering."

But Reille's opinion came too late. As early as the previous evening, the emperor had decided that the enemy army, in halting behind the ridge of Mont-Saint-Jean to await his attack, had put itself in a trap, and he interrupted the general with an exclamation of incredulity. (According to another version, Reille did not present his views to Napoleon, but only in private to d'Erlon; and when the latter suggested discussing these objections with the emperor, Reille replied, "What's the use? He wouldn't listen to us!") Not even a strange bit of news brought by his brother Jérome could disturb Napoleon's serenity. The previous evening, the prince had dined at the King of Spain Inn in Genappe; a few hours before, the Duke of Wellington, accompanied by his officers, had eaten lunch in the very same inn. A waiter told Jérome that during the meal the English had talked about the Prussians' planned march from Wavre to join the Allied army. But the incredulous Napoleon shrugged; after the trouncing they'd taken at Ligny, he declared, the Prussians would need at least two days to recover, and moreover Grouchy would take care of them.

The emperor's plan was as yet largely undefined; it would take a great deal of time and a great deal of work to unmask the strengths and weaknesses of Wellington's deployment. Napoleon said to his generals, "I'll bring my numerous artillery into play, I'll have my cavalry charge in order to force our enemies to show themselves, and when I'm quite sure of the position occupied by the English nationals, I'll march straight at them with my Old Guard." But over and above this way of proceeding, which may be considered routine, there were two things the emperor was sure of: This battle would save France, and it would go down in history. At ten o'clock, while the generals were remounting their horses to return to their troops, Soult wrote to Grouchy: "The Emperor directs me to inform you that at this moment His Majesty is about to attack the English army, which has taken up a position at Waterloo."

FOURTEEN

THE NUMBERS
IN THE FIELD

Many books about Waterloo give a precise tally of the armies in the field and their orders of battle, down to the last detail. The meticulousness exhibited in such books is seductive, until you notice that the careful figures of one scholar never agree with those of another. Moreover, the first of these books were published when the officers who had taken part in the battle were still alive, and they greeted with derision the scholarly writers' naive faith in the official numbers entered in the regimental rolls. When Major De Lacy Evans, the aide-de-camp in Sir William Ponsonby's cavalry brigade, read in a book that his brigade had gone into battle with 1,123 sabers, he objected: "I dare say it is all very right as a Return, but the 1,123 sabres were not on the field according to my humble recollection and belief." Recent scholars, basing their conclusions on the rolls, arrive at even greater numbers for the brigade, namely 82 officers and 1,233 men; and yet another officer, Captain Clark, declared, "With regard to the strength of the Brigade in the field on the 18th of June, I have never calculated it at more than 950, or at the utmost 1,000 swords." Similarly, Captain Rowan of the Fifty-second, reading in a colleague's memoirs that the regiment had gone into action with 1,148 men of all ranks, specified that this was a purely theoretical figure, corresponding to "about 1000 bayonets when in squares." The fact is that one must subtract from the rolls the officers' servants, who stayed behind with their commanders' horses and baggage; the soldiers charged with looking after the wounded and assisting the surgeons; all those assigned to guard depots, hospitals, or prisons, or to escort convoys; and last but not least, the absent without leave. The forces actually in the field were always quite inferior in number to the forces as they appeared on paper.

Bearing in mind that there are such limitations on the documents' reliability, we may hazard a guess as to the number of combatants each commander actually had at his disposition. The army with which Napoleon intended to assault the Mont-Saint-Jean ridge must have counted around 69,000 men, or—to be more precise—48,000 infantry, 14,000 cavalry, and 7,000 artillery with about 250 guns. This was not a particularly imposing army; at Wagram in 1809, the emperor had commanded 170,000 troops and 500 guns, and at Leipzig in 1813 he'd had a grand total of 195,000 men and 700 guns. At Waterloo, Napoleon's host more resembled the old-time armies, the ones from the days before the empire provoked half of Europe, both enemies and allies, into mobilizing their human and material resources and building up their military strength. Except for the cannon—the emperor always maintained an unshakable faith in the big guns, and he never stopped increasing their number—the forces under his command were roughly equivalent to those at Austerlitz ten years earlier, when the French army had fielded 73,000 men and 139 pieces of artillery.

Napoleon was wrong in thinking that Wellington's army outnumbered his. The number of men effectively available to the duke was nearly identical, around 67,000, of which 50,000 were infantry, 11,000 cavalry, and fewer than 6,000 artillery. Among these, the British accounted for no more than 24,000 men. Around 18,000 belonged to the army of the Netherlands, and 26,000 were divided among the four German contingents: the King's German Legion, with 6,000 men; the Hanoverian regulars, with 11,000; the army of the duchy of Brunswick, with 6,000; and the army of the duchy of Nassau, with nearly 3,000.[9] Although numerically equivalent to Napoleon's army, Wellington's was much inferior in artillery. The Allies had slightly more than 150 guns in the field, a hundred fewer than the French.

The weakness of the Allied army was increased by the presence of a large contingent of militia soldiers. While Napoleon could count on a line infantry of 48,000 men, Wellington had, in effect, barely 38,000; another 13,000 were inexperienced militiamen. This factor, together with the enormous disparity in guns, was the fundamental reason why Wellington had spent the previous day in continuous retreat and was preparing a defensive position that morning, while Napoleon was getting ready to attack, convinced that his adversary had committed a fatal error by accepting battle in order to protect Brussels.

But Wellington was counting on the arrival of the Prussians, which would change everything. Of course, Blücher's army was not so imposing as it had been two days previously, when it mustered around 95,000 infantry, 13,000 cavalry, and 5,000 artillery with 300 guns—that is, almost double the force that Wellington commanded. Allowing for the dead, the wounded, prisoners, and deserters, the disaster at Ligny and the subsequent retreat had cost the Prussians a good fourth of their entire army. Even in this condition, however, the remaining forces were more than sufficient to tip the balance in favor of Napoleon's adversaries, provided that they could reach the battlefield at Waterloo in time; Bülow's IV Corps alone, which had been marching on Waterloo since the first light of dawn, numbered something like 25,000 infantry, 3,000 cavalry, and 2,000 artillery with 88 guns.

Definitive victory or defeat largely depended on whether the Prussians would be able to keep their commander's promise to Wellington in spite of the mud-filled roads, the swollen rivers, and, especially, Grouchy's cavalry, which was still out there somewhere, looking for Blücher and his army. The Battle of Waterloo would also be a battle against the clock, and surely the importance of gaining time was what the duke had been thinking about earlier, when he spoke to Uxbridge of his confidence in his relatively few British troops. He knew they wouldn't run away, Wellington said, and it would take a good many hours to kill them all.

FIFTEEN

WELLINGTON'S DEPLOYMENT

At sunrise, neither of the two generals had the slightest idea of his adversary's deployment; some of Napoleon's troops were still on the march to La Belle Alliance, and Wellington's had bivouacked out of sight on the reverse slope of the ridge at Mont-Saint-Jean. Both commanders, therefore, made their dispositions on the basis of a hypothetical assessment of what might happen.

The method according to which Wellington ordered his units showed his concerns regarding the imminent struggle. Although the Allied army was subdivided into two combat corps and a reserve, this organization was more administrative than tactical and rarely respected on the battlefield, where the basic unit of maneuver was the division. When Wellington had the time to do so, he conveyed his orders through his two corps commanders, Lord Hill and the Prince of Orange, who were placed respectively on the right wing and in the center of his line; but in urgent circumstances, the duke gave his orders directly to the divisions, moving them about freely without taking into account to whom they belonged. Therefore, Wellington's deployment will be primarily referred to by the various army divisions.

The front that the duke proposed to defend formed an arc less than four kilometers (about 2.5 miles) long, decidedly narrow in respect to the conventions of Napoleonic warfare and the dimensions of Wellington's army. The battlefield at Austerlitz had extended over eight kilometers, and at Leipzig the front reached twelve kilometers in length. By defending a smaller front, the duke was able to deploy deeply and thus to hold a great number of troops in reserve. The cobblestone road that ran from south to north in the direction of Brussels formed the battlefield's natural axis; the center of the defensive line was represented by the intersection of this main road with the sunken lane called the chemin d'Ohain. This crossroads was shaded by a large elm that later came to be known as "Wellington's tree." Logically, therefore, the Allied forces would have been disposed in more or less equal numbers on both sides of the main road.

Wellington's dispositions, however, were completely different. On what was for him the left-hand side of the road, between the crossroads and Papelotte, along a front about two kilometers in length, the duke initially placed only two divisions, Picton's Anglo-Hanoverian division and Perponcher's Dutch-Belgians, that is, precisely those divisions that had been most severely tested at Quatre Bras two days before. In all, they represented about 11,000 bayonets, but only 7,500 of these infantrymen belonged to line battalions; the rest were militia. Perceiving that this was too small a force to hold a front two kilometers long, Wellington decided to add the two brigades of Sir Lowry Cole's division, only one of which—2,500 Hanoverian militia under the command of Colonel Best—was already in line; the other brigade, commanded by Sir John Lambert and much stronger in that it included more than 2,000 regular British troops, was still on the march from Brussels.

Since Sir Lowry Cole was off getting married in England, the duke put Lambert in command of both brigades and ordered him to prepare to take up a position in the line to the left of Picton's division. Even if Lambert's troops had reached their intended positions, the total strength of the left wing still would not have exceeded 16,000 bayonets and 33 guns. The three British cavalry brigades commanded by Vivian, Vandeleur, and Ponsonby were also deployed on the left, in a second line behind the infantry, and their 3,000 sabers represented a respectable reserve capable of mounting a counterattack should the opportunity arise. Nonetheless, the impression remains that Wellington did not expect to be attacked in force on that side, and in any case the roads coming from Wavre, on which the Prussian reinforcements he was expecting were supposed to appear, emerged in that sector of the field.

The center was much stronger than the left wing. Alten's Anglo-Hanoverian division—the Third British Infantry Division, a good 7,000 bayonets, all regular army troops—was deployed there, to the rear of the outpost represented by La Haye Sainte. Since the section of the front assigned to the Third was only a few hundred meters long, it was much better defended than the left wing. Behind Alten's men, in reserve, was von Kruse's First Nassau, another 2,500 bayonets, all regular army, although inexperienced. Lord Edward Somerset's heavy cavalry brigade, 1,000 sabers strong, was deployed in the same sector, and a little farther back was the entire Netherlands Cavalry Division, with another 3,400 sabers. A powerful concentration of 50 guns, some already in line and some in reserve, added to the robustness of Wellington's center.

The right wing was stronger still. Where the sloping ground descended in the direction of Hougoumont, in the château itself and in its park, along an arc that measured no more than a kilometer and a half—less than a mile—Wellington's front line was held by General George Cooke's Guards Division, a select group of 3,700 bayonets, along with nearly 1,000 German marksmen, experts detached from the divisions of Perponcher and Alten. Farther back, and partly in echelon to the right to prevent the enemy from turning the Allied flank by maneuvering along the road between Nivelles and Mont-Saint-Jean, were Mitchell's English brigade, Clinton's Anglo-Hanoverian division, and the Brunswick contingent. Posted far behind the front line, near the village of Braine l'Alleud on the Allies' extreme western flank, were the Dutch-Belgians of Chassé's Third Netherlands Division. All told, these units positioned in the rear formed a powerful reserve of some 20,000 bayonets, of which nearly 15,000 were regular army troops. The Anglo-Hanoverian cavalry brigades of Dornberg, Grant, and Arentschildt, together with the Brunswicker cavalry, added 3,700 sabers to a sector that, with its 74 guns, was much denser and far better protected than the left wing.

In short, Wellington's deployment was distinctly unbalanced, with a mighty, deeply echeloned right wing, a strong center, and a decidedly weaker left wing. Judging from these dispositions, the duke intended to hold at all costs the two outposts protecting his line, the farm of La Haye Sainte and the château of Hougoumont; he moreover expected—and feared—an attack on his right, and perhaps he also anticipated the necessity of opposing a movement to envelop his right flank and cut his lines of communication with the ports on the English Channel. By contrast, Wellington was much less concerned about his left flank, where he placed the troops that had been most severely bloodied at Quatre Bras, as if giving them a chance to catch their breath, and where he expected at any moment to see the vanguard of the Prussian columns appear.

All in all, the defensive position that Wellington assumed has always been deemed an excellent one. The two walled enclosures of Hougoumont and La Haye Sainte were veritable fortresses that he could hope to defend all day long from any frontal assault, and the ridge of Mont-Saint-Jean hid the majority of his troops from the enemy's view and gave them at least partial protection from artillery fire, even though an intense bombardment, with the enemy guns firing blindly over the ridge, was still capable of causing some casualties. At the time, though, some disagreed. Sir Thomas Picton, having ridden all along the Allied line, felt the necessity of remarking to Sir John Colborne, the colonel of the Fifty-second Light Infantry, "I never saw a worse position taken up by any army." But Sir Thomas was renowned for his ill humor; furthermore, at Quatre Bras a cannonball had cracked two or three of his ribs, and to avoid being sent back to Brussels, the general had mentioned his wound to no one except his servant. Under the circumstances, it's understandable that Sir Thomas may have been more irritable than usual.

SIXTEEN

NAPOLEON'S DEPLOYMENT

What would Napoleon do? Would he be able to take advantage of the weakness in his enemy's line and strike his vulnerable left wing, or would he try to maneuver around Wellington's right flank, as the duke feared? In truth, at ten in the morning Napoleon still had not decided what course of action he would take, for the good reason that he was totally ignorant of Wellington's deployment on the reverse slope of the Mont-Saint-Jean ridge. All the emperor knew was what a reconnaissance officer sent out shortly after dawn had reported, namely that the position was "defended by an army of guns, and by mountains of infantry." Therefore, the emperor deployed his troops as symmetrically as he could, not wishing to compromise any future developments, and retaining until the last moment the possibility of committing the bulk of his forces to the right, left, or center. Besides, this was Napoleon's normal way of opening a battle: He would evaluate all alternative possibilities, holding his decision in abeyance until he had gathered sufficient clues. The most significant feature of a Napoleonic plan was its resolute flexibility; thereafter, as the emperor liked to repeat, "execution is everything."

The deployment adopted by Napoleon was an expression of his insistence on remaining flexible. His right wing, whose assigned positions were in the fields beyond La Belle Alliance, to the east of the main road that divided the battlefield in two, was formed by d'Erlon's I Corps. Since this corps had taken no part in the bloody battles of Ligny and Quatre Bras, it was the strongest in the entire army: Its four divisions numbered around 16,000 muskets and 46 cannon, along with 1,500 cavalry. These latter troops were stationed on the extreme right, not far from Papelotte, keeping an eye on the enemy's outposts. On the left wing, west of the main road, Reille's II Corps took up its positions. Originally even stronger than I Corps, the II Corps was much reduced: Three of its four divisions had been damaged at Quatre Bras, and the fourth so thoroughly mauled at Ligny that it had been left there to get reorganized.[10] Nevertheless, Reille still had 13,000 bayonets, 1,300 cavalry, and 36 guns; by midmorning, his infantry, which had bivouacked at Genappe, was still taking up positions in front of Hougoumont, while the cavalry had already pushed farther on, in the direction of Braine l'Alleud.

In the center, along the road between Le Caillou and La Belle Alliance, the emperor massed his reserves. Had one or the other of his two wings proven unable to overcome on its own the Allied forces in its front, Napoleon intended to send in his reserves, counting on the impact of their attack to deliver the decisive blow. These troops included the VI Corps, commanded by Georges Mouton, Count Lobau, and the infantry of Drouot's Imperial Guard. From the beginning, Mouton's corps had been the weakest in the army, and then one of its three divisions had been detached to pursue the Prussians, so now it numbered only 6,000 muskets and 30 cannon, but these were fresh troops who had not yet been in combat. As for the infantry of the Guard, its three divisions had contributed to the victory at Ligny, but they had by no means fought themselves out, and with their 13,000 muskets—all select troops—and their 72 guns, they were capable of attacking with great force and delivering immense firepower.

The emperor deployed his numerous reserve cavalry according to the same principle of symmetry, which guaranteed him maximum flexibility and the possibility of intervening anywhere on the field. On the right, behind d'Erlon's infantry, he placed Milhaud's IV Corps, with its 2,700 cuirassiers, and the light cavalry of the Imperial Guard, under the command of Lefebvre-Desnouettes, with 2,000 lancers and chasseurs. On the left, supporting Reille's infantry, was Kellermann's III Corps, with nearly 3,000 cuirassiers, carabineers, and dragoons, and the Imperial Guard's heavy cavalry, commanded by Guyot, with horse grenadiers and dragoons numbering 1,600 sabers. Finally, there was one last reserve force in the center, behind La Belle Alliance, consisting of the two light cavalry divisions of Domon and Subervie, with a total of 2,000 lancers and *chasseurs*. In all, ten horse artillery batteries—a total of 60 guns—were attached to these various units.

SEVENTEEN

---•◆•---

"VIVE L'EMPEREUR"

While the troops were still marching into position, Napoleon mounted his horse to inspect the outposts one more time. The artillery officers had reported that the ground was drying out and that soon it would be possible to maneuver their heavy weapons. The valet Marchand stayed behind at Le Caillou, together with the coaches carrying the emperor's baggage and his cooks, who had received orders to have dinner ("a well-cooked shoulder of mutton") ready at six o'clock in the evening. Riding with the emperor and his adjutants was a local resident, a peasant named De Coster who owned a tavern on the road not far from Le Caillou. At five in the morning, the French had hauled him out of his bed and forced him to go with them; the emperor needed a guide. To keep De Coster from escaping, they tied his hands behind his back and hoisted him onto a horse that was attached by a strap to a light cavalryman's saddle.

As the emperor passed, the troops greeted him with mounting enthusiasm. The shouts of the men, thousands upon thousands of them, even drowned out the music of the regimental bands, whose members were playing their hearts out, sounding the glorious marches of the revolution and the empire. Everyone made an effort to get close enough to see Napoleon; for many, it was their first sight of him since his return from Elba. "He looked to me to be in the best of health, extraordinarily active and intense. Several times, he doffed his hat to us," a young officer later recalled; but then he added, with a touch of uneasiness: "He seems to be deep in thought and seldom speaks, except when he gives some sudden, terse order. As for his complexion, it's without color, almost waxen, not yellow, but rather white, like a Pascal candle." However, the great majority of the troops had no chance to observe Napoleon so narrowly, nor any occasion to conceive grounds for disquiet in his appearance. The infantry raised their shakos aloft on the points of their bayonets, the cavalry brandished their sabers, and from every section of the line there arose a mighty roar: "*Vive l'Empereur!*" An officer in d'Erlon's corps later wrote, "Never had those words been shouted with more enthusiasm; we were practically delirious."

In reality, this enthusiasm was not shared by everyone, and especially not by those soldiers whose stomachs were empty. An infantryman of that same I Corps recalled that a double ration of brandy had been issued that morning: "We would have been just fine with a chunk of bread, but there was no bread. You may imagine what kind of humor we were in. Many people say that we were filled with enthusiasm, that we were all singing, but that's a lie. Marching all night without rations, sleeping in water, forbidden to light fires, and then preparing to face grape and canister took away any desire to sing. We were just glad to pull our shoes out of the holes they sank into with every step. After passing through the wet grain, we were chilled and soaked from the waist down, and even the bravest of us looked discontented. It's true that the regimental bands were playing marches, and that the cavalry's trumpets and the infantry's drums mingled their sounds to grandiose effect, but as for me, I never heard anyone sing at Waterloo."

Whether sham or sincere, the enthusiasm with which the soldiers acclaimed their emperor that morning was the result of a well-orchestrated propaganda campaign. Napoleon had exerted every effort to ensure that the surge of excitement that had passed through France like an electric shock at the news of his escape from Elba did not subside, especially among the troops. Triumphant ceremonies, such as the presentation of the Eagles to the regiments of the reconstituted imperial army, were devised to galvanize the troops. These Eagles were fashioned of bronze and mounted, along with the French tricolor, on poles similar to those carried by the legions of ancient Rome; there was one Eagle per regiment, and the emperor had presented them to their respective units in a solemn ceremony on the Champs-de-Mars barely eighteen days before. Those regiments that had been absent from Paris at the time received their Eagles even later, on the eve of the campaign. On June 11, Colonel Fantin des Odoards, commander of the Twenty-second Ligne, presented the Eagle to his regiment, which was formed up in square. According to the colonel's emotional account of the scene, "This new standard, fresh from the gilder's studio, was solemnly blessed in the church of Couvins; then every soldier touched it with his hand and swore to defend it to the death." Although the men irreverently referred to the Eagle as "the Cuckoo," at Waterloo they would demonstrate that they took their oath seriously.

In the weeks preceding the battle, while he was still in Paris, Napoleon had increased the troops' enthusiasm by a massive distribution of decorations. In one incident, the emperor asked the colonel of the Ninety-third Ligne for the names of twenty soldiers, to whom he would award the Legion of Honor when the Ninety-third passed in review in the Place du Carrousel. At the ceremony, noticing that the colonel had submitted twenty-five names, Napoleon refused to confer the decoration on the last men in line and irritably threw away the list. One of the soldiers who watched their ribbons evaporate this way later wrote about the experience: "I could see the piece of paper on the ground, carried away by the wind, like my young man's dreams. I never in my life felt a sharper pain." Perhaps such public relations errors as this explain why not everyone in his secret heart shared the widespread enthusiasm for the emperor; nevertheless, it cannot be denied that Napoleon, during the course of the Hundred Days, managed not only to raise an army but also to galvanize it sufficiently to face the tests that awaited it.

Along the ridge occupied by the Allies, all eyes were fastened on the extraordinary spectacle presented by the enemy troops as they took up positions in full view little more than a kilometer away, with banners flying in the wind and bayonets gleaming in the sun; successive roars of enthusiasm burst from the men as the emperor, on horseback, reviewed one regiment after another. To the eyes of Lieutenant Wheatley, one of the many British junior officers who had joined the King's German Legion in the past few years, the vision of those dark masses of troops, outlined against the horizon and coming down toward him, "disjointing then contracting, like fields of animated clods, had a fairy look and border'd on the supernatural in appearance." Corporal Farmer of the Eleventh Light Dragoons, one of the regiments in Vandeleur's cavalry brigade, deployed on the extreme left of the Allied line, compared the descent of the seemingly endless columns to images seen in dreams. Ensign Macready of the Thirtieth Regiment, an extremely young officer who had been in the service for only a few months, realized that the sight of the French advance was giving him the shivers, and he thought that all the thousands of men crowded around him with their eyes fixed on the enemy must be feeling the same emotion.

In fact, some of them were feeling even stronger—and less honorable— emotions. In the Fortieth Regiment, a recruit who had never been in battle before approached Sergeant Lawrence, declaring that he had been taken ill and would have to fall out. "I could easily see the cause of his illness," Lawrence later recalled. "So I pushed him into rank again, saying, 'Why, Bertram, it's the smell of this little powder that has caused your illness; there's nothing else the matter with you'; but that physic would not content him at all, and he fell down and would not proceed another inch." The sergeant chose to overlook this behavior, for otherwise he would have been obliged to shoot the young man; sometime later, however, when the soldier again reported to the regiment, Lawrence handed him over to a court-martial, which sentenced him to 300 lashes. One of the troopers in the Sixteenth Light Dragoons jumped off his horse and took to his heels. According to Captain Tomkinson, the man was "deranged. He was an old soldier, yet not the wisest, and had been shoemaker to the troop for many years. The men after the day was over did not resent his leaving them, knowing the kind of man and his weakness." Another of Tomkinson's dragoons failed to get off so easily: Having absented himself without leave before the battle—he was off thieving—he was reported to the captain and, the morning after the battle, "booted" by his comrades-in-arms.

Many strove to identify Napoleon, aware that they were about to measure themselves, for the first time in their lives, against the great man himself. Their emotions were divided between the hatred and contempt officially directed at "Buonaparte" by British public opinion and the admiration they felt for him in their hearts, almost in spite of themselves. Even the simplest soldiers were conscious of these contradictory sentiments; sometime previously, Sergeant Wheeler had written to his family at home, couching his letter in his peculiar orthography: "The Emperor will most assuredly command the French Army, and it will require a General of uncommon skill to withstand so powerful a genus." There was all the more reason for officers to feel this way; Captain Mercer admitted that deep down he "had often longed to see Napoleon, that mighty man of war—that astonishing genius who had filled the world with his renown." Naturally, at that distance it was difficult to know with any certainty whether one had really seen the emperor or not. An officer of the Royal Scots "saw a cloud of staff moving about, following some person of rank, who stopped occasionally, as if to address the French troops. I could almost fancy I could distinguish the redingote and 'petit chapeau tricorne' of our imperial Enemy." Sir Hussey Vivian was positive he'd picked him out with his telescope before the attack began: "With a large suite of Officers, he rode amongst the Columns forming in the front of the British left, and was hailed with shouts of *Vive l'Empereur*. I fancied looking through my glass I could distinguish the little Hero, and, indeed, have little doubt of it."

When the last troops had reached their positions, shouting themselves hoarse all the while, Napoleon ordered Marshal Ney to remain on the field and coordinate the action; as for himself, the emperor intended to oversee the whole battlefield, and therefore he had decided to establish his headquarters on high ground almost two kilometers to the rear, near the Rossomme Farm. From there it was possible with a telescope to survey the entire horizon, from Hougoumont on the left all the way to the forest known as the Bois de Paris (or Fichermont) and the heights of Chapelle-St. Lambert, which obstructed the horizon on the right. In accordance with a well-established procedure, the emperor's aides set up a camp chair and a little table, on which they spread out his maps. Weary from so much riding, Napoleon sat down heavily and waited for the battle to begin. One of the young officers in his retinue noted, a little uneasily, that the emperor, in stark contrast with his enthusiastic troops, seemed all too listless.

EIGHTEEN

WHAT IS A BATTLE?

What exactly was a "battle" in 1815? The most acute description is given by Carl von Clausewitz in the fourth book of his treatise *On War*, published posthumously in 1832–5. In the following passage, the Prussian theoretician was not describing Waterloo in particular, but rather the general idea of a Napoleonic battle, which he knew well both from direct personal experience and from many hours spent in reflection. Clausewitz wrote:

What generally takes place in a major battle these days? Great masses of troops calmly position themselves in rank-and-file order. A relatively small proportion of the whole is sent forward, and these men are left to expend themselves in a firefight of several hours' duration. Now and again, combat is interrupted and displaced a little this way or that by small, isolated blows: infantry attacks, bayonet assaults, cavalry charges. If the engaged troops gradually wear themselves down in this way and lose some part of their fighting spirit, then they are withdrawn, and other troops take their place.

Thus the battle burns on slowly, with moderated intensity, like wet gunpowder, and when night spreads its dark veil and all grows calm, because no one can see anymore and no one wants to entrust himself to blind chance, then the estimates and evaluations begin: how many usable forces (that is, how many masses of troops not yet collapsed like blasted volcanoes) remain to one side and the other, how much territory has been won or lost, how secure is the rear. The impressions of courage and cowardice, cleverness and stupidity that individual officers believe they have gathered, both from their own men and from the enemy, are assembled into a general impression and combined with the results of the foregoing evaluations to arrive at a decision: either to abandon the field, or to renew the fighting the following morning.

Although in the case of Waterloo a sense of defeat overcame the French army before reaching its commanders and the decision to abandon the battlefield was taken by the troops themselves, more spontaneously and chaotically than Napoleon would have wished, Clausewitz's sketch corresponds better than one might think to the events of June 18, 1815. In fact, an earlier version of the definition of battle given above can be found in the book Clausewitz wrote before *On War*, titled *The Campaign of 1815 in France*, which dealt specifically with the Waterloo campaign:

> In every contemporary battle, the opposing forces are worn down during a long period of mutual destruction along the front line, where these forces are in contact. This phase of the conflict lasts for several hours, and the firefight results in minor oscillations, until one of the two sides finally receives a visible preponderance from its reserves—that is, from fresh troops—and thus is able to deal the decisive blow to the already wavering enemy.

A little farther on in the same book, Clausewitz wrote:

> Our battles last between half a day and an entire day. For what is by far the major part of the entire struggle, there is a slow attrition, a slow destruction of the two armies, which are in contact at points all along the battle line and which, like two incompatible elements, destroy each other at those points of contact. Thus the battle keeps burning slowly, moderately, like wet powder; and it's only when the major part of the forces on one side or the other has been consumed and rendered useless that a decision can be reached with the remaining troops.

Then chief of staff to Thielemann's corps, Clausewitz had seen hard action at Ligny and found himself in Wavre that June 18 morning, where he would remain all day long. His analysis is indispensable to our understanding of the way in which Napoleon conducted the Battle of Waterloo.

NINETEEN

---❖---

NAPOLEON'S ORDERS

Around eleven-thirty, or noon at the latest, Reille's infantry began moving toward the wood at Hougoumont, seeking contact with the enemy; almost at once the artillery on both sides opened fire in that sector of the field. All along the front, officers pulled their watches out of their pockets and took note of the exact time when the battle began. The watches of the British, regulated in accordance with the observatory in Greenwich, were an hour behind those of the French, a fact that helps to explain the extreme discordance in the various eyewitness accounts. On the east side of the battlefield, d'Erlon's infantry had not yet moved, and his artillerymen were still laboring to haul their guns through the mud and into their batteries, but it was clear that action would soon get under way there as well. The two generals, Reille and d'Erlon—respectively on the left and right of the French line and in charge of the II Corps and I Corps—were preparing to execute the emperor's orders. The rest of the army, including the Imperial Guard, Mouton's corps, and all the cavalry, remained in wait. But there has been debate over the exact instructions that the two commanders had received.

Napoleon's general order had been dictated at eleven and addressed to Marshal Ney, who was charged with coordinating the French offensive. In this order, the emperor decreed that the attack would start around one o'clock, with the goal of seizing the village of Mont-Saint-Jean, "at the intersection of the Nivelles and Brussels roads." The fact that the Allied troops, most of them invisible to the emperor, were actually deployed ahead of Mont-Saint-Jean, in the dead ground immediately behind the ridge, and the related possibility that Napoleon and his generals, striving to make their maps jibe with what they saw through their telescopes, confused La Haye Sainte farm with the village of Mont-Saint-Jean, are in the final analysis irrelevant, given that both places were on the main road to

Brussels. To make a breakthrough in this sector, the emperor ordered the three reserve artillery batteries of the I, II, and VI Corps to mass their heavy 12-pounder guns and bombard the center of the enemy position. Immediately after the bombardment, the left-hand division in d'Erlon's deployment was to advance, while his other divisions held themselves in readiness to support the attack; as to Reille's II Corps, it was to advance at the same rate as I Corps. On the back of the sheet of paper, Marshal Ney scribbled in pencil, "Count d'Erlon will observe that the attack is to commence from the left, not the right. Communicate this new disposition to General Reille."

This summarily formulated order from the emperor and Ney's cryptic addendum to it have caused rivers of ink to flow, though Napoleon's intentions seem clear. By sending forward both the I Corps and the II Corps, the emperor obviously planned to engage the enemy all along his front, searching for the point where his troops could break through. The order did not state where that point would be; since the emperor did not yet know where it would be found, he could not pinpoint it. His designation of Mont-Saint-Jean as the objective of his advance meant only that he planned no flanking maneuver to right or left, but rather a frontal assault. In any case, Reille and d'Erlon were not called upon to mount an immediate bayonet charge; they were to make gradual contact with the enemy and exert steadily mounting pressure upon his forces. This phase of the battle could go on for hours, while the conditions for a decisive thrust slowly emerged. Once combat was initiated, the enemy's reactions, the conduct of his troops, and the movements of his reserves would reveal to the emperor the time and place for the final attack.

But remaining open to all possibilities is not the same as refusing to consider the probable outcome, and clearly Napoleon expected d'Erlon's corps to be more completely engaged than Reille's. The wording of the order demonstrates that the emperor had given rather detailed thought to the movements to be undertaken by I Corps, while the indications for II Corps seem much more generic; moreover, the village of Mont-Saint-Jean, which had been chosen as the focal point of the attack, lay on the line of d'Erlon's advance, and there Napoleon ordered the massing of his 12-pounder batteries. Taking into account the little that he could foresee at that moment, the emperor apparently expected more decisive results from the advance of his right wing than from that of his left. In his memoirs, Napoleon claimed that he wanted to maneuver in such a way as to separate the English from the Prussians, cutting off Wellington's retreat to Brussels and pushing his army toward the sea; although the emperor's assertions cannot always be taken as the undiluted truth, in this case there is no apparent reason to disbelieve him.

Another fact demonstrates that Napoleon, while remaining ready for any eventuality, expected to break through Wellington's left wing: At the last moment, he changed his dispositions for I Corps, modifying the verbal orders he had given to his generals over breakfast at Le Caillou. Originally, d'Erlon's troops were to begin engaging the enemy on the right, around Papelotte, and the battle would then be extended gradually along the whole front, so that the final and probably decisive pressure would be exerted along the axis of the Brussels road, when the last of I Corps's divisions entered into action in that sector. But at some point, Napoleon must have experienced one of those supernormal intuitions that had produced so many of his great victories in the past. Looking through his telescope at what little could be seen of the enemy positions behind the ridge, the emperor realized that Wellington's left wing was the weak spot in his deployment, and resolved, therefore, to attempt a breakthrough there.

The proof of this lies in the note that Ney scribbled on the back of Napoleon's order: "Count d'Erlon will observe that the attack is to commence on the left, not the right. Communicate this new disposition to General Reille." The change evidently pertained to the order of advance that the four divisions of I Corps were to follow, and it could only have sprung from a decision to exert gradually increasing pressure against Wellington's left wing, starting from the center and working out. Threatened on its right by Reille's advance, pinned in the center by the offensive of d'Erlon's First Division, the enemy army would be driven in farther to its left, exactly where it was the weakest, after which the remaining divisions of I Corps would make a ninety-degree turn to the left and attack Mont-Saint-Jean, cutting the Brussels road and trapping the bulk of Wellington's forces.

The fact that the troops of Reille's II Corps, and not d'Erlon's, opened the battle, and did so an hour earlier than Napoleon had stipulated, has raised questions over what orders were sent to Reille. The instructions for II Corps—to advance at the same rate as I Corps—appear to be laconic, but Napoleon had spoken at length to Reille and his other division commanders—among them his brother Jérome—that morning and obviously felt no need to modify the arrangements made at that time. Reille was to advance, coordinating his movements with those of the I Corps; since the Hougoumont wood was in his front, it seems entirely credible that he would have been ordered to occupy it, as both Prince Jérome and Reille himself later affirmed. Reille understood, and explained to his officers, that the main effort was going to be made by d'Erlon's corps, and that their task was simply to occupy the woods as a cover for the advance of the French right wing. One of those officers, a *chef de bataillon* named Jolyet, confirmed that their orders were "to prevent the enemy from coming out on our left flank; for I had been well forewarned that the army was going to pivot on us, and consequently that it was imperative for us, at all costs, to hold our position," that is, to retain possession of the Hougoumont wood. The emperor and his generals knew from their maps that the wood was an inhabited place, even though the Ferraris-Capitaine map was imprecise on this point and gave the impression that Hougoumont was nothing less than a village. The château and various buildings of Hougoumont, hidden as they were by the alders of the park, were invisible from the French positions. For most of the junior officers and their men, therefore, what they had in front of them was simply a wood that they had to occupy because the emperor's plan required them to do so. Given that the emperor's general order called for the commencement of combat shortly after one o'clock, the fact that Prince Jérome's infantry started advancing toward the wood before noon, when d'Erlon's men had not yet got under way and the artillery bombardment had not yet begun, may come as a surprise, but in the end the discrepancy seems unimportant. Reille stated that he received the order to advance into the wood at a quarter past eleven, and therefore the most probable explanation is that Napoleon had decided to accelerate the pace of events: If II Corps wanted to remain in alignment with I Corps when the latter moved forward in its turn, then II Corps would have to clear the Hougoumont wood. And perhaps their hope that the wood was not even defended caused Napoleon and his generals to consider this movement as a plain and simple adjustment of their line, not the beginning of a battle, only to change their minds when the infantry's advance was greeted from the wood with a heavy barrage of musket fire.

TWENTY

NAPOLEONIC
INFANTRY TACTICS

I n order to appreciate what happened from the moment the battle began, some
fundamental principles of infantry tactics in the Napoleonic age are needed to
make clear how infantry was generally maneuvered and what options officers
had when they found themselves under enemy fire.

The infantry battalion, with its five or six hundred men, constituted the basic
unit of maneuver and could be deployed in different formations. Manuals
prescribed in detail the movements that had to be executed in order to pass most
quickly from one formation to another while causing the least possible confusion.
A great part of infantry training consisted in teaching the officers the correct
sequence of orders for every eventuality and in accustoming the soldiers to carry
out those orders rapidly and automatically, even when they were under fire.

The three basic combat formations for a battalion were the line, the column,
and the square. For a century and a half—ever since the musket had become the
foot soldier's main weapon—the line had been the normal combat formation used
by European infantry. A battalion deployed in line, two or three ranks deep,
covered a fairly broad front, a hundred meters or more. Thus disposed, every man
was able to shoot, and the battalion's firepower reached its maximum level. Under
normal conditions, the British infantry was trained to deploy in two ranks only;
this arrangement extended the line as far as possible and optimized the troops'
firing capacity. Continental infantry preferred the shorter, more solid three-deep
line. In reality, this difference proved unimportant at Waterloo, because although
the British infantry was excellently trained in shooting, it fought virtually the
entire battle in an emergency formation four ranks deep, renouncing—for reasons
we shall discuss—the firepower advantage that even its adversaries acknowledged.

The column, which had come into wide use during the Napoleonic Wars, was a more compact formation, broader than it was deep, that sacrificed the battalion's firepower for the psychological advantage of depth and mass. A French battalion in column consisted of nine ranks, lined up one behind the other; the battalion's total frontage was approximately forty meters, and if the troops closed ranks the column's depth could be reduced to only fifteen meters or so. The column was preferred by both the French and the Prussians for bayonet attacks, because it guaranteed moral support to the men, who were surrounded on all sides by a multitude of comrades, and because of the force of impact it could develop along such a narrow front. However, the column's firepower was comparatively reduced, and it offered enemy artillery an ideal target. The awareness of these disadvantages and the attempt to find a solution for them played an important role in the way the French generals fought the Battle of Waterloo.

But neither the column nor the line was a suitable formation for facing a cavalry charge. Gambling on its speed and the force of its impact, the cavalry could maneuver in such a way as to avoid the fire of the infantry and burst upon it from an unexpected direction. All training manuals emphasized the injunction that infantry soldiers facing cavalry had to form *square*, a term not to be taken in its literal geometric sense. The British manual of arms directed that a battalion, which comprised ten companies, should rather form what was called an *oblong*, with three companies in front, three in the rear, and two on each flank. The eyewitness account of a former staff officer stated that an unusual sort of oblong was also tried at Waterloo, with four companies front and rear and only one on each flank. Often two undermanned battalions were united in a single square; although even this maneuver was covered in the manual, the results could not have been regular, geometrically speaking. Casualties, too, made maintaining an ordered, symmetrical formation impossible.

The "square" therefore was a formation of variable geometric configuration, whose short side might cover as little as a dozen meters, while the long side could extend to sixty or seventy. In any case, the square enclosed many hundreds of men, crowded shoulder to shoulder and presenting four ranks of bayonets in every direction. Against such a formation, cavalry generally failed to charge home, because it was impossible to induce horses to impale themselves on a hedge of steel; and even occasionally the cavalry, instead of milling around at a distance, actually made physical contact with its adversaries, so many bayonets thrusting at each horse's chest made the outcome a foregone conclusion. That is, of course, provided that the men in the square kept their nerve; if instead they started wavering at the cavalry's approach and a soldier panicked and abandoned his post, the cavalry could force a passage amid the infantry, and in such cases the square inevitably collapsed.

On the battlefield at Waterloo, Wellington's foot soldiers had to remain in square for a great part of the day, and this explains why the infantry, even when it deployed into line, almost always adopted an unusual four-deep formation. The transition from a line of this type into square, and vice versa, was much faster, especially if the emergency necessitated a creative interpretation of the rules. At such times, the standardized, rote-learned procedures that guaranteed the automatic cooperation of so many men often clashed with the advisability of simplifying or ignoring those procedures, and this tension was one of the chief problems that armies of the time had to deal with. It is a veritable leitmotif in the accounts of the officers who fought at Waterloo.

In particular, the British troops in this battle often deployed from square into line without heeding the prescriptions of the training manual published by Sir David Dundas in 1788. At one point in the battle, the men of the 3/1st Foot Guards, under fire from some enemy troops, advanced to dislodge them. In order to drive off the enemy, one of the Foot Guards' officers explained, the battalion chose not to waste time by deploying into line—a maneuver that would have been imprudent at best, given the great masses of enemy cavalry that were roaming this part of the field. Instead, the guardsmen split the rear face of their square in the center; pivoting left and right, this face and the two lateral faces wheeled into line with the front face of the square, thus forming an irregular line four ranks deep. Later in the day, faced with the advancing Imperial Guard, the battalion commander had the idea of using the same unorthodox method once again. He was killed shortly thereafter, and twenty years later a colleague, despite the pity he felt for his fallen comrade-in-arms, still couldn't help being scandalized by the thought of such a flagrant violation of the rules: "The Duke of Wellington ordered the 1st Brigade of Guards to *take ground to its left and form line four deep*, which poor Frank D'Oyley did by wheeling up the sides of the Square, putting the Grenadiers and my Company (1st Battalion Company) in the centre of our line. What would Dundas have said!!!"

TWENTY-ONE

THE SKIRMISH LINE

Although the different infantry battalion formations absorbed the majority of an army's manpower, a successful outcome in battle depended on the cooperation between these mass formations and a minority of selected troops trained in individual combat. Even when deployed on the front line, an infantry battalion was never in direct contact with the enemy for very long. Most of the troops stood in formation, crowded together shoulder to shoulder; the noncommissioned officers strove to maintain proper alignment; in the midst of the ranks, the banners fluttered overhead; but only at critical moments did the battalion receive the order to advance with fixed bayonets while the drums beat the charge. Even the occasions when the troops fired their weapons—all together and at an officer's command—were relatively rare; an infantryman carried a leather pouch that contained, at the most, fifty or sixty cartridges, enough for thirty minutes of sustained fire. The emphasis that infantry training placed on developing the ability to shoot as rapidly as possible shows that the combat was expected to be brief and decisive.

Only a small number of men were actually in contact with the enemy throughout the battle, maintaining a constant if irregular fire. These soldiers, trained to fight in pairs and in open order, moved ahead of the main body and started the firefight as soon as they spotted the enemy's forward lookouts. During the latter part of the eighteenth century, the use of these skirmishers had become more and more general; they complemented the lines of infantry deployed in close formation and maneuvered in cadence by officers. In the French military, the number of such soldiers, known as *tirailleurs*, was steadily increased, so much so that they contributed heavily to the great victories of the revolutionary and Napoleonic armies. By the time of Waterloo, all European armies had so thoroughly integrated *tirailleurs* that their use was virtually automatic. Every line battalion present on the battlefield had a company of men, known as the light company, trained to perform this role. In the case of the German armies, each battalion had at least one squad of selected marksmen, the *Scharfschützen*, or sharpshooters. Agility and quickness were the chief physical qualities required of such soldiers; they were usually chosen from among those who happened to be both short in stature and crack shots.

These shooters or skirmishers were armed with the same smoothbore muskets as the line soldiers used, except that the skirmishers were trained to use them better. The British army had begun to introduce into some units the use of flintlock muskets with rifled barrels, which had far superior range and accuracy. These weapons were called Baker rifles, and they were carried by the battalions of the Ninety-fifth Rifles, an entire, elite regiment trained to fight in open order, and also by the light infantry of the King's German Legion. The French *tirailleurs* all used the ordinary 17mm caliber musket, which was decidedly more accurate and manageable than the standard-issue British musket, the 18 caliber familiarly known as "Brown Bess," to say nothing of the heavy 19 caliber musket carried by the Prussians. Speaking of the French, a British officer observed that "their fine, long, light firelocks, with a small bore are more efficient for skirmishing than our abominably clumsy machine," and he added that the Brown Bess too often displayed defects of manufacture. British soldiers, he said, "might be seen creeping about to get hold of the firelocks of the killed and wounded, to try if the locks were better than theirs, and dashing the worst to the ground as if in a rage with it."

Armed with rifled muskets or, more often, with smoothbores, the skirmishers awaited the signal to advance. When the officers blew their whistles, the men moved forward and formed the army's outpost line. Wellington's entire front was covered by a line of skirmishers a few hundred meters forward of the main positions. These men held their ground as best they could all day long, except when the approach of enemy cavalry or an advance in force by enemy infantry compelled them to withdraw to the nearest friendly formation. Similarly, every French attack was preceded by a thick chain of *tirailleurs*, who tried to beat the Allied skirmishers in a firefight and force them to evacuate the no-man's-land between the armies.

If skirmishers got the upper hand and advanced so far that the defensive battalions were in range, they began peppering the serried ranks with isolated, well-aimed shots designed to fray the nerves of men standing in a packed and unmoving mass and, if possible, to pick one of their higher officers off his horse, thus softening up the defenders before the real attack came. Artillery batteries, too, provided an ideal target for the shooters; when they drew within range of a battery, they would aim for the gunners or, at least, for the horses. Seldom could a battery commander allow himself to waste precious ammunition firing at such elusive targets; it was indispensable, therefore, to cover the batteries also with a screen of skirmishers solid enough to prevent those of the enemy from getting too near the guns.

This form of combat ate up skirmishers fairly quickly. The light companies were not adequate to their task, not even when they were reinforced, as was common practice in critical moments, by all the soldiers in the battalion who were distinguished for marksmanship. The first tactical problem that all armies tried to solve, therefore, was how to reinforce their skirmishers. The solution most widely adopted was to establish entire units trained to operate in open order and for that reason called light infantry; when judiciously placed, these battalions could support a line of skirmishers along an entire front, continually sending in men to replace the fallen or demoralized. The Prussians—whose infantry battalions had no light company, only a squad of *Scharfschützen*—went so far as to furnish each of their line regiments with a battalion of light infantry, known as fusiliers, so that in the Prussian infantry regiments the ratio of fusiliers to musketeers was one to two.

In addition, the Prussian army experimented with the even more drastic practice of training a third of all the men in their line battalions to fight as skirmishers. When continental infantry deployed in line to fire or to advance, the troops were normally disposed in three ranks; when necessary, the men in the third rank, where there was the greatest difficulty in firing effectively anyway, employed as reinforcements for the line of skirmishers. Although this measure could hardly be applied with insufficiently trained troops—those of the *Landwehr* (militia), for example—it nevertheless allowed the Prussian army of 1815 to attain a significant degree of tactical flexibility, covering its battalions with swarms of skirmishers even more numerous than the French.

Despite their exposure, the skirmishers did not bear the brunt of the fighting. Throughout the battle, until they ran out of ammunition, the big guns of both armies kept up a constant fire aimed at any available and appealing target, chiefly presented by the battalions of infantry and the regiments of cavalry drawn up in formation about a thousand yards away. Furthermore, the skirmishers, whenever they could, directed their fire against the formed-up troops, upon whom they could inflict considerable damage, officers being the targets of choice. When the commander in chief decided that the enemy troops in a certain sector had been sufficiently worn down by the firefight and that the time had come to seek a decisive breakthrough, the line infantry was ordered to move out, marching in step, and such an advance—in the open, under fire—was absolutely the worst moment for the soldiers, the time when they risked the greatest number of casualties. But it remains generally true that the persistent battle, the one that burned like wet powder all along the front, marking the line of contact between the two armies with an irregular series of gunshots and puffs of white smoke, was carried on by the skirmishers. Even Dundas's manual of arms acknowledged that the light infantry had "become the principal feature" of the British army, and this affirmation would have sounded even more self-evident to a French or Prussian officer.

Considering the effectiveness of the *tirailleurs*, one could ask why the whole infantry was not used in this way, and why instead most of the men were kept in closed order and maneuvered mechanically, according to the prescriptions laid down in the manual of arms. One answer is that innovations take hold only gradually, meeting stiff opposition before at last unequivocally establishing themselves: not until 1914 did the armies of Europe, by then carrying firearms incomparably more potent than those of Napoleon's day, realize the necessity of deploying all their troops in open order instead of closed formations. And yet the use of skirmishers with a battalion in formation fairly close behind them presented concrete advantages. Not every soldier had the intelligence necessary for operating with a degree of individual autonomy; most troops were kept under much better control if they were marching shoulder to shoulder and responding to their officers' rote commands. Furthermore, given that it took twice as long to train a good skirmisher as a regular infantryman, there was not enough time to prepare all the recruits for open-order combat. Not coincidentally, perhaps the most significant difference between regular troops and militia was that the latter, precisely because it was insufficiently trained, was nearly or completely useless as light infantry.

In addition, the close-order formation packed an undeniable moral wallop. The fire of several hundred men discharging their weapons all together on command had more of an impact, physical and psychological, than the individual fire of the skirmishers, even though theirs was much more accurate; and that multitude, marching to the attack with bayonets fixed and drummers beating the cadence, produced a shock effect—primarily psychological in this case—that no general could do without. The skirmishers themselves would not have fought without the reassuring certainty that the battalion was formed up behind them, offering a shelter they could run to in case of danger, especially if the rumble of hooves and the ring of sabers unsheathed announced the approach of enemy cavalry, for skirmishers dispersed about the countryside were certain to be massacred if cavalry took them by surprise.[11]

For their part, the light infantry units, accustomed to individual initiative and much more thoroughly trained in marksmanship than the line infantry, were the troops best adapted to defending or attacking fortified positions, where it wasn't possible to deploy the men in the formations recommended in the manual. As we shall see, the fights around Hougoumont and La Haye Sainte essentially involved light infantry, engaged in furious hand-to-hand combat in the gardens and orchards of the two farms, and inside the buildings themselves; not by chance had both Wellington and Napoleon from the start assigned the bulk of their light battalions to these two sectors, even at the cost of exposing other parts of their lines by stripping away indispensable skirmishers.

Understanding the grammar, as it were, of Napoleonic warfare provides insights into what happened on the battlefield at Waterloo, starting at noon on that June 18, when Reille's artillery opened fire on the enemy troops deployed on the high ground behind the château of Hougoumont, and his infantry columns, preceded by a host of skirmishers, started marching toward the farm, toward the hedges and ditches that marked the limits of its orchard and wood.

TWENTY-TWO

---•◆•---

HOUGOUMONT

The Hougoumont château was a robust noble residence and compound, entirely surrounded by walls, with stables, barns, sheds, and houses for the farmer and gardener. There was a massive wooden gate on the south side, leading to an inner courtyard, and the facade of the main residence, the château itself, faced north and the Allied lines. A covered, sunken lane, to become famous as "the hollow way," permitted the troops deployed on the high ground in front of the château to send its defenders ammunition and reinforcements at any moment. On the eastern side of the building—the right side, from the French viewpoint—was a large formal garden, whose walls extended eastward for some two hundred yards, and beyond it was an orchard. A spacious wooded park, on which Reille advanced, extended five or six hundred yards to the rear of the château, and next to the park were a couple of pastures. The whole was enclosed by extremely thick hedgerows and a flooded ditch to keep in livestock. This topography, however, was known only to the German infantrymen who were occupying the château; all the French could see from their lines were the trees of the wood.

In normal conditions, an attack was always preceded by a prolonged cannonade, but the French, unable to see the enemy, could not fire upon him, nor could they know for a fact that he was really there. Had they been a little more familiar with the position, they might have bombarded the château. Although the artillery of the time consisted mostly of smoothbore cannon that fired projectiles in a flat trajectory, every battery included one or two howitzers, specifically designed to fire in a high arc and strike concealed objects. But Reille judged it useless to open fire against a complex of buildings about which, except for what he could glean from the map, he knew practically nothing. The only thing to do was to send light infantry into the wood and see what would happen.

Reille's II Corps comprised three divisions. To begin the attack, he selected the one commanded by Prince Jérome, which with approximately 6,500 bayonets was also the largest, accounting for half of the corps. The prince's division, which occupied the extreme left of the French army, was deployed at an oblique angle to the southwest corner of the wood and covered a front about half a mile long. A soldier burdened with his equipment and marching in the mud would have taken at least ten minutes to traverse this section of the French line. Prince Jérome did not owe his command to any particular military ability; in fact, his performance as commander of the army of Westphalia during the Russian campaign—when he was king of that realm invented by his brother—had been a failure. Within the army, the prince was better known for his frequent duels and for a scandalous American wife, whom Napoleon had refused to allow into France. But his family ties were strong, and so Jérome had a division at his command, though the real work was handled by his second-in-command, General Guilleminot, who had been assigned to direct the prince.

Jérome's division was made up of two large brigades commanded by two barons, Bauduin and Soye. Both brigades contained expert regiments at full strength, composed in large part of Grande Armée veterans who had already fought against the British in Spain. The prince decided that General Bauduin's brigade would lead the advance into the wood. His men were particularly adapted to this sort of combat, including an excellent light infantry regiment of three battalions, the First Légère. Two days previously, the squares of this regiment, commanded by Colonel de Cubières, had thrown back Wellington's cavalry charges of Quatre Bras, and its fire had killed the young Duke of Brunswick. Bauduin ordered the colonel to advance his battalions to the edge of the wood and to send a line of skirmishers to explore it.

Cubières's men, like all those in Reille's corps, had bivouacked along the main road far behind the front lines. Awakened at five o'clock, they had marched north to Le Caillou, arriving at the farm in the early morning, when the emperor was still there. After a halt, they had started marching again and had barely taken up their positions before Hougoumont when the order came to advance into the park. While the *tirailleurs* of the First Légère, ahead of the columns, were running toward the wood, leaping the ditch, getting through the hedge, and darting among the trees, Reille's artillery started firing on the little that could be seen of the English line, deployed on the high ground on the other side of Hougoumont. Hearing this first cannonade, Ensign Leeke of the Fifty-second Light Infantry, a seventeen-year-old lad who had joined the regiment little more than a month before, convinced himself in his innocence that the enemy was firing at the Duke of Wellington, who as it happened had stopped with a group of his aides not far away. Shortly thereafter, he saw something go hissing through the grain. A sergeant wryly instructed him, "There, Mr. Leeke, is a cannon shot, if you never saw one before, sir."

In their turn, the British artillery positioned on the high ground began to fire at Cubières's battalions, which had advanced into the open while their skirmishers disappeared into the wood. The first balls struck the files of the First Légère with mortal precision, claiming many victims; battalions in column order always presented an excellent target to artillery. Therefore, to give their men some shelter from the bombardment, the French officers ordered them down into a little lane—sunken, like all those in the region—that ran right along their front; and since an intense exchange of musketry continued to resound ahead of them, the officers started sending a growing number of men into the wood, a few at a time.

TWENTY-THREE

THE DEFENSE
OF THE CHÂTEAU

As early as the previous evening, it had been apparent to Wellington that Hougoumont must be defended at all costs. The responsibility for this defense devolved upon the Guards Division, deployed on the high ground immediately facing the estate on the north. Each of the division's two brigades, commanded by Sir John Byng and Sir Peregrine Maitland, consisted of only two battalions, but they were much larger than normal and made up of troops selected and trained with the meticulousness that characterized the Guards; in reality, however, the majority of these men had received their baptism of fire only a few days before at Quatre Bras. In the evening of June 17, the division commander, knowing that he could send reinforcements into the château whenever he chose, had limited himself to occupying the buildings and grounds with his four light companies, each numbering about a hundred men. He placed two of these companies, commanded by Lieutenant Colonel Macdonell, in the main building and the garden, and the other two, under the command of Lieutenant Colonel Lord Saltoun, in the orchard. In reaching their assigned positions, the British had come upon a French patrol, which they had been obliged to chase off in a firefight before they could take possession of the château.

But before they defended the buildings they would have to defend the park, and Wellington had decided that German light infantry was better for this sort of combat than their British counterparts; the men in such German units were called *Jäger*, "hunters," and for good reason. By tradition, they were recruited among gamekeepers, and their dark green uniforms served to camouflage them among the trees. By order of the duke, some Hanoverian *Jäger* companies had been detached from their units the previous evening and sent to occupy the park on the south side of the château; but when Wellington examined the position on the morning of the battle, he became convinced that he needed more troops and ordered the 1/2nd Nassau, which belonged to the Prince of Weimar's brigade, to leave Papelotte and move into Hougoumont wood. When this battalion arrived with its seven hundred to eight hundred men, the Guards officers, believing they could leave to the Germans the responsibility of the defense of the château, withdrew their men from the premises and occupied a position nearby.

The selection of the Nassau battalion to defend the château and especially the park seems questionable in retrospect. Nassauer infantrymen did wear green uniforms and were officially designated as *Jäger*, which may have caused the Guards officers, according to some of their accounts, to see the new arrivals as light infantry. Instead, however, they were probably a normal infantry battalion, not at all trained for this type of combat. Major von Büsgen, who commanded them, took possession of the empty château and sent some of his men, including the light company, to the edge of the wood. At that moment there were about a thousand muskets at Hougoumont, of which perhaps half were defending the perimeter of the park.

The first French skirmishers understandably found it difficult to advance very far into the wood, requiring first Cubières's regiment and then Bauduin's entire brigade to send in increasing numbers of men. To get to the park, the *tirailleurs* had to cover a certain amount of open ground under the disagreeably accurate fire of the British artillery; once they were in the wood, which was not particularly thick, they found that the trees offered only partial shelter from the Germans' lively fusillades. Since all commanding officers of the time had to be able to move quickly on the battlefield, General Bauduin urged his men forward from horseback, thus presenting an excellent target; he was killed almost at once, the first of seven French generals who would be mortally wounded that day.

Even after Bauduin's death, however, his regimental commanders knew what they had to do: keep their troops under cover, as close to the wood as possible, and send in more and more men. Although the German defenders held on tenaciously, eventually the French were able to bring a considerably superior number of muskets to bear on them. Before long, the *Jäger*, running short of ammunition and demoralized by the growing number of enemies pouring into the wood, were driven back to the residence and the garden. The Nassauer's regiment had already been severely battered at Quatre Bras; at Hougoumont, many of the men managed to get inside the compound and kept on fighting, but some of them decided they'd seen enough and slipped away. Wellington himself observed their flight, but when he tried to stop a group of them, one fired a random shot in the duke's direction before taking to his heels. "Do you see those fellows run?" Wellington observed to the Austrian attaché, who happened to be by his side at that moment. "Well, it is with these that I must win the battle."

Thus the French light infantry reached the wall protecting the garden and the rear of the château. Since it was more than six feet high, this wall looked difficult to climb over; but farther along to the left, in the back of the building, there was a large entrance with a heavy door, and the orchard, which stood farther to the right, was not walled but merely surrounded by a hedge, albeit taller than a man and extremely thick. The French, therefore, went resolutely forward. All along the wall and the hedge, however, the surviving Germans were waiting for them, together with the light companies of the Guards, who had precipitously returned to their former positions as soon as the British generals realized that the Germans were evacuating the wood. In the course of the previous night, the Guards had had time to fortify the château by making loopholes in the rear of the building, barricading the big door, and building makeshift platforms that allowed the defenders to fire over the garden wall, while the French, when they emerged from the wood, found themselves in the open. Their first assault failed, and the *tirailleurs*, demoralized by their losses, fell back into the wood.

Up to this point, Wellington had remained on the high ground beyond Hougoumont, anxiously watching the development of the conflict. He then decided to push back and retake Hougoumont wood. For the most part, it was impossible for the British artillery to fire on the French, who were well hidden by the trees of the park; but Wellington had at his disposal a battery of six howitzers, under the command of Major Bull. The howitzers had been recently purchased, and this was the moment to see whether they were worth all the sterling they had cost. Cannon fired either cast-iron balls capable of killing or mangling many men at a time, one after the other, if they were struck while in formation, or canister— also called "case-shot"—which had an effective range of only three or four hundred yards. Howitzers, by contrast, could lob their shots in from a high angle, and they fired a different type of ammunition: explosive shells, which burst into fragments that could cause great slaughter, or the even more deadly shrapnel, an English invention, which exploded in midair, pelting a wide area with a murderous hail of musket balls. The only drawback to this technology—whose future was obviously assured—lay in the difficulty of adjusting the fuse so that the shell would burst at the proper distance from the ground. But Major Bull (one of the very few British officers of the time who wore a beard) knew his business. The shells and shrapnel began to explode above the *tirailleurs* hidden among the trees and in the midst of the infantry columns that had advanced as far as the hedgerows, and almost at once the French started retreating in disorder, while the Guards went forward with fixed bayonets and retook possession of the wood.

TWENTY-FOUR

————•◆•————

THE BOMBARDMENT IN THE HOUGOUMONT SECTOR

When he perceived that all the progress made by his men in more than an hour's hard fighting had been nullified, Prince Jérome must surely have felt frustrated. His brother—or so the prince asserted in his memoirs—had personally ordered him to take Hougoumont "at all costs." Obviously, he needed to send in more men; Soye's brigade, therefore, was ordered to move forward in support of Bauduin's. While Bauduin's battalions, feeling the effects of the losses they had suffered, stayed in the shelter of a sunken lane, Soye's men advanced into the open, and in their turn drew the fire of the British artillery. When they reached cover at the edge of the wood, the brigade sent in its skirmishers. Many trees were by then stripped of their branches and in some cases half down, and the *tirailleurs* who went forward among them once again gained numerical superiority and compelled the defenders to retreat to the château and the garden. There, however, the attack stalled, because taking the barricaded gate and the garden wall by storm was clearly impossible.

A bombardment by the French artillery broke the stalemate and allowed the embattled brigades to return to the attack. Right from the beginning of the action, Reille's guns had been firing at everything in sight, and even though the distance (a good thousand yards, on average) represented the limit of his 6-pounders' range, a disconcerting number of cannonballs nonetheless reached their targets. All the British eyewitness accounts confirm that the infantry massed on the high ground beyond Hougoumont came under fire from the very first moment and suffered a steady attrition that gradually began to wear on the men's nerves. The column of companies, the formation in which most of Wellington's battalions were deployed, waiting to enter into contact with the enemy, was a deep formation, with all ten companies lined up one behind the other, like rungs on a ladder. It was easy to maneuver units so deployed—a column could transform itself into a line in a few minutes and into a square in even less time than that—and therefore this was the ideal formation for waiting troops; but it certainly wasn't suitable for withstanding artillery fire.

The Twenty-third Fusiliers, whose position was behind the Guards, came under fire from some French guns that had been brought up as far as the Nivelles road; after several men had already been wounded, a ball scored a direct hit on a captain, killing him instantly, whereupon Colonel Ellis ordered his troops to lie down. The Fifty-first Light, holding the extreme right of the Allied line, west of Hougoumont, faced an expanse of grain fields, taller than a man, in the midst of which French skirmishers were hiding, and so the British regiment was under both musket and artillery fire. Sergeant Wheeler found the experience anything but pleasant, and the men of the Fifteenth Hussars, who had been detached to cover this flank, must have felt the same. "A shell now fell into the column of the 15th Huzzars and bursted," he recalled. "I saw a sword and scabbard fly out from the column. . . . grape and shells were dupping about like hail, this was devilish annoying. As we could not see the enemy, altho they were giving us a pretty good sprinkling of musketry, our buglers sounded to lie down." One after the other, all the regiments eventually took the same precaution, and all that multitude of soldiers lay facedown on the wet earth while French cannonballs whizzed over their heads.

A first consequence of the bombardment, therefore, was that the British infantry was kept under pressure and forced to remain under cover as much as possible. But, even more important for the French, their guns distracted the British artillery, which had demonstrated its effectiveness early in the attack, whenever Reille's battalions had exposed themselves in closed formation. Napoleon's artillery outnumbered that of his foe, and it had been ordered to deliver counterbattery fire—that is, to fire on the enemy's guns—whenever possible. Wellington, on the other hand, had expressly ordered his battery commanders not to let themselves be lured into artillery duels, which were a waste of precious ammunition. As Napoleon himself observed, for artillery to respond to enemy fire in kind was practically an automatic reflex. "When artillerymen are under attack from an enemy battery, they can never be made to fire on massed infantry. It's natural cowardice, the violent instinct of self-preservation: men immediately defend themselves from their attackers and try to destroy them, in order to avoid being destroyed themselves."

As soon as the British artillerymen in the batteries stationed behind Hougoumont realized that the French guns were firing on them, Wellington's prohibition was promptly forgotten. Captain Mercer's troop, placed at the end of the artillery line with orders to fire on any French cavalry that advanced too far, quickly came under fire and lost a few horses; since his battery had more than two hundred of them, they presented the most obvious target. Irritated, Mercer decided to flout his orders and opened fire against the French artillery ("a folly, for which I would have paid dearly had our Duke chanced to be in our part of the field"), but had to desist almost at once, because he realized he was drawing the attention of too many enemy batteries and risked getting the worst of it in a protracted duel. A short distance behind his troop, the infantry of the Fourteenth Regiment (waggishly nicknamed "the Peasants," because they were all extremely young recruits just arrived from rural Buckinghamshire) were lying on the ground, but still in square, as the French cavalry wasn't far away: Mercer caught glimpses of their lances, with their white and red banners flying above the fields of tall grain that bordered the Nivelles road.

Like Mercer unable to resist temptation, other battery commanders began to respond to the French fire. Captain Samuel Bolton, who commanded six 9-pounders drawn up six or seven hundred yards behind the château, detached three of them to engage a French battery that, according to one of his officers, "was committing great devastation amongst our troops in and near Hougoumont." Those three guns kept firing at the enemy battery for more than an hour, trying to force it to change position. However, the artillery support was scarcely appreciated by the British infantry deployed in that area of the field. Things were going fairly calmly for the Seventy-first Regiment, whose soldiers were lying in a hollow. But then Bolton's guns arrived and took up positions right in front of them, "which, attracting the Enemy's attention, brought down a heavy fire of shot and shell, very destructive in its consequences to our Columns lying in the rear," as an officer of the Seventy-first remembered with annoyance many years later.

Major Bull's howitzer battery, which had directed such effective fire against the French infantry that penetrated Hougoumont wood, also came under attack from the enemy artillery, and Bull, too, lost no time in responding in kind. Later, he justified his actions by declaring that no fewer than twenty-two French guns had been firing directly at his position. In the long run, the losses in men, horses, and wagons and the expenditure of shells wore down the battery to such a point that, no more than two hours after the beginning of the battle, Bull's guns were compelled to abandon the line of fire. Wellington, who was still in the area, was so irritated by the disobedience of his artillery that he gave his aides orders to place the first battery commander he came upon under arrest. The commander in question nevertheless succeeded in convincing the duke that his guns were firing at the enemy infantry and not—as most of his colleagues were doing—at the enemy artillery. Gritting his teeth, Wellington agreed to let the matter drop.

TWENTY-FIVE

THE ATTACK ON
THE NORTH GATE

Although the battle flared up throughout the Hougoumont sector between noon and one o'clock, for the majority of the soldiers massed there this meant only that they had to remain stretched out on the ground in hollows or sunken lanes, while every now and then a shell exploded in their vicinity or a cannonball passed hissing over their heads. The artillery was more and more engaged in dueling, battery against battery, while losses of men and horses mounted, guns overheated and became less accurate, and ammunition chests were emptied at an alarming rate. But this situation, which seemed to be a stalemate, actually favored the French infantry, which was no longer pinned down by the enemy guns. Though the French were incapable of taking the south wall of the château by storm, they could still maneuver around the flanks: through the pastures to their right, where Bull's howitzers had pounded them not long before, and through the stretch of flat country to their left, under cover from the horse artillery troops that had advanced beyond the Nivelles road.

Prince Jérome's division, therefore, began to maneuver. Having sent their light companies forward into the wood, Soye's battalions marched in column through the pastures, got past the hedges, and invaded the orchard. The British and German defenders commanded by Lieutenant Colonel Lord Saltoun were forced to abandon the orchard and were chased back into the hollow way that ran in front of the château. There, however, Soye's attack came to a halt. The so-called hollow way was deeply entrenched, bordered with thorny hedgerows, and defended by hundreds of muskets, as was the garden wall, and they were equally difficult to get over. Incapable of going forward, the French troops who had passed through the pastures and into the orchard started to engage the defenders in an intense firefight

94

that was unlikely to turn to their advantage. In an attempt to dislodge the defenders from their positions, the French hauled a cannon into the orchard. A worried Lord Saltoun responded by ordering his men to make a sortie and capture the gun, but the withering enemy fire compelled them to scamper back to their covered positions. Their young lieutenant colonel, commanding from horseback and offering the easiest of targets, escaped without a scratch, though in the course of several hours' fighting he had four horses killed under him. The cannon, however, proved less effective than the French had hoped, and the exchange of musketry went on, more or less inconclusively; but the French, being more exposed, suffered greater losses.

During this time, the troops of Bauduin's former brigade were also maneuvering, but over the flat land on the west side of the château. Captain Mercer, from his position on the high ground overlooking the Nivelles road, watched the French and British light troops engage in an interminable skirmish amid the tall grain. Under enemy pressure, the British skirmishers were obliged to give ground, not enough to endanger the position, but enough to allow the enemy infantry to maneuver unmolested on the plain. Colonel de Cubières, who had taken command of the entire brigade after Bauduin's death, had already lost many men in the wood, but he had enough left to try another way. His soldiers, less troubled by the British artillery, advanced in the open, went around the west side of the château, descended into a sunken lane, and found themselves in front of the north gate. This large wooden portal was the only means of communication between the Hougoumont garrison and the reserves deployed farther to the rear, and therefore it was not barricaded; a short while before, in fact, the Guards had brought an ammunition cart through the gate and into the farmyard.

The appearance of Cubières and his men before the north gate marked the most critical moment for Hougoumont's defenders, and it is no coincidence that more than one British officer, many years after the battle, still remembered the French commander on his horse, one arm in a sling because of a wound he had suffered at Quatre Bras two days before, urging on his *tirailleurs*.

Colonel de Cubières, baron of the empire, was by birth the Marquis Despans de Cubières and was, therefore, one of the many young nobles of the *ancien régime* (no more than children at the time of the French Revolution) who had sided with the emperor and made a career in the Grande Armée. When Napoleon had returned from Elba three months previously, the twenty-nine-year-old Cubières was second-in-command of the First Légère, and he had been present at the moral crisis of his soldiers, divided between the oath they had sworn to the Bourbons and their old loyalty to the emperor. Very soon after Napoleon's arrival in Paris, the regiment passed in review before him, and he asked who its commander was. Cubières took a step forward and said, "Sire, it's Colonel de

Beurnonville, but he's ill." Napoleon replied, "Beurnonville's not one of ours. From now on, it is you, Colonel Cubières, who will take command of the 1st Légère." Then the emperor walked away, bringing the colonel's protests to an end with a wave of his hand.

Napoleon's exit line is indicative of an often overlooked aspect of these events—how profoundly ideological was the 1815 Armée du Nord, which had been purged, insofar as possible, of everyone who was not "one of ours." But, even for those times, Cubières was an exceptional man, and he commanded an exceptional regiment. On May 2 the soldiers, like all French citizens, had been called to vote in a plebiscite on the so-called Acte additionnel, the new constitution that Napoleon had devised for France. In front of his regiment assembled on the parade ground, Colonel de Cubières declared that he would vote against the constitution because it gave the emperor too much power and could not be the foundation of a genuinely liberal France; furthermore, such a hastily arranged plebiscite was in itself undemocratic; and therefore he, Cubières, called upon the soldiers of his regiment to vote against the measure. The First Légère was the only regiment in the army to vote against the Acte additionnel, and it did so nearly unanimously. (The sole exception was a captain, who explained, "I love the colonel with all my heart, but when it comes to making constitutions, he's not so clever as the Emperor, who's made plenty of them.") Napoleon was not pleased with the regiment's vote—before very long, all record of it conveniently disappeared—but Cubières got off with a letter of censure and retained his command.

Lieutenant Colonel Macdonell's two light companies of British Guards were positioned outside the château when Cubières and his men arrived at the north gate. Surprised by the sudden appearance of the French, the Guards beat a hasty retreat, passing through the still-open gate into the farmyard. In the course of this brisk withdrawal, a British sergeant standing very close to Cubières fired on him and knocked him from his horse. The sergeant sprang into the saddle and urged the beast through the gateway, reaching the safety of the farmyard just before his comrades closed the big door. Cubières, who was only wounded, managed to rise to his feet and reach safety, and ever after he was convinced that the British, seeing how disabled he was, had deliberately refrained from shooting at him anymore. Many years later, when he was in the service of the pope as governor of Ancona, Cubières met an officer of the Coldstream Guards, a veteran of Hougoumont, and expressed to him his gratitude for their chivalrous conduct.

While Cubières was being carried to safety, the situation of his men could easily have become precarious; the only way to get in was to hack through the gate, and one of the officers of the First Légère, Lieutenant Legros, whose bulk and strength had earned him the nickname "l'Enfonceur" ("the Basher"), took a sapper's ax, positioned himself before the gate, and started hacking away. Once a sapper himself, Legros knew how to wield his instrument; soon he smashed through the wooden bar that held the gate closed. Then the rest of the barrier yielded to the pressure of many bodies, and a large number of Frenchmen burst inside. At the beginning of the savage melee that followed, the panicked defenders sought refuge in the surrounding buildings, leaving Legros and his men, for a brief time, masters of the yard. A Frenchman armed with an ax chased a German officer into one of the houses, caught up with him at the door, and chopped off one of his hands.

That morning, Müffling had expressed to Wellington some doubt about the defenders' ability to hold the château. The duke's only answer was "Ah, but you don't know Macdonell." At a moment of crisis, the lieutenant colonel proved himself worthy of his fame as one of army's most formidable warriors. Together with some other officers and a sergeant, the thirty-four-year-old Macdonell was able to fight his way through the enemy, close what was left of the gate, and set another timber in place, after which all the French who had entered the compound were killed, including Legros, except one: Rushing into the farmyard in time to see Macdonell, his face covered with blood, finish barricading the gate, Private Matthew Clay ran into a French drummer boy, whose life had been spared because of his age. Clay took the boy into his care and brought him inside the château, to the room where the wounded had been assembled, telling him to stay there and not to be afraid, because no one was going to hurt him. Meanwhile, the French troops who had remained outside the château compound, raked by the defenders' precise fire, were beginning to disperse, while those who tried to climb over the wall were struck down one by one.

But many *tirailleurs*, instead of withdrawing to their own lines, climbed the slope in the direction of the Allied positions, concealing themselves amid the high-standing grain. Directly above them, Lieutenant Colonel Webber-Smith had positioned the six 9-pounder guns of his battery. Like other British artillery commanders, Webber-Smith was completely indifferent to Wellington's orders prohibiting long-range dueling, and he immediately began firing at the French horse artillery batteries on the other side of the plain. The battery was fully engaged in the combat and had already suffered its first casualties when the French skirmishers hidden in the nearby grain suddenly opened fire. In the course of a few minutes, many gunners and horses were hit, and Webber-Smith had to give orders to limber up the guns and abandon the position before it was too late.

At this point Sir John Byng, who commanded the Guards brigade deployed on the rising ground behind Hougoumont, decided to counterattack in force to alleviate the pressure on the château's defenders. His two battalions—the Second Coldstream Guards and the 2/3rd Foot Guards—went down the slope in companies, one after the other, and reached the hollow way. Surprised by their arrival, the *tirailleurs* withdrew in disorder, abandoning even the orchard. After a brief fusillade, some of the guardsmen succeeded in entering the farmyard, the rest got into the garden through a small side door, and soon Lord Saltoun's exhausted men were relieved. Notwithstanding the losses suffered by the Allied troops, the château was now defended by more than 1,500 muskets, and the chances that the French might overrun it were more and more remote. Not coincidentally, at about one-thirty in the afternoon—precisely when the reinforcements were taking up their positions in and around the château—Wellington left the high ground above Hougoumont for the first time and went to oversee the center of his battle line, where the roar of cannon indicated another thickening storm.

TWENTY-SIX

THE GRANDE BATTERIE

A little after eleven in the morning, Count d'Erlon and his artillery commander, General Desales, were observing the French troops as they took up positions on the slope to the right of La Belle Alliance when they were joined by an imperial aide-de-camp, General de La Bédoyère.[12] He was carrying the order dictated by the emperor at eleven, commanding I Corps to begin the attack at one o'clock that afternoon in the direction of Mont-Saint-Jean, first sending forward the division on the left and then supporting it with the others in turn, from left to right. The order added that the three reserve artillery batteries attached to I, II, and VI Corps were to mass their powerful 12-pounder guns and attack the center of the enemy position.

After handing Desales the order, La Bédoyère verbally informed him that the emperor was putting him in command of all the artillery deployed in the center. This included not only the three reserve batteries but also I Corps's four divisional batteries, with seven or eight 6-pounders each. All these cannon would form a Grande Batterie of fifty-four guns, which Desales was to deploy in a single line halfway down the slope of La Belle Alliance. This arrangement sounded familiar to Napoleon's generals; the emperor hadn't been an artillery officer in his youth for nothing, and he had always taught that it was necessary to wear down the enemy with a bombardment before attacking him, and that this meant concentrating the highest possible number of guns on the point where the breakthrough was to be made.

A battery was an extremely cumbersome organization. Every 12-pounder piece required about fifteen gunners, many of whom shuttled to and from the ammunition wagons, which for security reasons were parked at least thirty or forty yards to the rear. For every gun, there were two or three wagons, each drawn by four horses, in addition to its limber. This, too, waited at a certain distance, with its six draft horses and their drivers. Each cannon weighed, on average, about a ton, and since there was no mechanism to absorb the recoil, the gun rolled back a couple of yards after every shot and had to be hauled back into position by the gunners. Main strength was also required to carry the cast-iron cannonballs from the wagons to the guns; each ball weighed about ten pounds. Obviously, every gun required a great deal of room to maneuver, so that a French battery with eight pieces, 200 men (gunners and drivers), and almost 150 horses ended up occupying a hundred-yard front, with a depth of around fifty yards. Once the 12-pounders were in position, mired in the sticky mud of the Flemish hills, moving them again was extremely difficult.

The position that Napoleon had chosen for the Grande Batterie presented advantages and disadvantages. The lay of the land, gradually sloping down toward the opposing lines, seemed expressly designed for deploying a great many guns directly in the face of the enemy, with a guaranteed effect on his morale; indeed, the accounts given by the British officers confirm that the arrival of the French batteries, which took up their positions one after the other, was observed with growing uneasiness. Captain Kincaid of the Ninety-fifth Rifles, who was stationed on a little hill a hundred yards behind La Haye Sainte, had been scanning the field with idle curiosity when he realized what was happening in the sector right in front of him, which until a few minutes before had been deserted. From that moment on, he was unable to take his eyes off the "innumerable black specks" which he could see "taking post at regular distances" in advance of the opposing line; "recognizing them as so many pieces of artillery, I knew from experience, although nothing else was yet visible, that they were unerring symptoms of our not being destined to be idle spectators."

Squinting through telescopes, the French artillery officers scanned the enemy position, trying to identify possible targets. A great many batteries could be seen all along the ridge of Mont-Saint-Jean, some out in the open, some covered by the hedges that bordered the sunken lane. Behind La Haye Sainte, nothing else was visible; to the right, however, a long line of infantry was in plain sight, deployed on the exposed forward slope of the ridge ahead of and below the British guns. It is doubtful that Desales's artillerymen knew that this line, part of Perponcher's Netherlands Division, represented only a fraction of the enemy's left wing, and that most of his soldiers were deployed farther back, lying on the ground on the reverse slope of the ridge, protected and invisible. Nevertheless, the French regarded this visible fraction as a target more than sufficient to justify the artillery concentration ordered by the emperor.

However, there was such a great distance between the mouths of the guns and the positions they were to attack that the French cannonades seemed more likely to affect enemy morale than anything else. At a thousand yards, not even 12-

pounders would fire their projectiles with any great accuracy, while firing 6-pounders at that distance was equivalent to shooting at random. But evidently Napoleon preferred not to risk his guns by sending them too far forward; the great concentration of fire from so many muzzles would compensate for the inaccuracy of their aim. Besides, the task of the Grande Batterie was, above all, to achieve a psychological effect; this is clear from the emperor's order to Desales, in which the latter is expressly enjoined to open fire with all his guns at the same moment, "to astonish the enemy and shake his morale."

One of Napoleon's artillery officers, however, was not content with morale-shaking. General Ruty, the overall artillery commander of the Armée du Nord, joined Desales as he was overseeing the deployment of his guns and observed that it would be a good idea to move the batteries forward during the course of the attack so that they would not have to fire from so prohibitive a distance. In anticipation of such an advance, therefore, Ruty ordered Desales to carry out a reconnaissance in the direction of the enemy lines and identify a suitable position. Convinced as he was "by theory and by practice" that moving so much artillery in the middle of a battle was always dangerous, Desales had his doubts, but nonetheless rode his horse down the slope, and within a few hundred yards, he discovered a spur of ground almost within musket range of La Haye Sainte. The terrain formed a natural platform on which he could deploy his guns in case of need.

His reconnaissance complete, Desales turned back to start the attack, assigning commanders to the different sectors of the Grande Batterie. Desales wanted the most expert of his subordinates, Colonel Bernard, to command the 12-pounder batteries, but the colonel had lost an eye at the siege of Zaragoza and, as he pointed out to Desales, was not the most suitable man for the job; at that distance, the 12-pounders were the only guns one could still try to aim. Therefore, the one-eyed man was given command of the 6-pounder batteries, and Desales put another colonel, younger and still all in one piece, in charge of the 12-pounders. The general then reported to Marshal Ney, who was caracoling impatiently in the center of the deployment, and informed him that, as far as the artillery was concerned, the battle could begin.

When the Grande Batterie opened fire between noon and one o'clock, fierce fighting had been going on around Hougoumont for some time; nevertheless, the roar of all those guns drowned out every other sound, and Desales felt the earth shuddering under his feet. From time immemorial, soldiers in the French army had referred to cannon with a nickname that mingled familiarity and revulsion—*le brutal*—and they were surely right. One of the first shots that struck the little hill where Captain Kincaid was stationed scored a direct hit on the only tree, sending a hail of branches showering down on the battalion's two medical officers, who had set up an aid station in that spot, believing it to be safe. However, Wellington's more experienced soldiers quickly realized that the enemy was carrying on this massive bombardment principally for psychological effect. An officer in Picton's division later recalled, "The greater part, fortunately, went over our heads, carrying one off here and there. This fire was much too high; the old hands said it was meant to intimidate, as usual."

The cannonballs and shells that passed high above the ridge nevertheless came down vertically upon the troops massed in the second line. Perhaps the French batteries at a certain point deliberately began firing as high as possible in order to reach the dead ground behind the ridge, especially after the Dutch-Belgian infantry, initially deployed on the exposed forward slope, hastily withdrew to a more sheltered position. Firing blindly in this way meant that actually hitting someone was a matter of chance, but the bombardment was so intense that the infantry soldiers stretched out on the ground behind La Haye Sainte and behind the chemin d'Ohain all the way to Papelotte nevertheless began to take losses. A few too many shots reached even the reserve cavalry deployed on Wellington's left wing several hundred yards behind the ridge, and Sir William Ponsonby, who commanded one of the two heavy cavalry brigades, had his men withdraw and search for less dangerous ground.

Any calculation of the intensity of the fire produced by the Grande Batterie can only be based on statistical averages, which are best treated with suspicion. Desales had twenty-four 12-pounder guns and thirty 6-pounders, to which were added the horse artillery's eighteen 6-pounders. The rate of fire was one shot per minute for the 12-pounders, which were more difficult to return to their positions after recoiling, and two per minute for the lighter guns, for a total of 120 shots per minute. However, the bombardment was dispersed along a front of more than two thousand yards, and the French gunners conscientiously did their best to pound it all. Even General von Vincke, who commanded the Hanoverian militia brigade stationed on the extreme left of Wellington's line, reported that the enemy batteries took up their posts at noon, and despite a distance of two thousand paces, which should have rendered them harmless, they were able to strike the rear of his position, behind his lines, so that the brigade medical station had to be moved farther back.

On average, therefore, one shot per minute was fired for every twenty yards of front. The front, however, was several hundred yards deep; the shots fired with the highest trajectories landed inside this rectangle at random, and the soaked, soft ground stopped projectiles from bouncing very far. This explains why the Allied losses seemed in the long run bearable, despite the fact that the occasional direct hit sent shivers down the spines of all those who had the misfortune to witness it. While Ponsonby's cavalry was withdrawing to a more

Right: Napoleon Bonaparte. *Painting by Robert Lefèvre.*

Below right: The elderly Field Marshal Gebhard Leberecht von Blücher.

Below: Arthur Wellesley, Duke of Wellington, 1814. *Painting by Sir Thomas Lawrence.*

Above: Napoleon giving orders to an aide-de-camp for Marshal Grouchy on the morning of the battle.

Below: General Reille, commander of Napoleon's II Corps. *Engraving by A. Tardieu.*

Below: Jérome Bonaparte, division commander and Napoleon's youngest brother. *Painting, 1808.*

Above: The Duke of Wellington outside his headquarters at Mont-Saint-Jean. *Painting by J. C. Aylward.*

Left: The ceremonial Eagle, mounted on a pole with the French tricolor.

Below left: A 12-pounder gun, one of *les belles filles de l'Empereur.*

Below: The crops of rye in June were almost as tall as the infantry soldiers who flattened them as they marched across the fields.

Inset above: British soldiers form a square to defend against cavalry attacks.

Main illustration: The French bombard Hougoumont, prompting the British artillery to open fire, against Wellington's orders.

Inset opposite: The Guards brigade attack the French to alleviate the pressure on the defenders of the château, just visible in the far right background. *Painting by Denis Dighton.*

Right: The battle around the farmhouse and stables at La Haye Sainte. *Painting by R. Knotel.*

Above: General von Bülow. *German engraving.*

Below: Marshal Grouchy. *Engraving.*

Above: Count d'Erlon holding his marshal's baton. *Engraving by Collier after Larivière.*

Above: "That old rogue," Sir Thomas Picton.

Below: The charge of the Scots Grays. *Painting by Lady Butler.*

protected spot, Lieutenant Wyndham of the Scots Grays, a young officer who had joined the regiment barely a month previously, came across five or six Scottish soldiers who were carrying one of their wounded officers to the rear. Wyndham was considerably shaken "when a shell came and fell near them and destroyed nearly the whole [party]." As soon as the French guns began their bombardment, the Allied batteries duly replied, once again ignoring the orders of the duke. Through his telescope, Desales saw that the enemy cannon were protected by the sunken lane as though by a trench and that it would not be at all easy to silence them. The French artillery was more exposed, and the first casualties weren't long in coming: A shell exploded a short distance from Desales, wounding all those around him. Struck in the shoulder by a shell fragment, the general felt himself to see if he was wounded, but to his relief he discovered that the fragment had lodged itself in the collar of his coat; however, his arm stayed numb from the contusion for a long time, and from that point on Desales maintained a healthy respect for the precision of the British counterbattery fire.

Although the French general could not know it, the situation on Mont-Saint-Jean ridge was even more disconcerting. With mounting uneasiness, the officers of the Allied infantry watched artillery caissons struck by enemy cannonballs blow up before their eyes; as the smoke cleared, they could see that some batteries, running short of ammunition, were harnessing horses to limbers and preparing to clear out of that inferno. Les belles filles de l'Empereur, "the Emperor's beautiful daughters"—as the French gunners affectionately called their 12-pounders—were doing their job well.

D'Erlon's infantry soldiers, massed immediately behind the guns, could tell from the movement of the couriers and the gesticulations of the commanders that the moment was about to arrive when they would begin marching toward the Allied positions and "comb their hair for them," as the soldiers said. Captain Martin of the Forty-fifth Ligne, a Swiss barely twenty years old, was in a good humor, and so were all his troops; the night had been horrendous, but morning had brought a little cow meat, which seemed delicious to such hungry men, and a great deal of brandy, of which all had drunk their fill. "We were all getting ready, cleaning our weapons, urging one another to do well so we could finish the campaign with this one stroke. Alas! We didn't know how right we were."

TWENTY-SEVEN

NEWS OF THE PRUSSIANS

On the high ground behind Rossomme farm, Napoleon waited for Marshal Ney to set d'Erlon's infantry in motion. Major Lemonnier-Delafosse, General Foy's aide-de-camp, was there, too, expecting the arrival of an artillery battery that he was to guide into position. While he waited, the major observed his emperor: "He was sitting on a straw chair in front of a rustic table and holding his map open on it. His famous spyglass was in his hand, and he often pointed it at various parts of the battlefield. When he rested his eyes, he picked up a wheat straw and put it in his mouth like a toothpick. To his left stood Marshal Soult, alone, awaiting his orders, while ten paces behind him all the members of his staff were grouped together on horseback. Sappers from the engineers were leveling the ground around and making ramps so that people could reach the Emperor more easily. . . . In the end, I had to go away with the artillery, and I never saw him again."

Napoleon didn't remain seated in his straw chair the whole time. De Coster, the guide, described how the emperor walked up and down, sometimes with folded arms, but more often with his hands behind his back, or with his thumbs hooked in the pockets of his overcoat; now he looked at his watch, now he took a pinch of tobacco, now he brought the telescope to his eye and surveyed the battlefield. During one of these surveys he seemed to catch a glimpse of something in the distance, on the right, something that hadn't been there before. The emperor asked Soult for his opinion, and after examining the horizon, the general affirmed that they were looking at troops in movement. The other officers hastened to point their telescopes, but since it was a hazy day, there was a variety of perceptions: One thought it was a grove of trees, while others saw troops at rest with their weapons stacked. But someone declared in agreement with Soult that not only were they troops, but they were moving in their direction.

Comparing what they saw with the map, the French calculated that if indeed they were looking at marching columns, the head of those columns must be approaching Chapelle-St. Lambert, a village four or five miles away, just on the other side of the River Lasne; which meant that they would be able to reach the extreme right of the French line, deployed in front of Papelotte, in about three hours. Soult suggested that it might be Grouchy's troops, and at first glance the hypothesis appeared to them plausible as well as pleasantly reassuring. But the fact that it was even taken into consideration indicates that the emperor and his general weren't working with their habitual efficiency. In fact, Grouchy's last dispatch, dated at six in the morning, revealed that at that time he was still in Gembloux; his plan was to march toward Sart-à-Walhain—that is, farther to the northeast—before turning northwest toward Wavre, after making sure that the bulk of the Prussian troops had retreated in that direction. Had the emperor bent over his map and calculated the distances with his compass, as had been his custom in the past, he would have seen at once the physical impossibility that Grouchy, given the time of his departure and the direction he proposed to take, could have already reached Chapelle-St. Lambert. But nobody took the trouble to make those calculations, and the dangerously vague idea that Grouchy would shortly appear on the horizon continued to waft through everyone's head.

In any case, the emperor, though still uncertain, ordered the two cavalry divisions commanded by Domon and Subervie to deploy as cover for the right flank as far as the Fichermont wood, which closed off the battlefield on that side. This decision suggests that Napoleon did not really believe that a threat was going to materialize from that direction; those six regiments of light cavalry, a little more than 2,000 horsemen in all, were certainly not the right troops to infiltrate the wood and deny the Prussian vanguard passage over the Lasne, and in fact they limited themselves to taking up positions on the near side of Fichermont. Had the emperor sent a couple of battalions of light infantry into the wood instead of cavalry, pushing out a line of skirmishers as far as the escarpment that overlooked the watercourse, General von Bülow's advance might have been delayed almost indefinitely. But evidently, Napoleon's intention was simply to reinforce the cavalry screen on that flank and multiply reconnaissances to identify the approaching troops, in the hope that they were really Grouchy's. General Domon himself interpreted his mission in the most optimistic sense: He told his officers that the battle was won, that their task was to implement the linkage with Grouchy's troops, and that they would sleep that night in Brussels.

Nevertheless, all uncertainty about the troops that could be glimpsed beyond the bell tower of Chapelle-St. Lambert was soon dispelled, because a squadron from the Seventh Hussars arrived, bringing the emperor a Prussian prisoner. They had been sent by their commander, Colonel Marbot, who had that morning been ordered to make a reconnaissance beyond the French right flank. Once they were through the Fichermont wood, the Hussars were to patrol the roads and the bridges over the Lasne and the Dyle in anticipation of making contact with Grouchy's vanguard. Marbot was an old fox who would later write one of the most colorful memoirs in the epic of Napoleon. He was also a soldier who knew his business; the first Prussian courier who tried to pass his way was caught and sent to the emperor, together with the dispatch he was carrying. It was a note addressed to Wellington, informing him that Bülow's corps, marching as promised to the battlefield, had reached Chapelle-St. Lambert. The prisoner, who spoke French, did not hesitate to assure the emperor that the troops visible in the distance were indeed the vanguard of Bülow's corps, that the entire Prussian army had spent the night at Wavre, and that during their march that morning, they hadn't encountered a single Frenchman.

By then, Wellington had been aware for some time that the Prussians were on the way. That morning, a Prussian Hussar officer at the head of a cavalry patrol had come into contact with a squadron of the British Tenth Hussars, which had been assigned to guard the extreme left of the Allied deployment. After communicating to Captain Taylor, commander of the British squadron, the momentous news that Bülow's corps was now nearing the battlefield, the Prussian and his patrol turned back. Taylor immediately sent one of his officers to inform the duke, and then he and the rest of his men began anxiously scrutinizing the horizon, waiting for the Prussian columns to appear. But their wait turned out to be disagreeably long, and the occasional arrival of one of the duke's aides-de-camp, sent out to Taylor's position to determine whether anything had finally appeared, did nothing but add to the captain's embarrassment. He saw—too far off for him to be able to do anything about it—some French cavalry leave the field on what appeared to be a reconnaissance mission, heading in the direction from which the Prussians were supposed to arrive; but of the Prussians themselves he saw no trace.

Nevertheless, word that the Prussians were coming spread rapidly among the Allied officers. Sir Augustus Frazer learned it from one of Lord Uxbridge's aides-de-camp, who was looking for the duke, wishing to report the news to him, and asked Sir Augustus to join him in the effort. Frazer diligently copied Captain Taylor's report, according to which Bülow and his troops had arrived at a place that Sir Augustus transcribed as "Occey"; afterward, when he tried to find the place on the map, he was predictably unable to locate it anywhere. In any case, Frazer galloped off in search of Wellington but stopped on the way to communicate the news to Sir Thomas Picton and lingered to discuss the situation with him and to adjust the position of some guns; when, much later, he finally found the duke and delivered Taylor's report to Wellington's secretary, Lord Fitzroy Somerset, the latter icily informed him that "his Grace was aware of it."

TWENTY-EIGHT

BÜLOW'S MARCH

Although no one realized it, the information that the Prussian officer had given Captain Taylor was excessively optimistic; General von Bülow's march turned out to be much more difficult than had been foreseen. The roads his troops were advancing on were dreadful; actually, they were simple dirt paths, in terrible condition after days of rain. To follow them, the troops had to go up and down hills, traverse densely wooded areas, and pass over streams and rivers so swollen that only a few bridges would allow the men to cross them safely. It was the third consecutive day of marching for the exhausted men of the IV Corps, most of whom were inexperienced *Landwehr* recruits, and hardly any of whom had had anything to eat that morning except a little bread and brandy. Furthermore, they had to haul along with them some eighty-eight artillery pieces—howitzers and cannon—while sinking to their knees in mud.

Worse yet, IV Corps, even though it was the only corps in the Prussian army whose troops were still fresh, was also the one that had bivouacked farthest away. The men began marching at the first light of dawn, but they had to go through the encampments of the other three corps, and then through the narrow lanes and alleys of the little town of Wavre, before they could even set foot on the first of the muddy tracks that would lead them to Waterloo. The main stone bridge across the Dyle was located in the center of Wavre, and the situation that developed there can be easily imagined by anyone who has ever been stuck in a traffic jam. At one point, a single 12-pounder gun broke an axle and blocked the entire column; the street had barely been cleared when a mill near the bridge caught fire, and the flames quickly leaped to the adjoining buildings. Since, at that moment, the bridge was crowded with ammunition wagons, panic spread through the troops, and the column dissolved into a mob of howling runaways; only with difficulty could their officers succeed in getting them in line again on the other side of the bridge. The cumulative effect of so many delays was such that the last of the four brigades of IV Corps got under way only at ten in the morning, by which time its men, having been roused at dawn, had been standing in formation for six hours. By then, also, Bülow's column was strung out about six miles long, and his vanguard had already reached Chapelle-St. Lambert.

If Bülow's troops, instead of stopping there, had gone down into the Lasne valley, crossed the river, and continued marching along the tracks that led to Fichermont wood, they would have met no resistance worthy of note and would have reached the battlefield by the early afternoon. Perhaps Bülow's personal characteristics had some influence on the caution of his movements; the general was already an elderly man, a fervent Lutheran, and a composer of religious music, and at the same time much smitten with his own rank and quick to take offense. Gneisenau, his equal in rank but not in seniority, never sent him orders without couching them in the most obsequious terms. But Bülow was also a good general; in 1813, he had routed Marshal Ney at Dennewitz—a feat that had won him, among other things, the title of count.

When Bülow reached Chapelle-St. Lambert, he saw nothing ahead of him but a steep slope, almost a precipice, where the path descended into the valley; beyond the swollen waters of the Lasne, there was an equally impracticable ascent, up which his guns would have to be hauled and pushed; and beyond that, a thick forest prevented him from seeing anything else. As if that weren't enough, the instructions transmitted by Gneisenau the previous evening expressly directed Bülow to advance only as far as Chapelle-St. Lambert and not to proceed beyond that place without first having verified that Wellington's army was indeed engaged in battle at Waterloo; for if at the last moment the duke had decided not to stay where he was and await Napoleon's attack, the Prussians would not have exposed themselves to it, either.[13]

Thus it is difficult to blame General von Bülow, arriving at Chapelle-St. Lambert with his vanguard and knowing that several hours would pass before his whole corps could be assembled there, for being wary of ordering his troops to advance beyond the village. The cannonade had yet to begin at Waterloo, and his orders expressly forbade him to proceed farther without knowledge that the battle was on. As he waited to acquire more information, Bülow decided that the enemy was too close for him to take any chances; he deployed his battalions in battle order, one beside the other, by having them pass from marching formation to attack columns eight ranks deep, preceded by a swarm of skirmishers, as prescribed in the Prussian manual.

The passage from column of march to deployment by battalions in attack column was one of the most complex maneuvers that troops of those days had to perform. All officers knew, or should have known, the proper sequence of commands, but it was a long process at best, all the more so with exhausted and for the most part insufficiently trained troops like those of the IV Corps. While the Prussian commanders were intent on this maneuver, the opening cannonade at Waterloo could be heard in the distance. This convinced Bülow that there was indeed going to be a battle, but it also reinforced his belief that it was imperative to deploy his troops in battle order before proceeding. Several hours therefore passed between the moment when an officer of the Prussian Hussars, at the head of his patrol, met Captain Taylor near Smohain, and the moment when Bülow's first battalions, having completed their deployment on the high ground behind Chapelle-St.-Lambert, began to advance. Around one o'clock, when Napoleon noticed that something was happening in that area, the line of Prussian skirmishers had just begun moving out to cross the Lasne and penetrate the Fichermont wood.

TWENTY-NINE

———◆———

NEW ORDERS
FOR GROUCHY

Napoleon's reaction to the discovery that the columns advancing toward his right wing were not Grouchy's after all constitutes one of the enigmas of the Battle of Waterloo. In his memoirs, the emperor maintained that he ordered Mouton's entire corps—or rather, his two remaining divisions, a total of 6,000 muskets and thirty guns—to leave La Belle Alliance, where the corps was lined up in front of the Imperial Guard, and take up a covering position on the right flank, facing the Fichermont wood. This was not a large force, but it was fresh, and the forty-five-year-old Mouton, whose heroism in the 1809 campaign had earned him the title of count de Lobau, was one of the boldest and most enterprising of the French generals. He could well have found a way to hold off the Prussians for a few hours, thus giving Napoleon enough time to win his contest with Wellington.

Yet Mouton's troops were not in position to oppose the Prussians when they finally emerged from the Fichermont wood several hours later. All the French managed to do, after much delay, was assume a defensive deployment much farther back than they could have wished. The account of Colonel Combes-Brassard, the VI Corps chief of staff, offered a credible explanation of this puzzling state of affairs and at the same time confirmed the unreliability of Napoleon's memoirs. Combes-Brassard wrote that Mouton's troops were indeed posted to the right wing in the early afternoon, but their mission was to support the attack of d'Erlon's I Corps, and they were all taken completely by surprise when the Prussians appeared on their flank. This interpretation accords perfectly both with a situation that arose in the meantime and with the available accounts of other eyewitnesses. In all probability, the transfer of VI Corps to the right wing was intended to reinforce d'Erlon's divisions, which were engaged in what the emperor at that moment considered the decisive attack; only later, in an attempt to avoid the accusation of having underestimated the threat posed by Bülow, would Napoleon claim that his maneuver had been directed against the Prussians right from the start.

Did the emperor do nothing to meet the gathering threat on his right flank? His calculation makes sense in light of another element that formed an integral part of it—the hope and perhaps expectation that Grouchy's columns would appear on the horizon and take the Prussian columns arriving from Wavre in the flank. That Napoleon cherished this illusion is quite clearly demonstrated by the orders he sent out at the time. When Marbot's Hussars arrived with their prisoner, the Prussian courier, Soult had just finished writing a message to Grouchy, dated "from the battlefield at Waterloo, at one in the afternoon," with orders to maneuver his troops in such a way as to approach Napoleon's army as closely as possible, and moreover "to be always prepared to fall upon any enemy troops that may try to annoy our right, and to crush them." The emperor had a postscript added to this dispatch: "A letter that has just been intercepted states that General Bülow is to attack our flank. We believe that we see this corps on the high ground at Saint-Lambert; therefore, do not lose an instant in drawing near to us, in order to join us and crush Bülow, whom you will catch in flagrante delicto."

Napoleon, in short, was persuaded that Grouchy would arrive on the battlefield in time to resolve any problem caused by the Prussian advance. He is inevitably accused of excessive optimism, but was his conviction genuinely unrealistic? Grouchy would have had to cover twenty-five kilometers, starting from Gembloux, where he spent the night, then passing by Sart-à-Walhain (in accordance with his plan as stated in his last dispatch) before reaching Chapelle-St. Lambert. Such a distance on paths and tracks in bad condition, in heavily wooded country, and with the River Dyle to cross would ordinarily have taken twelve or thirteen hours of march for a column of infantry with all its wagons and guns, but an energetic commander could have done it in less time. If Grouchy had in fact begun his march at six in the morning, as his dispatch claimed, his columns might have appeared in the neighborhood of Chapelle-St. Lambert in the late afternoon, in time to attack Bülow's flank and rear before the Prussian could have time to organize an attack of his own. More than one field marshal had successfully carried out undertakings of this kind.

This hypothesis, however, was based on the assumption that Marshal Grouchy, once he reached Sart-à-Walhain, would turn northwest immediately and cross the Dyle by the bridges of Mousty and Ottignies. (Not coincidentally, Napoleon had expressly included these two places among those he required Colonel Marbot's Hussar patrols to reconnoiter.) Only in this case could Grouchy's columns have appeared on the horizon in time, despite weary hours of marching, and engaged the Prussians, who would have been no less exhausted than the marshal's men. Yet, while Soult was adding the postscript to his one o'clock dispatch, Grouchy's columns had already advanced too far north to use those bridges, and the marshal, positively informed that the bulk of the Prussian forces were concentrated around Wavre, had decided to head straight for them and was continuing his northward march.

Grouchy has been harshly criticized for not having heeded the advice of his subordinates, who wanted to march not northward but westward, where the thunder of cannon fire was growing increasingly intense; but the orders Grouchy had thus far received from Napoleon left the marshal no other option, and the emperor should have known this. The previous day, when he charged Grouchy with pursuing the retreating Prussians, Napoleon had stressed to him the necessity of maintaining contact at all costs with the enemy: Follow him closely, the emperor said, "with your sword against his back." At that moment, everyone in the French command was convinced that the Prussians were retiring on Gembloux and Namur—that is, toward the east—and Grouchy had naturally sent his columns marching off in that direction. The emperor's following dispatch, dated from Le Caillou at ten in the morning and received by Grouchy in the early afternoon, acknowledged that at least a part of the Prussian forces had instead headed north, toward Wavre, but nevertheless obliged the marshal to follow them in the same direction rather than turn west toward Waterloo. ("His Majesty desires that you direct your movements toward Wavre . . . pushing before you the units of the Prussian army which have taken that direction, and which are supposed to have halted at Wavre, where you must arrive as soon as possible.")

While Napoleon's ten o'clock dispatch, in addition to the instructions above, enjoined Grouchy to maneuver in such a way as to approach the main French force and to stay in contact with its operations, the emperor clearly wanted Grouchy to make this approach by way of Wavre. At ten o'clock, in fact, far from suspecting that they had already begun marching on Waterloo, Napoleon was still convinced that the Prussian columns were beating a breathless retreat. He knew that the Prussians could, theoretically, have turned west at Wavre, but he believed that the appearance of Grouchy's cavalry would be enough to send the enemy fleeing northward again. Grouchy, he thought, who would occupy Wavre, seize its bridge, and then, finally, turn west to bring the weight of his troops to bear on the battle. Around one o'clock, when Napoleon realized that things were not going as planned and that the Prussians were on the point of threatening his right wing, he sent Grouchy a fresh dispatch, very different from the previous one. The only urgent requirement of these new orders was that Grouchy should head for Waterloo at once in order to take Bülow "in flagrante delicto"; but the emperor forgot that the marshal was still obeying his earlier orders and would continue to do so for many hours before the new dispatch could come into his hands.

If anyone should be held responsibile for the misunderstanding, therefore, it is Napoleon, not Grouchy; the emperor knew the orders he had sent the marshal, and had he checked them against a map, he could not have expected any help from Grouchy, who at that moment was marching north to reach Wavre "as soon as possible." Even if he met no opposition, Grouchy could not have arrived at Chapelle-St. Lambert before night. Of course, he could have decided to disobey the orders, as his corps commanders proposed, but Grouchy had just been promoted to marshal and was exercising an independent command for the first time in his life; not surprisingly, he chose the more prudent course.

Napoleon declared, in his memoirs, that he told Soult, "This morning we had ninety chances in our favor; now we have sixty against forty. And if Grouchy redresses the grievous error he made yesterday by wasting time in Gembloux and sends his troops quickly, our victory will be all the more decisive, for Bülow's corps will be completely destroyed." As is often the case in the emperor's memoirs, these words must have been a mixture of recollections, some authentic and some conveniently revised; the allusion to the "grievous error" has all the appearance of having been imagined in the years following the event, after the legend of Grouchy's fatal delay had already been created. But the hope that the marshal, in spite of everything, could still arrive in time to destroy not only Wellington's army but also Bülow's corps seems to reflect what was going through Napoleon's mind while Mouton left to reconnoiter the ground where he would have to deploy his corps, Desales's guns continued to pound away at Wellington's position, and d'Erlon's infantry, stirred by the rhythmic beating of its drums, prepared to advance against La Haye Sainte.

THIRTY

LA HAYE SAINTE

The center of the Allied front was held by German troops. To the right of the Brussels road (from Wellington's point of view), a brigade of the King's German Legion was deployed, commanded by Colonel von Ompteda. This brigade contained four battalions, one of which was inside the buildings of La Haye Sainte. Farther to the right was another German brigade, composed of Hanoverian regulars: five battalions under the command of General Count Kielmansegge, a Saxon noble famous for his hatred of Napoleon and for his scandalous separation from his wife, who by contrast was an enthusiastic admirer of the emperor and had her permanent residence in Paris. In all, these two brigades counted fewer than five thousand muskets, since none of the battalions of the King's German Legion, which had been partially demobilized the previous year in the belief that Europe was entering a long period of peace, could field as many as four hundred men.

The main road formed the boundary between these troops, which belonged to Sir Charles Alten's division, and those of Sir Thomas Picton's division, which was deployed to their left. Since the main road cut into the hill at this point like a deep furrow, Picton's men (except for the 1/95th, which was stationed right beside the road) were not involved in the defense of La Haye Sainte. The troops of Ompteda and Kielmansegge, after sending out a line of skirmishers to take up positions in the ravine at the bottom of the slope, were deployed in columns of companies; a traumatic encounter with French cavalry at Quatre Bras had left their officers rather nervous, and so they had decided to keep their men in this formation, which could be transferred into squares in a matter of seconds, rather than to deploy them in line. To avoid offering too conspicuous a target to enemy artillery, the men had been ordered to lie down on the reverse slope of the ridge. Two batteries, each with six 9-pounder guns, were positioned a few dozen yards ahead of them, on the face of the slope that descended toward the enemy. The battery on the right was German, commanded by Captain Cleeve, and it, too, belonged to the King's German Legion; the one on the left, just behind the farm, was a British battery commanded by Sir Hew Ross.

Colonel von Ompteda had posted a battalion of light infantry, the Second KGL, under the command of Major von Baring, to garrison La Haye Sainte farm. There were fewer than four hundred of these German riflemen, with their dark green uniforms and their special training in marksmanship, and they represented the first obstacle in the path of the French attack. Like the British fusiliers of the Ninety-fifth Rifles, the men of the KGL's light infantry carried, instead of the common smoothbore musket, the Baker rifle; its grooved barrel permitted accurate fire at up to two or three hundred yards from the target, so that irregular fire from these rifles was much more deadly than that of the smoothbores used by the line battalions. However, since it was rifled, the Baker had an essential shortcoming: because the ball had to be forced down a grooved bore, and because riflemen did not use prepared cartridges, but a more old-fashioned procedure that involved pouring powder from a flask, the loading process was much slower. As a result, troops armed with Baker rifles could fire only one shot per minute, as opposed to the two or even three shots that could be fired by musketeers. Since for the military leaders of the day the importance of rapidity in firing was an indisputable dogma, nobody had ever considered arming the entire infantry with rifled muskets, and this fact led to a further drawback: Troops armed with rifles needed special munitioning, as they were unable to use the ammunition issued to the other troops, a decisive problem in the fight for La Haye Sainte.

Although the farmhouse at La Haye Sainte was a respectable edifice, as a defensive position the farm was in no way comparable to the château of Hougoumont. The rustic house, the stables, and the barn—all of them built of brick and stone and covered by tiled roofs—faced a walled courtyard. The main gate opened directly onto the road. On the other side of the barn, the side closest to the French, there was an orchard surrounded by a hedge, and there was a kitchen garden behind the house. That morning, upon being informed that they would have to defend the farm, Baring's men had set about fortifying it, but the results weren't as satisfactory as at Hougoumont. The greatest problem had been caused by the troops themselves: The previous evening, in a conspicuous demonstration of improvidence, they had torn down the barn door, which faced the fields to the west, and burned it as firewood to cook their soup. The farm, therefore, was open on that side. The mule that was carrying the battalion's entrenching tools had gone lost the previous day, so there was not so much as an ax to work with, and the battalion's sappers, who could have offered valuable assistance, had been sent to Hougoumont. The riflemen did what they could, opening three loopholes in the walls, but they could build no firing platforms, because all the available lumber, including the farm carts, had been burned during the night.

Behind the house, not far from the kitchen garden but on the other side of the main road, three companies of the 1/95th Rifles occupied a hillock or knoll that, along with the sandpit that had been excavated at its base, offered an excellent position for crack sharpshooters, who could keep the road under fire. Sir Andrew Barnard had deployed the other half of his battalion a little farther back, along the chemin d'Ohain, and had ordered his adjutant, familiarly known to everyone as Johnny Kincaid, to command the advanced position. Since morning, the men of this battalion had been piling up tree branches and debris from the farm on the road, in an effort to erect an abatis, or barricade, that would obstruct the passage of enemy cavalry. Captain Kincaid was observing the work with satisfaction, when to his surprise a troop of British light dragoons passed that way and charged through the abatis, scattering it like straw. But the riflemen were stubborn, so they gathered their materials once more and again blocked the road. Despite their efforts, one of Wellington's aides-de-camp, Lieutenant Cathcart, would later remark of this barricade, "If I recollect right it was not much of a one at any time." Rather more than to this pile of bushes and branches, the defense of the position was entrusted to the rifled muskets of the Ninety-fifth, perhaps the most elite unit in the entire British army, and to two of Sir Hew Ross's two artillery pieces, which he had deployed on the road itself, next to the sandpit.

THIRTY-ONE

THE FIRST ATTACK
ON LA HAYE SAINTE

A little after one o'clock, in accordance with Napoleon's orders—which required I Corps to begin its attack from the left, directly south of La Haye Sainte, and to extend it gradually rightward—the first of d'Erlon's divisions, under the command of Donzelot, advanced against Baring's and Kincaid's riflemen. Although d'Erlon's four divisions were identical in structure—each division had two brigades, each brigade had two regiments, each regiment had two battalions—Donzelot's division was the strongest; many of its battalions comprised six or seven hundred men, whereas the others ranged between four and five hundred. More important, one of the division's two brigades, namely that of General Schmitz, included the only light infantry regiment assigned to I Corps, the Thirteenth Légère, and was therefore particularly suited to make an assault upon La Haye Sainte.

The old, experienced Donzelot sent forward his two brigades; Schmitz's headed straight for the orchard, and Aulard's advanced farther to the right, with the idea of bypassing the southern boundary of the farm and attacking its eastern flank. At that moment, the sunken position of La Haye Sainte unexpectedly revealed itself to be dangerous for the defenders: Baring, who was in the orchard with half of his men, was surprised to see the line of enemy skirmishes appear, already within musket range, and he had barely had time to order his troops to lie down and hold their fire, so that their volley would have a greater effect when the *tirailleurs* started firing first. Baring later reported, "The first shot broke the bridle of my horse, and the second killed Major Bösewiel, who was standing near me." The French, obviously, were aiming at officers. The fusiliers in the orchard fired back, but at that relatively close range the superiority of their Baker rifles was more than offset by the greater time it took to reload them. The defenders, moreover, were heavily outnumbered by the attacking skirmishers, and it quickly became clear that any further defense of the orchard was out of the question. The French generals also realized this, almost at once ordering their men to advance in column. Soon, "demonstrating the greatest contempt for our fire," they burst into the orchard.

The sapper companies of I Corps were at the head of the column. These units were made up of men selected for their physical strength and equipped with axes; the emperor had expressly ordered them to be ready to construct barricades around the conquered buildings and prevent the enemy from reoccupying them. One of Marshal Ney's aides-de-camp, Colonel Levavasseur, had come upon these troops a few minutes previously, sitting at their ease behind a rise in the ground while awaiting the order to attack. The officer in command, recognizing that the colonel was wearing the uniform of an aide-de-camp and was therefore an influential person with access to the powerful, decided that this was his chance to get himself noticed and earn a promotion; he approached Levavasseur, therefore, handed him his visiting card, and exclaimed, "*Monsieur aide-de-camp*, please take this, here is my name!" Then he ordered his drummers to beat the charge and led his sappers toward the orchard.

When the French burst in, the surviving fusiliers took to their heels and sought refuge in the barn; Baring followed them, still on his horse. A musket ball broke the animal's leg, Baring was thrown to the ground, and he quickly ordered his adjutant to dismount and took his place. Though he thereby offered the enemy a conspicuous target, it was unassailable dogma that a battle leader had to remain on horseback, and for good reasons: He could see much farther from the saddle, and he could be seen more easily by his men, thus positively and decisively reinforcing their morale. Once they had retreated to the barn, the German riflemen quickly regained their courage, and their fire successfully checked the French in the orchard. French soldiers tried to set the building ablaze, but all the straw had been removed during the night and the barn was empty, so for the moment, the fire failed to catch.

Meanwhile the other French brigade, commanded by Aulard, had advanced in column along the road. When they came to the abatis, preceded by a line of skirmishers, they were compelled to move farther to the right and into the fields east of La Haye Sainte, while accurate fire from the riflemen in the farm and the sandpit claimed the first victims. Lieutenant Graeme of the King's German Legion was stationed behind the abatis with a squad of fusiliers, and he was surprised by the great number of skirmishers in front of the enemy column, "as thick almost as an advancing line of our troops." Despite the heavy fire, the French skirted the barricade and attacked the farm; Graeme and his men barely had time to enter the yard by the main gate and close it behind them. Then they climbed onto the roof of a structure that stood next to the wall, and which everyone called the piggery. From the roof, the riflemen could keep the road under fire even better than they could from behind the abatis, and with relief they watched the French give them a wide berth, not even trying to climb the wall or break through the gate, and continue up the slope toward the sandpit.

From atop the knoll, Kincaid had watched with mounting concern as the French columns took up positions right in front of him; now, urged on by the obsessive rolling of the drummers and by cries of "*Vive l'Empereur*," shouted in unison from hundreds of throats, the French began to advance again. The closer they got, the louder they shouted; Kincaid attributed this to a mistaken belief that such roaring could scare his troops into running away. With true British pride, he compared the noisy advance of the French to the somber silence with which his men, around him and down the slope in the sandpit, awaited the attack. In the beginning, the *tirailleurs*, though numerous, were held in check by the riflemen of the 1/95th. Firing from such a position of advantage, they soon reduced the enemy to silence. But Aulard's response was to send his column forward, and despite the terrible losses they suffered, they passed through the skirmish line and in a few instants reached the mound and the sandpit. Outnumbered and overcome, Kincaid's riflemen ran from their positions and joined the rest of the battalion, lying down on the ridge behind them. Before clearing off in their turn, some of the riflemen's officers effectively exchanged a few saber blows with the officers who were leading the enemy column. The two guns that Sir Hew Ross had positioned on the road had been destroyed almost at once by the fearfully concentrated fire of the Grande Batterie.

THIRTY-TWO

CRABBÉ'S CHARGE

From the viewpoint of the German generals observing the situation from the Mont-Saint-Jean ridge behind La Haye Sainte, the moment was critical. A French column had occupied the orchard and chased the British from the knoll and the sandpit, and the enemy skirmishers were already moving toward the kitchen garden behind the farmhouse, threatening to take the defenders in the rear; despite the fire from the roof, other *tirailleurs* had managed to reach the wall and were firing into the courtyard through one of the loopholes opened by Baring's troops that morning. Most of the men in this second French column, however, were in the fields on the other side of the road and therefore the responsibility not of the Germans but of Sir Thomas Picton. For their part, the Germans had to reinforce Baring's men, who were at risk of being overwhelmed in the barn. It was decided to send a battalion forward, and for this duty General Kielmansegge selected one of his two battalions of light infantry; once again, these were the most suitable troops for the ground that was being fought over. The nearly six hundred men of the Lüneburg battalion, commanded by Colonel von Klencke, rose to their feet, advanced up the reverse slope to the crest of the ridge, crossed it, and began to descend the open slope west of La Haye Sainte. Some witnesses say they moved out in line; according to others, they were in open order; in any case troops attacking downhill, especially inexperienced troops, would have been hard-pressed to maintain an ordered formation.

The arrival of reinforcements convinced Baring that the time was right for a counterattack. Therefore, he and his men issued from the barn and had the satisfaction of seeing the *tirailleurs*, temporarily overwhelmed, disperse and turn back. His satisfaction, however, did not last long. An officer rushed out of the building and notified him that enemy troops were behind the house, occupying the garden. Shortly after receiving this news, Baring, who because he was on horseback had a view of what his men could not yet see, looked to his right and discovered that a mass of French cuirassiers had suddenly appeared on the horizon. Given the configuration of the terrain, they would have been only a few hundred yards away, moving rapidly toward the German troops through the high grain.

One of the important rules followed by Napoleonic generals was that cavalry should be kept close at hand to support advancing infantry. While d'Erlon's soldiers were taking up their positions for the attack on La Haye Sainte, Marshal Ney gathered all the cavalry colonels and had them detach from their regiments a certain number of squadrons that would be directly under his command. Seizing the occasion, Ney gave over command of these squadrons to one of his adjutants, Colonel Crabbé, and ordered him to cut down everything in his path. Forty-seven years of age and therefore Lord Uxbridge's exact contemporary, Crabbé (a Belgian, curiously enough, and a native of Brussels at that) was a veteran cavalry officer. Between Hougoumont and La Haye Sainte, the terrain formed a kind of elongated hump: The ground rose from the château, crested, and then sloped down again toward the farm. No one in the fields immediately west of La Haye Sainte could see what was happening on the other side of this crest, and so the French cuirassiers were shielded from the enemy's sight. Crabbé formed up his squadrons in column, one behind the other, and advanced over the dead ground on the Hougoumont side of the hump. And then, suddenly, they appeared on Baring's flank.

Of all the forces at a Napoleonic commander's disposal, the cuirassiers were capable of producing the weightiest impact. In 1815, there was already a recognizable tendency in many armies, which would grow progressively stronger until the First World War, to reduce the distinction between heavy cavalry, whose main purpose was to smash enemy lines, and light cavalry, which was mostly used to make reconnaissance and to provide cover for forward positions. But the French cuirassier was unquestionably the incarnation of heavy cavalry. Like their mounts, cuirassiers were of greater than normal stature, and they rode protected by helmets and cuirasses. In prior years, Napoleon's standards had required recruits to be at least 1.8 meters (about 5 feet 10 inches) tall and veterans of at least twelve years and three campaigns; even though the reconstituted cavalry of 1815 could not allow itself such demanding criteria, the cuirassiers were still veteran, physically powerful, and privileged warriors who received special pay. Each man with all his equipment weighed more than three hundred pounds, and he mounted a horse sufficiently robust to carry that kind of weight, even if only for short distances, at a gallop.

The force of impact generated by cavalry, provided it was engaged at the proper moment, was out of all proportion to its numbers. Had this not been the case, after all, governments would not have spent so much money on maintaining mounted troops, which represented a heavy cost to the national treasury. After Napoleon returned from Elba, he authorized the expenditure of a million francs for the purchase of horses; this sum sufficed to acquire just over six thousand animals, more than two-thirds of which were for the light cavalry. Horses that could be used by the heavy cavalry cost more than triple the price of the others. A single cavalry regiment consumed four metric tons of fodder every day; putting such a regiment in the field and maintaining it for the duration of a campaign cost as much as it did to equip and maintain twelve infantry battalions. A single cuirassier cost the state the equivalent of twenty infantrymen. Nevertheless, the results obtained were generally worth the expense.

When he saw the cuirassiers descending the slope, Major von Baring realized at once what was about to happen. He shouted to his men to form ranks around him and fall back immediately into the barn, but the catastrophe overwhelmed them all before they could obey him. When the German soldiers heard the sound of the horses' hooves, they did the first thing that skirmishing troops caught in the open by cavalry tended to do, which was also the worst choice they could make: They started running for their lives. Most of them tried to reach the ridge, where in the meantime the other battalions, realizing the danger, were beginning to form squares. Baring had not been in command of his battalion for very long, and his men were not familiar with his voice, which could not have been easy to hear in these circumstances; in any case, no one rallied to him. In a few seconds, the cuirassiers caught up with the fleeing troops and began sabering them. Colonel von Klencke was cut down and his battalion destroyed: According to the rolls compiled after the battle, 228 men of the Lüneburg battalion were lost at Waterloo, including dead, wounded, and missing. This figure by itself is equivalent to nearly half of Klencke's force; add the men who were taken prisoner and released later in the evening as well as those who simply vanished until the following day, and the battalion had ceased to exist. One of its two colors fell into the hands of the French and was recovered only after the battle.

Baring's men fared little better. The major, who was on horseback, managed to reach the crest, but in the meantime *tirailleurs* had occupied the kitchen garden, and they shot down many of the KGL riflemen as they ran past. Seized by the general panic, a number of the troops who were in the farm buildings and the yard also took to their heels and joined the mad dash for the ridge. Fortunately, a small group of men remained inside the farm: Lieutenant Graeme and a dozen fusiliers were on the roof of the piggery, while Lieutenant Carey and Ensign Frank, with another squad, were in the farmhouse itself.[14] For the moment, their fire made it difficult for the *tirailleurs* to get out of the garden and the orchard and continued to inflict casualties on Aulard's columns, which were mounting the slope beyond the sandpit; but the situation made it seem quite unlikely that the defense of La Haye Sainte could last for long.

Meanwhile, the French cuirassiers continued their gallop up the slope of the ridge, where Kielmansegge's and Ompteda's battalions, formed up in square, were waiting for them. Quite soon, however, it became clear that the French had no intention of charging all the way into these formations. How many squadrons Colonel Crabbé had with him is unclear, but there were probably only four or five, no more than half a thousand sabers. It hadn't been necessary to employ them all in the destruction of the Lüneburgers; when cavalry squadrons charged, one after the other, with their men deployed in two lines, each squadron covered a front at least fifty or sixty yards long, so that two or at the most three squadrons would have been sufficient to assail the unfortunate Hanoverian battalion in front and flank. In any case, however, Crabbé no longer had troops fresh enough to launch a serious attack on the enemy squares, especially since the cuirassiers' chargers were winded by the time they reached the ridge. Captain von Scriba, who was in a large square formed by two Hanoverian battalions, saw the French move forward at a trot, take a few losses caused by the massed fire from the squares, and then, still forty or fifty paces away, change direction and disappear without even trying an attack.

Scriba's recruits, most of them boys and young men in their first battle, watched the departure of the French cavalry with relieved shouts of "Hurrah!"; but their joy was at the expense of Sir Hew Ross's men, positioned a little farther on, who were continuing to fire their four remaining guns from the slope behind La Haye Sainte. As the cuirassiers came back down from the ridge, they suddenly found themselves in the midst of the battery, and many gunners were cut to pieces before they could run to the nearest squares, as they were instructed to do in cases of this kind. The survivors flung themselves into the shelter of the sunken lane or under their own cannons, where the cuirassiers' sabers couldn't reach them. At the same time, the first French cavalry troops were urging their mounts across the main road and reaching the sandpit, which was occupied by *tirailleurs*; La Haye Sainte was surrounded.

THIRTY-THREE

———•◆•———

D'ERLON'S ADVANCE

Wꜰile the fight was raging around the farm, Wellington, who up to that moment had been observing the defense of Hougoumont, must have realized that the enemy's main push was going to be made much farther to the left; he galloped along the line, followed by the throng of his adjutants, to get a better view of what was going on. The group halted under the great, solitary elm, visible for miles around, that marked the intersection of the main road and the chemin d'Ohain. From this crossroads, a few hundred yards behind La Haye Sainte, Wellington and his companions could see the entire French line, including the farmhouse inn of La Belle Alliance, which with its whitewash and its tile roof marked the center of Napoleon's position. Farther to the left, in plain sight, d'Erlon's other divisions were following up Donzelot's advance; they, too, were drawing near the Allied line, crowded so thickly together that the entire hollow between the two ridges seemed to be full of soldiers on the march.

It was past one-thirty, and the fight around La Haye Sainte had been raging for some time, when Ney gave d'Erlon the signal to bring his other divisions forward. And so they advanced, descending the slope, crossing the boggy lowland, and mounting the opposite slope: first, Quiot's division, with Bourgeois's brigade farther forward and Charlet's in support, and next, Marcognet's division, with Grenier's brigade farther forward and Nogues's in support. Still farther down the line, the first of Durutte's two brigades had just started to move out, and the second was preparing to follow it (as we have seen, the emperor had ordained that the attack was to develop progressively from left to right). The drummer boys, marching in groups behind each battalion, beat the *pas de charge* over cadenced, unison shouts of "*Vive l'Empereur!*" Some officers, riding out in front of the ranks with their sabers unsheathed, barked out the most characteristic words of encouragement used in the imperial army, words that even British veterans remembered having heard many times and that always made a deep impression on them: "*L'Empereur récompensera le premier qui avancera!*"[15]

D'Erlon had concentrated an astonishing number of muskets in a little space. All together, the front occupied by these six brigades, plus Aulard's brigade at La Haye Sainte was about a thousand yards wide, starting from the Brussels road and stretching east, and in that relatively restricted space d'Erlon had massed twenty-eight battalions, which included some fourteen thousand men. All this infantry took about twenty minutes to traverse the lowland—flattening, as they marched, the fields of rye, whose crops had stood almost as tall as a man that morning—and climb the opposite slope to the Allied positions. D'Erlon's troops marched through the mud at a rhythm of seventy-six steps per minute, as prescribed by French regulations, in cadence with the monotonous roll of the drums.

The formation in which d'Erlon and his commanding officers deployed their men has been the subject of much contention. Customarily, a battalion of French infantry advanced in column, just as the First Légère did in attacking Hougoumont; an attack column was nine ranks deep, and at least the first two or three ranks, the most numerous, contained fifty or sixty men each, spread across a front some forty yards wide. That morning, however, d'Erlon had breakfasted with his emperor at Le Caillou, and after the breakfast he had joined the other generals in a discussion of their respective experiences in facing British infantry. All agreed that it would be too risky to attempt to deploy their troops into line when they were already under enemy fire; it was much preferable to advance in line rather than in column. That way, every battalion, after having sent out its *tirailleurs*, would be formed in only three ranks, with a frontage of nearly a hundred yards, and it would be capable of almost three times as much firepower as a column, since every man in the line's three ranks would be able to fire his weapon.

There was a single—but weighty—objection to an advance in line: The French infantry was accustomed to the deeper formation, the column, which guaranteed an indispensable boost in morale, since every soldier had an impenetrable mass of comrades behind him, supporting him and pushing him forward. That morning at Le Caillou, however, the French generals must have remembered the days before the introduction of the column formation, when the revolutionary armies had achieved the same effect on morale by having their battalions advance in line, one behind the other. D'Erlon decided that the divisions of Quiot, Marcognet, and Durutte, which represented the main attack force, would adopt this formation: Each brigade would form a column of four battalions in line, one behind the other, with barely five or six paces between them. There would be a total of six massed brigades in echelon, each with a front about a hundred yards wide, spread out over an arc barely a thousand yards long, and d'Erlon expected they would exert such pressure on the Allied line that it would break; moreover, the casualties suffered in the firefight by the lead battalion in each column would be easily made up by advancing the second battalion into the front line.

Naturally, all twenty-eight battalions had sent out their *tirailleurs*; they amounted to something like 2,500 men and advanced in front of the columns in open order, but close enough together to form an unbroken chain. D'Erlon, unlike Reille at Hougoumont, was not just feeling out the situation; he had received orders to launch a breakthrough attack and open a breach in Wellington's line. If up to this point the battle had burned—to return to Clausewitz's image—irregularly, like wet powder, now the tempo of events was about to undergo a dramatic acceleration. The swarm of skirmishers was necessary to drive the enemy skirmishers from their hiding places, whether lying on their bellies amid the standing grain or crouched behind the hedge of the chemin d'Ohain, and to disturb the firing of the artillery batteries posted along the crest of the ridge; but at the moment of impact, the marching columns would reach the skirmish line and pass through it (as Aulard's column had already done at the sandpit), assaulting the enemy position with all the weight of their close-order battalions.

The first commander charged with defending the ridge in front of them was a Dutch officer, General Baron Perponcher-Sedlnitzky. His Second Netherlands Infantry Division constituted the Allies' first line of defense, a line so extended that Perponcher's two brigades ended up separated, and each had to fight on its own: The one on the left, in fact, commanded by Prince Bernhard of Saxe-Weimar, had entrenched itself in the Papelotte area, while the one on the right, commanded by Graaf van Bijlandt, was deployed in front of the chemin d'Ohain, on the exposed slope in the very face of the enemy. One battalion of Bijlandt's brigade, in open order, formed the chain of skirmishers, another three battalions were in line, and only one was held in reserve. In order to cover such an extensive front, these 2,500 men had been commanded to deploy in two lines, in the British manner, rather than the three favored by continental armies. The brigade covered almost the entire front that was about to receive d'Erlon's attack; the rest of the first line, on Bijlandt's right, was held by only four hundred men of the Ninety-fifth Rifles, First Battalion, commanded by Sir Andrew Barnard and positioned on the high ground above the sandpit.

The Dutch position was an unhappy one, all the more so because Bijlandt's brigade, formed entirely of inexperienced troops (more than half of them militia), had been sorely tested at Quatre Bras. Of its five battalions, one existed only in name, a handful of men gathered around a standard, and the other four were also decidedly below strength. Exactly why these troops found themselves in front of the sunken lane, rather than in the shelter of the thorny bushes and willow trees that bordered it, is the topic of a discussion that has not yet ended. Since General van Bijlandt's light infantry battalion, the Twenty-seventh Dutch Jäger, had been chosen to form the forward skirmishing line defending the entire left wing, he had probably preferred not to spread out his exhausted battalions but rather to deploy them close to one another. Besides, the habitual practice of keeping infantry hidden behind features of the terrain, where the troops lay on the ground until the last moment, was one of Wellington's characteristics but was much less popular with continental generals; and so after Perponcher, who commanded the Netherlands division, had been informed that his troops were to constitute the first line of defense, he simply did what anyone else would have done in his place.

A little farther back, on the reverse slope of the ridge, the commander responsible for the second line was none other than Sir Thomas Picton. Two of his brigades, those commanded by Sir James Kempt and Sir Denis Pack, were exactly on the line of march of the leading French columns; farther to the left two brigades of Hanoverian militia, commanded by Colonel Best and General von Vincke, were deployed. Since d'Erlon's divisions, in accordance with the orders they had received, were tending to converge toward the left, pointing in the direction of Mont-Saint-Jean village, the brunt of the attack, once the Netherlanders' resistance had been overcome, was destined to fall essentially on the brigades of Kempt and Pack, whose men, except for those of the Ninety-fifth's First Battalion, were lying on the ground perhaps a hundred yards behind the sunken lane. These brigades comprised eight battalions of select troops, all English and Scottish veterans of the campaign on the Iberian Peninsula, and their generals, including Picton, were well known for combativeness: They were all "fire-eaters," as their soldiers said, and they also shared such character traits as impatience and irascibility. But both brigades had been badly mauled at Quatre Bras, so much so that their battalions were reduced to no more than four hundred men each; three of Pack's four battalions had lost their commanders, and the brigade as a whole had lost nearly two-thirds of its officers. All things considered, Picton and Perponcher could rely on barely six thousand muskets to cover the eight or nine hundred yards of front toward which "Johnny"—the British veterans' slang for the enemy; in this particular case, the fourteen thousand troops of d'Erlon's I Corps—was marching up the slope.

There were also guns defending the Allied position, but not enough of them. At the crucial moment, the artillery deployed along the front attacked by d'Erlon came to twenty-nine pieces at most, and the majority of the batteries were no longer operating at full efficiency. Captain Stevenart's Belgian battery had lost six of its eight guns at Quatre Bras, and a junior officer was commanding the two that were left, because Captain Stevenart had been killed as well. Captain Braun's

Hanoverian battery had lost all six of its guns at Quatre Bras, and they had just been replaced the previous day with six old British 6-pounders. Another Hanoverian battery, commanded by Captain von Rettberg, had already used up half its ammunition at Quatre Bras.

On the other hand, the majority of the guns had been posted not on the exposed forward slope but behind the chemin d'Ohain. In some cases, the gunners had forced open a passage for their cannon through the hedge that bordered the sunken lane. This explains why, when Desales's guns opened fire on the Allied position, none of the batteries was wiped out, except for the two pieces that Lieutenant Colonel Ross had posted on the main road. All the same, the Allied gunners' situation was anything but comfortable, and their accounts of the battle clearly evoked the frightening intensity of the French fire. Even before Braun's battery took up its position, it had already lost its commander, wounded by a shell fragment in the thigh; the guns had not yet been unlimbered when a shell blew up one of the limbers, destroying the gun and killing three gunners and four horses; and when the first French *tirailleurs* advanced, the junior officer who had taken command of the battery was killed, too.

All this notwithstanding, during d'Erlon's advance the Allied artillery, firing over the heads of the Dutch-Belgian infantry deployed below them, opened broad gaps in the compact ranks of the attackers; yet the latter closed up and continued their serried march, undeterred. Supposing that all the Allied guns had fired without interruption on d'Erlon's columns from the moment they began to march until the moment when the gunners had to abandon their pieces, about a thousand cannon shots would have been fired against those fourteen thousand men, a rate of one shot per second. However, the rapidity and efficiency of fire diminished under stressful conditions, while an extremely high percentage of shots generally missed their targets; in addition several Allied batteries, despite their orders, were in fact chiefly engaged in artillery duels with the Grande Batterie. Thus, the ordeal faced by the attackers was less intense than it could have been and was not enough to stem that human tide.

Captain Duthilt, an aide-de-camp on the staff of General Bourgeois, was amazed by the soldiers' enthusiasm; from the start, they moved out in double time, marching on the heels of the *tirailleurs* and bellowing shouts of triumph. Very soon, however, the heavy, viscous mud clogged their steps and slowed their advance; gaiters came apart, and some men even began to lose their shoes. Corporal Canler of the Twenty-eighth Ligne, feeling his foot coming out of his shoe as he marched, noticed that the instep straps on one of his gaiters had broken; he bent down to adjust them, and as he did so, a violent blow struck his shako: A bullet had passed completely through it, just grazing his skull. The corporal, with no time to stop and reflect, hurried, limping, back to his place. In fact, the officers "kept shouting the same awful order: 'Close ranks!'" every time a gap opened in the formation, and the men, as though intoxicated by those urgent cries and by the dismal rolling of the drums, kept marching up the slope. Despite the strenuous efforts they were making, their roars of enthusiasm were so deafening that it became hard to hear the officers' commands. "Soon there was a bit of confusion in the ranks, especially after the head of the column drew within range of the enemy's fire," Captain Duthilt later recalled; but the French advance seemed unstoppable, all the same.

THIRTY-FOUR

THE ATTACK ON
THE SUNKEN LANE

The sparse line of skirmishers covering the Allied front was quickly overwhelmed by the much more numerous enemy. Meanwhile, the Dutch generals had had sufficient time to realize that Bijlandt's brigade, deployed in line on the exposed side of the slope without any defenses, did not have the slightest chance of withstanding the attack. Belatedly, the generals decided to withdraw the brigade to the sunken lane. The inexperienced Netherlands battalions, in blue uniforms that closely resembled those of the French, had already stayed too long in their initial positions, exposed to the cannonade of the Grande Batterie, and their withdrawal was likely not executed in good order. Seeing the Netherlanders withdraw, the British soldiers behind them jeered and hooted pitilessly, and even a few volleys were fired.

When the line of French skirmishers, closely followed by the leading columns, approached the batteries stationed behind the sunken lane, a wave of panic began to spread among the artillerymen, too. Sir William Gomm, a member of Wellington's staff, saw two cannon being moved back in great haste at the enemy's approach, and he couldn't help noting that this withdrawal was carried out with "considerable bustle." But the majority of the guns were simply abandoned, not that the gunners could have done anything else; at that point, it was up to the infantry to repulse the attack and regain possession of the sunken lane, and therefore of the guns. At least one artillery sergeant thought such a recovery so unlikely that he spiked his gun before abandoning it, rendering it useless in the time-honored way, by driving a spike down the vent at the back end of the barrel. Since it was through this vent that the powder was lit, spiking a gun prevented the enemy (or anyone else) from using it.

The bulk of Picton's infantry was deployed at least a hundred yards behind the chemin d'Ohain and the thick, thorny hedge that lined it, and the soldiers remained there, flat on their stomachs, as long as they could, to reduce the casualties caused by the artillery barrage. Naturally, the result of this rearward deployment, which was necessitated by the concentration of guns that Napoleon had brought to bear on that sector of the Allied line, was that d'Erlon's columns were able to reach the hedge without having to face the disciplined musket fire of the British troops, only the disordered volleys of the Dutch infantry, which had just withdrawn to the sunken lane. With the exception of the pickets, who were soon overwhelmed by the French skirmishers, the only British soldiers in a position to see d'Erlon's advancing columns were the fusiliers of the 1/95th, armed with their short, deadly Baker rifles and already engaged in holding off the first of the attack columns, commanded by Baron Aulard.

Unlike the other brigades, Aulard's advanced in column, headed by the two battalions of the Fifty-first Ligne, and behind them the two of the Nineteenth Ligne. Despite the losses they suffered from the fire of the British fusiliers in front of them and from the fire of the German troops on the roofs at La Haye Sainte, the French stormed the sandpit and the mound behind it, forcing the outpost stationed there under Captain Kincaid to abandon the position in great haste. The rest of the battalion, stationed in the sunken lane, ought to have held out longer, but it had already suffered heavily from artillery fire, and when these troops saw Kincaid's unit falling back, they experienced a moment of panic. Kincaid barely had time to urge his horse through an opening in the hedge before he discovered, to his dismay, that Sir Andrew Barnard had been wounded and was unable to continue in command, that his second-in-command had already been incapacitated in his turn, and that the remainder of the battalion was retreating in some disorder, heading for the rear. Kincaid shouted to the men to halt, and since they were, after all, experienced veterans, he managed somehow to get them formed up in line a short distance from the road.

He did so just in time, for the Fifty-first Ligne had reached the hedge and overrun the abandoned guns, and with the British infantry finally in sight, the French were briskly maneuvering to change from column of attack to a deployment in line. This maneuver, which officers learned by heart and men repeated a thousand times on the drill field, required the companies deployed in the second and third ranks to advance at an oblique angle until they were aligned with those in the front rank and thus able to fire on the enemy without obstruction. Before his troops discharged their weapons and everything disappeared in a thick cloud of smoke, Kincaid had time to see the advancing French quickly spreading out, "cheered and encouraged by the gallantry of their officers, who were dancing and flourishing their swords in front." Another officer in Kempt's brigade also remembered with admiration "the gallant manner the French officers led out their Companies in deploying." Evidently, there was an instant in which the two opposing forces looked one another in the eyes from a distance that was probably no more than fifty or sixty yards. This moment lasted long enough to become indelibly stamped in the memory of many a soldier; at the time, of course, smoke enveloped everything.

When the French column appeared, the troops in the other battalions of Kempt's brigade rose to their feet and opened fire as well. Under these withering volleys, delivered at such close range, the Fifty-first Ligne's deployment into line was brusquely interrupted, as was that of the Nineteenth, which came up behind the Fifty-first and was trying to deploy farther to its right. The brigade commander, Aulard, was killed, and then or shortly thereafter the commander of the Fifty-first, Colonel Rignon, met the same fate. The French companies took shelter behind the hedge, each man responding as he might to the enemy fire. The British infantry was not deployed in the usual line formation, two ranks deep, which would have permitted it to develop maximum firepower to the front, but rather in the more cautious four-rank line, because the British commanders feared an attack by the French cavalry while their men were engaged in opposing the infantry's advance. This was an understandable decision, but it also explains why Picton's men did not automatically gain the upper hand in the first exchange of fire. Incredulous, Kincaid realized that the ranks of his riflemen were growing dangerously thin; Picton must likewise have assumed that something was amiss, because he spurred his horse into the midst of Kempt's men and ordered a bayonet assault: "Charge! Charge! Hurrah!"

Counterattacking with fixed bayonets after a brief exchange of fire was the British infantry's favorite tactic. In this case as in others, faced with a thousand redcoats advancing toward them at full speed, the enemy began here and there to halt—but not everywhere—and kept up their fire throughout. Upon reaching the sunken lane, the troops of the Thirty-second Regiment found themselves in the midst of the enemy, who were retreating down the slope; the ensign who carried the regimental color fell wounded, and Lieutenant Belcher seized the standard. As he looked around for another ensign, he was suddenly confronted by a French officer, whose horse had just been killed under him. Instead of running to safety, the Frenchman barred Belcher's way, took hold of the standard, and started to pull it away from him, while Belcher, taken by surprise, grabbed a handful of silk and hung on. The Frenchman tried to unsheathe his saber with his free hand, but before he could do so the color-sergeant struck him in the breast with the long pike that was the emblem of the noncommissioned officers of the British infantry, and which was ordinarily used for dressing ranks. Someone cried out, "Save the brave fellow!" but it was too late; another British infantryman had already leveled his musket and killed the wounded officer.

A little farther left, the Scottish troops of the Seventy-ninth Regiment, the Cameron Highlanders, encountered such heavy fire that they chose to stop before reaching the hedge, content to respond with volleys of their own. In contrast to the standard British regiments, whose men came from all corners of the kingdom, the Camerons were an exceptionally homogeneous unit: The great majority of the soldiers were Scots, and no fewer than nine of their officers belonged to Clan Cameron. This was, in short, one of those units in which the relationships of blood and patronage among the men and their commanders guaranteed an uncommon degree of cohesion. Moreover, even the English officers least inclined to appreciate the northern barbarians had to admit that they made extraordinary defensive soldiers. Tomkinson of the Sixteenth Light Dragoons, for example, believed that Scottish troops were the best in the army in situations calling for coolness, steadiness, and obedience to orders; he thought them less valuable in skirmishes or, more generally, in any kind of combat where quickness of reaction was called for. But the Camerons had lost nearly half of their personnel at Quatre Bras, and the regiment, like others that had taken part in that battle, was still in shock from the carnage. Their French attackers seemed to have no intention of giving up easily, and Wellington himself, who wasn't far away from the struggle, noticed that after a while the Camerons "seemed to have had more than they liked of it."

When Sir Thomas Picton saw, to his horror, that the Scots were starting to disband, he signaled to the first officer he came across, ordering him to go and stop them. The general was not known for mildness of manner (he was, in the duke's pointed judgment, "as rough and foul-mouthed a devil as ever lived"), and in this case, too, his language matched the drastic occasion. But while he was speaking to the officer, who was the famous Captain Seymour, Lord Uxbridge's aide-de-camp and "the strongest man in the British army," Sir Thomas was struck in the head by a musket ball that passed through his top hat. He fell from his horse, and a moment later Seymour's horse was mortally wounded and collapsed, too. The captain disentangled himself from the carcass just in time to see one of his soldiers already bending over the general's body and emptying his pockets. Seymour recovered Sir Thomas's purse and eyeglasses from the thief and called his aide-de-camp, Captain Tyler, but the two officers quickly realized that nothing could be done for Picton, who was dead. Tyler remembered the evening of Quatre Bras, not forty-eight hours before, when the general had confessed to having left his home with the feeling that he would never return to it again; after surviving the dangers of that battle, however, Picton had started to believe that no one would succeed in killing him.

THIRTY-FIVE

—•◦•—

THE FIREFIGHT ALONG
THE CHEMIN D'OHAIN

While the brigades of Aulard and Kempt—both of them severely battered and neither of them deployed in a formation prescribed in the manuals—continued firing at one another amid the smoke on both sides of the sunken lane, Quiot's battalions were also mounting the slope a little farther on; the first brigade, commanded by Bourgeois, had nearly crested the ridge. In front of them, Bijlandt's brigade was rapidly losing cohesion. Withdrawn at the last moment to the shelter of the sunken lane, deployed in a two-rank formation unfamiliar to them, and running short of ammunition since the enormous expenditure at Quatre Bras, they were, predictably enough, unable to develop sufficient firepower to stop Quiot's veterans. By this point, most of their officers were already dead or wounded, including General von Bijlandt, and the brigade was under the command of Colonel De Jongh of the Eighth Dutch Militia, who had been wounded in the battle of Quatre Bras and had ordered his staff at Waterloo to tie him to the saddle. When the first French regiment, the 105th Ligne, appeared before them, most of the Dutch stopped fighting and ran away. Only the brigade's single Belgian battalion, the Seventh, remained in position and kept firing, while the last companies of Kempt's brigade began to turn toward their left, where they could see the French advancing along their flank and clearing the hedge.

Among the officers of the Seventh Belgian line, there was one Lieutenant Scheltens, who until the previous year had been a sergeant in one of the grenadier regiments of the Old Guard. He had fought in Napoleon's armies from Spain to Russia before taking service with the new Belgian army, where professionals of his caliber were fully appreciated. "The battalion," Scheltens later recalled, "remained

134

lying down behind the road until the head of the French column was a pistol-shot away. Then the line received the order to rise and commence firing, and the French committed the error of halting in order to reply to our fire." A "pistol-shot" was, in fact, just a few paces. According to Scheltens, "We were at such close quarters that when a musket ball wounded Captain L'Olivier in the arm, the paper wad from the cartridge was left smoking in the fabric of his coat sleeve."

Such firefights as this, where two lines of men stood upright and shot at one another from a few dozen yards away, are perhaps the most incomprehensible aspect of the Napoleonic battle. Admittedly, the mass-produced muskets used by the armies of the day were inferior weapons and soldiers were not taught to aim, so that, beyond a certain distance, their fire was pretty ineffective. In 1814, barely a year before Waterloo, Colonel Hanger, a veteran of the Revolutionary War in America, published a pamphlet in which he declared, "A soldier's musket if not exceedingly ill-bored (as many are), will strike the figure of a man at 80 yards, perhaps even at 100; but a soldier must be very unfortunate indeed who shall be wounded by a common musket at 150, provided his antagonist aims at him; and as to firing at a man at 200 yards with a common musket, you may just as well fire at the moon." But great distances were not involved in this firefight, where hundreds of men discharged their weapons all together, without aiming, at a distance of less than a hundred yards, and at a target which, to all appearances, it was impossible to miss.

The most curious generals of the day had even developed tests to show how many projectiles could reach their target in such a situation. The Prussians, for example, had held test firings at a hundred paces, using a wooden target six feet tall and thirty feet long—more or less equivalent to the frontage of a French battalion in column—and had concluded that at least two-thirds of all bullets fired struck the target. In the English tests, carried out on the firing range of the Tower of London, three-quarters of the balls fired in a volley from a hundred yards away hit the target, which was fifty yards long. Based on these numbers, two battalions of between four and five hundred men each, shooting at one another across a space of a hundred yards, could have achieved mutual annihilation in the course of a minute. But in reality, such firefights could go on for ten minutes, and perhaps even longer, and yet there was no annihilation. The Cameron Highlanders, who engaged in a combat of this sort under unfavorable conditions and who, according to the duke himself, got more of it than they wanted, suffered about 175 casualties, both dead and wounded, over the entire day at Waterloo—a great many, to be sure, but still fewer than half of those who had answered roll call that morning.

Apparently, the results obtained from the tests conducted on parade grounds and firing ranges had little to do with reality, and during a real battle, operating under severe stress and completely enveloped and blinded by the smoke from their own muskets, the majority of soldiers fired without hitting anyone. In England a historian calculated that the most plausible number of target hits at 100 yards was not 75 percent, as in the tests, but more like 5 percent. Someone else reached the conclusion that, over the course of a whole battle, one musket ball out of every 459 fired struck a man; as small as this number may seem, it's probably not far from the truth. Another student of the battle, considering that the opposing forces at Waterloo engaged in many short-range firefights, figured there was one casualty for every 162 shots fired. In addition to these calculations, Perponcher's division used up more than five hundred thousand cartridges in the course of the battles of Quatre Bras and Waterloo and suffered around 2,200 casualties, which means it took one casualty for every 227 shots fired, and this figure doesn't allow for the large percentage of casualties that were actually caused by artillery.

When two battalions engaged one another in such circumstances, the result was not their immediate mutual destruction (which explains why a firefight at relatively close range was even considered possible, and even more, why the troops' entire training was aimed at developing an optimal rhythm of fire and the ability to resist panic in such circumstances). Instead, the soldiers kept shooting at each other for rather a long time, all the while completely hidden by smoke, while each battalion lost, perhaps, three or four men per minute, until the feeling that the enemy's fire was more effective and that the danger level was getting a bit too high spread through one or the other of the two battalions, causing it to begin a disordered retreat. The fact that Bourgeois's men, having reached the hedge, opted for a firefight instead of a bayonet assault is perhaps less strange than it appeared to Scheltens; after all, the French generals had decided to send their men forward in line for just this eventuality. Moreover, although the Belgian officer could not know this, Quiot's other brigade, the one commanded by Charlet, was already mounting the slope a little farther to the right and would go into action in a few minutes, opening fire or leveling their bayonets and advancing on the enemy's flank. The center of Picton's line would probably not have been able to withstand this new pressure, since this was exactly the type of situation in which soldiers, realizing that the odds were changing in the enemy's favor, would usually decide to save their skin.

A British brigade was deployed nearby, practically elbow to elbow with the Belgians, under the command of General Sir Denis Pack, and three-quarters of its troops were Scottish veterans; but Marcognet's entire division was advancing upon them. It, too, was deployed in two columns, commanded by Grenier and Nogues. Like Kempt's, Pack's men had lain down at some distance from the sunken lane and remained there for a long time, but then they had deployed in line, four ranks deep, with the front of each battalion extending no more than fifty or sixty yards, and advanced to one side of the hedge, while the French were approaching it from the other. Grenier's infantry, with the Forty-fifth Ligne at the head of the column, reached the hedge with their muskets still on their shoulders. Having got through, they were crossing the lane when they realized that the enemy infantry was deployed in their front. The Scots fired a volley before the French could level their muskets, and for a moment the head of the column seemed to break up; but the French fired an answering volley almost at once, and theirs was equally deadly.

The first Allied battalion, part of the Scottish Forty-second Regiment (the Black Watch), advanced almost as far as the hedge, stopped short, and renounced the idea of crashing through it. Afterward, one of the regiment's sergeants explained that the Scots, whose legs were naked under their kilts, had not dared plunge into the thick, thorny bushes. A more likely explanation is that they were stopped and even thrown back by the enemy's fire, because Pack, who was advancing in the midst of the following battalion, the Ninety-second (Gordon Highlanders), began to shout: "Ninety-second, everything has given way on your right and left and you must charge this column." But the Gordons, who like all the brigade's other battalions had lost nearly two-thirds of their officers at Quatre Bras, had already spent too much time exposed to artillery fire and seen too many comrades killed without having yet fired a shot. Rather than advance with lowered bayonets as their general hoped, they too opened fire, inevitably getting the worst of the exchange, so that they started to fall back in disorder, while the men of the Forty-fifth Ligne burst through the hedge en masse, yelling in triumph.

From his chair on the heights of Rossomme, Napoleon could see nothing of this, except for the white smoke that enveloped the entire ridge. Around La Haye Sainte, where the fighting had been going on longer, the smoke was not moving forward; there, evidently, the Allies were putting up a stiffer resistance. But farther to the right, the combat had advanced beyond the sunken lane, and it was clear that the French had captured the crest of the ridge and were gradually pushing the enemy back. Excited, the emperor decided that the time had come for him to draw a little closer to the battlefield. He mounted his horse and prepared to move, with all his aides-de-camp, his chair, his table, and his map, to the high ground at La Belle Alliance, about a mile and a quarter ahead and a little more than three-quarters of a mile from the enemy lines. The unfortunate De Coster was obliged to go along, and when a few stray balls started whizzing by not far from them, he began fidgeting and squirming to such a degree that the emperor scolded him: "Come, my friend, don't lurch around like that. A musket ball can kill you from behind just as easily as from in front, and the wound it makes is much worse."[16]

When the emperor dismounted at La Belle Alliance and went back to surveying the battlefield through his telescope, things seemed to be turning out as he had predicted. Almost everywhere, and more and more clearly as the eye swung from left to right, the smoke was advancing, a sign that the pressure being exerted by d'Erlon's troops was proving irresistible. Despite the iron discipline of the British army, each of Wellington's men engaged in the combat on the Allied side of the sunken lane must have already realized that the possibility of his being the next to fall dead or maimed was increasing every minute, while his cartridge-pouch was becoming steadily lighter. When a comrade was wounded, those near him felt more and more strongly the temptation to drop everything and help him to safety behind the lines. It wouldn't have taken much for this urge to gain the upper hand of an entire battalion or possibly even of a brigade, and had Picton's men begun to disband, there would have been no troops to take their place, because Wellington had not massed any reserves in that sector. At two o'clock in the afternoon, along the chemin d'Ohain between La Haye Sainte and Papelotte, the French were winning the Battle of Waterloo.

THIRTY-SIX

---·•◆•·---

THE INTERVENTION OF
THE BRITISH CAVALRY

In that critical moment on the ridge, while Bijlandt's and Pack's troops were
starting to fall back and disperse under the French fire, the most senior general
present was the Earl of Uxbridge. Wellington was not far away; by then, he had
reached his command post, under the elm at the crossroads behind La Haye Sainte,
and he would remain there for a great part of the afternoon. But from that position,
in the midst of the gunpowder smoke that was now spreading its grayish-white
tentacles everywhere, and while the shells of the Grande Batterie were exploding at
an implacable rate all around him, the duke could not fully assess what was
happening to his left. His attention must have been mostly absorbed by the attack
on La Haye Sainte, by the *tirailleurs*, who had already surrounded the farm and
seized the kitchen garden, and by the cuirassiers, who had made a threatening
advance to the crest of the ridge. Until someone arrived with the news, Wellington
could not know that Picton had been killed, nor that his entire left wing, whose
weakness was due to his dispositions, was on the point of breaking up under the
pressure of d'Erlon's columns.

The Earl of Uxbridge, too, was a recent arrival in that part of the field, having
come from inspecting the cavalry deployed behind Hougoumont—another
indication that the British generals were concentrating all their attention on their
right flank. The insertion of cavalry into a battle required, above all, firsthand
observation and a sense of timing, and the prompt decision of an officer in the
field could count for more than the judgment of his commander in chief.
Knowing this, Wellington had explicitly authorized Uxbridge, as commander of
the cavalry, to employ it without waiting for instructions or permission. Shortly
after his arrival on the high ground above La Haye Sainte, west of the Brussels

road, Uxbridge saw Crabbé's cuirassiers advance close to the Allied squares. Avoiding a direct clash with them, the French turned, went back down the slope, and set about sabering Sir Hew Ross's gunners. Without any more reflection than was absolutely necessary, the commander of the Allied cavalry decided that his men must charge and throw back the enemy; since the strongest of his ten brigades was close at hand, deployed behind Ompteda's and Kielmansegge's squares, Uxbridge galloped over to its commander, Lord Edward Somerset, whose men made up the Household Brigade, so called because it was constituted of former Guards regiments. Uxbridge ordered Somerset to wheel his troops into line and prepare to charge.

It is not clear how aware Uxbridge was that the greater danger was looming farther to the east, on the other side of the main road, where the advancing French infantry had already occupied the chemin d'Ohain. The earl must have had the feeling that he was ordering a potentially decisive charge, and that it would have to be carried out in force without any economizing of his resources. Therefore, he spurred his horse across the cobblestone road and up to where a second brigade of heavy cavalry was deployed in reserve behind Picton's infantry. Because of its three dragoon regiments, this cavalry force was known as the Union Brigade: One regiment was English (the First Dragoons or Royals), one Scottish (the Second Dragoons or Scots Grays), and one Irish (the Sixth Dragoons or Inniskillings). Lord Uxbridge rode up to the brigade commander, Sir William Ponsonby, and ordered him to prepare his troops to charge; then the earl rode back to the Household Brigade, determined—like the Hussar he had been and still remained, despite his forty-seven years—to lead the attack of the Guards cavalry himself.

The two brigades of heavy cavalry that were about to go into action constituted a powerful striking force. Their horses, whose tails were docked in accordance with British practice, were probably the best in the world at a time when all the continental armies were feeling the effect of the dreadful equine destruction occasioned by the wars of the last three years, beginning with the Russian campaign. Prussia, for example, where horse-breeding had never been very good in the first place, had come out of the defeat of 1806 impoverished and had sharply scaled back its expenditures on heavy cavalry; there was none at all attached to the army that had been entrusted to Blücher's command. All the Prussian cavalry present at Waterloo was mounted and equipped according to the more modest light cavalry standards. Even the French cuirassiers were no longer mounted on the powerful animals that would have been required to maximize their force of impact, but rather on beasts of generally mediocre quality; furthermore, many French regiments at Waterloo were considerably under-strength, precisely because of the scarcity of adequate mounts. By contrast, Great

Britain had always possessed excellent horses, along with the financial means to obtain more of them wherever they might be found. Captain Tomkinson of the Sixteenth Light Dragoons observed that during the Waterloo campaign the horses in his regiment—which were newly arrived from England, and at a time of year when horses normally reach peak physical condition—were in excellent form, and this must have held true to an even greater degree for the animals in the service of the heavy cavalry.

Although the British cavalry enjoyed the advantage of magnificent material, its technical capabilities were rather less striking. Lieutenant Waymouth of the Second Life Guards, who took part in the great charge of Somerset's brigade, thought the swords issued to his men greatly inferior to those of the French cuirassiers, because the British weapon was a full six inches shorter; another officer described the sword used by the British cavalry as a "lumbering, clumsy, ill-contrived machine. It is too heavy, too short, and too broad." But the major problem was the way of wielding this sword, as prescribed by British regulations, with the elbow bent and the point upraised. It was "the custom of our Service," remarked Waymouth, "to carry the swords in a very bad position whilst charging, the French carrying theirs in a manner much less fatiguing, and also much better for attack or defence." The fact is that the French cavalry had perfected its technique by dint of the experience gained in years and years of uninterrupted campaigning; the British cavalry was almost completely lacking in such experience.

To the defect of inexperience, the British officers added an educational background and a value system in which competence and professionalism did not receive pride of place. The most extreme case of contempt for danger coupled with irresponsibility was probably that of Colonel Lord Portarlington, commander of the Twenty-third Light Dragoons. The evening before the battle of Waterloo, Portarlington left his command without permission and went to Brussels; when he returned to the field late the following morning, he arrived too late to rejoin his regiment. Desperate, and realizing too late that he'd thrown away his honor, the colonel attached himself to another regiment, fought in its ranks the whole day, and had his horse killed under him; despite his efforts, however, his absence from the regiment he was supposed to command was unpardonable, and Portarlington was obliged to resign his commission.[17]

A marginal case, without a doubt; but let us consider another one. Major Thornhill of the Seventh Hussars, Lord Uxbridge's old regiment, was chosen by the earl as one of his first aides-de-camp. Thornhill recalled that when he delivered Uxbridge's order to charge to one of the regiments of the Household Brigade, the Royal Horse Guards or "Blues," the commander of the regiment, Sir Robert Hill, "most kindly and courteously" invited him "to join them in the charge." The major accepted the invitation without a second thought and accompanied the Blues as they charged down the slope; his horse was killed, and the fall stunned him so badly that he was unable to remember what happened afterward. Apparently, it had not occurred to him for an instant that, as Lord Uxbridge's aide-de-camp, he should return at once to his commander, nor does the evidence suggest that it occurred to Sir Robert Hill, either. The concept of professionalism as we understand it today was as yet practically unknown, particularly among British cavalry officers; in its place was the code of honor, and that was deemed sufficient.

This handicap became more glaring in direct proportion to the number of units engaged, since it was precisely in the coordination of units and in the prudent management of reserves that the officers' lack of training made itself felt. "Our officers of cavalry have acquired a trick of galloping at every thing," Wellington complained. "They never consider the situation, never think of manoeuvring before an enemy, and never keep back or provide for a reserve." As for skill in maneuver, the British cavalry was so inferior to the enemy that whatever physical advantage the British enjoyed was canceled out; in the duke's view, though one British cavalry squadron could hold its own against two French squadrons, it was best for the British to avoid encounters when the opposing forces consisted of four squadrons each. The enemy was of the same opinion; though expressing due respect for the magnificent horses of the British and the fearlessness of their officers, General Foy maintained that for all practical purposes, the French cavalry was superior to theirs. As we shall see, the final outcome of the great charge ordered by Uxbridge did nothing to refute these judgments, even though the action was, on the whole, an astonishing success and in all probability saved Wellington from defeat.

Taken together, the two cavalry brigades that Uxbridge was preparing to set in motion counted around two thousand sabers. This figure is lower than the one attested to by the rolls, but based on the accounts of officers who took part in the battle the number of men actually present was much inferior to the number that appeared on paper. Moreover, in the case of the cavalry, the measure of forces actually available was not provided by the number of men but by the number of horses, which was usually even lower. On the rolls, the Sixteenth Light Dragoons numbered 31 officers and 402 men, but Captain Tomkinson affirmed that the regiment landed in the Netherlands with 330 horses, of which only 320 remained on the morning of the Battle of Waterloo; this means that no more than three-quarters of the men can have really taken part in the fighting. In April, when the first units had just begun to disembark in Belgium, the minister had informed Wellington that, after the reductions in strength decided at the end of the preceding war, the cavalry regiments could not allow themselves more than 360 horses each, and they would not have been able to increase that figure in such a short time. Therefore, every British cavalry brigade should be estimated as having contained about a thousand sabers at the most, even though the rolls yield numbers a good 20 or 30 percent higher.

Be that as it may, two thousand sabers added up to a considerable force, capable in some circumstances of deciding the outcome of a battle. Somerset's and Ponsonby's brigades comprised nineteen squadrons in all, of which no more than three were held in reserve, a decision that violated every rule of prudence. The squadron was, for all intents and purposes, the cavalry's principal tactical unit, and each included more than a hundred horses; when it was in line and waiting for the order to charge, it occupied a front of at least fifty yards. If collisions and injuries were to be avoided, horses could hardly be kept shoulder to shoulder at a trot, and so this front was destined to widen considerably when the riders spurred their mounts forward. For entire squadrons as for individual cavalrymen, a certain amount of space was indispensable. Taking these distances into account, we can conclude that the charge of the two brigades covered a front at least a mile wide; and given that the width of the entire battlefield was not above two and a half miles, such a charge must have made a huge impact.

And so the British dragoons, who until that moment had been stretched out on the ground among their horses to reduce the damage from the cannonballs that fell among them from time to time, climbed into their saddles at the bugle call. Following the familiar orders of their officers, they lined up two ranks deep by platoons, one squadron after another, noisily drew their swords from their scabbards, and set off at a walk, advancing toward the smoke and the firing. Their state of mind must have resembled that described by all those who have lived through such an experience: the exciting sensation that now the game is on, it's do or die, joined with the feeling of power and almost of invincibility that a rider feels when he's in the saddle and his mount begins to pick up speed. Lord Uxbridge, in his Hussar's uniform, rode ahead of the Household Brigade. Only much later did it occur to him that perhaps, as commander in chief of the Allied cavalry, he would have done better to remain behind and oversee the handling of his reserves.

On the other side of the main road, Sir William Ponsonby was preparing to order the Union Brigade to move out, and meanwhile he was thinking about his beautiful charger, a magnificent animal too expensive for Ponsonby to risk getting him killed, considering that the War Ministry would reimburse him only twenty pounds sterling, the standard price, which represented barely a fraction of the horse's real value. Sir William had been concerned about this matter for some days; only the night before last, he'd tried to purchase another horse, but he and the owner—an infantry colonel wounded at Quatre Bras—had been unable to agree on the price. The prospect of risking his precious purebred was troubling Ponsonby more than ever, so he decided to take his servant's horse, a hack of little value, and send its rider to the rear. While absorbed in these cogitations, he perhaps forgot to notify the colonel of the Scots Grays that his regiment was to remain in reserve, in accordance with the dispositions made that morning; or perhaps the idea of not taking part in the grand charge was simply too much for this colonel and his officers. In any case, when Sir William gave the sign, the Grays spurred their mounts ahead with the others, and the Union Brigade advanced in a single line, without leaving so much as a squadron in reserve.

When they came to within a hundred yards of the chemin d'Ohain, the brigade halted to allow the retreating infantry to reach safety by passing through the intervals between squadrons. In order to choose the most opportune moment to signal the attack, Ponsonby rode up to a vantage point on the crest of the ridge. The French artillery continued to pound the ridge, and a cannonball that passed too close spooked Sir William's nag; the sudden movement caused the general's cloak, which he was wearing thrown over his shoulders but not fastened, to slide to the ground. Ponsonby saw that the moment he was waiting for had come—the enemy infantry was engaged in crossing the sunken road, which in that sector ran a little below the crest—but he hated to lose his cloak, so he ordered his aide-de-camp, Major De Lacy Evans, to give the signal while he dismounted and collected the item. De Lacy Evans took off his hat and waved it, ordering the charge, and the brigade began to move.

While the Inniskillings were beginning to gather speed, many of them saw a man on horseback in civilian clothes waving his hat, too, and shouting, "Now's your chance!" Next to him, likewise on horseback, a boy with one arm in a sling and a bandaged head stood upright in his stirrups, thoroughly excited. The man shaking his hat was His Grace, the Duke of Richmond, who although he possessed the rank of general had been assigned no command in Wellington's army. Nevertheless, he had come to Waterloo to observe the battle, in which three of his sons were serving as aides-de-camp. The boy beside him was Lord William Pitt Lennox, at fifteen the youngest of the three, a cornet in the Blues and aide-de-camp to Sir Peregrine Maitland. A few days before, the teenager had fallen from his horse, breaking his arm, cracking his head, and losing the sight in one eye; but when he learned that Maitland's other aide-de-camp, the eighteen-year-old Lord Hay, had been killed at Quatre Bras, young Lord Lennox had insisted on returning to service, thus demonstrating his adherence to the English aristocracy's code of honor.

That morning, therefore, the boy had presented himself to Sir Peregrine with his slung arm, his bandaged eye, and his cracked skull; but since the general would not permit him to serve in his present state, the fifteen-year-old had resigned himself to watching the battle at his father's side. Whenever the duke, heedless of the bullets that were whistling all around, stopped to converse with one general or another, Lord William had all he could do to steady his frightened horse, which seemed on the point of bolting off and perhaps carrying him into the midst of the French; but he felt immense pride when his father turned to him and said, "I'm glad to see you stand fire so well." Then the cavalry began to move forward, and the boy remained there, tingling with excitement, standing straight up in his stirrups to see what would happen.

THIRTY-SEVEN

———◆•◆•◆———

THE CHARGE OF THE
HOUSEHOLD BRIGADE

The terrain over which Lord Edward Somerset's brigade was advancing was not ideal ground for a cavalry charge. The squadrons had to descend a gradual slope, muddy and slippery, ascend the opposite slope to the crest of the ridge, and there get past the complex obstacle presented by the sunken road and the thick bushes that bordered it. Since the chemin d'Ohain was too wide to leap over, the horses would have to go down one side of the lane and up the other, passing through the thorny bushes twice. Even before they could reach the hedge, the cavalry had to move through the Allied infantry; as soon as the foot soldiers heard the bugles and the horses' hooves behind them, they tried to open lanes for the cavalry to pass. According to Lord Uxbridge's personal account, under such conditions the cavalry could not charge at a gallop, sweeping down en masse like an avalanche, but rather came on in a succession of more or less isolated squadrons, which barely managed to reorder their line and go into a trot before falling one by one upon the enemy. "The ground was dreadfully broken," Uxbridge remembered, "and upon a very active horse I was much put to it to descend it. Towards the bottom of the slope I found our Infantry mostly in line, but getting into squares to receive the Enemy's Cavalry, and making intervals for us as our Squadrons presented themselves. Thus we passed through the Infantry as fast and as well as we could (but necessarily not with exact regularity), when, again forming, we instantly charged."

In spite of the difficulty of the terrain, the charge was admirably timed. Crabbé's cuirassiers were still scattered about the slippery slope, not having had time to reorder their ranks after their charge, and small groups of them were starting to cross the main road. This in itself presented a formidable obstacle, running as it did between two steep banks, each higher than a man. The French had no hope of resisting the sudden attack; caught between the charging British, who fell upon their left and rear, and the enclosure of La Haye Sainte, which barred the way on their right, they spurred their horses forward, trying to reach the main road. But the passage was so narrow and the road so deeply embanked that many of them were struck down before they could cross it, while others tumbled down the slope, clogging the roadway with a tangled mass of dead and dying horses and men.[18] Captain Kelly of the First Life Guards, a noted swordsman, charged the colonel of the First Cuirassiers, felled him with a rain of saber blows, and then dismounted to rip off his victim's epaulets, which he kept as a trophy. Kelly remained convinced that he had killed this officer, but in fact the colonel was only stunned. His name was Michel Ordener, and at barely twenty-eight years old he was already a veteran of eight campaigns and a count of the empire. He returned to action shortly afterward, survived the battle, and died in 1862.

Pursuing the cuirassiers, part of the British cavalry came in their turn to the top of the bank that sloped down to the main road. Some of the riders descended into what was by now a shambles of dying men and horses and continued the massacre of the fleeing enemy. Other British cavalry would perhaps have halted before the obstacle presented by the road, but the French skirmishers posted in the kitchen garden at La Haye Sainte, in the sandpit, and on the little knoll behind it started firing on the British with deadly precision, so that their only choice was to push forward. Several hundred cavalry got across the road as best they could, mounted the opposite bank, and clashed with the cuirassiers who had crossed the road a few minutes earlier. The encounter, a saber fight, was brief and exceedingly violent; one of the combatants was Corporal Shaw of the Second Life Guards, the famous boxer. Shaw was one of the best-known men in an army that knew how to appreciate the pugilistic sport. For a man of his enormous stature, he also excelled at wielding his saber, and he was feeling especially bellicose, having swallowed a vast quantity of brandy that morning. Surrounded by French cuirassiers, he was seen slashing and hacking so rapidly that he unsaddled one after another, felling no fewer than nine, or at least that is what was said after the battle. But as he fought, a cuirassier withdrew a little distance from the melee, raised the short carbine issued to all cavalry troopers, took careful aim, and shot Shaw off his horse. The boxer dragged himself to the wall of La Haye Sainte, where he died from loss of blood.[19]

Eventually, however, the surviving cuirassiers were routed, and they scattered in all directions. By that time, they had lost their commander, as Colonel Crabbé had been mortally wounded in the melee. A single cuirassier, isolated from the rest, galloped so far along the ridge that he ended up behind Pack's men, who were deployed in line beside the sunken lane. Enraged at seeing his path obstructed in this way, or perhaps simply because he'd lost his head, the Frenchman charged the infantry, wheeling his saber. Since he was coming upon them from behind, there was a chance that he might get through; but a soldier shot the cuirassier's horse dead, ran out of line, killed the man with a few bayonet thrusts, searched him quickly, stole his purse, and ran back to his comrades.

As they were chasing the cuirassiers, the British dragoons suddenly came upon the flank of Aulard's brigade, which was already having difficulty staving off Kempt's counterattack. Again this time, the psychological effect was immediate and catastrophic: Overrun first by their own fleeing cuirassiers and then immediately afterward by multitudes of British dragoons, whirling their sabers in hot pursuit, the two battalions of the Fifty-first Ligne, which had been in the front line since the beginning of the battle and had already suffered heavy losses, as well as the two battalions of the Nineteenth Ligne, which were deployed to the right of the Fifty-first, allowed themselves to be seized by panic and ran headlong from the field. From the walls of La Haye Sainte, the German fusiliers enthusiastically greeted the arrival of the dragoons, who galloped along the perimeter of the farm, sweeping aside everything in their path. Lieutenant Waymouth of the Second Life Guards had enough time to recognize an officer of the King's German Legion whom he knew by sight, Lieutenant Graeme, at his post on the roof of the piggery. Shortly thereafter, Graeme and his men went down into the courtyard, opened the gate leading to the road, and issued forth to mop up the French, who threw away their weapons and surrendered voluntarily rather than face the saber-strokes of the cavalry.

Captain Kincaid and his riflemen also watched with immense relief as the cavalry rode into the midst of their enemies and put them to flight. The captain was mounted on his mare in a gap in the hedge, and a moment before he had noticed, to his alarm, that some cuirassiers were coming straight at him; but when he tried to draw his saber, he found that the rain of the previous night had rusted it into his scabbard so tightly that he was unable to pull it out. Although Sir James Kempt in person had ordered him not to move from his position, Kincaid was hastily considering the pros and cons of disobeying, when suddenly the cuirassiers were overwhelmed by the British cavalry and thrown back among their own infantry, transforming it at once into a throng of fugitives. Recognizing the helmets of the Life Guards, Kincaid admitted to himself that they were real soldiers, after all, and not—as he had sometimes thought—just manikins good for nothing except parades in Hyde Park. The French column had been routed in an instant. "Hundreds of the infantry threw themselves down and pretended to be dead, while the cavalry galloped over them, and then got up and ran away," Kincaid later recalled. "I never saw such a scene in all my life."

The rout of the French infantry was not total everywhere; some soldiers rose to their feet and started firing at the backs of the British cavalry, and here and there a rider was dragged from his horse and hauled away as a prisoner—for example, Lieutenant Waymouth, who fell badly wounded by a saber blow from a cuirassier and remained a prisoner in enemy hands for several weeks. While Captain Irby of the same regiment was returning from the charge, his horse was killed under him and he was captured and taken away; the next day he managed to escape from a cellar where he and other prisoners had been confined. On the whole, however, the charge had been a complete success, and Aulard's brigade had practically ceased to exist. Over the course of the day, the Fifty-first and Nineteenth Ligne regiments lost a total of seventeen officers killed and twenty-four wounded—that is, nearly half of the regiments' officers, an extremely high percentage.

The other squadrons of the Household Brigade, having driven the cuirassiers toward the *chaussée*, the cobblestone main road, continued charging down the slope with Lord Uxbridge at their head and attacked the skirmishers of Schmitz's brigade, who were stationed near the enclosure of La Haye Sainte. Uxbridge observed that all the enemy troops in his front gave way immediately. As unlikely as it was that a line of skirmishers would have so much as considered standing up to a force of six or seven hundred cavalry, coming down upon them from higher ground at increasing speed, nevertheless, the fire of the French skirmishers, who hid amid the stubble and along the walls of the farm, must have been horribly efficient. Sir Robert Hill, commander of the Blues, saw the commanding officer of the First Life Guards fall dead from a musket shot while leading his men at the beginning of the charge. The colonel of the King's Dragoon Guards was also killed almost immediately, and his body was later found a short distance from La Haye Sainte; in launching the charge, he had cried out to his men, "On to Paris!"

Perhaps the loss of so many officers can partly explain why the British dragoons, having routed Crabbé's cuirassiers, kept on charging, not because they had received precise orders to do so, but from sheer force of momentum. They swept away isolated skirmishers, but they never came upon any objective that could justify prolonging the action. "After the overthrow of the Cuirassiers," Lord Uxbridge wrote, "I had in vain attempted to stop my people by sounding the Rally," but no one heeded the call. As often happened in such cases, the charge had broken up into a vast number of isolated combats, which occasioned a few strange episodes. Lieutenant Story, who had recently returned to service after having been a prisoner of the French for a full seven years, was about to strike an enemy soldier with his saber when the man threw away his musket and begged for mercy, assuring Story that he knew him well. The incredulous lieutenant recognized a French soldier he had known when he was a prisoner in the fortress of Verdun. Story spared him and his companion and sent them to the rear as prisoners.

The net result of the extended charge was that the surviving *tirailleurs* got themselves under some kind of cover, Schmitz's battalions formed square near the orchard of La Haye Sainte, and the cavalry found itself at the bottom of the slope with blown horses—all force of impact gone—and exposed to the accurate fire of the enemy massed on the opposite slope. At that moment, by his own later admission, Lord Uxbridge realized that the commander in chief of all the Allied cavalry should not have been where he was. For the moment, though, his troubling premonitions were quelled by the extraordinary success of the charge, and by shouts of triumph coming from the other side of the main road, indicating that the Union Brigade, whose charge had begun a little later, had met with the same success.

THIRTY-EIGHT

---◆---

THE CHARGE OF
THE UNION BRIGADE

L ike Somerset's men, Ponsonby's had also been obliged to pass through the ranks
of their own infantry before coming into contact with the enemy. Often, it was
rather the case that the infantry, already in full retreat, withdrew to the rear,
passing through the intervals between one squadron and another. In places where
the infantry was still holding its position, the light cavalry went right over them;
when the Scots Grays moved through the ranks of the Ninety-second, for example,
the exultant cries of the highlanders mingled with the curses hurled at them by the
soldiers their horses knocked down. Through the din of the charge, the bagpipes'
familiar lament augmented the Grays' excitement; one of them recognized the
Gordons' piper, who was standing on a hillock a little apart and playing the old
Scots song "Johnny Cope, Are Ye Wakin' Yet?" The story that some of the infantry,
in a frenzy of enthusiasm, caught hold of the cavalry's stirrups and charged with
them into the fight, shouting "Scotland forever," forms part of the patriotic
mythology of the Battle of Waterloo.

Once through the infantry, it was not necessary for the Union Brigade's
squadrons to get across the chemin d'Ohain and reorder their line before
charging, because the French were mostly past the sunken lane when the British
troopers suddenly appeared out of the smoke, whirling their sabers above their
heads. Assaulted frontally and without warning by about a thousand cavalry, the
divisions of Quiot and Marcognet disbanded rapidly. Lord Uxbridge later wrote,
"My impression is that the French were completely surprised by the first Cavalry
attack. It (our Cavalry) had been rather hidden by rising ground immediately
before their position. I think the left wing of our Infantry was partially retiring,
when I determined upon the movement, and then these 19 Squadrons pouncing

downhill upon them so astonished them that no very good resistance was made, and surely such havoc was rarely made in so few minutes."

Sir William Ponsonby's aide-de-camp, De Lacy Evans, was so struck by the speed of the catastrophe that he concluded that the French columns must have been composed of inexperienced recruits. "The Enemy's Column, near which I was, on arriving at the crest of the position seemed very helpless, had very little fire to give from its front or flanks, was incapable of deploying, must have already lost many of its Officers in coming up, was fired into, close, with impunity, by stragglers of our Infantry who remained behind. As we approached at a moderate pace[20] the front and flanks began to turn their backs inwards; the rear of the Columns had already begun to run away."

In truth, however, d'Erlon's was a solid infantry, with a large proportion of veterans, enthusiastically devoted to the emperor. The first of the two regiments of Bourgeois's brigade, the 105th Ligne, was in fact noted for its fanaticism: On the march to the Belgian border, the men of the 105th had assaulted and demolished a newly constructed house decorated with paintings of the Bourbon lilies, and the local authorities had been obliged to arrest the unfortunate owner in order to calm the soldiers' fury. But in these circumstances—faced with a massed cavalry charge, deployed in a formation unsuited to such an attack, and having just emerged from a debilitating firefight—any infantry would have been routed.

The first regiment of the Union Brigade, the Royals, fell on the 105th Ligne, which had got through the hedge and were pushing back the Belgians of the Seventh. Each of the three squadrons of the British regiment spanned some fifty yards, and thus they attacked the French line, no more than eighty yards long, in both front and flank. When the French realized their danger, the cavalry was less than a hundred yards (and therefore only a few seconds) from impact; Captain Clark, who commanded the central squadron of the charging cavalry, saw the enemy give signs of panic but nevertheless fire a volley that brought down some twenty dragoons. This feat, performed under such extreme conditions, offers a final confirmation of the effectiveness of the French musketry. Then, since there was no time to do anything else, the infantry took to their heels, seeking the safety of the hedge and the sunken lane. An instant later, the dragoons were upon them, sabering their victims without pity, even though at that point many of the French had thrown down their weapons and were trying to surrender. According to Clark's account, the whole French column got "into one dense mass, the men between the advancing and retiring parts getting so jammed together that the men could not bring down their arms, or use them effectively, and we had nothing to do but to continue to press them down the slope."

The captain had been in the melee for some minutes when he saw the officer who bore the Eagle of the 105th Ligne trying to carry it to the rear and safety. The loss of an Eagle was considered a disaster for an imperial regiment, and capturing one was the fervent desire of all who fought against Napoleon. Captain Clark immediately ordered his squadron, "Right shoulders forward, attack the Colour," and spurred his horse in that direction. Upon reaching the French officer, who was turned the other way, Clark ran him through with his sword. When the man fell, the captain reached for the flag, but his fingers only grazed the fringe, and he gave a frenzied cry: "Secure the Colour, secure the Colour, it belongs to me." One of his men, Corporal Styles, seized it before it fell and turned it over to Clark. In the excitement of the moment, the captain tried to break the Eagle off its pole so he could put the trophy inside his coat, but the corporal said to him, "Pray, sir, do not break it," and the captain, regaining some of his composure, agreed to desist, saying, "Very well, carry it to the rear as fast as you can, it belongs to me."

The Royals' charge sealed the destruction of Bourgeois's brigade. At the end of the day, the 105th Ligne would mourn the loss of twelve officers killed and twenty wounded out of a total of about forty; Colonel Genty, who commanded the 105th, was wounded and taken prisoner, and both battalion commanders were killed. The Twenty-eighth Ligne, which was slightly behind the 105th, fared little better. Having avoided capture by the skin of his teeth, Corporal Canler was limping to the rear, stopping every now and then to rifle the pockets of some dead officer, without making any distinctions between Britons and French. As he made his way, Canler came upon his colonel, who was galloping back and forth and shouting, "To me, 28th! To me!" in hope of gathering together a few of his men. His efforts, however, were unsuccessful; no one, not even the corporal, paid him any attention. A little later, while wandering "somewhat randomly" with a couple of comrades, Canler encountered a general, who stopped them and asked where they thought they were going. To avoid trouble, the men declared that they were trying to rejoin their unit, but the general shook his head. "It's useless," he told them. "Your regiment is scattered." Unlike the losses suffered by the 105th, those of the Twenty-eighth comprised more fugitives than dead and wounded, but in any case, Bourgeois's brigade was hors de combat.

In the center, the Inniskillings obtained a rather less triumphant success, because their charge was directed against the other brigade of Quiot's division, the one commanded by Colonel Charlet, which had stayed back in support. This meant that the Inniskillings had to cross the sunken lane and then go partway down the slope before they made contact with the French, who thus had more time to prepare some resistance or to run away. In fact Charlet's two regiments, the Fifty-fourth and the Fifty-fifth Ligne, made little attempt to resist, and the Inniskillings, howling their wild Irish "Hurrah!" routed them. Though heavy, the losses in Charlet's regiments did not compare to those in Bourgeois's, which were literally cut to pieces by the British sabers.

The combat included dramatic moments for soldiers on both sides. Muter, the Inniskillings' colonel, saw "an Infantry French soldier on his knees, deliberately taking aim at the Adjutant of the Inniskillings, who was close to me, in the *midst* of one of the French Columns, and sending his bullet through his head." The Inniskillings took fewer prisoners than the other regiments in the Union Brigade, and it was the only one of the three that did not capture an Eagle from the French. Writing many years later, Colonel Muter still couldn't get over this failure, and his chagrin was increased by the legend that was repeated around the regimental table, namely that a trooper of the Inniskillings had indeed seized an Eagle, but then naively allowed himself to be tricked out of it by a corporal from another regiment.[21]

The most dramatic charge of all was that of the Scots Grays. Mounted on their powerful gray steeds, made to appear even more impressive by their bearskin caps, the Scottish dragoons bore down upon the men of Grenier's brigade, who were crossing the sunken lane. For a moment, the French infantry, and particularly its leading regiment, the Forty-fifth Ligne, seemed able to repulse the attack with the massed fire of its muskets, and the Grays' advance—made at a moderate trot because of the nature of the terrain—gave some companies enough time to fire more than one volley. Lieutenant Wyndham remembered noticing "the extraordinary manner in which the bullets struck our swords as we ascended," saw several of his men shot from their horses, got through the hedge, and shortly thereafter was wounded himself. Another officer turned to Captain Cheney and blurted out, "How many minutes have we yet to live, Cheney?" The captain coldly replied, "Two or three at the very utmost, most probably not one."

The majority of the French troops, however, found that the cavalry was upon them before they saw it coming, as Captain Martin of the Forty-fifth Ligne related: "A hollow road, lined with hedges, was the only obstacle still separating us from them. Our soldiers didn't wait for the order to cross it; they hurled themselves at it, jumping over the hedge and breaking ranks in order to rush upon the enemy. Fatal recklessness! We struggled to bring them back into order. We brought them to a halt in order to rally them. . . . Just as I finished pushing a soldier back into his rank, I saw him fall at my feet, struck down by a saber blow, and I quickly turned around. The British cavalry were charging us on all sides and cutting us to pieces. To avoid the same fate, I could only rush into the midst of the crowd. We found ourselves defenseless, exposed to a ferocious enemy. They even cut down the boys who served as our pipers and drummers." Actually, though, many French troops were able to surrender, throwing their muskets to the ground and unfastening their crossbelts—or perhaps the Grays' blades were not as sharp as they once were. At the battle's end, Grenier's brigade counted only three officers killed and fifty-nine wounded, an exceptional disproportion. An officer of the Gordons, from his position on the high ground, watched the Scots Grays as they "actually walked over this Column," and this is probably the most objective description of what happened; in the end, therefore, the death toll wasn't extremely high—partly because of the smoke, which covered everything in an instant—but Grenier's brigade was nonetheless crushed.

In this case as in the case of Bourgeois's brigade, the lead regiment, which had led the victorious attack, which had been the most exposed, and which had suffered the most casualties, was the regiment most thoroughly routed when the turning point came; moreover, it suffered the shame of losing its regimental Eagle. Sergeant Ewart of the Scots Grays, a giant well over six feet tall, had just decapitated a French officer with a saber blow and was looking about him in search of other victims when he saw the Eagle of the Forty-fifth Ligne swaying over the heads of the fleeing French infantry. Ewart spurred his horse, caught up with the standard-bearer, exchanged a few saber strokes with him, and finally, having split his opponent's head open, triumphantly took possession of his war trophy. This was the second Eagle captured during the Battle of Waterloo, and it would be the last: a testament to the obstinacy with which the French, even in the moment of final defeat, continued to defend their "Cuckoos."

Immediately after overwhelming Grenier's brigade, the Grays attacked the first regiment of Nogues's brigade, the Twenty-first Ligne. Since it was still some three to four hundred yards from the sunken lane, the Twenty-first had time to observe what was happening and quickly form square. As the British dragoons drew near in what was by then almost complete disorder, they came under fire from the square, which struck down a great many horses and men. Lieutenant Wyndham, despite having received one wound, continued to charge together with his men; he was wounded again, this time in the foot, and compelled to leave the battlefield. But the impetus of the oncoming British dragoons was so great—as was, in all probability, the terror of the French recruits, given what was happening all around them—that the square broke up as the cavalry advanced, and the Twenty-first was overwhelmed. Its colonel, a veteran of the revolutionary wars named, ironically enough, Carré ("Square"), was wounded and captured; a great many of his soldiers threw away their muskets and fell on their knees, begging for mercy. One of the Grays' officers remembered that the French "cried out 'Prisoners!' and threw down their arms, and stripped themselves of their belts and ran to our rear. Ay, they ran like hares!"

In the meantime, the Royals and the Inniskillings had followed the fleeing infantry all the way to the bottom of the slope. There they, too, like the Household Brigade on the other side of the main road, came under fire from some enemy infantry formed on the opposite slope. The squadron commanders tried to assemble their men and lead them back to their lines, but the regiments were so widely dispersed that only a few troopers could hear these orders. Those few, commanders and men, retired back up the slope, pushing their prisoners before them.

Many French soldiers who had thrown themselves on the ground or raised their hands started gathering up their muskets and firing again. Captain Clark found the enemy lacking in a sense of fair play: "The French on this occasion behaved very ill, many of our soldiers falling from the fire of men who had surrendered, and whose lives had been spared only a few minutes before." He was attacked by a Frenchman who leaped to his feet, pointed his musket at the captain's head, and pulled the trigger; a sudden turn of the head saved Clark's life, but the ball carried away the tip of his nose.

Infantry units from the brigades of Ompteda, Kempt, Bijlandt, and Pack were already advancing in support of the cavalry, and they completed the roundup of prisoners. This advance, however, was carried out in the utmost confusion: The British infantry fired on the Belgians, whose blue uniforms resembled the enemy's, and shortly thereafter, having realized their error, they mistook French troops for Belgians and let them get away. An officer went so far in pursuit of the fugitives that eventually they ganged up on him and took him prisoner, stripping him of nearly all his clothes and leaving him in his shirt. The ferocity of the action seems to have been equal to the confusion. The Scottish troops of the Forty-second Regiment had lost their colonel, Sir Robert Macara, at Quatre Bras; wounded in the battle, he was being carried off the field when French cavalry surrounded his party and cut it to pieces. Now, some of the Scots shouted, "Where's Macara?" as they bayoneted unarmed French soldiers who were trying to surrender. Sergeant Robertson of the Gordons heard a Frenchman who spoke excellent English offer his money and his watch to whoever would agree to protect him. Lieutenant Scheltens saved the lives of two French officers who gave him a secret Masonic sign as they were surrendering; fortunately for them, the Belgian was a Mason, too, and he made sure they were brought to the rear, among at least two thousand French troops taken prisoner and escorted behind the Allied lines. "They were, generally speaking, fine soldierlike men," observed a British officer, "but appeared a little cast down from their want of success."

Durutte's division was the only one in d'Erlon's corps that escaped the disaster. According to Napoleon's orders, this division was to go into action last, and so it began its march after the others. The French troops advanced toward the high ground where two brigades of inexperienced Hanoverian militiamen, commanded by Colonels Best and Vincke, awaited the attack with mounting anxiety.

The state of mind that prevailed in this sector of the Allied line—which up to now had been the least engaged—is illustrated by the vicissitudes of the surgeons attached to Vincke's brigade. Having set up their dressing station in the rear, they were ordered to withdraw farther in order to be safe from the artillery bombardment. They complied, found a peasant's house that suited their purposes, and were preparing to operate on the first casualties when they heard shouted warnings that they had to leave the house at once. One of the physicians, Dr. Oppermann, went outside to see what was happening and met the brigade's chief surgeon, who told him, "You will have to fall farther back." The surgeons obeyed, and after a march of some ten minutes they halted and finally set about their work. Troops wounded by artillery attacks and by the fire of the *tirailleurs* were carried by comrades all the way to this spot, and no doubt some healthy men took advantage of the opportunity to abandon the front lines. According to Oppermann's account, "[The surgeons] worked together for half an hour. Outside, however, the tumult was continuing to increase, and I was forced to make a quick decision, because men on horseback were arriving every minute, totally in the grip of panic and shouting, 'Back! Back! Move it! Move!'" Eventually, the surgeons cleared off completely and did not stop until they reached Brussels. In the turmoil, they lost all their expensive instruments, for which the War Ministry later obliged them to pay.

But General Durutte either did not wish to commit his entire division or had insufficient time to do so. After a march of many hours that morning, his men had taken up their positions in the front line only a short while before, and Durutte later admitted that he had only half believed that an attack organized in such a way could succeed in the first place. Properly concerned about the strong force of enemy pickets he glimpsed on his right, among the hedgerows and walls of the farms of Papelotte and La Haye and even beyond them as far as the Fichermont wood, he kept a part of his force in reserve, and this prudent approach led to a reduction in the damage done by the British cavalry when it appeared in that part of the field and put an end to the French advance. Durutte's men promptly formed square and repelled the uncoordinated attempts to charge them made by a few isolated groups of Grays. An officer in Pack's brigade, stationed a few hundred yards away, noticed that the Dragoons had lost nearly all cohesion: "Flushed with their victory, they galloped up by twos and threes, and even singly, to the French columns, prancing about, and brandishing their swords, as if in defiance. An officer was attempting to bring them off: I could distinctly see a French soldier level his piece, fire, and bring him rolling to the ground." When the British cavalry finally withdrew, Durutte's men remained practically the only organized force left in d'Erlon's corps. In the course of a few minutes, five other French brigades had been transformed into a mob of fugitives.

THIRTY-NINE

━━━━━━◆•◆━━━━━━

DRAGOONS AGAINST GUNS

The Scots Grays, who according to Lord Uxbridge's orders were supposed to remain in reserve, were instead the regiment that kept charging longest. While the officers of the Royals and the Inniskillings, satisfied with the results of the action and worried about the losses they had suffered, tried to reassemble their scattered squadrons and lead them back up the slope, Colonel James Hamilton of the Grays decided that he and they had not yet had enough.

At the age of thirty-eight, Hamilton had a curious history. He was born in a British army encampment during the American Revolutionary War. He returned home with his father, a sergeant named Anderson, and grew up like any other child of the Glasgow slums. But General Hamilton, who had commanded Sergeant Anderson's former regiment, took young James Anderson under his protection and sent him to school at his own expense; eventually, he assumed full responsibility for the boy, raised him in his own house with the help of a spinster sister, and in the end adopted him and gave him his name. When James was sixteen, General Hamilton bought him an officer's commission in the Scots Grays. Twenty-two years later, James Hamilton was the commander of the regiment; the Scots Grays were his entire life, and this was the first time that he led them into battle, because during his tenure the regiment had never before been sent outside the United Kingdom. Their zeal to show at last what they were worth, together with the total lack of experience on the part of both Hamilton and his officers, explains what happened next. Having sighted the guns of the Grande Batterie in the distance, the colonel decided to capture them. He resolutely spurred his horse in that direction, followed by a large part of his regiment.

The attack on the Grande Batterie is one of the more obscure episodes in the Battle of Waterloo. Very few accounts were left by eyewitnesses who actually took part in the action, and yet historians generally take it for granted that the cavalry reached a great many guns and rendered them useless. Lord Uxbridge himself wrote that his men seized ("or rather passed," he prudently adds) a vast number of guns, but as to the effective results of the charge, he is reduced to quoting a French general, whose name he does not recall, who is said to have told him that the charge put forty guns out of action. The most vivid account was provided by one of the Grays' noncommissioned officers, Corporal Dickson. The corporal remembered Colonel Hamilton in the act of indicating the objective to his men, and he gave a particularly raw description of the dragoons' behavior once they got among the guns: "Such slaughtering! We sabred the gunners, lamed the horses, and cut their traces and harness. I can hear the Frenchmen yet crying 'Diable' when I struck at them, and the long-drawn hiss through their teeth as my sword went home. The artillery drivers sat on their horses weeping aloud as we went among them; they were mere boys, we thought."

From the absence of eyewitness accounts by members of the other regiments, it seems that no other cavalry followed Colonel Hamilton and the Scots Grays to the guns in their half-mad charge. Considering that none of the guns could be taken away, and that a short time later the surviving Grays had hastily to abandon the position, one could reasonably conclude that the Grays' attack was without significance, and accept Napoleon's curt summary of the matter, according to which the British cavalry restricted itself to taking momentary possession of a few cannon that were quickly recaptured. But another account, from a most credible source—General Desales—confirmed that the British cavalry's sudden appearance in the midst of the guns of the Grande Batterie did indeed produce a disastrous effect, not so much for the material losses the Grays inflicted as for the panic that seized the gunners, just as it had seized the infantry a few minutes before.

Desales was engaged in coordinating the fire of the more than fifty guns the emperor had put under his command when the chef d'escadron, Waudré, who commanded I Corps's two horse artillery batteries, came to notify him that the enemy was deploying great masses of cavalry. The worried Waudré asked the general whether they should inform the emperor. With some impatience, Desales told him to return to his post, because the emperor had an excellent telescope and surely needed no advice from them. Then Desales turned back to his artillery and decided that the time had come to carry out the order he had received and begin moving the guns forward, one battery at a time under the covering fire of the others. He rode over to Marshal Ney to inform him of what he intended to do, but shortly after he arrived at the marshal's side, Desales noticed that the colonel in command of the three 12-pounder batteries had already moved them on his own initiative; in fact, they were taking up their new positions, a few hundred yards farther down the slope, almost level with La Haye Sainte. Desales anxiously followed these movements. With relief, he watched the guns get into position and reopen fire, but just as he relaxed, Marshal Ney cried out, "They're charging you!"

In that instant, the routed French infantry surged around the guns, followed by the British cavalry. The French gunners had stopped firing, "for fear of killing our own" (although Captain Martin was convinced they had fired into the mass for a little while, killing many of his men), and a moment later they were swept away in the rout. It took but a few minutes for the British dragoons to pass the line of 12-pounders and, in the midst of the crowd of fugitives, to reach the 6-pounder batteries, which were still in their original positions. Most of the gunners took to their heels as the dragoons sabered horses and men. Desales claimed he rushed into the center of this disaster, took command of one of the 12-pounder batteries, redeployed it along the main road, and immediately started firing on the cavalry; but in spite of his efforts, the panic that had overcome the gunners could not be calmed.

In the end, when the Scots Grays abandoned the position, the French guns were all still in place because the dragoons had no means of carrying them away. Had the surviving gunners come back into line, the damage would have been small, "and honorable men should have returned to their post, because not one piece, not one caisson had been taken by the enemy." Instead, Desales concluded bitterly, most of the runaways did not show their faces again. The colonel who had brought the 12-pounder battery into its new position tried in vain to call back the fugitives and was the only battery commander to report to Desales. The general, beside himself, received the officer with an angry exclamation: "Monsieur! When one has committed such a military error as this, he does not report, he gets himself killed!" Years later those ill-judged words, uttered in the excitement of the moment, continued to prick Desales's conscience. The colonel was little more than a boy and full of fervor; he had been promoted a few months previously by Napoleon in person, when the emperor passed through Grenoble after his flight from Elba. "The poor young man! He galloped away at once. I heard nothing more about him."

This account, given by the commander of the Grande Batterie, is in complete accord with the one an anonymous general gave Lord Uxbridge in a conversation that took place some time after the battle. According to this general, the charge had rendered forty guns useless, a declaration that justifies the suspicion that he may have been Desales himself. Perhaps the general, exasperated at the cowardice of the gunners and desirous of saddling them with the responsibility for the disaster, exaggerated the number of batteries that remained effectively out of commission. The catastrophe of the Grande Batterie did not really have a decisive material effect, because Napoleon was in possession of immense reserves of cannon, more, in fact, than he could possibly deploy on such a narrow front. But from a psychological point of view, the panic that seized Desales's artillerymen, just as it had seized the infantry, was an ominous sign.

FORTY

---·•◆•·---

JACQUINOT'S LANCERS

However good his telescope may have been, Napoleon, from his position on the ridge at La Belle Alliance, had not had sufficient time to forestall the disaster. But before the enemy cavalry had reached the end of its ride, stopping to catch its breath in the shallow valley or among the guns of the Grande Batterie, the emperor was already reacting. He ordered Milhaud's corps, which constituted the cavalry reserve of the right wing, to counterattack. General Farine, who had already been wounded at Ligny and would soon receive another wound at Waterloo, and General Travers, with their four cuirassier regiments, ten fresh squadrons totaling almost 1,300 sabers, set out in pursuit of the exhausted British cavalry, whose troops were remounting the slope in disorder, trying to return to their original positions.

From his position on the extreme right of the French line, in front of Papelotte, General Jacquinot, commander of I Corps's light cavalry, had also watched incredulously as the rout unfolded, and had immediately wheeled his squadrons into line to intervene. One of his four regiments, Colonel Marbot's Seventh Hussars, had been detached to reconnoiter the Prussian advance. Jacquinot held another in reserve, but he sent his two regiments of lancers—some seven hundred riders in all—galloping into the fray. For some time, Napoleon had been increasing the number of French cavalry units armed with lances, following the examples of the Austrian uhlans and the Russian Cossacks. As the new weapon was nearly nine feet long, weighed seven pounds, and had a steel point on a wooden staff, it was awkward to carry, and cumbersome, it had its detractors, and the British cavalry had not yet considered adopting it; but Jacquinot's men would demonstrate the lance's terrifying efficiency. The two regiments fanned out and started a mopping-up operation over the entire length of the ground where catastrophe had struck the I Corps only a few minutes previously.

The commanders of the British cavalry quickly realized that their men, and particularly their horses, were in no condition to withstand this double counterattack. When Lord Uxbridge saw the cuirassiers advancing, he hastened to turn back and summon his reserves to intervene. Although he had forgotten to give the appropriate orders, he expected—or so he later said—that the other cavalry brigades deployed in that sector would have moved forward to support the great charge, but to his dismay he discovered that none of them had moved. When he reached the crossroads behind La Haye Sainte, he met Wellington, surrounded by his aides-de-camp and a crowd of foreign military attachés, and he saw to his relief that this whole "*Troupe dorée*," as he called it, was rejoicing in the success of the charge. "They thought the battle was over," he recalled. And so, although his conscience was telling him that he been wrong to lead the charge in person instead of staying behind to coordinate the reserves, he stayed there with the others to see what would happen.

On the other side of the battlefield, across the main road, Sir William Ponsonby had also seen that things were taking a turn for the worse. For some time, he and his adjutants had been signaling frantically to their troopers to stop their wild career, but so great was the excitement of the pursuit that no one paid the officers any heed. Major De Lacy Evans reported, "Our men were *out of hand*. The General of the Brigade, his staff, and every Officer within hearing, exerted themselves to the utmost to re-form the men; but the helplessness of the Enemy offered too great a temptation to the Dragoons, and our efforts were abortive." Soon, Ponsonby and his officers became aware that the French lancers were coming threateningly close, advancing in good order, their long lances decorated with red-and-white pennons. "If we could have formed a hundred men," Evans observed, "we could have made a respectable retreat, and saved many; but we could effect no formation, and were as helpless against their attack as their Infantry had been against ours. Everyone saw what must happen."

Sir William and his staff, vainly pursuing the Scots Grays, rode into the midst of the French guns. "Finding that we were not successful in stopping the troops, we were forced to continue with them in order to continue our exclamations to halt, as we all, except I suppose the Cornets, saw what would happen," reiterated Major Evans, still obsessed, many years later, by the memory of that foreseen disaster.[22] An instant later, Jacquinot's lancers fell on them, and everyone had to try to save his own skin. "Those whose horses were best or least blown, got away. Some attempted to escape back to our position by going round the left of the French Lancers. All these fell into the hands of the Enemy." De Lacy Evans and a few others galloped all the way to the main road, dodged the fire of the French infantry who were still posted around La Haye Sainte, dashed down the slope, and somehow made it to safety.

Sir William Ponsonby, however, together with his brigade adjutant, Major Reignolds, made a dash around the other side, and a lancer quickly began pursuing them. While they were crossing a plowed field, Sir William's second-rate got stuck in the mud; in an instant, the lancer was upon him. Against a man armed with a lance, the general's saber was worth nothing, so Ponsonby threw it away and surrendered. Reignolds came to his aid, but the lancer compelled both of them to dismount under the threat of his lance. The man was nervous and excited at having captured what was obviously an important prize. Sir William must have had a bad presentiment, because he took out his watch and a miniature portrait and passed them to his adjutant, asking him to deliver them to Lady Ponsonby. At that moment, a small group of Scots Grays happened to pass a short distance away, saw the three, and galloped shouting in their direction, with the idea of liberating the prisoners. In a flash, the Frenchman killed the general and his brigade major with two blows of his lance, then boldly charged the oncoming dragoons, striking down three in less than a minute. The others abandoned the combat, completely incapable of holding their own against the enemy's deadly weapon.

In the hands of Jacquinot's veterans, the lance showed its frightening effectiveness. "I had never before realized the great superiority of the lance over the sword," recalled Durutte, who saw everything from his position on the high ground in front of Papelotte.[23] In the memoirs of Waterloo, the French lancers, galloping at will over the battlefield, sending saber-armed cavalry fleeing before them, and calmly stopping to finish off the wounded without even having to dismount, appear as an image of vivid horror. Wyndham of the Scots Grays saw the lancers pursuing British dragoons who had lost their horses in the charge and were trying to save themselves on foot. He noted the ruthlessness of the lancers' pursuit and watched them cut their victims down. "At Brussels, some weeks afterward, I found many of our men with 10 or 12 lance wounds in them, and one man, *Lock*, had 17 or 18 about his person, and lived afterwards to tell the story." Corporal Dickson remembered how his friends, after their horses were killed, had been surrounded and struck down, one after the other; he seemed to see them still, slipping in the mud and trying to ward off the lance blows with their hands.

An officer in the Grays who had the good luck to survive the combat with a minor wound, Lieutenant Hamilton, revealed that the French lancers held a special place in their enemies' imaginations even before the battle. "One of the red lancers put his lance to my horse's head, I made a cut at his arm as I passed him; and as I did not look behind me to see whether I had struck him or his lance, I should not have known that I had struck his arm, had I not in recovering my sword thrown the blood on my white pouch belt. On inspecting my sword I saw that I had succeeded in wounding the lancer and possibly thus saved my own life. My fears were, when I saw him thrust at my horse's reins, that he would shoot me with his pistol, having heard of the red lancers sometimes doing so." Although this recollection betrays some confusion between the lancers of the Imperial Guard, who wore red uniforms, and those of the regular cavalry, whose uniforms were green, it's obvious that Napoleon's lancers obviously struck the British imagination as exotic, vaguely barbaric enemies, exactly as the kaiser's uhlans were considered at the outbreak of the First World War. This explains why the lancers remained so vivid in the memories of the survivors—much more so than, for example, Milhaud's cuirassiers, and yet the latter made at least an equal contribution to the pursuit and destruction of the British heavy cavalry.

The attack practically wiped out the Scots Grays, against whom the lancers were initially sent. Of the twenty-four officers who had taken part in the Grays' charge, eight were wounded and eight killed, and the lower ranks suffered more or less the same proportion of losses—a terrifying rate, given that usually the wounded greatly outnumbered the dead. Colonel Hamilton's body was found the next day, missing both arms, with a bullet in the heart, and with his pockets emptied by thieves; someone swore he had seen the colonel, armless, guiding his horse with the reins between his teeth, before he disappeared for good. The other two regiments of the Union Brigade suffered comparable casualties, around six hundred dead and wounded out of fewer than a thousand, a percentage that makes the famous charge of the light brigade at Balaklava pale by comparison. As for the Household Brigade, Lord Edward Somerset, after escaping the pursuit of the cuirassiers, succeeded in redeploying several squadrons, particularly those of the Blues, in their original positions. At the beginning of the action, the Blues had been in the second line, and thereafter had maintained a certain order; but of the squadrons that had charged in the first line, fewer than half the men turned back.

Considered on the whole, Uxbridge's charge, despite its extraordinary initial success, had concluded with the destruction of the two brigades engaged. As Captain Kincaid coldly observed, the heavy cavalry never knew when to stop, and they had "burnt their fingers." Tomkinson, who had watched the whole spectacle from his brigade's position on the heights behind Papelotte, commented that it couldn't have ended any other way, since the men of the two cavalry brigades, as well as a great many of their officers, had gone into combat for the first time in their lives, and they had not had the least idea what they should do after their initial impetus was exhausted. But Tomkinson was also sure that the enemy was killing prisoners: After the battle, only one or two men reported out of an entire squadron of the First Dragoon Guards, and to Tomkinson it was inconceivable that all the others would have been killed without anyone trying to surrender.

Almost certainly some of the troopers who were taken prisoner were in fact massacred either immediately after they were captured or later, in cold blood. General Gourgaud, the emperor's aide-de-camp, was escorting a British dragoon to the rear when an infantry sergeant stepped out of formation, struck the man down with the butt of his musket, and killed him with bayonet thrusts before Gourgaud had time to stop him. The endless lists of missing on the rolls of the Household Brigade—124, in the case of the First Dragoon Guards—are the only record of a large number of men who literally vanished during the great charge, probably much the way the general's prisoner did; their bodies were never identified.

FORTY-ONE

"TU N'ES PAS MORT, COQUIN?"

W hen they saw the French lancers attack and overwhelm the winded squadrons of the heavy cavalry, the commanders of some of the light cavalry brigades deployed behind the Allied front decided on their own initiative to intervene in the fray. The old and quarrelsome Sir John Ormsby Vandeleur moved two of his three regiments forward, the Twelfth and Sixteenth Light Dragoons, prudently holding the third in reserve. Some of his squadrons left soon enough to participate in the defeat of the French infantry; the troops they attacked were Durutte's, and although on the whole his soldiers were able to maintain cohesion and fall back without ending in a rout, even this last French division was compelled to return in haste to its starting point, leaving a great number of prisoners in enemy hands. In the course of the confused struggle, the commander of the Sixteenth was almost killed by a ball that entered his back and passed completely through him. Since a wound of this sort did not seem particularly honorable, the officers of the regiment concluded that the colonel had fallen victim to what would today be called "friendly fire": The shot that struck him came from the Allied infantry stationed behind him on the ridge.

The clash between Vandeleur's regiments and Jacquinot's lancers reached heights of extreme ferocity, as Sir Frederick Ponsonby, commander of the Twelfth Light Dragoons and a distant cousin of Sir William, learned firsthand. Two evenings before, Ponsonby had roamed over the battlefield at Quatre Bras, examining the corpses of cuirassiers to determine whether or not their cuirasses were musket-ball-proof. At last he found one with three holes through it that answered his question, and he concluded that not even Napoleon's famous cavalry was invincible; but an enemy more dangerous than the cuirassiers was waiting for him on the battlefield at Waterloo. In combat with Jacquinot's lancers, he was wounded in both arms and lost control of his horse, which carried him into the midst of the enemy, one of whom finally felled him with a saber cut to the head. When he regained consciousness, he was lying in the mud, and he struggled to raise himself; a passing lancer saw him move and gave him a thrust through the back, crying out, "*Tu n'es pas mort, coquin?*" The steel point entered under his shoulder blade and punctured a lung. The colonel, who was only thirty-two years old, felt his mouth fill with blood and lost consciousness, convinced that the end had come.

The Twelfth Light Dragoons offered a clear example of how, after a single charge and a brief combat, a cavalry regiment could become practically unusable, out of proportion to the losses it officially admitted having sustained. At the moment when they mounted their horses, the three squadrons contained a total of 310 cavalrymen; when the regiment reassembled after the combat, it could muster only two half squadrons, a total of ninety-four men altogether. While over the course of the day the regiment recorded forty-five dead and sixty-one wounded—a high casualty rate—this was still less than half of the total missing after the first charge. The initial casualty rate was swollen to more than twice the actual figure by the number of men taken prisoner, of those who had become isolated and were unable to rejoin their units until the next day, and above all of those who had lost their horses and were therefore of no more use. A cavalry regiment was a bit like a single-shot weapon; you could use it only once.

Along with Vandeleur's troopers, the Netherlands Cavalry Division played an important role in putting an end to the incursion of Napoleon's cavalry. This division was commanded by General Baron de Collaert and deployed on the reverse slope of the ridge, in the direction of the village of Mont-Saint-Jean. The British officers made no effort to hide the mistrust they felt for these politically suspect allies, whose desertion rate was decidedly anomalous. For example, like many Belgian units the Eighth Hussars, a regiment recruited thanks to the commitment of a great landowner, the Duc de Croy, who virtually considered it his property, had been equipped haphazardly, so much so that at an inspection in March fewer than half of the men were supplied with horses. Perhaps this disorganization was one of the reasons that the regiment had lost more than two hundred deserters since January, but a factor of at least equal importance was the hostility of the Belgians toward the Dutch, coupled with the bond that many Belgians still felt with imperial France. During the course of the long day at Waterloo, another thirty-three Hussars went over to the enemy, openly justifying their desertion with their refusal to fight against their former comrades-in-arms.

Despite this problem, however, the Netherlands cavalry performed well in its first charges of the battle, until attrition rendered it, for all practical purposes, useless; the officers in particular gave proof of a combativeness worthy of the Napoleonic veterans they were. Baron de Ghigny, who commanded one of the two light brigades, decided on his own initiative to cross the main road and intervene against Jacquinot's lancers. The first of the baron's two regiments—the aforementioned Eighth Hussars—descended the slope in good order. Their commander was Colonel Duvivier, who until the previous year had commanded a regiment of light cavalry in Napoleon's army, and who was an officer of the Legion of Honor and a baron of the empire. Now Duvivier led his Hussars in a charge against the scattered groups of French light cavalry, which had dispersed after their charge. The ground was so trampled that it was almost impassable, and the conflict did not last long, but it was enough to persuade Jacquinot's lancers to return to their original positions, thus putting an end to the action in this sector.

On the other side of the field, west of La Haye Sainte, General Trip van Zoudtlandt, who had been a colonel in the French army until the past year and bore the scars of a wound received at Berezina, advanced with his three regiments of heavy cavalry carabineers, two Dutch and one Belgian, against the emperor's cuirassiers, who were ascending the slope in pursuit of the remnants of the Household Brigade. The forces were more or less equal, about 1,200 sabers on each side, but the cuirassiers were riding uphill and were already in some disorder when they appeared in front of the line of enemy cavalry, which had just got into motion. A French officer rode ahead, advancing until his horse was practically touching muzzles with those of the Netherlanders; then he rose in his stirrups, brandished his saber, and challenged any enemy officer to fight with him. A Belgian lieutenant, also a veteran of Napoleon's armies, accepted the challenge—this sort of thing was not at all rare on the battlefields of those days—and for a few moments, in the no-man's-land between the battle lines, these two exchanged furious saber-strokes. Each was wounded, but the Belgian had the worse of it and fell, pierced through. Then the two lines clashed, and the combat became general until the French cuirassiers, finding themselves at a disadvantage, abandoned the field and withdrew to the bottom of the slope.

With the disordered saber duels between Milhaud's cuirassiers and Trip's carabineers on the slippery slope west of La Haye Sainte, the colossal cavalry action that had begun with Crabbé's charge and continued with Lord Uxbridge's great countercharge seemed to have exhausted itself. But the cuirassiers had been checked only momentarily; judging by the haste with which their officers were pushing them back into line, they had just begun to fight. It might have been three o'clock in the afternoon, or four o'clock at the latest, which meant that there would be five or six more hours of daylight. Along the ridge, Wellington's army was still deployed in a purely defensive position and appeared incapable of mounting anything beyond counterattacks. The experience of the last hours suggested that dislodging the Allied forces would not be as easy as having breakfast; but the French still believed that the battle could be won.

PART THREE

"A Stand-up Fight Between Two Pugilists"

FORTY-TWO

"IT DOES INDEED LOOK VERY BAD"

When the cavalry duels stopped for a moment in the no-man's-land between the two armies, it seems unlikely that the men on the battlefield had any sensation of the pause so often spoken of by historians. Rather, the memoirists give the impression that everyone at Waterloo was in a state of high tension the whole time, without a moment to draw a calm breath; moreover, there was no spot on the battlefield where one was ever safe from a hurtling cannonball or from a sharpshooter's bullet, fired from his hiding place among the stubble some one or two hundred yards away. Around the fortified positions of Hougoumont, La Haye Sainte, and Papelotte, violent fighting continued between the defenders barricaded in the buildings and the swarms of *tirailleurs* posted outside; along the entire front, other skirmishers were moving across no-man's-land—covered with dead or dying men and horses—trying to gain ground and push their line of outposts forward.

Sir Frederick Ponsonby was an involuntary witness to this type of combat. When he regained consciousness, he found himself wounded and immobilized in a sector of the battlefield patrolled by enemy skirmishers. One of these threatened to kill him and demanded his money; Ponsonby let himself be searched, the man found what he was looking for, and he went away. A second skirmisher with the same intentions arrived on the scene but left disappointed after an even more meticulous search of the colonel's person. Finally, an officer passed his way at the head of a group of soldiers, gave Ponsonby a swallow of brandy, ordered one of his men to put a knapsack under the colonel's head, and then departed, apologizing for leaving him there: "We must follow the retreating English." Still later, another *tirailleur* came by and decided to use the immobile

171

Ponsonby as a screen. He stayed for a long time, reloading and firing over the colonel's body again and again, "and conversing with great gaiety all the while." At last he went away, but not before assuring Ponsonby that he should not worry: "You'll be happy to hear that we're going to withdraw. *Bon soir, mon ami.*"

The French artillery also kept stubbornly pounding the enemy position. As soon as the cavalry fighting subsided, Napoleon concerned himself with returning the Grande Batterie to action. Fortunately for him, the Imperial Guard, which was lined up along the main road, had such a quantity of guns and so many caissons that his forces were able to reconstitute the battery quickly. The officers recruited infantrymen from nearby formations to give the gunners a hand in maneuvering their pieces, and the firing recommenced with the same intensity as before. The Allied counterbattery fire was equally intense, despite Wellington's orders, and General Desvaux de Saint-Maurice, the Guard's artillery commander, was killed by a cannonball while overseeing the placement of his 12-pounders. The interruption in the bombardment had been so brief that no one on the Allied side of the battlefield had even noticed it—a further inducement to reevaluate the significance of the British cavalry charge against the guns of the Grande Batterie.

As far as the Duke of Wellington could tell with his telescope, the French reserves formed a mighty force, even though some units were moving toward the Fichermont wood to take up new positions, anticipating the long-awaited Prussian advance. By way of contrast, his own defensive line, despite its success in repulsing d'Erlon's attack, was starting to become perilously thin: Picton's battalions, commanded by Kempt after Sir Thomas's death, were at the end of their strength, and Alten's troops—against whom a great part of the murderous enemy fire had been directed—were hardly in better shape. Therefore, all the infantry units still being held in reserve behind Wellington's center were ordered into the battle line to fill up the gaps opened by the French attack.

Sir John Lambert's brigade, more than two thousand muskets strong, took up a position behind La Haye Sainte. His three veteran regiments were recently arrived from America, where they had taken part in Sir Edward Pakenham's campaign in Louisiana, including the disastrous Battle of New Orleans, in which that general, Wellington's brother-in-law, had met his end. Their officer corps was considerably reduced, so much so that the Irish troops of the Twenty-seventh Regiment (also called Inniskillings) were commanded by a captain; but a healthy infusion of recruits had filled out their ranks. Two days before, Lambert's men had still been in Ghent; they had spent most of the previous night marching through the forest of Soignes, forcing a passage for themselves through the refugees who thronged the road. When they reached the village of Waterloo, the men of Lambert's brigade sank down to sleep in the fields and stables. A short time later, half awake and stupefied with exhaustion, they were marched in great haste and under artillery fire along the final stretch of the main road until they came to the Mont-Saint-Jean crossroads. The Inniskillings went into position behind what was left of the 1/95th (whose troops had retaken the sandpit and the knoll behind it), and Lambert's other two regiments deployed farther to the rear. In order to offer a less conspicuous target to the enemy artillery, the men were ordered to lie on the ground, where many of them would soon have fallen asleep had the appearance of a few squadrons of enemy cavalry not compelled them, from time to time, to get to their feet and form square.

Farther right, Colonel von Kruse's Nassau contingent, nearly as strong as a brigade with its three battalions—almost 2,500 bayonets—was ordered to advance into the front line and take up a position between the squares of Kielmansegge's brigade and those formed by Halkett's troops. The Nassauers, almost all of them inexperienced recruits, wearing their characteristic green uniforms, massed into squares around their flags of pale yellow silk. Theoretically, the position they occupied was in dead ground behind the ridge, where the terrain should have protected them from the artillery bombardment; in fact, however, bombs and shells rained down on them so thickly that it seemed the French had managed, somehow or other, to see them after all. The colonel decided that if his men were offering too visible a target, it was the fault of the white cloths covering their shakos, and he ordered these covers removed. It was true that the shakos cost the treasury money, and also true that it was better not to ruin them, but in so grave a situation, potential damage to headpieces seemed a trivial concern.

Wellington also sent a part of the reserves into line on his right wing, where the pressure against the Hougoumont stronghold showed no signs of letting up. Masters of the no-man's-land around the château, the *tirailleurs* occupied a dominant position from which they were able to keep the interior of the compound under fire while remaining hidden in the tall grain; they "never distinctly showed themselves," observed one of the defenders. But "they annoyed us very much by firing at the door which communicated between the courtyard and the garden, and of which they could see the top." The duke ordered the First King's German Legion Brigade, commanded by Colonel Du Plat, to advance slowly in square—thus avoiding surprises from enemy cavalry—and send his light companies into the farm buildings. Shortly thereafter, the same orders were transmitted to Colonel Olfermann, who since the death of the Duke of Brunswick at Quatre Bras had taken over command of the Brunswick contingent, which was deployed in reserve in the same sector. Olfermann sent forward his five battalions of light infantry, at least one of which still included a number of veterans of the wars in Spain. Having halted in square on the high ground behind the château, these troops also began sending in skirmishers in twos and threes, as needed, in order to maintain a constant volume of fire from the walls of Hougoumont and keep Reille's skirmishers pinned down.

Between three and four in the afternoon, of the 83 infantry battalions that constituted Wellington's army, the duke had 60 in line, and of these, 17 had by then been severely mauled. He still had 23 battalions in reserve, the minimum he would have needed to maintain his optimism. For his part, Napoleon had so far engaged 57 of his 103 battalions, of which a goodly number were so battered that they could no longer be used in an offensive; but the emperor still had 46 fresh battalions, among them the 22 of the Imperial Guard. The emperor, therefore, also had reason to be optimistic, all the more so because the hypothesis of a Prussian offensive against his right wing had not yet materialized. The outcome of the battle was, in truth, hanging by a thread.

The enormous number of *tirailleurs* in action in no-man's-land, together with the intensity of an artillery bombardment the likes of which none of them had ever experienced, had caused an unusual pessimism to spread among the British officers. While Captain Mercer was speaking with his superior officer, Colonel Gould, the latter confessed that he found their situation desperate. Not the least of his reasons was his belief that the only road through the forest would be bottled up in an instant. "It does indeed look very bad," Mercer concurred. Then, trying to say something encouraging, he suggested that the duke, in one way or another, would get them out of their present difficulties. "Meantime gloomy reflections arose in my mind, for though I did not choose to betray myself (as we spoke before the men), yet I could not help thinking that our affairs *were* rather desperate, and that some unfortunate catastrophe was at hand. In this case I made up my mind to spike my guns and retreat over the fields, draught-horses and all, in the best manner I could, steering well from the highroad and general line of retreat."

The rumors flying around Brussels during the late afternoon and evening, gradually increasing as the first wounded officers arrived from the battlefield, were likewise indicative of a mood that was anything but optimistic. A Member of Parliament, one Mr. Creevey, who found himself in the city with his entire family, breathed a sigh of relief when he saw the prisoners from d'Erlon's corps arriving, escorted by a squadron of the Life Guards; but then he ran into another parliamentarian, who had been on the battlefield and who assured him that the battle could not have gone worse for the Allied side. A wounded soldier whom he met shortly thereafter confirmed this gloomy assessment, declaring that the French were advancing so irresistibly that he knew not what could stop them. Creevey next went on to the home of an acquaintance, where he found a young officer, wounded and on the point of collapse, who predicted that the enemy would enter Brussels that evening. Deeply agitated, Creevey was returning home when a message reached him from a friend, Sir Edward Barnes, Wellington's adjutant general; Barnes had been wounded, and he requested that the Creeveys put him up in their house. The bearer of the message, Major Hamilton, assured

Creevey that the battle was lost, declared that Sir Edward, even though he was known in the army as a "fire-eater," was of the same opinion, and advised Creevey to leave Brussels at once. Each of these viewpoints, of course, was conditioned by personal experience and in some cases by the shock of wounds received; nevertheless, taken together, they confirm that the morale of the British officers on the battlefield was low.

However, the emperor, too, was beginning to find himself in a tight spot. The defeat suffered by d'Erlon's troops limited Napoleon's possibilities: With I Corps decimated, he could no longer consider maneuvering against the enemy's left wing. Because of the way the battle had gone thus far, and because of the position of his reserves, which had reached the battlefield by the Brussels road and were massed between Le Caillou and La Belle Alliance, Napoleon had no other choice but to concentrate his efforts against the center of Wellington's line. In other circumstances, perhaps he would have been able to maneuver his troops, but there was not enough time—no more than six hours of light remained—and the terrain, trodden into a quagmire by so many shoes, would no longer allow him to move troops and guns quickly enough. Maneuvering was out of the question, but the emperor still had enough troops to get the job done; he would have to take Hougoumont or La Haye Sainte, or if possible both, and then make a breakthrough in the center of the enemy's line.

When Wellington saw that the French were preparing to attack his center once again, he permitted himself an unflattering remark about Napoleon: "Damn the fellow, he is a mere pounder after all," he muttered, almost disappointed to discover that his adversary, in the end, had not proved equal to his fame. Like many English gentlemen, the duke was an ardent enthusiast of the pugilistic sport, and it was natural for him to fall into the language of boxing when describing a battle. In a letter to a friend a few days later, he wrote, "Never did I see such a pounding match. Both were what boxers call gluttons."[24]

Somewhat later, Major Harry Smith also commented on the battle in boxing terms: "It was as a stand-up fight between two pugilists, 'mill away' till one is beaten." And indeed, after d'Erlon's promising maneuver came to such an unexpected and inglorious end, the struggle at Waterloo ceased almost completely to be a battle of movement and was transformed into a series of monotonous and repetitive frontal engagements. This fact explains why all accounts of the battle fell increasingly into repetition and confusion as the afternoon wore on. But given the results of the battle to this point, and especially given the condition of the ground, not even Napoleon could devise a different way of proceeding.

FORTY-THREE

PAPELOTTE

T he rout they had suffered notwithstanding, the troops of I Corps managed almost at once to put the enemy under renewed pressure from the first and last of d'Erlon's divisions: The former, commanded by Donzelot, was in action around La Haye Sainte, and the latter, under Durutte, was in the sector that included Papelotte farm. This sector was defended by Prince Bernhard of Saxe-Weimar's Netherlands brigade, actually made up of Germans in the Orange-Nassau and the Second Nassau regiments. The prince's direct superior was General Perponcher-Sedlnitzky, but the general spent almost the entire day with his division's other brigade, the one commanded by Bijlandt, so Prince Bernhard essentially operated as an independent commander. The troops under his orders were excellent, and they had already performed well two days previously at Quatre Bras, where the prince's spirit of initiative had made no small contribution to saving the day. Since one of his five battalions had been detached and sent to Hougoumont by Wellington's order, Prince Bernhard was left with about three thousand muskets, a quarter of them carried by *Landwehr* troops, to oppose any possible French effort to turn the Allies' left flank.

Prince Bernhard had installed his brigade in the two farms of Papelotte and La Haye, in a group of houses a little farther east, which the maps of the period designate as Smouhen or Smohain, the same name as the muddy little stream that rises nearby—and in the old medieval château of Fichermont. This series of four built-up areas extended along a line about three-quarters of a mile long, a boggy landscape of sunken lanes bordered by hedges and shrubs, impracticable for horses and ideal for defense. After posting his skirmishers as far forward as possible in the swampy hollow that marked the boundary of his position, the prince stationed one or more companies in each of the four groups of buildings and held the major part of his forces in reserve, almost as far to the rear as the chemin d'Ohain; from this spot, he could send reinforcements in any direction, as needed.

Durutte's skirmishers had already made contact with the Nassauers' outposts during d'Erlon's ill-fated advance. In the beginning, this was only an exercise in prudence, undertaken by Durutte to protect his own right flank from surprise; but after the failure of the main offensive, the French general concentrated all his efforts on a serious attempt to drive the enemy outposts from the Papelotte sector. Durutte opened fire against the enemy position with the guns at his disposal, apparently one of the Imperial Guards' 12-pounder batteries. The Nassauers, who were in the open, withdrew after the cannonballs began mowing down their first victims, lay down behind the walls and hedges of the farm, and waited. Then Durutte sent his line of skirmishers forward; the German skirmishers stationed among the stubble and in the ditches opened fire; and the combat flared up along the whole front.

Among the houses of Smohain and around the walls of Papelotte, the fighting was no less fierce than it was at La Haye Sainte, but since the position was less important, and especially since British troops were not involved, few eyewitness accounts of what really happened remain. At one point, the men of the Orange-Nassau regiment realized that they were almost out of ammunition; not far away, the men of the Second Nassau still had a good supply but were unable to share it, as they were armed with French muskets and the Orange-Nassau troops carried English muskets. A drummer boy named May, a young lad of fourteen years, ran all the way to the line of Hanoverian troops stationed on the high ground behind them, filled his haversack with cartridges, and ran back to hand them out.

When he had finished the distribution, he went back a second time; a stray ball struck him in the hip, but the force of the projectile was nearly spent, and the boy almost failed to notice it ("I found it later in my underwear"). The third time, Prince Bernhard saw him running down the slope with his haversack full of cartridges and told him that now there were enough, and that he must not expose himself to further danger. May slung his drum back over his shoulder and went to rejoin his comrades.[25]

In spite of the fierceness of the struggle, all records suggest that only one of Durutte's two brigades was deployed in the Papelotte sector; skillfully massing the skirmishers of his other brigade, he used it to keep the pressure on Colonel Best's inexperienced Hanoverian infantry, which was occupying high ground a little to the rear. At the end of the day, this brigade was still almost intact before Napoleon transferred it to the La Haye Sainte sector for use in the final offensive. Given that Durutte did not attack Prince Bernhard's three thousand muskets with more than two thousand of his own, it is not surprising that he failed to dislodge the Nassauers from their fortified positions.

Besides, Durutte could not have been expected to do more; after the failure of d'Erlon's offensive, his division was evidently required to perform one role only, namely that of protecting the army's right flank against any enemy initiatives. Turning the Allies' left had been judged impossible as early as that morning, when a cavalry reconnaissance revealed that the Smohain, although a narrow, shallow stream, was very muddy, and that crossing it under enemy artillery fire would be too risky. Therefore, in that part of the field, the goal of the French offensive was only the consolidation of Durutte's positions, and its outlook was essentially defensive. What Durutte did not know was that one of the dirt roads coming from Wavre went through Smohain, and down it were marching the Prussian columns. Had he known this, he would have seen the vital importance of at least seizing the stone bridge that passed over the little stream and occupying the surrounding houses.

FORTY-FOUR

————◆————

THE SECOND ATTACK
ON LA HAYE SAINTE

In the La Haye Sainte sector, the French quickly prepared to go back on the offensive. After the British cavalry charge, the defenders of the farm had gone out among their dead and wounded enemies, marveling at how many there were, but they soon returned to the farm and barricaded themselves in the buildings. Lieutenant Graeme and his men were again stationed on the roof of the piggery when he saw a single cuirassier approaching at a trot along the main road. When he got close, the man began waving his sword, as though in greeting; thinking he was a deserter, Graeme ordered his men to hold their fire. The cuirassier rode up all the way to the abatis that was blocking the road, raised himself in his stirrups as though trying to see over it, then suddenly wheeled his horse and galloped back toward the French lines. The riflemen fired after him, but, as the lieutenant concluded with some admiration, "in the hurry I believe the gallant fellow luckily escaped our shots."

By the time Major von Baring returned to the yard in La Haye Sainte, he was convinced that holding the farm much longer was unthinkable with only his single battalion, and he requested his superior, Colonel von Ompteda, to send him two more companies of riflemen. These reinforcements amounted to fewer than 150 Baker rifles, which joined perhaps an equal number remaining from Baring's original command; with these troops, the major fortified his position as best he could, except for the orchard, which he decided not to reoccupy. He was just in time, because two columns of French infantry, preceded as usual by a swarm of *tirailleurs*, were once again advancing on both sides of the farm and threatening to surround it.

Astonishing the German major with the contempt they showed for his men's deadly fire, the French were at the walls of the farm in an instant, trying to force their way inside. A ferocious combat ensued, particularly around the few loopholes that Baring's men had opened that morning in the wall of the farmyard. The French grabbed the barrels of the defenders' muskets, tried to wrest them out of their hands, and eventually succeeded in gaining control of one of the loopholes. Then a French soldier standing outside the wall started firing into the yard through the loophole, using the loaded muskets that his comrades passed him, one after the other. On the west side of the farm, the French tried to enter the barn, and in a few minutes a great many corpses were piled up in the doorway, which the defenders kept under fire. As more attackers arrived, they used the piled bodies as protection, firing into the farmyard from behind them.

Baring's horse was killed, and the major went down with it. The major's servant, convinced that he was dead, seized the opportunity and abandoned the position at once, so that when Baring rose again to his feet he found that he no longer had either his servant or his spare horse. However, by then a good many other officers had been knocked out of their saddles, and the major soon found a new mount in the farmyard. His servant's bad behavior notwithstanding, Baring was touched by how faithfully his riflemen executed his orders and those of the other officers, in a situation where the probabilities of survival were getting lower and lower: "These are the moments when we learn to feel what one soldier is to another, what the word 'comrade' really means," he observed in his report.

For a long time, a KGL rifleman, Private Lindau, watched an enemy officer on horseback as he trotted back and forth across the fields in front of the farm, urging his men to attack. Lindau waited until the Frenchman drew within rifle range, waited some more, and finally fired. The officer's horse fell mortally wounded, dragging down its rider in the fall. Soon afterward, when the riflemen made a sortie from the main gate of the farm, scattering the French skirmishers who had advanced along the road, Lindau ran to his man and began searching him, quickly ripping away the golden chain that held his watch. But the officer, who was only stunned, raised his saber, hurling insults at the private, who unceremoniously killed him with the butt of his Baker. Then he cut off the bag attached to the officer's saddle and was about to pull a gold ring off his finger when his comrades shouted to him, "Come on, leave that! The cavalry's coming!" Lindau ran for the farm, carrying his booty, and just managed to reach the yard before the gate was bolted behind him.

In fact, during the *tirailleurs'* repeated attacks, French cavalry was always present in force on the slope that led to the farm, passing it several times on the way to harass the Allied squares deployed farther to the rear. How much of this activity was undertaken by the cuirassier generals on their own initiative and how much was ordered by Marshal Ney or even by the emperor himself is unclear. Milhaud's cuirassiers—those who remained after the destruction of the detached squadrons led by Crabbé—were the chief participants in the attack: perhaps some twenty squadrons in all, battle-weary, but still almost two thousand sabers strong.

Obviously, this cavalry did not advance all together, nor would it have been possible to do so, given the immense front it covered; the infantry squares deployed behind La Haye Sainte received charges involving several hundred cavalrymen at a time, succeeding one another as regiment after regiment sent a few squadrons forward and held the rest in reserve. Particularly in the case of troops who had received little training, the tension caused by the approach of cavalry often induced men massed in squares to fire too soon, and while the foot soldiers were busy reloading their muskets, the cavalry could take advantage of their mistake by advancing, in the hope that the infantry, aware of being temporarily disarmed, would allow itself to be seized by panic. When the cuirassiers presented themselves before Kielmansegge's squares, his Hanoverian officers strove to prevent their men from firing too early; in one of the squares, Captain von Scriba heard the pistol-armed commander threaten to shoot anyone who fired before the order was given.

Scriba saw the cuirassiers "advance at a trot and stop some 70 or 80 paces away. The temptation to fire was great, but the whole square remained motionless with weapons cocked." The French got jumpy and advanced a little closer, then decided to forgo the charge and trotted away, turning around the corner of the square. At this point, the Hanoverian recruits were ordered to fire. "Led by a brigade general, the cavalry passed at a distance of six paces along the right side of the square, which I commanded," Scriba wrote. "I noticed that all the men on the right side aimed their muskets at the general's horse when the order was given to fire, and he moved away from the danger." As was so often the case, the troops' fire turned out to be ineffective: "The cavalry suffered some losses in this attack, but not so many as I believed it should, given the close range. This made me think that our men were aiming too high. From then on, the officers kept warning them not to."

Sergeant Lawrence, standing with the Fortieth in their square a little to the rear, was unimpressed by the cuirassiers' first charges, though their magnificent helmets and gleaming cuirasses did impress the sergeant and his men, who genuinely believed that the cuirassiers were "Bonaparte's Bodyguard." The British officers, overestimating the enemy's armor, which they were seeing for the first time, ordered their troops to aim not at the riders, but at the horses, and when the cuirassiers came within range, the infantry squares shot down so many of their mounts that the stricken animals impeded the progress of the others and the charge had to be aborted. "It was a most laughable sight to see these Guards in their chimney armour—trying to run away, being able to make little progress and many of them being taken prisoner by those of our light companies who were out skirmishing. I think this quite settled Napoleon's bodyguards, for we saw no more of them," Sergeant Lawrence concluded with satisfaction.

However, not all the squares got off so easily, especially when the French cavalry succeeded in coordinating its action with that of the infantry. One of the battalions in Ompteda's brigade, the Eighth KGL, was composed of German veterans of the Spanish wars; under normal circumstances, they could have withstood the cuirassiers' threatening maneuvers indefinitely. But the legionaries got into difficulty when, preparing to fight a solid line of advancing French infantry, they were surprised by the arrival of cavalry. Since a firefight between the two infantry formations—Allied square vs. French line—would have been decidedly unequal, with all the advantage going to the French, Colonel von Schroeder had ordered his men to deploy into line. But just as the troops of the KGL battalion, already under fire and in growing disorder, were trying to obey him, the enemy infantry opened their ranks to allow some cuirassier squadrons to pass through. Caught in the act of changing formations, the battalion was smashed, Schroeder was mortally wounded, and a triumphant cuirassier carried off the battalion's color. Still, the men of the KGL were veterans, and after they had taken to their heels to escape the cuirassiers' sabers, their surviving officers managed to reorder their ranks and lead them back, one way or another, to their position in the battle line; "but now the square was much smaller than before," one of them recalled.

The French had once more seized the initiative; in order to snatch it back from them, the British commanders decided they needed to send in the cavalry again. Somerset's brigade—or what remained of it—had barely had time to redeploy behind La Haye Sainte when one of Lord Uxbridge's aides arrived, carrying the order to charge. The three squadrons of the Blues, the only ones that were still more or less intact, charged down the slope, and once again, through sheer momentum, got the best of the enemy squadrons in front of them and momentarily cleared the field. The French infantry crowded around the walls of La Haye Sainte had to run for cover, and the second attack on La Haye Sainte, like the first, was broken off. But it was clear that there would not be much of a pause; as soon as the French cavalry reordered their ranks, they would advance once more, and the siege would begin anew. Major von Baring's men greeted the retreat of the enemy cavalry with howls of derision from the roofs and walls of La Haye Sainte, but the major had begun to be worried about running out of ammunition; when he ordered a tally, he discovered that they had already consumed more than half their supply. An officer sent back to the brigade command to ask for an emergency delivery was told not to worry; the battalion would be receiving fresh ammunition in a little while.

FORTY-FIVE

---•◆•---

THE GREAT FRENCH CAVALRY ATTACKS AGAINST THE ALLIED SQUARES

While Major von Baring was counting the ammunition in his men's cartridge pouches, all the Allied officers stationed along the Mont-Saint-Jean ridge between La Haye Sainte and Hougoumont, a front a mile long, realized with mounting concern that the French cavalry was preparing to advance in even greater strength. Alongside Milhaud's indefatigable cuirassiers, who were about to ride up the slope for the third time, the emperor was sending into line the light cavalry of the Imperial Guard, a division under the command of General Lefebvre-Desnouettes. This most elite division comprised the light cavalry regiment known as *chasseurs à cheval*, which with 1,200 sabers was by itself as strong as three or four ordinary regiments, and a regiment of lancers with more than 800 men, one of whose squadrons, was still composed of Polish veterans who had shared Napoleon's fortunes since the campaign of 1806–7 and had followed him to Elba. All told, a tide of at least 3,500 horses was about to surge up the slope through the slippery mud and attack the enemy line. The cavalry was so numerous that the squadrons quickly extended out to the left, threatening not just the infantry battalions deployed behind La Haye Sainte but Wellington's line, all the way to the high ground behind Hougoumont.

Faced with this enormous force of cavalry massing but a few hundred yards away, the infantry stationed along the ridge could do nothing but stay in their squares and wait. Gradually, as the attacks developed, Wellington sent more and more reserves into the line of battle; in the end, he would have hardly any left. The three infantry battalions of the Brunswick contingent's Second Line Brigade

183

moved up behind Halkett's squares; Adam's British brigade formed four squares in support of the squares formed by Maitland's and Du Plat's brigades; Detmers's brigade of Netherlanders, called back from the extreme right, deployed four of its battalions in the same area of the field; and even Vincke's brigade, with its four battalions of Hanoverian militiamen, was withdrawn from the extreme left and redeployed in two squares as a reserve force in the center, on the reverse side of the slope a little south of Mont-Saint-Jean farm. Over the course of that afternoon, a total of thirty-six squares—of which twenty were German, twelve British, three Dutch, and one Belgian—faced the charges of Napoleon's cavalry.

To protect them from the artillery bombardment, the squares were deployed on the reverse slope, where only rebounding cannonballs and blindly fired shells could strike them. Insofar as possible, the squares were positioned in a checkerboard pattern to maximize the effect of their fire. The idea was that whenever a squadron of French cavalry, cresting the ridge and confronting a square, should decide against charging and ride past or around, it would find itself faced with another and end up caught in a crossfire. Although fire from infantry squares had little effect, in the long run a situation of this kind was destined to take a toll on the attackers without leading to any tangible result. Wellington and his British and German generals anticipated such an inconclusive struggle as they peered through their telescopes at the French cavalry, massing at the foot of the slope. According to contemporary military theory, their expectations were correct: in a manual published in Paris in 1813, General Thiébault declared, if infantry formed two lines of squares deployed at the proper intervals and supported by artillery, "I cannot imagine what cavalry would be able to accomplish against them."

Napoleon later tried to dissociate himself from the great cavalry attacks against the Allied squares; he let it be understood that they had been carried out without his authorization, or at least too soon. But such a large movement could not have been undertaken a few hundred yards from the emperor's chair without an explicit order from him. More likely, Napoleon was unable to appreciate the depth of the infantry masses that Wellington had deployed on the back side of the ridge, and believed he could achieve a decisive breakthrough, as had happened at Eylau, where a cavalry charge, involving more or less the same number of sabers, had broken up the Russian line. That Napoleon believed this is demonstrated by a few sentences that Las Cases recorded on St. Helena not a year later, when the emperor confessed his regret that Murat, who had commanded his cavalry in so many battles, had not been with him that day. Murat would have succeeded, Napoleon said, "and with that, perhaps, he would have given us the victory. For what was it that we needed to do at certain points in the battle? Smash three or four British squares."

If Napoleon was responsible for not having verified in person the solidity of the enemy line, which was formed in such a way that his own manuals would have shown him the impossibility of breaking it, then the person who was perhaps to blame for not having properly explained the situation to him was his representative in the field, Marshal Ney. But "*le rougeaud*", "the Redhead," as his troops called him, was anything but a student of military theory, and he laughed at manuals. Ney spent the day engaged in urging his squadrons forward, saber in hand, and in getting horses shot under him, each time emerging miraculously unscathed; apparently, he too believed a breakthrough was possible. If the cavalry, observing a wavering square, perhaps one made up of recruits, could have managed to get among them and scatter them in a rout, a breach would have been opened in Wellington's line; and if the same sequence could be repeated in several neighboring squares, the breach would have become impossible to close.

In the beginning, the squares were not alone in facing the tide of advancing cavalry, even though in the end everything really did come down to that. There were six or seven Allied artillery batteries posted on the crest of the ridge, and much farther forward, almost at the bottom of the slope, every officer who commanded a square maintained a line of skirmishers, continually engaged in exchanging fire with the corresponding enemy line. The artillery officers and the officers in charge of the light companies all had received precise orders should the enemy cavalry advance— to keep firing until the last possible moment and then to abandon their positions and take refuge in the nearest square, since neither a line of skirmishers nor a battery of guns had the least possibility of holding off attacking cavalry. Repulsing the attack was the job of the squares; when that was accomplished, the gunners were to return to their pieces and open fire on the retreating cavalry. Then, using caution, the line of skirmishers could also be reestablished.

In fact, the attack of the French cavalry was carried out with such violence and with such a numerous force that many skirmishers, surprised in the open, were slaughtered before they had time to retreat. When Macready, the young officer who commanded the light company of the Thirtieth Regiment, assembled his men for roll call the morning after the battle, he discovered that, of the fifty-four troops present in the ranks the previous day, only ten remained; he didn't know, he said, whether to laugh or cry. Later, Macready went over the battlefield, searching for any of his men who might still be alive. The youth was able to find only one, and that one so severely wounded that he would not survive long. He was "a good religious soldier," Macready wrote, with "life enough left in him to give me the disgusting details of their butchery."

The artillery, too, found that obeying the instructions they had received was not easy. In a letter written some time afterward to Lord Mulgrave, master-general of the ordnance, Wellington himself, still frothing with rage, alluded to their difficulties. "The French Cavalry charged, and were formed on the same ground with our artillery, in general within a few yards of our guns. We could not expect the artillery men to remain at their guns in such a case. But I had a right to expect that the officers and men of the artillery would do as I did, and as all the staff did, that is to take shelter in the Squares of the infantry till the French cavalry should be driven off the ground, either by our cavalry or infantry. But they did no such thing; they ran off the field entirely, taking with them limbers, ammunition, and everything; and when in a few minutes we had driven off the French cavalry, and could have made use of our artillery, we had no artillerymen to fire them; and, in point of fact, I should have had NO artillery during the whole of the latter part of the action, if I had not kept a reserve in the commencement."

The same thing happened to the British artillery that had happened to the Grande Batterie a short while before, further testimony to the terrifying impact on gunners of a cavalry charge. In at least two cases at Waterloo, the battery commanders themselves, seeing the cavalry advance, gave the order to limber up the guns and transport them to the rear. One of these, Captain Sinclair, had already lost four guns in a clash with the French in Spain two years previously, and the consequences for his career had been distinctly negative. There was no lack of extenuating circumstances, but Wellington remained furious. A few months later, when there was talk of giving the artillery officers who had been present at Waterloo a cash reward, the duke expressed his unequivocal opposition to the idea.

Having routed skirmishers and artillery, the French cavalry was in possession of the Mont-Saint-Jean ridge. The uphill charge had surely tired their horses and disordered their ranks, and then, in front of them, were Wellington's squares, each one formed by a troop of a few hundred men crowded close together around a flag or banner, all with fixed bayonets, those in the first two ranks down on one knee, the others on their feet. We do not know exactly what orders the cavalry generals had been given, nor whether Marshal Ney had ridden that far with them (though in all probability he had), but they could scarcely have been told anything other than that they had to break up those squares. At that moment, they were more than three thousand strong, the cavalry of the Grande Armée, the most famous mounted force in the world. The officers of the cuirassiers, of the *chasseurs à cheval*, and of the lancers dressed the ranks of their men, brandished their sabers, and led them forward.

For almost all the squares, the first attacks were the ones that came closest to causing panic. Many soldiers in the British and German squares were young recruits under fire for the first time. An officer of the Royal Engineers who had taken refuge in one of the squares remarked, "The first time a body of cuirassiers approached the square into which I had ridden, the men—all young soldiers—

seemed to be alarmed. They fired high and with little effect, and in one of the angles there was just as much hesitation as made me feel exceedingly uncomfortable." Private Morris of the Seventy-third wavered for a moment when a "considerable number of the French cuirassiers made their appearance, on the rising ground just in our front, took the artillery we had placed there and came at a gallop down upon us." Morris was so awestruck by the sheer size of the men and the horses, by the shining helmets and the steel cuirasses, that he thought, "we could not have the slightest chance with them."

The same sentiment prevailed among people who were much more experienced than the nineteen-year-old Morris. In the yard at La Haye Sainte, Major von Baring ordered his fusiliers to fire at the serried ranks of cavalry riding past the farm, but he watched the enemy horsemen continue their advance "without even noticing" this fire and boldly attack the squares. "I could see all this going on, and I'm not afraid to admit that my heart sank more than once," Baring later recalled. Some distance away, on the high ground behind Hougoumont, Captain Mercer was still talking with Colonel Gould when he saw the enemy cavalry come back up the slope and overwhelm the guns of the batteries posted in the first line, and for an instant he had the impression that the infantry squares, too, had disappeared under the countless whirling sabers. "The only objects were a few guns standing in a confused manner, with muzzles in the air, and not one artilleryman," Mercer wrote. "And now we really apprehended being overwhelmed, as the first line had apparently been. 'I fear all is over,' said Colonel Gould, who still remained by me. The thing seemed but too likely, and this time I could not withhold my assent to his remark, for it did indeed appear so."

But if the squares were not broken or at least pushed back, the capture of the guns meant nothing, and a charge against a line of squares, more than just blind momentum, rather resembled a risky psychological game. The French cuirassiers were assembled in plain view on the crest of the ridge, little more than a hundred yards away from the nearest squares, far enough that it would have been useless for the infantry to start shooting at them. When a squadron had chosen its objective and was ready to move, it set out at a walk, superior officers in front, their sabers unsheathed. If, at this point, the men in the square started to fidget a bit too much, the cuirassiers' officers could risk accelerating the pace to a trot, which meant that the infantry had time to fire one volley only. Should that volley be fired badly—too soon or too high—the cavalry could pass to a gallop, and then the infantry soldiers, in all probability, would lose their nerve and clear off, and the inevitable result would be a massacre. However, if the infantry, kept in place by the blows and curses of its officers and sergeants, remained steadfast and held its fire until the last possible moment, the cavalry would usually slow its pace, veer to the right or left before impact, and ride off in search of another target. In this case, the soldiers in the squares could shoot with impunity, and the cavalry would receive the full force of the infantry's fire.

Yet for an infantry square, victory meant only a moment's breathing space before another cavalry squadron appeared, while defeat meant destruction and death. By contrast, a squadron could lose many such games before its offensive capacity would start to be seriously reduced by the weak fire of the squares. But the balance was redressed in favor of the defenders in that the cavalry—considered in purely physical terms, as a striking force—did not have the slightest chance of breaking up a square by dealing out saber-strokes; horses could not be persuaded to plunge into the midst of bayonets. "The horses of the first rank of cuirassiers, in spite of all the efforts of their riders, came to a standstill, shaking and covered with foam, at about twenty yards distance, and generally resisted all attempts to force them to charge the line of serried steel," wrote Ensign Gronow, who spent several hours in the square of the 3/1st Foot Guards. All in all, the final outcome depended exclusively on the courage of the infantry: If it kept its nerve, nothing could happen to it, while the courage of the cavalry, in and of itself, was not enough to guarantee victory.

Between four and six o'clock in the afternoon, on the slope that descended from the north side of the chemin d'Ohain to Mont-Saint-Jean, countless games of this type were played out, and the British and German infantry—thanks to tough training, the energy of the officers, and the courage of the men—held fast for the duration. Captain von Scriba described how the officers were able to compel their recruits to hold their fire until the cuirassiers were only twenty or thirty paces away; the ensuing volley, though ineffective in terms of accuracy, was enough to disperse them and force them to withdraw. The French quickly regrouped and began to advance again, but this time, when they reached the same distance from the square as before, the foot soldiers, miraculously restrained by their officers, continued holding their fire, unnerving the cuirassiers so thoroughly that they changed direction and rode away harmlessly along the sides of the square.

Sometimes, this psychological game took on comedic rhythms. The Duke of Wellington recalled having seen some squares which "would not throw away their fire till the Cuirassiers charged, and they would not charge until we had thrown away our fire." But variations were introduced into the game. Having realized that the squares' tactic was to hold their fire until the very last moment, the cuirassier commanders started to send individual riders forward. These urged their horses very close to the enemy and took aim with the short carbines they all carried. A cuirassier did this at serious risk to his own skin; had a square responded to his aggression with an exasperated volley, he would surely have been cut down. But that was exactly what the French officers wanted, for it would give their men an opportunity to charge the infantry before they had time to reload their muskets. The British and German officers found it necessary to send some selected marksmen out of the square—with all the risks such exposure entailed—in an attempt to keep the cuirassiers and their carbines at a distance.

Everywhere, the commanders' abilities, as well as their nerves, were stretched to the limit by this type of combat. Not far from La Haye Sainte, a cuirassier squadron charged the square of the Fifth KGL several times. Repulsed every time, the riders took shelter in a fold of the ground while their commanding officer quite coolly remained in the open, riding around the square, on the lookout for the favorable moment to order a fresh attack. Colonel von Ompteda, commander of the Second KGL Brigade, who had taken refuge in this square, asked several of the battalion's elite marksmen to shoot the French officer down, but they all missed him. Finally, after the square had been charged for the fifth time, a rifleman from another regiment, John Milius, who had been wounded in no-man's-land and dragged to the relative safety of the square, offered to try his hand. One of his legs was broken, and he had lost a great deal of blood; but he had himself carried to the front rank, got the French officer in the sights of his Baker rifle, and killed him with one shot.

Though the French cavalry was not making much progress, Wellington's situation was precarious. The enemy had overwhelmed his defensive line, his guns were temporarily lost, and he and all his generals were compelled to seek protection inside the squares, from where it inevitably became more difficult to exercise command. As Wellington remarked a few weeks later in a letter to Lord Beresford, the enemy cavalry were moving among the Allied troops as though they were their own. If at this moment Napoleon had sent forward the infantry of the Imperial Guard, which constituted the principal reserve force still available to him, the line along the ridge could have been definitively occupied and the Allied guns rendered useless, and in all probability the French would have won the Battle of Waterloo.

The emperor has always been criticized for not having used his reserves in support of the cavalry; in the end, it has often been said, this excessive caution cost him the battle. Concern for the Prussian columns that were approaching from the east may have played a part in his failure to act; at that moment, the vanguard of those columns was just beginning to emerge from the Fichermont wood. In light of what happened later, it is also probable that as long as Hougoumont and La Haye Sainte were still putting up resistance, the emperor intended to postpone the final attack; he knew how risky it would be to insert the bulk of his forces into such a narrow space while at their back those two bastions remained in enemy hands. But perhaps an even more convincing reason for his inaction lies in the fact that the fighting around the squares took place on the side of the ridge that Napoleon could not see. Until Marshal Ney or the cavalry commanders communicated with him, the emperor was unable to know what was going on. A few years previously, Napoleon would have jumped on a horse and gone to see for himself; but he was forty-six years old, and he was tired. He remained seated on his camp chair near La Belle Alliance, chewing on straws and waiting for news.

FORTY-SIX

---◆◆◆---

"WHERE ARE THE CAVALRY?"

The only force that could try to drive the French cavalry from the ridge and give the squares a chance to breathe was the Allied cavalry, and Lord Uxbridge engaged it without reserve. Between La Haye Sainte and Hougoumont, the cavalry brigades of Grant, Dornberg, and Arentschildt had seven regiments in all, four British and three KGL; there were, as well, the Brunswick contingent's Hussar regiment and a regiment of Hanoverian volunteers, the Cumberland Hussars. Collaert, the commander of the Netherlands cavalry, had another seven regiments; most of these, however, had already been battered in their recent charge. All the same, the total number was imposing: more than six thousand sabers, of which at least half were still fresh. Yet almost all of Uxbridge's troopers were light cavalry, and he could not have hoped to engage them in large numbers against the cuirassiers or the lancers of the Old Guard. He preferred to post his horsemen behind the squares, near enough for the infantry to feel their reassuring presence; then, when the occasion presented itself, in the moment when the enemy cavalry could be surprised, when it was scattered and falling back after an unsuccessful charge, he would launch a few squadrons in a counterattack.

In more than one instance, these counterattacks were successful, even though the Allied cavalry, both British and German, continued to demonstrate the same dauntless contempt for orders and the same lack of foresight that their colleagues had shown earlier in the battle. At one point in the conflict, General von Dornberg decided to attack a cuirassier regiment with two regiments of his own, the Twenty-third Light Dragoons, a British unit, and the First Light Dragoons of the King's German Legion; his forces, therefore, outnumbered the enemy by two to one. Should the French begin to fall back, Dornberg cautioned his commanders, only one squadron from each regiment was to pursue them; the others were to re-form their ranks and stay under cover. The first squadrons

191

of the French regiment, attacked on both flanks, were indeed put to rout, whereupon Dornberg's entire cavalry, forgetful of his orders, dashed after the fleeing enemy.

But the French colonel, unlike his adversary, was holding some squadrons in reserve, and these broke up the Allied pursuit; immediately thereafter, while the British and German cavalry were remounting the slope in disorder and on blown horses, a fresh cuirassier regiment appeared and blocked their way. Dornberg's squadrons launched a desperate charge; the French came to a halt, drew their swords, and awaited the enemy unmoving. At the moment of impact, the light dragoons realized that their curved sabers were no match for the cuirassiers' long swords, nor could they penetrate the French cuirasses. Seeing that his men were losing heart, General von Dornberg tried to lead some of them against the enemy flank. "At this point, I was pierced through the left side into the lung. Blood started coming out of my mouth, making it difficult for me to speak. I was forced to go to the rear, and I can say nothing more about the action."

Dornberg's mournful account recalls the Duke of Wellington's caustic comments about his cavalry's ability to maneuver, and it was echoed by others. Major von Goeben of the Third KGL Hussars tells how Lord Uxbridge in person ordered two squadrons to attack two regiments of French cavalry that were remounting the slope: "This attack was made, and that part of the enemy force that the two squadrons could reach was brought to a standstill and then violently thrown back. However, since the enemy line was so much stronger, these same squadrons were then outflanked on both sides and suffered a considerable loss in officers, men, and horses." When the German regiment, which had begun the day with at least 500 sabers, re-formed its ranks behind the protection of the squares, no more than 120 men were still in their saddles.

Both the material superiority of the French cuirassiers, with their heavy armor, and the tactical ignorance of too many British and German officers were regularly confirmed in almost all the conflicts. Not content with the previous action, Captain von Kerssenbruch—who had succeeded to the command of the Third Hussars after a cannonball killed their colonel—wished to attack the flanks of several cuirassier squadrons. Kerssenbruch's men, however, quickly got the worst of the encounter, the captain was killed, and the surviving Hussars, together with the cuirassiers pursuing them, ended up among the squares. The Allied infantry fired, persuading the French to fall back, but many of them, carried along by their own momentum, passed beyond the enemy lines. When the Hussars attempted to regroup and re-form their ranks, they discovered that there was a cuirassier in the midst of them; since he refused to surrender, they tried to cut him down with their sabers, but his stout helmet and cuirass resisted many blows, and it was a good while before he finally fell.

This phase of the battle proved to be rather frustrating for many officers of the Allied cavalry. Captain Robbins of the Seventh Hussars, Lord Uxbridge's pampered personal regiment, remembered little else but that he and his men, having dismounted in order to offer a less conspicuous target, had been moved back and forth several times, always under the fire of the enemy artillery. "Much annoyed by shot and shells, and still seeing no Enemy, yet losing many men and horses, we were again moved." Robbins and his men took cover in the sunken lane, but not even this was safe: "Some guns of the Horse Artillery had just been obliged to withdraw, the Enemy's Guns having exactly got their range and doing great execution." The regiment was finally ordered to mount and engage the enemy cavalry, which was advancing near Hougoumont château. There was barely time to see that their adversaries were the lancers of the Imperial Guard, deployed in three ranks, moving forward "as steadily as if on a field day," and then the Hussars charged. In this attack, Robbins says, he "was wounded and fell." Thus "obliged to leave the field," he was "unable to give any account" of what happened after that.

Not surprisingly, the Allied cavalry eventually began to lose heart. The few remaining squadrons of the Household Brigade were sent forward in yet another disastrous charge, after which they were obliged to form up in the rear, deploying in one line instead of two, in order to "make an impression." One of a small number of surviving officers confessed, "Fortunately for us, nobody attacked us." Shortly thereafter, Lord Uxbridge rode over to Trip's brigade and ordered it to charge, then unsheathed his saber and set off at a trot. His adjutant, Captain Seymour, hurried after him to point out that no one was following him. Infuriated, Uxbridge turned back, but despite his efforts, he could not persuade the Netherlanders to move.

A little while later, Uxbridge saw the Cumberland Hussars showing clear signs of agitation and beginning to fall back without having received any order to do so. The earl immediately sent Seymour to see what was going on. The Hussars were an all-volunteer German unit, in their first battle. They had remained under the artillery bombardment for a long time, but it had not occurred to their officers—who were as inexperienced as they—that they could reduce casualties by having their troopers dismount. Lieutenant Waymouth of the Second Life Guards remembered seeing them sitting motionless in their saddles at a point in the battle when the entire British cavalry had dismounted and taken shelter under their horses; the captain wondered in amazement what was wrong with the German cavalrymen, allowing themselves to be slaughtered like that. Now, however, the Hussars had had enough; their commander, Colonel von Hake, explained to the incredulous Seymour that since his men were volunteers and their horses were their own property, he didn't think he could compel them to remain in the battle line. The captain ordered them to halt but achieved no result; he spoke of the honor of the regiment, grabbed the bridle of the colonel's horse, told him through his teeth what he thought of him, and finally implored him at least to deploy his men in the rear, out of range of the enemy guns; but nobody listened to Seymour, and the regiment dispersed. A number of officers and men, outraged by the cowardice of their comrades, left their ranks and attached themselves to other regiments; the rest abandoned the field and galloped all the way back to Brussels.

After the battle, this episode was much publicized, and Colonel von Hake had to go in front of a court-martial, which expelled him from the army with ignominy. Yet at this point in the battle, not even the British cavalry felt like fighting anymore. Lord Uxbridge's exhortations met the same obstinate reluctance everywhere, and in the end his chagrin was so great that he declared himself ashamed to be an Englishman. The infantry packed into their squares probably had never felt any great love for the cavalry, and they expressed the same opinions as the earl. In the square in which the Duke of Wellington himself had taken refuge, the men were so exasperated at the sight of the cuirassiers, calmly riding past them a short distance away, that someone began to shout, "Where are the cavalry? Why don't they come and pitch into those French fellows?"

In the end, the principal function that Wellington's cavalry was able to carry out during the attacks of the French cuirassiers was to take up position behind the squares, particularly those composed of recruits, and prevent the soldiers—using the flat of their swords, if necessary—from being seized by panic and running away. Deployed in a double line, their horses' muzzles almost touching the backs of the foot soldiers in the rearmost rank, the cavalry regiments occupied so much space that it was physically impossible for the infantry to creep away, even though many soldiers, especially those in the most vulnerable positions, were sorely tempted to try. Sergeant Cotton of the Seventh Hussars remembered, "At times it was quite amusing to see some of the foreign troops cut away from the angles of their squares, and our staff-officers galloping after them to intercept their flight. It was surprising to see how readily they returned to their squares."

FORTY-SEVEN

"VOUS VERREZ BIENTÔT SA FORCE, MESSIEURS"

More than the threat from the French cavalry, the most severe trial for the infantry was the continuous artillery bombardment, which had intensified to coincide with the advance of the cavalry. Compelled to remain on their feet in serried ranks, the men were much more exposed than before to the cannonballs that came bounding down the slope and to the fragments of the exploding shells that the French howitzers were blindly firing over the ridge. The recorded recollections of the survivors leave the impression that just about everyone in the squares was engaged in counting the dead and wondering when it would be his turn. Tom Morris, who was still keeping watch over the Seventy-third's liquor supply, stared in fascination at a shell that had fallen not far away, and as the fuse burned down, he wondered how many men it would kill. "The portion which came to my share, was a piece of rough cast-iron, about the size of a horse-bean, which took up its lodging in my left cheek; the blood ran copiously down inside my clothes, and made me feel rather uncomfortable. Our poor captain was rather frightened, and several times came to me for a drop of something to keep his spirits up. Towards the close of the day, he was cut in two by a cannon ball." The men did not mourn the captain, because he was sixty years old, he had forgotten all the maneuvers, and two days before, at Quatre Bras, had the sergeants not corrected his mistakes, he would have led the whole unit to its doom.

In one of the Hanoverian squares behind La Haye Sainte, Captain von Scriba coolly kept tabs on the number of cannonballs that were falling among his men at horribly regular intervals. "Around half past two," he wrote,[26] "our gallant commander lost his horse to a cannonball. He immediately mounted Major Müller's horse. A few minutes later, he saw a riderless horse roaming around,

195

ordered it caught, and gave the Major his horse back. Not fifteen minutes after that, our well-beloved Lieutenant-Colonel von Langrehr lost his right leg, which was shattered by a cannonball. He remained on his horse. With a few touching words, he bade us farewell and turned over command of the Square to Major von Schkopp." Then Langrehr quietly left the field and died a little behind the lines.

While waiting for the cannonball that sooner or later must have his name on it, Captain von Scriba observed with some consternation the Nassau square deployed next to his own. Ever since the French artillery had adjusted its fire, the Nassauers had begun to grow agitated, and the order to remove the cloth coverings of their shakos had not sufficed to calm them down. "When the cannon fire recommenced, we were greatly distressed to see our neighbors to the right, the Nassauers, waver and fall into some disorder; but the efforts of the gallant Nassauer officers, who gave their subordinates an excellent example, succeeded in bringing the men to a halt and leading them back to their former places. This unfortunate incident was repeated once or twice, under identical circumstances. Their losses were visibly quite considerable." Fortunately for the Allies, there were no squadrons of enemy cavalry near enough to take advantage of the situation in either one of these cases. Furthermore, even though some French batteries had maneuvered in such a way that the squares were visible to them, their guns were still posted at a great distance, and they ceased firing when the cavalry made its advance. The bombardment resumed only after the gunners saw the cavalry fall back, and this is certainly one of the circumstances that saved the Allied line from destruction.

The officers in some squares, seeking to protect their men from the hail of cannonballs and shell fragments, ordered them to lie down. (Such a precaution was, of course, impracticable when enemy cavalry was in sight.) Lieutenant Pattison of the Thirty-third recounted the strange fate of three officers, who "were lying on the ground close to one another in the centre of the square": "I was standing up, much interested in what was going on to our left, when a missile, supposed to be the fracture of a shell, hit Hart so severely on the shoulder as to cause sudden death, and passing over Trevor, scooped out one of Pagan's ears. He got up staggering and bleeding profusely, when I with other assistance placed him on a bearer to carry him to the rear. The men thus employed had hardly left the centre of the square, when a cannon-ball hit one of them and carried off his leg. Another man took his place, when he was then carried in safety to the village of Waterloo, where medical attention was paid to his wound."

A few hundred yards away, Adam's battalions were taking the same punishment. Ensign Leeke, who carried the regimental color of the Fifty-second, observed that "standing to be cannonaded, and having nothing else to do, is about the most unpleasant thing that can happen to a soldier in a regiment."

Officers generally lay down on the ground along with their men, but the officers entrusted with carrying the banners and the noncommissioned officers assigned to escort them were forced to remain on their feet. One of Leeke's sergeants, seeing a ball coming straight at him, avoided it "by stooping just as he saw it in line with him at some little distance; this was quite allowable when his comrades were lying down at their ease."[27]

A short time later, it was Leeke's turn. Mesmerized, the ensign watched the servers of a French gun many hundred yards away load their piece and fire it. With his young eyes, he could see the ball itself as it issued from the mouth of the cannon and headed straight for him. For an instant, he wondered if he should do something and whether he should move, but mentally answered both questions in the negative and remained dutifully immobile, clutching the standard of the regimental flag. "I do not exactly know the rapidity with which the cannon-balls fly, but I think that two seconds elapsed from the time I saw this shot leave the gun until it struck the front face of the square. It did not strike the four men in the rear of whom I was standing, but the poor fellows on their right. It was fired with some elevation, and struck the front man about the knees, and coming to the ground under the feet of the rear man of the four, whom it severely wounded, it rose and, passing within an inch or two of the Colour pole, went over the rear face of the square without doing further injury. The two men in the first and second rank fell outward, I fear they did not survive long; the two others fell within the square. The rear man made a considerable outcry on being wounded." Episodes such as this remained fixed in the memories of the survivors, perhaps obscuring the long periods of time in which not a single ball fell on the square. In the end the losses suffered by these regiments were much lower than certain accounts suggested. Nevertheless, psychologically speaking, theirs was a formidable ordeal.

In the late afternoon, Sergeant Lawrence of the Fortieth was ordered to perform the duty of "color-sergeant." As he recalled many years later, "This, although I was used to warfare as much as any, was a job I did not at all like; but still I went as boldly to work as I could. There had been before me that day fourteen sergeants already killed and wounded while in charge of these Colours, with officers in proportion, and the staff and Colours were almost cut to pieces. This job will never be blotted from my memory; although I am now an old man, I remember it as if it had been yesterday. I had not been there more than a quarter of an hour when a cannon-shot came and took the captain's head clean off. This was again close to me, for my left side was touching the poor captain's right, and I was spattered all over with his blood. The men in their tired state were beginning to despair, but the officers cheered them on continually throughout the day with the cry of 'Keep your ground, my men!' It is a mystery to me how it was accomplished, for at last so few were left that there were scarcely enough to form square."

By contrast, the morale of the French was rising again at this point in the afternoon. When a cuirassier officer, unsaddled and dragged by force into a square, was asked by the British officers how many forces Napoleon had in the field, he "replied with a smile of mingled derision and menace: '*Vous verrez bientôt sa force, Messieurs.*'" A few hundred yards away, General Desales had retaken command of the reconstituted Grande Batterie and was directing his fire against the Allied squares behind La Haye Sainte when Marshal Ney approached him. "Have you ever seen a battle like this one? What fury!" Ney said joyously. After the heavy blow delivered to d'Erlon, everything seemed to be going well again, and the marshal was in the best of humors. "Tonight," Ney said to Desales, "you'll come and sup with me in Brussels."

FORTY-EIGHT

BLÜCHER ATTACKS

The French would have felt much less confident had they known that Prussian officers, having passed unmolested through the Fichermont wood, had been watching them through their telescopes for several hours. Sometime past midday, Major von Falkenhausen, leading a patrol of uhlans, went as far as the main Brussels road south of La Belle Alliance, behind Napoleon's entire army; there they captured a few thunderstruck French soldiers, who informed them that the emperor was in action and that the Imperial Guard was with him. Farther north, General von Valentini, Bülow's chief of staff, together with a few adjutants, entered Fichermont and encountered a farmer, who was seized, set on an artillery horse, and made to accompany the Prussians to the edge of the wood. The ripening grain in the fields was taller than a man, and the red coats of a few British deserters could be glimpsed, like bright poppies among the standing crops; but there was no trace of the French.

Pleasantly surprised by the enemy's absence, Valentini was questioning the farmer about the best road to take for Smohain when someone cried out that enemy lancers were approaching. Valentini and his group started to gallop away but saw that the cavalry was Falkenhausen and his uhlans, returning from their incursion. Once he was certain that none of the enemy was to be found anywhere in the Fichermont wood, Valentini pushed on beyond it, dismounted, and studied the horizon with his telescope. Here and there he spotted a few French sentries, but none of them thought to look to the right, in his direction. Somewhat later, Prince August of Thurn and Taxis, who was the Bavarian representative in Blücher's headquarters, reached the edge of the wood and was able to overlook the battlefield all the way to La Haye Sainte, which was enveloped in smoke. "Hard to believe as it may be, we could see into the rear of the enemy (a distance of about $1^{1}/_{2}$ hours' march), and could even make out with our telescopes how the wounded were being carried back."

Finally, Blücher himself arrived. That morning, the old man had arisen at dawn, rudely chasing away the physician who tried to rub some ointment into his aching shoulder with the comment: "If I must go into eternity, it makes no difference to me whether I go anointed or unanointed. And if things go well today, soon we'll all be washing and bathing in Paris." He dictated a combative letter to Müffling—"Ill and old as I am, I will nonetheless ride at the head of my men to attack the enemy's right wing at once, should Napoleon make any move against the Duke. If the French do not attack today, then in my opinion we should attack them together tomorrow"—and set out to catch up with his vanguard.

Together with Gneisenau and Bülow, the field marshal gave the unsuspecting enemy's rear positions a thorough examination; but despite the favorable situation, Napoleon's reserves, massed behind La Belle Alliance, looked impressive, and someone remarked that the prospect of having to face them was by no means a happy one. The majority agreed, however, that Napoleon, should he discover the threat to his right, would most likely redouble his efforts to break through Wellington's line, and Blücher curtly replied that the emperor had more than enough troops to do so. Among the Prussian staff officers, faith in the Allies' ability to resist was at a minimum. But Blücher had kept the duke informed of his progress during the course of the morning, and at one point Müffling, accompanied by some German officers from Wellington's staff, had arrived to discuss the situation. They had pointed out that a Prussian intervention was indispensable to saving the day and that Blücher could hold back no longer. The field marshal therefore ordered Bülow to resume the march and occupy the Fichermont wood in force.

The vanguard of the Prussian IV Corps, halted at Chapelle-St. Lambert, had been granted a few hours' time to catch its breath. The troops, in large part *Landwehr* militiamen, very much needed the respite. They also could have used something to eat, but they had no means of cooking anything and moreover there was no water. Many men used their mess tins to collect rainwater from the puddles and mixed it with ground coffee, sugar, and rum as their principal nourishment in view of the battle awaiting them. Thus, when the Prussians finally got under way again, the bulk of their troops took several hours to cross the Lasne Valley—which the rain of the previous night had turned into a bog—and then the broad area of dense forest, interrupted by occasional clearings, that constituted the Fichermont wood. The cannon sank up to their axles in mud; the horses slipped and stuck in mire; the soldiers cursed and tried to persuade their officers that the way was impassable. But Blücher was on horseback in the midst of them, and someone swore he heard the old man cry out, "Come on, boys, don't say it can't be done. I promised my brother Wellington. Do you want to make me a liar?" Finally, at four in the afternoon, half the infantry and almost all the cavalry of Bülow's corps were in position inside the margin of the wood; so covered with mud as to be unrecognizable ("they all looked like mulattoes"), they were nonetheless ready to surprise the enemy and fall upon his exposed right flank.

At first, the Prussian generals had agreed to assemble all of IV Corps at that point before starting the attack; but although part of his infantry and almost all of his artillery was still on the way, Blücher decided he could not wait any more. From all appearances, Wellington could not hold out much longer, so the Prussian commander ordered his troops to attack forthwith. As far as the old prince could see from his observation post, the Fichermont wood was the entrance to a stretch of upland bounded on the left by the valley of the Lasne and on the right by the valley of the Smohain. Although both these watercourses were barely streams, easy to ford in normal circumstances, their steep banks and marshy surroundings made them significant obstacles. But once beyond the forest, the Prussian generals could see the battlefield. Because the courses of the two streams diverged more and more, the plateau widened out considerably, so Blücher's officers would have all the maneuvering room necessary to deploy their troops and attack the French right flank, in keeping with his pledge to Wellington. According to the Prince of Thurn and Taxis's estimate, the battlefield was an hour and a half's march away; in that time, if nothing stopped them, the Prussian cavalry would reach La Belle Alliance.

In the beginning, nothing seemed capable of stopping them. Only when the first Prussians emerged from the wood did the French generals appear to realize the danger they were in and try to do something about it: up to that moment, as Bülow wrote in his report the next day, the enemy had "inexplicably neglected" his right flank and "did not appear to be paying any attention to our existence." This testimony confirms that Mouton's troops were at that moment deployed in support of the right wing, which had been so fearfully weakened after the defeat of d'Erlon, and that the general and his men were facing Wellington's positions without receiving any warning that the Prussians might appear on their flank. When Colonel Combes-Brassard, Mouton's chief of staff, saw troops issuing from the woods, he galloped closer to see who they were and discovered, to his dismay, that the soldiers were Prussians. "Their arrival took place without our having received any order from the Emperor. Our flank was turned."

Around four-thirty, when Bülow's line began to emerge in force from the Fichermont wood, only Domon's and Subervie's squadrons of lancers and *chasseurs à cheval* were properly positioned for an attempt to stop his advance, and in fact they were used unsparingly. The cavalry patrols that formed the Prussian vanguard were attacked and dispersed; these skirmishes proved fatal to the commanders of both the cavalry brigades that Bülow had sent ahead, a fact that confirms the deficient tactical abilities of the inexperienced Prussian cavalry.

But after each action, the French cavalry had to retire under the fire of the enemy batteries, which were taking up positions at the edge of the wood. Covered by that fire, the line of Prussian skirmishers began to spread out, and soon it extended across the whole plateau, touching the Smohain on the right and the Lasne on the left, along a front nearly a mile and a half wide.

The direction their advance would take had been debated in the earlier messages exchanged between Wellington and the Prussian generals by way of Müffling. Once emerged from the wood, Bülow could head his columns either northwest, toward Smohain, to establish contact with Wellington's left wing, or southwest, in a direction that would increase the distance between him and his ally but threaten the enemy's rear. The dirt tracks would permit both maneuvers, and at first Bülow tried to advance in two directions at once. One result of this was an incident involving the men led by Prince Bernhard of Saxe-Weimar: The Prussians advanced across the difficult terrain, broken by countless hedges and ditches, glimpsed in the distance a body of blue-uniformed infantry carrying equipment quite similar to that of the French, and immediately opened fire; the Nassauers replied in kind, and the shooting went on for at least ten minutes before the officers on both sides realized their mistake and succeeded in enforcing a cease-fire.

Bülow felt he could head for Smohain, enter the sunken road, and follow it to the positions of Pack's, Bijlandt's, and Kempt's exhausted brigades, whose places the Prussians would then take; this sort of relief was what Wellington had had in mind when he arrayed his forces. Anticipating Prussian reinforcements, he had deliberately undermanned his weak left flank. But that morning, Bülow and Müffling had also agreed that an advance along the chemin d'Ohain would be possible only if the road were not threatened by the enemy; should the contrary be the case, it would be much better to direct the Prussian offensive farther south, diverging from Wellington's line and attacking the French on the flank and perhaps even in the rear. Therefore, when he saw that La Haye Sainte and Papelotte were under attack, the Prussian general concluded that maneuvering along the sunken road was too dangerous, recalled the troops who had already set off in that direction, and turned the head of his columns definitively southwest.

Given the terrible gaps that had been opened in his infantry, Wellington at that point would have greatly preferred that the Prussian battalions join his forces and take up positions alongside his. Captain Seymour was ordered to ride to Bülow at once and present this pressing request. Early in the aide's mission, his horse was killed under him; another officer left in his place, managed to find the Prussian general, and conveyed to him the duke's wishes. But the British officer's efforts met with little success. Bülow had no intention of passing up an opportunity to attack Napoleon in order to play a purely defensive role, which would moreover have placed him under Wellington's orders; in any case, he told the officer that it was too late to change his plan of advance. All he could do was to write a message to Blücher and recommend that he send another corps in the direction of Smohain; Bülow's push would be made farther south. Later, the Prussian general wrote about emerging from the Fichermont wood and seeing the line of the horizon "marked by the Brussels road, running up to a crest where we could make out in the distance the farm called La Belle Alliance, built in a dominating position. This clearly visible spot was pointed out to all the troops as the common objective of our attack."

The charges of Domon's and Subervie's cavalry had gained Mouton the minimum amount of time needed to redeploy his troops at right angles to those of d'Erlon and face the growing thrust of the Prussian columns. One of the most expert French commanders, he did what he could, and his troops fought well, but theirs was a hopeless mission, especially in open country like the terrain west of the Fichermont wood. Mouton had fifteen battalions in all, many of them understrength, with little more than six thousand muskets and thirty guns; the six light cavalry regiments of Domon and Subervie added two thousand sabers and twelve guns. When Bülow came out of the Fichermont wood with only half his infantry, he nevertheless had eighteen full-strength Prussian battalions, a total of twelve thousand muskets; his cavalry numbered eight regiments with more than three thousand sabers, even though many squadrons had been scattered since morning on reconnaissance missions; and of his eleven batteries, though a few remained mired in the mud of the Lasne, Bülow eventually managed to deploy eight, with a total of sixty-four guns.

However brave and lucky a general Mouton may have been, he had no chance of standing long in open country against forces that outnumbered his own by two to one. For a brief time, his artillery kept up a lively fire against the advancing Prussian columns, but when he realized that the enemy line was much more extensive than his and threatened to envelop his flanks, Mouton properly ordered his troops to fall back. Repeated charges by Domon's and Subervie's cavalry slowed down the enemy advance, as the Prussian cavalry continued to demonstrate their ineffectiveness against their French counterparts, who were led by such men as Colonel Sourd, of the Second Lancers. Just the previous day, as a consequence of a violent clash with British cavalry, the surgeon Larrey, chief of Napoleon's medical service, had amputated Sourd's arm, but he insisted on maintaining command of his regiment and in fact led his men all day long. Nevertheless, though such actions as gallant cavalry charges might impede or stall Bülow's advance, they could not stop it. Slowly but surely, as the opposing outposts engaged in a continuous, debilitating skirmish, the Prussians gained ground. "Our skirmishers had gained a solid position," Bülow reported. "The artillery advanced with the rapidity that the situation required, passed the skirmishers, and opened fire on the enemy at close range. The line of massed battalions followed, and behind them came our supporting cavalry, who watched over the chain of skirmishers as they moved forward."

The Prussians' advance, which inclined more and more toward the southwest, threatened to bring them behind the French lines and bottle up Napoleon's army. Mouton's corps retreated in good order, maintaining its line of skirmishers and keeping up a steady fire from all available guns; Prussian losses were beginning to exceed those of the French, but Mouton could not halt, because the enemy was threatening to envelop his right wing. In the late afternoon, Prussian cannonballs started falling on the Brussels road, not far from the emperor's command post, and a couple of them went through the roof of the inn at La Belle Alliance, which was by then filled with wounded French soldiers and with surgeons intent on their sanguinary work. By turning his telescope in the direction the shots came from, Napoleon could see the Prussian skirmishers moving steadily southward along the road that formed the principal axis of their advance. This road descended toward the Lasne, and soon the Prussians would reach the first houses of the village of Plancenoit, which stood near the north bank of the little river.

FORTY-NINE

PLANCENOIT

Plancenoit was the largest population center in the region; traversing it from one end to the other, on foot and at a good pace, would have taken five or six minutes. It was, therefore, a full village, with a cobblestone street, a parish church built of stone, and a walled cemetery, whereas Smohain and Mont-Saint-Jean were nothing but small groups of houses. The inhabitants of Plancenoit had abandoned it the previous day, and French soldiers had spent the night in the houses, burning doors and shutters to keep warm. When the Prussians arrived, however, the village was empty. It was also frighteningly close to the rear of Napoleon's lines: After the last houses of Plancenoit, the road climbed a gentle slope for less than a kilometer—perhaps a thousand yards—before intersecting the main road behind La Belle Alliance itself. Other tracks, winding among the hills, met the Brussels road farther to the rear, at Rossomme or even at Le Caillou. Mouton would surely occupy and defend Plancenoit, recognizing that the village offered him the only favorable position for opposing the enemy advance; but from what Napoleon could see with the aid of his telescope, the general clearly did not have enough troops to hold out for very long. And should the village be lost, he knew the enemy troops would quickly continue up the slope until they found themselves within a musket shot of the main road, menacing the French reserves' flank and rear.

Reluctantly, the emperor decided that part of the Imperial Guard would have to be diverted in that direction to prevent the Prussians from seizing the village. The twenty-two battalions of the Imperial Guard were all the fresh infantry that Napoleon had left to deliver the decisive attack against Wellington's line, and every battalion subtracted from that effort would reduce the probability of victory; but the emperor had no choice. He ordered Duhesme, the commander of the Young Guard Division, to take his eight battalions and occupy Plancenoit. The guardsmen on both sides of the Brussels road had spent the day sitting on

205

the ground or on their knapsacks, smoking, chatting, and waiting for their turn to come. As always, the Young Guard occupied the positions farthest front, because it got sent into action first; and in this case, too, the guardsmen had to form ranks at the commands of their officers, and start marching, not toward the enemy in their front but toward the enemy who was about to appear on their right. Duhesme's division, together with three artillery batteries totaling twenty-four guns, moved in the direction of Plancenoit, where his four thousand muskets would join Mouton's six thousand.

In the fight for Plancenoit, Blücher's army would display all its positive qualities and all its limitations. From the viewpoint of morale, boh officers and men were animated by a fanatical hatred of the French; it had sustained them through the rigors of a long march through mud since dawn, and in the late afternoon it inspired the Prussian troops to fight with particular ferocity. The struggle in and around the houses of the village, captured, lost, and recaptured one by one, was bloody, with quarter neither asked nor given, just as the Battle of Ligny had been two days before. At the same time, too many of the Prussian troops were *Landwehr* recruits, insufficiently trained and lacking in cohesion. Bülow's was the only corps in the army in which *Landwehr* soldiers made up as much as two-thirds of the infantry; and the sudden collapses and moments of unjustified panic that the Prussian side experienced again and again during the course of the fight for Plancenoit probably had their origin in the excessive number of inexperienced regiments. Müffling explained to Wellington, "Our infantry doesn't possess the same physical force and capacity to resist as yours. Most of our troops are too young and inexperienced."

On the tactical level, the Prussian army had made some significant innovations: The lines of skirmishers they engaged were more numerous and better conducted than in any other army, and this fact surely explains why it was so difficult for Mouton's men, right from the beginning, to stem the Prussian advance. But the *Landwehr* regiments were incapable of sustaining this kind of combat at the same level as troops of the line, and none of them included the fusilier battalion that was otherwise an integral part of every Prussian infantry regiment. In short, Bülow's corps had proportionately fewer trained skirmishers than the other corps, and they had to cover a rather wide line of advance. When they arrived before Plancenoit, the Prussian skirmishers had already exhausted much of their ammunition and a great deal of their offensive capacity, so that the assault on the village was carried out less tactically than it should have been.

The Prussian reformers had also developed an attack formation for their brigades that was conscientiously taught to every officer. Their methods constituted a genuine innovation: Coordination between the lines of skirmishers and the battalions marching in column behind them was blended into a system simple enough to be learned and put into practice in any circumstances. At the same time, it provided brigade commanders with a certain model to follow when the time came for making decisions. But IV Corps's advance had begun along too broad a front, and the Prussian generals quickly began to detach two or three battalions to cover their flanks, some in the direction of Smohain and some toward the Lasne. Carrying out these maneuvers made the formation ordained in their manuals no longer feasible, and this departure from usual practice also contributed to a certain disorder, a certain improvisatory character in their attacks.

Finally, the inexperience of a great many of the troops and of their officers manifested itself in excessive waste of ammunition. Even before starting the assault on Plancenoit, some regiments indicated that they had nearly exhausted their supplies of cartridges in the prolonged fight with Mouton's line of *tirailleurs*. In like manner, the Prussian artillery was not used at all economically, and Clausewitz criticized it harshly in his history of the campaign: "We keep too much artillery in reserve, and we replace a battery whenever it has used up all its powder and shot; as a consequence, many batteries try to get rid of their ammunition quickly." The result, in the Prussian general's cold-eyed judgment, was that the French artillery, with fewer guns, regularly caused much more damage than its Prussian counterparts managed to inflict. Farther on in the same text, Clausewitz expatiated on this conclusion in terms that seem to be a direct comment on what happened at Plancenoit: "We use up our troops too fast in stationary combat. Our officers call for support too soon, and it's given them too readily. The consequence is that we suffer more dead and wounded without gaining any ground, and we transform our fresh soldiers into burnt-out husks."

When Blücher gave the order to attack Plancenoit, only half of IV Corps's infantry was in a position to participate in the action: General von Losthin's Fifteenth Brigade and Hiller's Sixteenth. The corps's other two brigades were still on the march to the front line, though by then they were fairly close. On paper, a Prussian brigade was a powerful force, equivalent to a division in any other army, with nine infantry battalions. The Fifteenth Brigade, however, had borne the brunt of the fighting to this point and was already considerably weakened, while one of its battalions had had to be taken out of the line because the troops had completely exhausted their supply of cartridges. As for the Sixteenth Brigade, it had detached almost all of its skirmishers to cover the left flank, where a wooded slope descended rapidly to the Lasne. Nevertheless, without waiting for reinforcements, the Prussian generals ordered the attack. "Our generals were too committed to the idea that making an advance is better than standing and firing. Everything should be done in its own time," Clausewitz observed.

On the right wing, the Fifteenth Brigade found itself facing the weaker of Mouton's two divisions, which was deployed on the slightly higher ground just outside Plancenoit. The Prussian muskets outnumbered the French two to one, but the French were fresher, they had more ammunition, and their artillery was more experienced. General von Losthin had only one line regiment, the Eighteenth, which until three months previously had been a reserve regiment, recruited among the Germans and Poles of Posnania, and whose troops were still wearing old gray uniforms cobbled together from oddments.[28] The brigade's *Landwehr* troops were also composed of Germans and Poles, in this case from Silesia, all of them traditionally faithful to the king. Therefore, even though they had been on the march since four in the morning, had eaten nothing all day, and were nearing the end of their cartridge provision, they went forward with enthusiasm.

The Prussian attack, however, broke up almost at once. One after another, the skirmishing platoons of the Eighteenth ran out of ammunition and beat a retreat; here and there, their rearward movement was sufficiently disorderly to oblige units of the Prussian cavalry, which was deployed in the rear, to ride forward and escort the skirmishers back to the relative safety of their lines. Officers started asking for volunteers to exit the ranks and advance to reinforce the skirmishers' line, but not even this measure was likely to produce much forward progress; on the contrary, there was a risk that the French might make an advance themselves. Lieutenant Culemann watched an enemy officer who kept urging his men to counterattack by shouting, "*Vive l'Empereur! En avant, mes braves!*" The lieutenant called for the battalion's best marksman, Sergeant Walter, and demanded he unhorse that officer. While the sergeant was preparing to fire, a musket ball struck his left hand. Culemann, who was likewise on horseback, rode up to Walter and offered him his stirrup as a support; and the sergeant, although wounded and bleeding, got the French officer in his sights and shot him down. Mouton's men, well aware of their numerical inferiority, gave up the idea of advancing farther, but the Prussians weren't making any progress, either. General von Losthin was an experienced commander; nevertheless, considering the fact that he was sent into retirement three months after the battle, the way he led his brigade that day is open to question. In any case, one thing is certain: The Prussian attack in that sector stalled completely.

In Plancenoit, at least at first, things seemed to be going better. Colonel von Hiller, who commanded the Sixteenth Brigade, had his men advance in column, without the benefit of a strong line of skirmishers. (He had detached all of them to other parts of the field.) The Prussians moved past the first houses of the village, and there they clashed with the second of Mouton's two divisions, which had barely taken up positions in time. Despite the heavy losses inflicted on them by enemy snipers stationed in the houses, the Prussians fought their way to the village's central square, where the church and the cemetery were located. There they found themselves facing the Young Guard, which was hurrying in its turn to occupy Plancenoit. In the confused clash that followed, the Prussians were routed, and after trying without success to defend the last houses on the outskirts of the village, they were obliged to retreat all the way back to open country.

In a fury, Blücher rode among the men of the Sixteenth Brigade and tried to rally them. He personally explained to Colonel von Hiller that the Allied victory depended on the capture of Plancenoit and that his troops must therefore make another advance. While Hiller's Westphalians and Silesians reordered themselves a good distance from the village and prepared to go back on the attack, a courier arrived with a message from Wavre and delivered it to the field marshal. General von Thielemann, who had been left at Wavre with his corps to cover the Prussians' rear, reported that Grouchy was attacking him with a numerically superior force and asked for help. Blücher held an agitated consultation with his chief of staff. As the historian Peter Hofschröer later wrote, the Prussians' situation was anything but happy: "Blücher's main attack was faltering, his reinforcements were coming up too slowly, his ally's defences were showing signs of crumbling under the French assault, and now his line of retreat was in danger of being cut." The two Prussian generals knew they had no choice; at that moment, sending reinforcements to Thielemann was out of the question. "He won't get so much as a horse's tail," Blücher exclaimed. Gneisenau expressed this thought in more formal terms, but his response to the III Corps commander was chilling all the same: "You must contest every step the enemy takes, because even the heaviest losses sustained by your corps will be more than compensated for by a victory against Napoleon here."

FIFTY

---◆---

"I'LL BE DAMNED IF WE SHAN'T LOSE THIS GROUND"

While Mouton's men were taking up positions in Plancenoit and contesting the Prussian attack, the French cavalry continued charging the Allied squares. Despite mounting losses, which had caused several regiments to abandon the action already, pressure from the French had not diminished, because Napoleon had ordered his other reserve cavalry corps, commanded by Kellermann, to replace Milhaud's corps. Kellermann's corps had been heavily engaged at Quatre Bras, but its remaining dragoons, cuirassiers, and carabineers still amounted to 3,500 sabers. Guyot's Heavy Cavalry Division of the Imperial Guard was also sent into line and was soon participating in the charges. This division's two regiments, the Horse Grenadiers and the Empress's Dragoons, accounted for another 1,600 sabers between them. Even though each Guard regiment had detached one squadron to join the emperor's escort, the total number of French cavalry troopers engaged at one moment or another against the Allied squares that afternoon rose above 8,000.

In his memoirs, Napoleon maintained that Guyot allowed himself to be drawn into the combat without having received any explicit orders to attack the Allied squares. However, the cavalry of the Imperial Guard never went into battle without a direct order from either its commander or the emperor in person. At the Battle of Wagram in 1809, this inviolable practice aroused the ire of Marshal Macdonald, who came within a hair of accusing a Guard general of cowardice because he refused to charge without the requisite order from on high. On balance, therefore, Guyot's declaration—that in the late afternoon the emperor ordered him to put the troops of his division at the disposal of Marshal Ney, which was equivalent to authorizing their immediate employment in the charges—seems credible. Only later, reflecting on this and other aspects of the battle that commentators had most criticized, did Napoleon become convinced that his cavalry had been uselessly sacrificed, and his memory of what had happened was deliberately manipulated to dissociate the emperor's responsibility.

The infantry massed in the squares continued to stand fast, but their steadiness was waning. Ensign Gronow of the First Foot Guards later wrote, "Our squares presented a shocking sight. Inside we were nearly suffocated by the smoke and smell from burnt cartridges. It was impossible to move a yard without treading upon a wounded comrade, or upon the bodies of the dead; and the loud groans of the wounded and dying was most appalling. At four o'clock our square was a perfect hospital, being full of dead, dying, and mutilated soldiers." During one of the cuirassiers' charges, Wellington himself took refuge in a square. He was "accompanied only by one aide-de-camp; all the rest of his staff being either killed or wounded. Our Commander-in-Chief, as far as I could judge, appeared perfectly composed; but looked very thoughtful and pale."

Having seen the difficulty of breaking up the squares by brute force, the French riders deployed a new tactic: They approached at a walk, or at most a trot, and when they were ten or fifteen paces away, they fired their carbines. "But their fire produced little effect, as is generally the case with the fire of cavalry," Gronow commented. "Our men had orders not to fire unless they could do so on a near mass; the object being to economise our ammunition, and not to waste it on scattered soldiers. The result was that when the cavalry had discharged their carbines, and were still far off, we occasionally stood face to face looking at each other inactively not knowing what the next move might be."

Not far away, Captain Mercer's battery also came under attack from isolated cavalrymen armed with carbines. Mercer was so anxious to prevent his men from wasting ammunition on them that he began riding back and forth in front of the guns. A mounted grenadier deliberately took aim at him, fired, and missed. Mercer wagged a finger at him, signaling "No," and called him a scoundrel, loudly and in French. The man laughed and started to reload. "I certainly felt rather foolish at that moment," Mercer confessed, "but was ashamed, after such bravado, to let him see it, and therefore continued my promenade. As if to prolong my torment, he was a terrible time about it. To me it seemed an age. Whenever I turned, the muzzle of his infernal carbine still followed me. At length bang it went, and whiz came the ball close to the back of my neck, and at the same instant down dropped the leading driver of one of my guns (Miller), into whose forehead the cursed missile had penetrated."

For a large part of the day, Mercer's battery had remained in a relatively calm position, in reserve behind Hougoumont; but then Sir Augustus Frazer, commander of the horse artillery, came galloping up and ordered the captain to move his battery into the front line. "I rode with Frazer, whose face was as black as a chimney-sweep's from the smoke, and the jacket-sleeve of his right arm torn open by a musket-ball or case-shot, which had merely grazed his flesh." Frazer had Mercer take up a position just behind the sunken lane, between two squares of Brunswicker troops, informing him that enemy cavalry would charge him in a few minutes, and commanding him and his gunners to take refuge in the squares in such an eventuality.

"We breathed a new atmosphere," Mercer remarked. "The air was suffocatingly hot, resembling that issuing from an oven. We were enveloped in a thick smoke, and, *malgré* the incessant roar of cannon and musketry, could distinctly hear around us a mysterious humming noise, like that which one hears of a summer's evening proceeding from myriads of black beetles. . . . it seemed dangerous to extend the arm lest it should be torn off." Mercer's men had barely started unlimbering the guns and hauling them into their battery positions when the Imperial Guards' mounted grenadiers rode up the slope, apparently in their direction, "the two Infantry Squares at the same time commencing a feeble and desultory fire; for they were in such a state that I momentarily expected to see them disband. Their ranks, loose and disjointed, presented gaps of several file in breadth, which the Officers and Sergeants were busily employed filling up by pushing and even thumping their men together; whilst these, standing like so many logs, were apparently completely stupefied and bewildered. I should add that they were all perfect children. None of the privates, perhaps, were above 18 years of age."

The least experienced troops had clearly arrived at the limit of what they could stand, and a few squares actually began to break up. In the rare cases in which a French battery advanced far enough to stop firing blindly and start aiming at visible targets, the Allied losses became catastrophic. The most exposed of Kruse's three battalions—the 1/1st Nassau, which had been moved forward to a position in the front line, found itself the target of just this type of fire, coming from French guns that had advanced to within three to four hundred yards. The Nassauers could plainly see that the British batteries deployed in their front had been abandoned, and this made the enemy fire all the harder to bear. When a cuirassier squadron calmly rode up to a spot about a hundred yards away and halted there, waiting, almost daring the young recruits to fire on them, the Nassauers began to show signs of panic. Seeing their agitation, the cuirassiers charged, destroyed part of the square, and took many prisoners.

The French artillery fire also opened a gap in the ranks of the 3/1st Foot Guards. This gap was wide enough to allow two cuirassier officers to penetrate the square, shouting and brandishing their sabers. Had some of their men gone in behind them, they would have had a good chance of smashing the formation; but evidently the two officers had got too far in front of the rest of their squadron, or perhaps nobody had the courage to follow them. Urged on by their sergeants, the Foot Guards closed the gap, while their officers, in the center of the square, shot the two cuirassiers to death with their pistols. Hardly an inexperienced

German battalion, the Foot Guards were the most rigidly trained infantry that Wellington had in the field, and even these troops had a narrow escape. Gronow, fascinated, witnessed the entire scene, and he was so struck by it that he noted the names of the two officers who had liquidated the intruders, both of whom were killed in their turn before evening.

At several times British and German generals maneuvered the squares, trying to obstruct the movements of the cavalry and, if possible, to seize the initiative. Well-trained troops could advance in square, however slowly. Captain von Scriba's square had repulsed several attacks before being ordered by the Prince of Orange to advance against the enemy cavalry, which was lining up a short distance away and preparing to charge. Surprised by this unexpected move, the cavalry scattered under the fire of the square, and the Germans continued their advance. Almost at once, however, the French artillery and the *tirailleurs* stationed outside the wall of La Haye Sainte adjusted their fire, taking aim at the German square. For a few minutes, the officers tried to hold their position, but in the end, they realized that their men would be routed if they stayed there. The order was given to retreat, but not before Major von Schkopp, who commanded the square, was hit, along with several others. "Many of the soldiers on that flank were knocked down or wounded or killed, or were rendered momentarily numb with shock."

On the high ground behind Hougoumont, the British infantry's difficulties were multiplied by the *tirailleurs*, who advanced through the tall crops every time the cavalry charges provided a moment's respite. To counter this threat, the battalions of Adam's brigade were deployed in lines four deep, so that they could deliver a volume of fire with some effect when the enemy advanced too far. Even in this formation, however, the men grew more and more impatient, and every so often one of them abandoned his position, ran forward, and fired his musket at the enemy. General Adam was so infuriated by his men's indiscipline that he confronted them on horseback with his saber drawn, even going so far as to strike one of them on the head with the flat of his sword by way of persuading him to rejoin the ranks. Finally, Wellington ordered the brigade to move forward beyond the gun line and definitively drive off the French skirmishers, who were making life difficult for the artillery, too. "I'll be damned if we shan't lose this ground if we don't take care," said the duke to his secretary, Lord Fitzroy Somerset.

Captain Mercer was obliged to hold his battery's fire when Wellington, "with a serious air, and apparently much fatigued," rode past, right in front of Mercer's guns, and then the captain watched Adam's infantry ascend the slope behind him, reach the crest, and head down the other side, toward the enemy. Mercer noted how even so straightforward a maneuver was rendered laborious by the dreadful condition of the ground: "His Grace was soon followed by a line of Infantry, who ascending the slope with *ported* arms, ankle deep in a tenacious clay and struggling with the numerous obstacles encumbering the ground, presented but a loose and broken front, whilst the feeble hurrahs they sent forth showed how much they were out of breath with their exertions."

The advance of Adam's brigade was, on the whole, a good move; in case of a renewed cavalry attack, the enemy would have been unable to capture any guns. Furthermore, the ground in that sector descended rapidly, so the British gunners could have continued to fire over the heads of the infantrymen. Obviously, however, the position of Adam's men became still more dangerous. Private Lewis of the 2/95th Rifles watched apprehensively as his comrades fell with disagreeable frequency all around him. A shell fragment wounded the man in front of him; Lewis closed up, and his unit began to move, but before they had gone twenty paces a volley of flanking fire cleanly removed the nose of the man next to him. Shortly thereafter, a cannonball struck the man on Lewis's left, tearing off his arm just above the elbow; the injured soldier clutched Lewis, soaking his trousers with blood, before falling to the ground. Then Lewis's battalion was ordered to advance past the guns, only to find itself immediately charged by enemy cavalry.

These were the first charges that had assaulted Adam's battalions directly, and the British officers and their men, like others before them that afternoon, were relieved to discover that cuirassiers were not, after all, as great a threat as they seemed. Ensign Leeke watched them advance: "They came on in very gallant style and in very steady order, first of all at the trot, then at a gallop, till they were within forty or fifty yards of the front face of the square, when, one or two horses having been brought down, in clearing the obstacle they got a somewhat new direction, which carried them to either flank of the face of the square, which direction they one and all preferred to the charging home and riding on to our bayonets." Writing a letter home a few days later, Private Lewis boasted that the cuirassiers of "Boney's Imperial Guard," with all their gleaming armor, had charged his battalion only to discover that they could do nothing against it.

In addition, Lewis's account confirmed that the cuirassier's new tactic of employing their short carbines had, in fact, some effect. "They fire on us with their carbines, then immediately do an about-turn while a comrade at my side collapses with a bullet full in the stomach and blood coming out of him as from a stuck pig. He barely had time to say, 'Lewis, I'm done for!' before he died. We continued firing at the Imperial Guard as they withdrew, and while I was reloading my rifle a ball struck it just above my left hand, breaking the ramrod and bending the barrel so much that I couldn't ram the cartridge down anymore." Perhaps Private Lewis added a little color to his narrative in order to impress the relatives he was writing to, but surely the confused succession of charges and firefights was proving destructive to the squares no less than to the squadrons attacking them.

FIFTY-ONE

---•◆•---

THE NIVELLES ROAD

T he only attempt the French cavalry did not make was the one that Wellington most feared: to outflank his right wing west of Hougoumont, where the high ground defended by the Allied infantry descended rather steeply into a valley traversed by the Nivelles road. In that sector, the lancers and *chasseurs à cheval* attached to Piré's division remained in sight all day long, their long lances visible over the tops of the tall grain; every now and then, they advanced as though they were going to attack, but the intention of this maneuver was only to draw the fire of the enemy batteries and, if possible, to keep a few regiments of British cavalry busy on that end of the field, their attention distracted from more important sectors. Although Piré's men intervened occasionally to rescue some *tirailleur* squads from difficulties, the division as a whole held its position and never advanced. Thus in that part of the battlefield, much of the day was spent in an uninterrupted succession of skirmishes, in which neither side achieved any sort of decisive result.

Among the eyewitness accounts of the battle, those left by soldiers in the regiments stationed along the Nivelles road stand in sharp contrast to the rest. These sources do not seem to be describing a great battle, but rather a combat of outposts, or sometimes a guerrilla action. Sergeant Wheeler of the Fifty-first Light Infantry was posted with two men "behind a rock or large stone, well studded with brambles. This was somewhat to our right and in advance. About an hour after we were posted we saw an officer of Huzzars sneaking down to get a peep at our position. One of my men was what we term a dead shot, when he was within point-blank distance. I asked him if he could make sure of him. His reply was 'To be sure I can, but let him come nearer if he will, at all events his death warrant is signed and in my hands, if he should turn back.'" When the French officer was close enough, a single shot killed him, "and in a minute we had his body with the horse in our possession behind the rock. We had a rich booty, forty double Napoleons and had just time to strip the lace of the clothing of the dead Huzzar when we were called in to join the skirmishers."

Although the troops stationed in this sector took insignificant casualties in comparison with those engaged in other parts of the field, this war of ambushes and surprises was nonetheless fought ruthlessly. The British Hussars of the Seventh stayed in their saddles for a long time in an area where they apparently ran little risk; one sergeant was even accompanied by his wife, who was mounted on a pony. Suddenly, however, Hussars started falling, but no one could tell where the shots were coming from. The sergeant's wife got scared, and her husband began rudely insulting her; finally, a disgusted officer ordered him to send her to the rear. In the end, someone noticed that the irregular fire was coming from a field of rye, taller than a man, not far away on their left. A Hussar squadron rode into the field, surprised a group of *tirailleurs*, and hacked them to death with their sabers.

The most famous episode from this sector of the battlefield involved a cuirassier squadron that charged into the Allied squares and then tried to return to their own lines by retreating along the Nivelles road, only to find it blocked by a barricade of felled trees, and behind them a company of the Fifty-first. Sergeant Wheeler was there, and he left a graphic account of what happened: "There were nearly a hundred of them, all Cuirassiers. Down they rode full gallop, the trees thrown across the bridge on our left stopped them. We saw them comming and was prepared, we opened our fire, the work was done in an instant. By the time we had loaded and the smoke had cleared away, one and only one, solitary individual was seen running over the brow in our front. One other was saved by Capt. Jno. Ross from being put to death by some of the Brunswickers. I went to see what effect our fire had, and never before beheld such a sight in as short a space, as about an hundred men and horses could be huddled together, there they lay. Those who were shot dead were fortunate for the wounded horses in their struggles by plunging and kicking soon finished what we had began. In examining the men we could not find one that would be like to recover, and as we had other business to attend to we were obliged to leave them to their fate."

This incident made such an impression that no fewer than five witnesses recalled it spontaneously many years later, all but one of them insisting that the cuirassiers had been totally destroyed. The only man to provide a different version was Captain John Ross himself, the commander of the company stationed at the barricade. According to the captain, the cuirassiers—about seventy in all— had broken into one of the squares and there surrendered; then, however, finding themselves under the weak escort of a few light dragoons, the French had decided to tempt fate and tried to escape along the Nivelles road. Alerted to their approach by the irregular fire that accompanied their passage, Captain Ross posted his men behind the barricade and opened fire on the French when they arrived. The officer commanding the cuirassiers, realizing that the British dragoons were in close pursuit, preferred not to fall back into their hands and offered Captain Ross his sword. "There were twelve horses and eight Cuirassiers killed on this occasion, and the remainder, about sixty, were dismounted, taken, or dispersed," the captain concluded. The discrepancy between his numbers and those of Sergeant Wheeler is emblematic of the uncertainties involved in trusting the memories of the people who were there.

FIFTY-TWO

---•◆•---

"INFANTRY! AND WHERE DO YOU EXPECT ME TO FIND INFANTRY?"

Although weakened, the Allied cavalry deployed in support behind the squares kept trying to coordinate their own actions with those of the infantry and make the French squadrons pay a heavy price for their attacks. A Hanoverian officer had the impression that the enemy cavalry were deliberately drawn to within musket range by the feigned attacks of the British cavalry, and he observed that in the long run these maneuvers wore down the cuirassiers, who continued to attack but with steadily decreasing élan. Major von Goeben of the Third KGL Hussars also noticed that the enemy's desire to advance started to diminish after a while. Repeatedly, some squadrons of the Imperial Guard's *chasseurs à cheval* rode up to within three or four hundred paces of his regiment, which had been reduced to some eighty men. "Their officers were wearing tall, broad bearskin hats, and on several occasions some of them rode up to us, challenging the officers of our regiment to single combat. As they were much stronger, the regiment could not accept the honor, and the enemy cavalry accomplished nothing other than to offer their big bearskin hats as targets to some of the sharpshooters in this Hanoverian Field Battalion."

In theory, the Imperial Guard's famous Red Lancers, armed as they were with their long weapons, should have been able to drive their attacks into the enemy ranks, as indeed they tried to do; but in reality the squares had so many bayonets confronting each rider that it was simply impossible to urge the horses close to them. Captain de Brack, a squadron commander, saw some of his exasperated lancers rise in their stirrups and hurl their lances like javelins at the enemy. The

Red Lancers charged, among others, a Brunswicker square, but even in this case they were unable to get close enough to do much harm. As soon as the charge was repulsed, two of the German foot soldiers stepped out of formation and ran over to a French officer who was trapped under his fallen horse. They cleaned out his pockets and then shot him in the head with his own pistol amid shouts of "Shame! Shame" from nearby British troops.

In time, there were so many dead or dying men and—above all—horses around the squares that advancing past them was becoming physically difficult. The centers of the squares were also filled with wounded and dying soldiers, and because the enemy cavalry continued roving in the vicinity, the infantry could not send wounded officers to the rear, as was the custom in the British army. As for wounded enlisted men, no one even tried to evacuate them from the squares. The cavalry, however, paid an even higher price: The fire from the squares, though slow, irregular, and inefficient, began to tell in the long run. Gronow declared that he would never forget the strange sound—like "the noise of a violent hailstorm beating upon panes of glass"—that his guardsmen's musket balls made as they struck the enemy's cuirasses; he added that the cavalry charges, which the men had so feared at first, eventually became a relief, because when the cavalry advanced, the enemy artillery was obliged to stop firing.

Others make the same observation. The Royal Engineers officer who took refuge in a square quickly realized that the cavalry's horses would not dare to come into contact with the bayonets: "Now and then an individual more daring than the rest would ride up to the bayonets, wave his sword about and bully; but the mass held aloof, pulling up within five or six yards, as if, though afraid to go on, they were ashamed to retire. Our men soon discovered they had the best of it, and ever afterwards, when they heard the sound of cavalry approaching, appeared to consider the circumstance a pleasant change (from being cannonaded)!" Reynell, commander of the Seventy-first—whose position a short distance from the Hougoumont hedge was the farthest advanced of any regiment in Adam's brigade—wrote of "repeated *visits* from [the enemy's] Cuirassiers. I do not say *attacks*, because these Cavalry Columns on no occasion attempted to penetrate our Square, limiting their approach to within ten or fifteen yards of the front face, when they would wheel about, receiving such fire as we could bring to bear upon them, and as they retired, *en passant*, that from the neighbouring Square." Macready of the Thirtieth observed that his men "began to pity the useless perseverance of their assailants, and, as they advanced, would growl out, 'here come those d———d fools again.'"

In the late afternoon, as the sun was slowly starting to sink toward the horizon, the morale of the troops standing in the squares began to rise again. By contrast French cavalry officers, despite the fearlessness to which every enemy/Allied account of the battle paid tribute, were having more and more trouble gathering their men, whose numbers were steadily declining, and leading them in yet another advance. "In the midst of our terrible fire," Gronow later recalled, "their officers were seen as if on parade, keeping order in their ranks, and encouraging them. Unable to renew the charge, but unwilling to retreat, they brandished their swords with loud cries of 'Vive l'Empereur!'" The initial period of equilibrium had passed, and the number of those who sensed this shift grew steadily.

The British artillery had played a role in wearing down the cavalry's striking power, but less than has been generally supposed. One factor is found in Sir Augustus Frazer's description of the problems with the British guns, "which, by recoiling, had retired so as to lose their original and just position. But in a deep stiff soil, the fatigue of the horse artillerymen was great, and their best exertions were unable to move the guns again to the crest without horses; to employ horses was to ensure the loss of the animals." Thus the guns in many batteries were no longer on the crest of the ridge, as they had been in the beginning; many must have slid back down the reverse slope, from which they were no longer able to fire on the cavalry as it fell back.

More significantly, and contrary to the romanticized image of valiant British gunners returning to their weapons between one charge and the next and blasting away at the retreating enemy, the cavalry charges penetrated so far behind the Allied lines that disorganization and panic spread among the gunners. Wellington explicitly stated that many of them, having once abandoned their posts and reached safety, never returned to their guns until the end of the battle. According to Tom Morris, in at least one case exactly the opposite happened: When some French cavalry overran a battery posted within a few dozen meters of the squares, artillerymen rode with them, turned one of the guns around, and fired it point-blank at the enemy. Several loads of case-shot, colloquially known as "grapeshot," opened broad gaps in the ranks of the Seventy-third, and one demonstration of the steadiness of the British infantry is the fact that after every shot the men closed up their ranks, drawing their wounded into the center of the square and throwing their dead outside it, without allowing the French cavalry to exploit their temporary advantage.

Major Lloyd's battery, which had been stationed in front of Halkett's squares since morning, was one of the few whose gunners did indeed return to their weapons in the intervals between one charge and the other and fire case-shot into the rear of the enemy cavalry as they retreated in disorder down the slope. One of Lloyd's subordinates recalled, "In general, a Squadron or two came up the slope on our immediate front, and on their moving off at the appearance of our Cavalry, we took advantage to send destruction after them, and when advancing on our fire I have seen four or five men and horses piled upon each other like cards, the men not having even been displaced from the saddle, the effect of canister." And yet on at least one occasion the battery commander, seeing that the enemy cavalry was in retreat, rode back to the guns only to discover that none of his gunners had followed him. Lloyd dismounted, determined that the cannons were all loaded—a measure of how precipitously the gunners had abandoned them—and fired one of the guns himself, then another; at last, unable to do anything else, he mounted his horse once more and returned to where he had left his men.

The battery that inflicted the most damage on the French cavalry was the only one whose gunners, contrary to orders, remained with their weapons throughout the struggle instead of taking refuge in a nearby square. Captain Mercer had so little confidence in the young German recruits formed up in the squares closest to him ("the young sourkrout-squares") that he decided not to send his gunners to shelter in their midst. "To have sought refuge amongst men in such a state were madness—the very moment our men ran from their guns, I was convinced, would be the signal for their disbanding." Had Mercer's battery been posted on the forward slope, such a decision would have been impossible; but his guns were farther back, right in line with the squares, and protected by the high bank of the sunken road. The captain ordered his men to prime their pieces with double loads of shot and grapeshot, and they repulsed several charges of the Imperial Guard's *grenadiers à cheval*; eventually, there were so many dead horses in front of Mercer's guns that the enemy cavalry, even if they still wanted to, could no longer reach his position.

In two hours of incessant charging, the French cavalry regiments lost so many men and horses that their value as a striking force was gone. The twenty regiments that took part in the charges were led by a total of slightly more than 500 officers; of these, some 50-odd were killed at Waterloo, and about 250 were wounded, including one of two corps commanders, five of six division commanders, ten of twelve brigade commanders, and eleven of twenty colonels. In Napoleon's cavalry, senior officers commanded from the saddle, led all charges, saber in hand, and paid the same price as their men. To these human losses, which exceeded 50 percent, were added the even greater losses in horses. It seems reasonable, therefore, to conclude that by six in the evening no more than a quarter of the troopers from the Imperial Guard cavalry divisions and from the corps commanded by Milhaud and Kellermann were still mounted on their horses and capable of wielding their sabers—a level of loss that would have destroyed the cohesiveness and morale of any unit whatsoever, including the most battle-hardened, rendering it effectively useless.

Given the final result of the battle, the protracted action against the Allied infantry squares must surely be considered a fatal error that consumed Napoleon's powerful cavalry without achieving any concrete result. There is no doubt that the emperor had only an imperfect idea of the nature of Wellington's deployment, and that Marshal Ney and his generals continued to attack without ever questioning whether what they were doing had any genuine probability of success. But the real blunder lay in the failure of the French to engage the Imperial Guard infantry in support of the cavalry. In his memoirs, Napoleon maintained that this was in fact his intention, but that the cavalry attacked too soon, before the infantry could support it. Taking account of the emperor's habitually guarded and ambiguous language, this statement probably indicates that Napoleon, at the moment when he should have decided to send in his reserves, hesitated and ultimately refrained from doing so. In the culminating stages of the cavalry attacks, Ney sent a message to the emperor, asking for some infantry support, and Napoleon sent back a famous reply: "Infantry! And where do you expect me to find infantry? Do you want me to manufacture some?"

The Middle Guard and the Old Guard were in fact still available to the emperor at that moment; but with the Prussians threatening his flank, the doubts that had thus far stopped him from engaging his reserves had become still more persuasive. He could not have been certain that the forces he had detached to protect his right would be enough to stop the Prussian advance, and Napoleon could not afford to leave himself without reserves to face Bülow's attack, should the Prussian general's troops overrun Plancenoit and threaten to cut the main road behind La Belle Alliance. In addition, the Allied garrisons in Hougoumont and La Haye Sainte were still putting up resistance, and the emperor was even less disposed than before to send his last reserves into the abyss between those two strongholds; the capture of one or the other was an indispensable condition for his signaling the final advance. By this time, barely enough fresh troops for one last offensive thrust remained to Napoleon, and he had to make that thrust at the proper moment. On that sweltering afternoon, exhausted like everyone else from the effects of a virtually sleepless night and the enervating tensions of the day, and accustomed to believing that the Old Guard should be engaged only in the final stages of a battle, Napoleon hesitated. In the end he decided to wait, perhaps already feeling the uneasiness, the growing disquiet that would lead him before many days passed to convince himself that the cavalry attacks had been launched too soon, and that it was all Ney's fault if the premature maneuver had been executed without success.

FIFTY-THREE

THE LAST EFFORT TO TAKE HOUGOUMONT

T hough the multiple charges of the French cavalry failed to accomplish their goal of achieving a breakthrough in the center of the Allied line, they had a further purpose, which has not always received sufficient emphasis. The charges were also intended to maintain the pressure that the infantry troops of Reille and d'Erlon were putting on Hougoumont and La Haye Sainte. To Napoleon, this pressure was destined, sooner or later, to provide the turning point in the battle by opening up enough space for him to launch his final attack. The cavalry therefore made a significant contribution to the emperor's purpose, not only by nailing the entirety of Wellington's troops to their positions and preventing any movement of his reserves, but also by coordinating their own action with the infantry's, both in the area of Hougoumont, where the French offensive was ultimately defeated, and at La Haye Sainte, where, around six o'clock in the evening, it finally attained success.

The attack against Hougoumont had been sustained by the *tirailleurs* of Prince Jérome's division, and then by those of General Foy, all afternoon long. These two commanders have been accused of prolonging a hopeless attack, thus wasting their troops without any positive result, and of acting without specific orders. In reality, Napoleon could see perfectly well what was happening at Hougoumont, just as Foy, with the aid of a spyglass, could see him so clearly that he could distinguish his every gesture. ("I saw him walking back and forth, wearing his gray overcoat, and often bending down to the little table where the map was spread out.") The prosecution of the assault on Hougoumont was an integral part of Napoleon's strategy, and that afternoon the emperor in person sent a specific order to the generals charged with conducting the attacks: Even if they had not yet used their artillery against the château because it was almost invisible amid the thick vegetation, they were to assemble their howitzers and fire incendiary shells at the buildings so as to set them on fire.

Having received the emperor's order, Reille transmitted it to his battery commanders, who opened fire on the château with such precision that a fire began to burn inside Hougoumont almost immediately, starting first in a pile of straw in the yard, then spreading to the barn roof and from there to the roof of the main house. The garrison had to detach more and more men in an attempt to contain the blaze and save the wounded; a number, however, were burned alive, along with the officers' horses, which were being kept in the barn. Seeing the flames rising from the château, Wellington hurriedly wrote an order to the commanding officer of the garrison, whose name he did not know, notifying him that he had to hold his position at whatever cost; he was to evacuate burning structures, but as soon as their roofs fell in, his men were to reoccupy the ruins. Little by little, the soldiers abandoned the most threatened buildings, returning as soon as the fire finished consuming them; within a short time, almost the whole château was reduced to a charred ruin, above which hung an immense cloud of black smoke. Only the chapel was spared by the blaze, a fact that did not fail to impress the soldiers, since it seemed that the crucifix hanging above the entrance had kept the flames at bay.

Along the walls of the château and in the orchard, which was by then razed to the ground, the French infantry continued to close in. Several times, the defenders had to evacuate the orchard and take shelter in the nearby hollow way, but the sustained fusillade from the garden wall again and again prevented the enemy from advancing. When fire began to consume the buildings, Foy's grenadiers moved forward once more, and under cover of flames and smoke they managed to penetrate into the farmyard through a small side door. Firing from the windows of the main house, the defenders held the French in check until the Guards Division could mount a counterattack and drive off the invaders. The woodland and the pastures attached to Hougoumont were all so thoroughly in French hands that their artillery batteries had advanced all the way to the hedges, and the French guns, posted just a few hundred yards away from their targets, were holding the Allied squares under fire on the high ground behind the château.

The charges of the cuirassiers carried them deep into the Allied lines and caused disorder even in the rear of Wellington's position. Along the road to Braine l'Alleud, several hundred yards beyond Hougoumont, Du Plat's brigade was still deployed in reserve, occupying the same positions it had held since morning, when, he reported, "there appeared suddenly on our left flank a regiment of enemy cavalry." The cavalry attacked a British square deployed a little to Du Plat's left; the French were repulsed, but the German officers could not help concluding from this action that "the enemy appeared to be getting the upper hand." If the

French, by dint of gaining ground, had succeeded in isolating the perimeter of Hougoumont, the defense would have been pushed dangerously close to collapse, as it would no longer have been possible to send companiès of skirmishers and carts of ammunition into the château to sustain the defenders' fire. For precisely this reason, Colonel Du Plat received orders to move his troops as far forward as possible, that is, as far as the hollow way, which had become the garrison's vital artery. Lieutenant Hesse of the Second KGL had been relieved to see the cuirassiers falling back, but "soon after that an adjutant rode along the front and shouted 'advance if you please!'"

Du Plat's four battalions literally had to fight their way to their new positions close to the hedgerows of Hougoumont. Still in column, the battalions had almost reached the chemin d'Ohain and were mounting the slope when, Hesse reported, "a column of enemy cuirassiers surprised us." The four light companies, which had been detached from the battalions and were hastening ahead to enter the grounds of the château, were attacked in their turn. "We still had plenty of ammunition and produced an almighty fire aimed at the cavalry, whereupon the same turned around." Resuming their advance, the Germans had barely arrived at the top of the slope when a regiment of cavalry in rapid retreat passed through their ranks at a gallop, pursued by French cavalry. Captain Sympher, commander of a KGL horse artillery battery that was accompanying the brigade's advance, "made a few lucky shots causing gaps so that the cavalry turned back." When they finally drew close to the château, Du Plat's men found themselves confronting Foy's *tirailleurs*, who were stationed behind the enclosure; but the Germans were forced to remain in square in order to fight off the cuirassiers, who continued to make threatening advances. As soon as the cavalry withdrew, the French skirmishers behind the hedge subjected the legionaries to a deadly accurate fire.

The accounts left by Du Plat's officers provide poignant testimony to the largely unsung ordeal of the German veterans, who were worn down by slow attrition during the course of the afternoon, all the while holding their positions and preventing the enemy from reaching the hollow way and isolating the defenders of Hougoumont. Their tenacity is all the more worthy of note in that they fought within a blinding cloud of smoke, in irregular formations that one of their officers described as "disbanded battalion squares," and without any orders from above, because "the Brigadier was already killed and each battalion had to help itself." Colonel Du Plat had been mortally wounded in the beginning of this confused and bloody action, and Captain Cordemann of the Third KGL confirmed that the combat was conducted without any superior officer's direction, "partly because it was not audible as a result of the uninterrupted thunder of the cannon and various other noises, making it incomprehensible, and partly because the battalion often did not know who the actual commanding officer was. The captains made every effort under these circumstances to inform the people of dangers and of enemy attacks, and to maintain order." When enemy cavalry prepared to charge, "we reminded the people again how they were to comport themselves: thereupon, the soldiers on their own loaded a second round and fired on the charging enemy at about 50–60 paces, independently, like hunters, so effectively that the same retreated with great loss." On the whole the men of the King's German Legion held their positions, preventing the enemy infantry from gaining ground and repulsing one cavalry charge after another; but after a while the legionaries' numbers were so diminished that two of their battalions had to be combined to form a single square, and all of the KGL officers' horses had been shot down by the *tirailleurs*.

Despite this support, there were moments when enemy pressure became so intense—the rear entrance to the château was among the favored targets—that the garrison inside Hougoumont was in serious danger of being cut off. The indefatigable Captain Seymour was charged with finding some ammunition and getting it hauled into the courtyard at Hougoumont, where the defenders' cartridge supply was starting to run low. Having encountered a soldier from the ammunition train driving a full munitions wagon, Seymour explained to him what he needed; the man whipped his horses and descended straight down the hill toward Hougoumont's front gate. He became the target of a fire so heavy that Seymour could not but admire his courage, though the captain thought there was little chance that the man's horses would get to the château alive; nevertheless, the wagon reached the gate, and the defenders received the ammunition they so desperately needed.

In the Hougoumont sector, the French charges, mostly carried out by the Imperial Guard cavalry, were regularly coordinated with the action of the infantry troops occupying the pastures and part of the orchard. At first, the British cavalry enthusiastically rushed into a countercharge, hoping to hurl back the pointed thrusts of the enemy; but they paid a heavy price for their zeal. More than once the troops of a British regiment, descending the slope at a trot, unexpectedly found themselves under fire from the *tirailleurs* hidden in the tall grain and were obliged to return in great haste to their starting positions in order to avoid being trapped and cut off by the enemy closing in behind them; in other instances, the retreating French cavalry drew their pursuers into range of Reille's infantry squares, with consequences invariably disastrous for the British. Lieutenant Lane of the Fifteenth Hussars described how two squadrons of his regiment charged the *grenadiers à cheval* of the Imperial Guard, who, however, refused the combat. "Our next attack (in line without reserve) was [on] a square of French Infantry, and our horses were within a few feet of the Square. We did not succeed in breaking it, and, of course, suffered most severely. At the close of the Battle, the two Squadrons were dreadfully cut up."

Soon after, General Adam was ordered to send his regiments forward to relieve Du Plat's exhausted battalions. Their positions—near the northeast corner of the Hougoumont orchard—were taken by a Scottish light infantry regiment, the Seventy-first, formed in square and supported by two companies of the 3/95th Rifles. A thick line of gray-coated French skirmishers suddenly appeared out of the smoke right in front of the Scots. The French, too, were caught by surprise, but they opened fire on the Seventy-first at once; rather than respond to the enemy fire, the Scottish veterans coolly began to maneuver, redeploying into line. An officer of the Rifles observed, "the French and 71st were closer than I ever before saw any regular formed adverse bodies, and much nearer than troops usually engage."

Seeing that the British infantry was in square in a very advanced position on the flank of Hougoumont, Reille had decided to attack in force. He employed for this purpose not only Foy's division but also Bachelu's, the last of his three divisions, which added three thousand muskets to the attack. Though these troops had spent the day until then in formation with their weapons on their shoulders ("Rumor had it that we had been forgotten," said Major Trefcon, the division chief of staff), Bachelu's men had suffered such terrible losses two days earlier at Quatre Bras, and this day had remained so long under enemy artillery fire, that their offensive spirit had been extinguished. For a moment, it seemed as though the French infantry, advancing in column behind a thick screen of *tirailleurs*, would succeed in coming into physical contact with the enemy; as they were moving into musket range, Foy, who was one of the most popular generals in the French army, clapped his adjutant, Major Lemonnier-Delafosse, on the back and said, "Tomorrow you'll be in Brussels, and promoted colonel by the Emperor!"

But Adam's brigade contained 2,500 men, all light infantry, a third of them armed with Baker rifles, and they quickly redeployed into the four-deep line formation adopted everywhere on the field that day by the British infantry; their fire—aided by that of the guns posted behind them—stopped the French attack at once. A shell fragment wounded General Bachelu in the head and killed his horse, and another fragment from the same shell wounded General Campi, the commander of one of Bachelu's brigades. General Foy took a bullet in the shoulder while trying to stop his men from running away, and shortly thereafter, the attackers returned in haste to the low-lying ground from which they had set out. Major Lemonnier-Delafosse had fallen from a fatally wounded horse; as he rose to his feet, he saw half a loaf of bread attached to a dead soldier's knapsack: "I seized the bread and devoured it. 'Devoured' is the right word; for two days I had nourished myself on nothing but beer."

Hardly had the French infantry disappeared back into the smoke when the Scotsmen of the Seventy-first saw cavalry bearing down upon them; they barely managed to form square in time, and General Adam himself was obliged to take refuge in their midst. After the cavalry, impotent against a square, beat a retreat, the Scots officers realized that the enemy *tirailleurs* were still stationed in the vicinity and had the Seventy-first under fire. The regiment accomplished a miracle: It advanced in line, driving the enemy before it, sent its skirmishers forward to occupy part of the orchard, and then quickly formed square again as soon as the enemy cavalry showed itself. Less experienced soldiers—the Brunswickers, for example—would never have been able to maneuver like this, in the face of the enemy and under fire; the troops of the Seventy-first, a veteran light infantry regiment, completed the maneuver and stood firm. Due in large part to this regiment's steadfastness, the French, despite the incessant charges of the Guard cavalry and the repeated attempts of Reille's infantry, never succeeded in isolating the perimeter of Hougoumont. More or less at this point in the struggle, General Adam heard Wellington mutter, almost to himself, "I believe we shall beat them after all."

This was not the only case in which the British infantry showed itself capable of changing coolly from line into square and of advancing or retreating as needed, still keeping square. Lord Saltoun, who had returned to the high ground with the survivors of his light company, watched the 3/1st Foot Guards maneuver to escape the combined action of the cavalry and the *tirailleurs*. "During the Cavalry attacks on the centre a great number of the Enemy's sharpshooters had crept up the slope of the hill, and galled the 3rd Battalion, who were in square, very severely. . . .The Third Battalion, who suffered severely from this fire, wheeled up into line and drove them down the hill and advanced to a point . . . and there re-formed square."

Historians have often stated, that the French attack against Hougoumont was a gigantic waste, in which a small number of defenders kept engaged and eventually defeated an immensely superior enemy host. However, from Napoleon's point of view, the offensive against the perimeter wall of the Hougoumont château represented only one aspect of a much broader maneuver, whose objective was to drive in Wellington's entire right wing, and the duke, knowing what was at stake, responded in kind. While the Hougoumont defenders never had, at any given moment, more than two thousand muskets within the perimeter of the château, the total number of soldiers in all the battalions that were committed to this action was much higher. Early in the day, the position was defended by Major von Büsgen's 1/2nd Nassau, reinforced by a few companies of Hanoverian *Jäger*; almost immediately, the Germans were joined by the two Guards battalions of Sir John Byng's brigade; during the course of the action, Du Plat's brigade and the Brunswick light infantry brigade sent all their companies into the château; and at the end of the day, these troops were in such bad shape that Wellington found it necessary to reinforce them with the last reserve he had available in that sector, the Hanoverian *Landwehr* brigade commanded by Colonel Hew Halkett, Sir Colin Halkett's brother. Since this officer outranked the various lieutenant-colonels of the Guards Division who were present at the scene, he assumed command of the château late in the afternoon, posting a battalion in the orchard, two in the hollow way, and one outside the grounds but near the wall.

Reille's corps exerted pressure not only on the troops inside the perimeter of the château but also on all the Allied infantry deployed in that sector, keeping them constantly engaged until the very last phase of the battle. Clearly, the disproportion of the forces involved in the struggle for Hougoumont is nothing but a legend of historiography. In the course of the day, the French employed the three divisions of II Corps in this sector, for a total of thirty-three battalions and some fourteen thousand muskets. Against them, Wellington committed the brigades of Byng, Du Plat, Adam, and Hew Halkett, five Brunswick battalions, one from Nassau, three companies of Hanoverian *Jäger*, and two companies from Maitland's brigade, amounting to twenty-one battalions—six British and fifteen German—and a total of twelve thousand muskets. Moreover, during the afternoon various artillery batteries that were in action around La Haye Sainte, including those of Rogers and Sinclair, were ordered to redeploy in the Hougoumont sector, a sign that the château continued to be of such concern to Wellington that for its sake he weakened his center, not without unfortunate consequences. Therefore, the downside for Napoleon did not consist in the fact that Hougoumont had kept a disproportionately high number of his troops engaged against a paltry enemy force, but rather in the fact that the château, in the end, did not fall.

The buildings were the key, and there the garrison stood firm, even though at certain moments they felt isolated and almost abandoned. At one point, Lieutenant Colonel Hepburn, who was inside the château, found himself commanding Byng's entire brigade, the general having been obliged to take over command of the Guards Division after General Cooke was wounded. Nevertheless, Hepburn later admitted, "I knew nothing of what was passing elsewhere." According to Major von Büsgen, who commanded the Nassauers, "Neither when I was detached to Hougoumont, nor during the combat, did anyone tell me from whom I was supposed to take orders. Given the intensity of the fighting and the limited field of vision, which was obstructed by trees, hedges, and walls, I was unable to see anything that was happening beyond them." But in the midst of the smoking ruins, among heaps of charred rubble where the ground underfoot was still burning hot, in the boggy mud of the hollow way, and amid the disfigured remains of the orchard's apple trees, the defenders of the château stood fast to the end, while along the south wall every attempt on the part of the *tirailleurs* to penetrate the enclosure resulted in fresh piles of corpses. Napoleon's final attack would not pass through Hougoumont.

FIFTY-FOUR

———•◦•———

THE CAPTURE OF
LA HAYE SAINTE

The success the emperor needed to continue his offensive came on the other side of the battlefield. While Reille's skirmishers were being held in check before the walls of Hougoumont, d'Erlon's finally succeeded in capturing La Haye Sainte. Hougoumont was a much more substantial complex, and even after a significant portion of the buildings burned down, it could still shelter a garrison of two thousand soldiers; within the perimeter of La Haye Sainte, Major von Baring did not have and perhaps could not have had more than a few hundred.

Moreover, Wellington had massed his men in such numbers behind Hougoumont that the French cavalry charges never were able to cut off the garrison from the bulk of the Allied army, even though the château was far from the duke's main line; all afternoon, reinforcements and ammunition carts continued to enter the farmyard through the north gate. By contrast, behind La Haye Sainte, where the bombardment of the Grande Batterie was most intense, Wellington's line had grown so thin that the combined pressure of the cavalry charges and the swarm of skirmishers sent forward by Donzelot continually brought the garrison to the verge of isolation. As long as the Allied cavalry conserved enough forces to be able to launch occasional countercharges, the situation remained fairly fluid, and the German battalions of Ompteda and Kielmansegge carried out counterattacks from time to time, sending reinforcements into the farm. But as the interventions of the Allied cavalry grew less frequent, Ompteda's and Kielmansegge's troops were reduced to playing a purely passive role, formed in square on the ridge behind La Haye Sainte and trying to stand fast. From the late afternoon on, Baring and his men, besieged inside La Haye Sainte, received no more orders or reinforcements; the Baker rifle ammunition, which the major had most insistently requested, never came.

Left: Marshal Ney.

Below: French cuirassiers charging a Highlanders' square. *Painting by Félix Philippoteaux, 1874.*

Left: Colonel von Ompteda.

Below: Nassauers defending their position at La Belle Alliance. *Painting by R. Knotel.*

Above: Blücher orders his men to attack Plancenoit. *Painting by Adolf Northern.*

Below: An officer of the mounted chasseurs of the Imperial Guard. *Painting by Gericault.*

Above: Napoleon, viewing the attack on his Imperial Guards through a spyglass. *Painting by James Atkinson.*

Below: Colonel Hew Halkett captures the French general Cambronne. *Painting by R. Knotel.*

Above: "No cheering, my lads, but forward, and complete your victory!" Wellington signals the general advance on Waterloo. *Painting by James Atkinson.*

Right: The Earl of Uxbridge, commander of the Allied cavalry. He lost his leg at Waterloo when it was shattered by a piece of shot that narrowly missed Wellington. *Painting by Peter Edward Stroehling, c. 1816*

Below: The surgeon's saw used to amputate Lord Uxbridge's leg.

Left: The famous meeting between Wellington and Blücher, depicted here in front of the inn at La Belle Alliance.

Below: General von Gneisenau.

Below: Napoleon among his men as he faces defeat. His carriage awaits his flight. *Painting by Ernest Crofts.*

Above: Napoleon Bonaparte burning the eagles and standards of his Imperial Guard after the battle.

Above: A burial party at work near La Belle Alliance, seven days after the battle. *Engraving by E. Walsh, drawn on the spot.*

Below: British soldiers removing French cannons, July 1815.

Baring was reflecting on this state of affairs, which to him seemed inexplicable—given that he had already sent three officers, one by one, to renew the request—when he perceived that the French outside the farm, exasperated by the defenders' resistance, had finally decided to resort to the method already used by their comrades at Hougoumont: They were setting the place on fire. The barn, which was the most exposed of the buildings, started burning at once and disappeared from sight in a cloud of dense black smoke. Fortunately, La Haye Sainte was well supplied with water, and the defenders, using the field kettles that formed part of the Nassauers' gear, managed to put out the blaze; but the barn, whose door had been missing from the start, became harder and harder to defend, despite the tenacity of the Germans. Baring saw Private Lindau, his head swathed in a bloody bandage, take shelter behind the small back door of the barn and from there keep the main entrance under fire, preventing the French from bursting in. The major's admiration was all the greater because he knew the man had in his pocket a bag stuffed with gold coins looted from a French officer who had been struck from his horse shortly before, and thus Lindau was risking not only his skin but his booty. Struck by so much selflessness, and seeing that the soldier's bandage was not stopping his bleeding, the major ordered him to leave his position and have his wound seen to, but Lindau refused to go, muttering, "He would be a scoundrel that deserted you, so long as his head is on his shoulders." "This brave fellow was afterwards taken, and lost his treasure," Baring noted sympathetically.

At that moment, Baring's situation became desperate. A count of the ammunition remaining to his men revealed that they each had only three or four shots left. The newest arrivals, the Nassauers, had much more ammunition than this, but it did no good, because their musket cartridges were unusable in Baker rifles; as to the Nassauers themselves, Major Baring preferred, in his account, not to elaborate on their performance, but they were inexperienced recruits, surely incapable of adequately replacing the riflemen. The farm was enveloped in the thick smoke of the fire, and the French, having successfully brought forward some artillery pieces to within sight of the external wall, were beginning to breach it. Although the defenders were taking advantage of every moment of respite to fill up the breaches with debris, it was evident to Baring that, under these conditions, they would not be able to last very long.

Baring ordered one of his officers to try to deliver a message to Colonel von Ompteda, explicitly putting him on notice that the garrison would not be able to withstand another attack. When the *tirailleurs* started making a fresh attack on the barn and the fire flared up again, and while his soldiers were using up their last grains of powder, Baring wrote another note, insisting that if he didn't receive some ammunition he would be forced to abandon his position. Meanwhile, the

French, seeing that the defenders' fire was growing steadily lighter, attacked the side of the farm nearest the road, and some sappers armed with axes started knocking down the carriage gate. Finally, as the men of the Thirteenth Légère were scaling the walls and bursting into the farmyard, Major Baring made the most difficult decision of his life: "Inexpressibly painful as the decision was to me of giving up the place, my feeling of duty as a man overcame that of honor, and I gave the order to retire through the house into the garden."

This turned into not so much a retreat as a disorganized flight, with the French, enraged by the defenders' obstinate resistance and determined to give no quarter to any of them, hot on their heels. The passage through the house was narrow, and many prisoners were taken; the most fortunate suffered a thrashing, followed by a brutal march to the rear of the French lines, but others did not fare so well. Some of the wounded vainly cried out in French, "Pardon!"—the conventional plea of one begging for his life—but they were finished off with bayonets. Ensign Frank, with one broken arm, took refuge in the house, hid behind a bed, and stayed in his hiding place until evening; when two fusiliers tried to hide in the same room, the French burst in behind them, crying out, "Pas de pardon à ces coquins verts!" and shot both of them to death. Lieutenant Graeme found his way blocked by an officer and four men; the officer grabbed him by the collar while one of the men thrust at him with his bayonet, but Graeme was still holding his sword and parried the blow. The officer, who had let him go, seized his collar again and gave him a jerk, whereupon Graeme twisted out of his grasp and took to his heels. With shouts of "Coquin!" the French fired after him, but they did not pursue him, and Graeme was able to rejoin his commanding officer. Baring led the lieutenant and the few other survivors of the garrison in a sprint up the slope and into the two companies of the First KGL Light Battalion, which were formed up in a small square behind the hollow way. "Although we could not fire a shot," he remembered, "we helped to increase the numbers."

Private Lindau took refuge with some comrades and an officer behind the fence that closed off a corner of the farmyard, and there they surrendered to the French. Pricking them with bayonets, their captors made them jump the fence to exit their hiding place, all the while furiously screaming, "En avant, couillons!" As soon as they reached the road, they were stripped of all they had, and Lindau lost his bag of gold, as well as two watches. The violence of their treatment exasperated the prisoners to such a degree that a few of them began to stoop down and gather stones to defend themselves; but the officer, a captain, managed to calm them, thus saving the whole lot from being massacred. Among their captors, the prisoners recognized an officer whom they themselves had captured a year before "in the Jewish cemetery in Bayonne." In an effort to protect the prisoners, this man ordered that they were not to be robbed, but his soldiers responded to this prohibition with catcalls and whistling. At last, the prisoners were turned over to a group of cuirassiers, survivors of the afternoon's fighting, who were ordered to escort them to the rear. "Most of the French cuirassiers had bandaged heads. They forced us to run as fast as their horses, and when a man from the first battalion couldn't run fast enough, they killed him with a saber blow."

As was the case in the Hougoumont sector, around La Haye Sainte the French succeeded in coordinating their infantry with their cavalry much more effectively than they managed to do in any other part of the battlefield. Despite hours of charging, the cuirassier squadrons of Milhaud and Kellermann appeared once again at the crest of the slope as soon as Donzelot's skirmishers took possession of the farm. Lieutenant Graeme had no time to take a breath before the cavalry charged the square he had just taken refuge in. To his relief, the riflemen stationed in the hollow way still had enough ammunition to keep the French at a distance, but meanwhile the *tirailleurs* had approached so close under the protection of the cavalry that the position of the square was rapidly becoming untenable. At this moment, Graeme was standing with other officers on the edge of the hollowing road, swinging his cap in the air to cheer on his men, when a musket ball shattered his right hand and he was obliged to quit the battlefield.

The *tirailleurs'* advance after the fall of La Haye Sainte was so sudden as to provoke panic and consternation among the Allied troops. Noticing that the defenders' fire was lessening, Wellington had ridden to a dangerously advanced position well past the sunken lane in order to see if he could discern a way to send the garrison more ammunition, and he remained there until the first enemy skirmishers appeared from around the corner of the house, close enough to take aim at him. Only then did the duke and his aides decide that the time had come for them to withdraw, but there was only one passage in the thick hedge bordering the chemin d'Ohain, and it took several moments for everyone to get through. As Lieutenant Cathcart, the last man, was awaiting his turn and keeping an uneasy eye on the approaching *tirailleurs*, only two hundred yards away, one of them fired at him. The ball struck his horse, which crashed to the ground; Cathcart tried frantically to make the animal rise again, but then he realized that it was too badly wounded. Leaving it there to die, Cathcart bolted through the hedge behind the others.

At this point, the generals observing the action from the ridge behind La Haye Sainte began to lose their heads. Sir Charles Alten rode up to Colonel von Ompteda and ordered him to recapture the farm with the only battalion he had left that was still near full strength, the Fifth KGL. The idea of descending the slope with a single battalion, exposed both to the enemy infantry, which was now entrenched behind the walls of La Haye Sainte, and to the cuirassier squadrons that were patrolling the area, struck Colonel von Ompteda as so risky that he did the unthinkable: He objected to the order and told his general that he thought the situation precluded an advance. The Prince of Orange, who outranked both of them even though he was only twenty-three years old, curtly ordered Ompteda to obey. "Well, I will," the colonel replied, and summoned Colonel von Linsingen, the battalion commander, and murmured to him, "Try to save my two nephews." Like many senior officers in a period when patronage and nepotism of the most blatant sort were the order of the day, Ompteda had procured officers' commissions in his unit for a couple of his nephews, aged fourteen and fifteen; evidently he was afraid that he was about to get them killed.

Until this moment, Lieutenant Wheatley of the Fifth KGL had remained in square with the rest of his battalion, comforting himself with frequent pinches of tobacco and mental recitations of some of Robert Southey's verses. Suddenly, the order came to deploy into line and advance at a walk; when his men were some sixty yards away from the enemy, Ompteda had the bugler sound the charge and urged his horse into the midst of the thick line of French skirmishers. The *tirailleurs* scattered, and Wheatley had just taken off in pursuit of a drummer boy, who was trying to escape by jumping a ditch, when French cavalry appeared on the battalion's flank and charged home. Wheatley heard someone cry out, "Cavalry! Cavalry!" but paid no attention, determined as he was to seize the drummer boy, who was caught in some brambles; but as the lieutenant reached out for his prey, a blow to the head with the flat of a sword knocked him unconscious to the ground. Colonel von Ompteda was encircled by enemy infantry, and the French officers, amazed by his courage, shouted to their men to take him alive; but Ompteda, who was by then, like his colleagues, beside himself, started aiming saber-strokes at the heads of the men surrounding him, and someone lost patience. When Lieutenant Wheatley regained consciousness, the colonel lay dead two steps away from him, with his mouth open and a hole in his throat, and Wheatley himself was a prisoner. Colonel von Linsingen had seized the commander's two nephews and hauled them to safety; the rest of the battalion had been cut to pieces, and its standard had been lost.

Captain Kincaid, who was stationed a short distance away with the survivors of the 1/95th Rifles, witnessed the destruction of the Hanoverian battalion. From where he stood, it seemed to him that their doom had come upon them with lightning swiftness. The cuirassiers came within range of Kincaid's men, who were about to open fire on them when some British light dragoons appeared. These horsemen went among the enemy, but apparently without much enthusiasm. "A few on each side began exchanging thrusts; but it seemed likely to be a drawn battle between them, without much harm being done," Kincaid wrote. In the end, the riflemen lost patience and started firing into the melee, and the cavalry on both sides cleared off in a moment. In an impotent rage, Kincaid watched the retreating cuirassiers as they leaned down from the saddle, saber in hand, and stabbed at the wounded Allied soldiers who were lying on the ground.

This and other firsthand accounts leave the impression that the French cavalry, despite the effects of an entire afternoon of continuous combat, still retained a capacity for action that their Allied counterparts had by then lost. Sir Colin Halkett, in an effort to raise the spirits of the few remaining men in his battalions, tried to lead a Netherlands cavalry regiment deployed behind them in a charge; but after a few steps the Dutch-Belgians stopped, refusing to go any farther, turned their horses around, and headed back. Halkett's infantry squares, formed nearby, grew indignant at this behavior and started firing at the retreating horsemen, bringing many down from their saddles. General van Merlen's Second Light Cavalry Brigade, composed of the Belgian Fifth Light Dragoons and the Sixth Dutch Hussars, conducted themselves more honorably, charging the French artillery that was taking up positions beside La Haye Sainte; but the results were no better. Van Merlen, whom Napoleon had created a baron of the empire barely three years before, was killed when a cannonball struck him in the abdomen, and his brigade fell apart: Colonel Van Boreel, who commanded the Hussars, tried to take over command of the brigade, but the survivors of the Fifth Light Dragoons refused to obey a Dutchman and joined another light brigade, which was commanded by the Belgian Baron de Ghigny.

By this point, the Netherlands Cavalry Division was so badly damaged that it could no longer be considered operational: Ghigny's brigade had lost more than half of its men. The division commander, Baron de Collaert, seriously wounded by a shell fragment, had been compelled to leave the battlefield. His division, which was the last cavalry reserve available behind the center of Wellington's line, was for all practical purposes useless, and the French cavalry, although crippled by their losses and weakened by fatigue, remained masters of the field. Sir James Kempt, in command of the division that had been Picton's, watched in consternation as La Haye Sainte fell into the hands of the enemy. Kempt was about to order Sir John Lambert to counterattack with the Twenty-seventh and recapture the farm, but almost at once he was compelled to the realization that it would be impossible for the Twenty-seventh or any other regiment to abandon their formation in square, because the enemy cavalry had them surrounded.

——— •◆• ———

FIFTY-FIVE

THE ADVANCE OF THE FRENCH ARTILLERY

After La Haye Sainte fell, the French generals were finally able to do what they had not dared until that moment: to bring forward their artillery, supported by those cuirassier squadrons that still had enough men in the saddle and sufficiently fresh horses to keep fighting. A few guns were advanced all too daringly, and the gunners paid the price for their recklessness. The French unlimbered two pieces, brought them into battery right in front of the 1/95th Rifles, and began firing canister at Kincaid's riflemen, but the battery was so close to them that the fire from their Baker rifles struck down most of the gunners within a few minutes, reducing the guns to silence. In general, however, the French brought forward so many guns and such an apparently inexhaustible supply of munitions that the Allied skirmishers found it difficult to maintain their advanced positions. The French even fired canister at the skirmishers, a rare indulgence of ammunition, and this ostentatious abundance of firepower wore on the morale of the already decimated skirmishers deployed ahead of Wellington's line.

After every cavalry charge up to this point, Lieutenant Pratt, commander of the light company of the Thirtieth Regiment, had successfully led his men out of their square and returned to a more advanced position, almost at the bottom of the slope. But once the French artillery advanced, his every attempt to move his troops forward was greeted with a regular barrage of case-shot. Pratt tried to stand fast, but he was well aware that before long he would have to retire and leave the enemy master of no-man's-land. "It was at this period that I was wounded," he noted, "and, of course, I ceased to be an eye-witness of what took place afterwards." The Seventy-third, which formed a single square with the Thirtieth, had no more skirmishers to send out, and so the captain who was in command of the regiment at that moment asked for volunteers willing to make a foray out of the square with him. Tom Morris and his brother William, together with a few others, agreed to accompany him, but they were hardly out of the square before case-shot felled almost all of them. The two Morrises, the only members of the party to emerge unscathed, took the captain by the arms—one of his legs was broken—and carried him to the rear.

Ensign Macready, who had taken over command after Pratt was wounded, decided that the few men remaining in his unit would be of more use inside the square, where they could fill the gaps made by the canister. After some time, "French artillery trotted up our hill, which I knew by the caps to belong to the Imperial Guard," Macready reported, "and I had scarcely mentioned this to a brother officer, when two guns unlimbering at a cruelly short distance, down went the portfires and slap came their grape into the square. They immediately reloaded, and kept up a most destructive fire. It was noble to see our fellows fill up the gaps after each discharge." As Macready had supposed, his men were much needed in the square, however guilty the young officer may have felt for exposing them to danger like that. "I had ordered up three of my light bobs [infantrymen], and they had hardly taken their places when two falling sadly wounded, one of them (named Anderson) looked up in my face, uttering a sort of reproachful groan, when I involuntarily said, 'By God! I couldn't help it.'" Lieutenant Rogers, who was in the same square, remembered those two French guns very well: "Every discharge made a regular gap in the square. It surprised me with what coolness our men and the 73rd closed them up."

The conduct of the noncommissioned officers, particularly those veterans who had fought in Spain, contributed decisively to keeping their men at their posts. Sergeant Major Ballam of the Seventy-third was pale as a corpse when he addressed the commander of the regiment, murmuring, "We had nothing like this in Spain, sir." And yet, having watched one of the men duck from time to time when the balls flew too close, Ballam stepped over to him and bawled him out: "Damn you, sir, what do you stoop for? You should not stoop if your head was off!" The man, a thin-skinned fellow, took this reprimand badly. A few moments later, a ball hit the sergeant major in the face, killing him instantly, and the soldier leaned over his disfigured corpse and exclaimed, "Damn it, sir! What do you lie there for? You should not lie down if your head was off!"

Slightly farther east, the officers of the 1/1st Nassau, which had already been nearly overwhelmed by a cuirassier charge, watched horrified as a French battery boldly advanced to within three hundred yards and opened fire on the square with case-shot. In the course of a few minutes, the battalion took so many casualties that the commander, Major von Weyhers, ordered his recruits to charge with fixed bayonets and capture the French guns. Dazed by the din and the smoke, the Nassauers had barely started moving when the major was cut down by case-shot. His men halted and hesitated; then most of them turned back, but two companies started firing a disordered volley at the French gunners. An instant later, a squadron of cuirassiers appeared from behind the guns and overwhelmed the Nassauers, cutting them down with their sabers. The Nassauer officers, whose professionalism must have been truly extraordinary, managed to halt the flight of the survivors and form them back up into something that once again resembled a square.

Wellington's artillerymen also noticed, even though it seemed impossible, that the enemy fire had become still more intense. Captain Samuel Bolton, on horseback amid his guns, was talking with Lieutenant Sharpin, who was standing beside the captain's horse with his hand on one of the stirrups. Sharpin later recalled, "The shot from a French Battery at that time flew very thick among us." A ball passed right between the two officers, and Bolton, with admirable coolness, "remarked that he thought we had passed the greatest danger for that day." Scarcely had he spoken when another ball struck the ground in front of him and bounded up, smashing the horse's shoulder and crushing the captain's chest. Man and beast collapsed in a single heap, and when the gunners succeeded in pulling Bolton out from under the animal's carcass, the captain was dead.

Another French battery advanced to a position on the flank of Captain Mercer's battery and opened fire from less than five hundred yards away. "The rapidity and precision of this fire was quite appalling," Mercer reported. "Every shot almost took effect, and I certainly expected we should all be annihilated. Our horses and limbers, being a little retired down the slope, had hitherto been somewhat under cover from the direct fire in front; but this plunged right amongst them, knocking them down by pairs, and creating horrible confusion. The drivers could hardly extricate themselves from one dead horse ere another fell, or perhaps themselves. The saddle-bags, in many instances were torn from the horses' backs, and their contents scattered over the field. One shell I saw explode under the two finest wheel-horses in the troop—down they dropped." Under the pressure of the French fire, Mercer's battery was literally pushed back, because his guns recoiled with every shot, and his surviving gunners were too exhausted to haul them forward again. In the end, Mercer noted, his pieces "came together in a confused heap," well back from their original position and "dangerously near the limbers and ammunition wagons, some of which were totally unhorsed, and others in sad confusion from the loss of their drivers and horses, many of them lying dead in their harness attached to their carriages." Later, when the order came to change position, Mercer did not have enough horses left to move his guns.

Only the extraordinary discipline of the artillerymen made it possible for some batteries to maintain their positions. Captain Rudyard, who served in Major

Lloyd's battery, described the scene: "The ground we occupied was much furrowed up by the recoil of our Guns and the grazing of the shot, and many holes from the bursting of shells buried in the ground. As horses were killed or rendered unserviceable, the harness was removed and placed on the waggons, or elsewhere. Our men's knapsacks were neatly packed on the front and rear of our limbers and waggons, that they might do their work more easily. Every *Gun*, every carriage, spokes carried from wheels, all were struck in many places." Rudyard much admired the fact that the Duke of Wellington, the Prince of Orange, and their staffs were often in the rear of the battery under fire, taking the same chances, running the same risks. "I saw the fore-legs taken from the horse of one of his Highness's A.D.C.'s at the shoulders, and [he] continued rearing for some time with his very fat rider, dressed in green. My own horse was shot through by a 9-pounder shot behind the saddle flap, and did not fall for some time."

The Allied line was exposed not only to artillery fire but also to the musketry of a multitude of *tirailleurs*, who became masters of all the dominant positions behind La Haye Sainte, from the farm itself to the mound overlooking the sandpit, all of which had been occupied that morning by British and German fusiliers. "We began to be annoyed also by a well-directed fire from behind a small hillock, almost in the heart of our position," one of the officers in Peck's brigade later recalled. "A knowing, enterprising fellow, holding the post of La Haye Sainte, which we had lost, had sent a strong detachment, which got to the hillock under cover of the brow, and opened a kind of masked battery upon us." The fire of these *tirailleurs* took a heavy toll, especially on the Twenty-seventh Regiment, the Inniskillings, who had been stationed in the most exposed place of all: in the northeast corner of the crossroads, barely two hundred yards behind La Haye Sainte and right beside the knoll on whose top French skirmishers had been posted. The Inniskillings remained there, formed up in square, until the evening, obedient to Sir James Kempt's orders to not abandon their position at any cost; only their presence in that spot prevented the enemy from penetrating deep into the center of the Allies' defensive line. In three or four hours, without ever moving a step, the regiment lost more than two-thirds of its men, the highest casualty rate of any battalion that fought at Waterloo. According to Kincaid, by seven in the evening "the twenty-seventh regiment were lying literally dead, in square, a few yards behind us." At that point in the battle, the regiment was commanded by a lieutenant, and eight of his ten companies were commanded by sergeants.

During the course of those few hours, remarkable things happened in the Twenty-seventh's square, one of which involved a soldier's pregnant wife, who had stayed with him rather than take shelter in the rear; she busied herself with caring for the wounded until a shell fragment struck her in the leg. Her husband fared worse: He lost both arms. In British military historiography, the tragedy of the Inniskillings has come to symbolize the most inhuman aspect of Waterloo: As John Keegan has suggested, the men must have been extremely tired, having marched some fifty-six miles in the previous seventy-two hours and slept very little, and their exhaustion may have helped them endure the horror to which they were subjected. Twenty years later, when Captain Siborne started building his grand model of the Battle of Waterloo, Sir John Lambert insisted that the knoll where the French skirmishers were stationed had to be represented, "as it was so important in that part of the line, and so honourable and fatal to the 27th Regiment, which kept its formation and lost more men and Officers than any Regiment during the day, and would otherwise have afforded an opportunity to the Enemy to have made an impression in a very serious part of the Line."

A great number of Wellington's generals and aides were killed or wounded in this particular phase of the battle, particularly in the area behind La Haye Sainte. The duke's secretary, Lord Fitzroy Somerset, who was at his side a short distance behind the crossroads, was struck in the arm by a musket ball fired from the roof of the farm and had to be carried to a field hospital, where the surgeons cut off the injured limb. One of the aides-de-camp, Lieutenant Colonel Canning, was preoccupied with keeping some German troops in line—they were on the verge of disbanding—when a musket bull penetrated his abdomen; a witness reported that the colonel, "although perfectly collected, could hardly articulate from pain." Canning was "raised to a sitting position by placing knapsacks around him," but "a few minutes terminated his existence." Another of Wellington's aides, Sir Alexander Gordon, who was also the duke's personal friend, had a leg shattered by a cannonball while he was encouraging a Brunswick square that had begun to waver; he was carried back to Waterloo and his leg amputated, but he did not survive the night. The quartermaster general, Sir William de Lancey, a young man of thirty-four whom Wellington had described as "the idlest fellow I ever met," was struck off his horse by a cannonball that passed so close to him it caused serious internal injuries; although no trace of the damage could be seen on his person, he was to die a few days later in the arms of his wife, whom he had married only two months before the battle. Having watched one of the squares in General Kielmansegge's brigade backing up under a pelting fire of canister and ordered the general to put a stop to this retreat, Sir Charles Alten was wounded by a shell fragment and obliged to leave the field; Kielmansegge took over command of the division, or what was left of it, but soon afterward he too was wounded; Colin Halkett became their new commander—though by this point almost nobody remained for him to command. A little farther to the west, a cannonball had pulped the right arm of the commander of the Guards Division, Major General George Cooke.

At this critical moment, the German infantry stood fast, but barely, and only thanks to the laborious efforts of its officers; but the British infantry gave a clear demonstration of the tenacity for which it was justly famous. Macready noted, "[The battle] had now become what I more than once heard the smothered muttering from the ranks declare it, 'Bloody thundering work,' and it was to be seen which side had most bottom, and could stand killing longest." His men would have greatly preferred to attack the French guns, whose positions were only a few hundred yards away, but they could not, because the French cavalry was always hovering near their cannons, ready to strike, while the Allied cavalry had disappeared from the battlefield. Another officer reported, "Our men were saying it was bloody murdering work, and growling much at not being allowed to charge." At one point, Wellington himself took refuge in this square, and some of the men started to complain aloud: "Are we to be massacred here? Let us go at them, let us give them *Brummagum!*"[29] The duke heard them and replied at once, "Wait a little longer, my lads, you shall have at them presently."

In truth, the situation could not have lasted much longer. In the square formed by the 3/1st Foot Guards, the sergeants were standing behind their men, leveling their pikes to compel them to remain in formation. "The fight, at one time, was so desperate with our battalion," a sergeant remembered, "that files upon files were carried out to the rear from the carnage, and the line was held up by the sergeants' pikes placed against their rear—not for want of courage on the men's parts (for they were desperate), only for the moment our loss so unsteadied the line." The Hanoverian square where Captain von Scriba was posted came "under artillery fire again" and "lost its original shape; at first, it became an irregular triangle, and then a mass closed up on all sides, without any identifiable shape." All along the front, in the centers of infantry squares filled with the dead and wounded, suffocated by smoke, and running shorter and shorter on ammunition, a growing number of officers were becoming convinced that the battle would be lost. In a letter to his brother, Ensign Howard of the Thirty-third confessed, "I thought that things were going badly"; the surviving officers decided to send the battalion's colors to safety in the rear, and soon afterward the same was done with all the colors from Halkett's brigade, a measure that was without precedent. Captain Kincaid, who was still holding the sunken lane behind the knoll with a handful of riflemen, was "weary and worn out, less from fatigue than anxiety." When he looked around, peering through the increasingly dense smoke, he could see nothing but the dead and the dying: "I had never yet heard of a battle in which everybody was killed, but this seemed likely to be an exception, as all were going by turns."

FIFTY-SIX

THE RENEWED ATTACK ON PLANCENOIT

According to tradition, more or less at this time the Duke of Wellington was heard to say, "Night or the Prussians must come." The absence of news from those allies was all the more frustrating because the Prussian vanguard, which hours before had advanced as far as Papelotte, had disappeared back into the woods, and despite their promises, no Prussian troops had come marching in after them. "The time they occupied in approaching seemed interminable," Wellington later wrote. "Both they and my watch seemed to have stuck fast." Certainly, the smoke rising in the distance around the bell tower of Plancenoit church and the sound of cannonading off to the south might have indicated to him that the Prussians were already in action; but for the moment the duke could not perceive any visible consequences of their intervention for the desperate battle that was being fought on the ridge.

In fact, although Wellington could not know this, there were already consequences, and they were decisive. That morning, along the main Brussels road between Rossomme and La Belle Alliance, Napoleon had massed thirty-seven battalions, which were supposed to constitute his strategic reserve, to be sent forward at the opportune moment to break through the weakest point in the Allied deployment; of these thirty-seven, no fewer than twenty-three, already withdrawn from the reserve and sent to stop the Prussian advance, were slowly being consumed in the combat around Plancenoit. On the Prussian side, the last two brigades of IV Corps, exhausted by their interminable slog through Belgian mud, had finally arrived in front of the village; one of these brigades, General von Ryssel's Fourteenth, was incomplete, having left two battalions behind at Wavre, but old Blücher nonetheless had at his disposition the equivalent of thirty-four battalions, or something like twenty-four thousand muskets, against the ten thousand that formed the French defensive line. Obviously, since both sides had already been severely battered, and since the Prussians, as they advanced, had scattered their forces to a much greater extent than had been the case with the French, these figures are uncertain, but they are indicative of the enormous numerical disproportion between the two sides.

The Prussians returned to the attack, led this time by the two battalions of the Eleventh Infantry, commanded by Colonel von Reichenbach. This regiment, recruited in Silesia, had been part of the regular army since its reconstitution in 1808, and it was the first seasoned Prussian line regiment that Blücher had been able to put on the battlefield that day. The two *Landwehr* regiments that made up Ryssel's brigade along with the Eleventh were also probably of good quality, having been recruited in Pomerania, one of the most patriotic regions of the old Kingdom of Prussia.[30] Under this redoubled pressure, Duhesme's troops were forced to abandon the first houses on the edge of the village, and the battle started to rage again in the narrow streets of Plancenoit, with the bloody ferocity of a house-to-house struggle fought with bayonets and musket butts. Carried forward by their numbers and their enthusiasm, the Prussians reached the village center, and there, around the church and the walled cemetery, the combat became even more savage; but in the end, worn down by the terrific fire that the French poured into them from the houses and the graveyard, Blücher's men were once again driven out of the village.

The tenacity of the defenders of Plancenoit was notable. The southernmost houses of the village, where there was a palpable danger that the advancing Prussians might debouch upon the flank or even in the rear of the French, were defended by the Fifth Ligne, which was no ordinary regiment. Its troops had been deployed by their monarchist officers a few miles south of Grenoble on March 7, with orders to bar the way to Napoleon, who had escaped from Elba and disembarked in France barely a week before. Napoleon had approached the regiment alone and, standing a few meters from the soldiers' musket barrels, had asked, "Would you fire on your emperor?" whereupon the troops revolted against their leaders and carried him in triumph. Remarkably, Colonel Roussille, though he disapproved of his men's defection, asked Napoleon to allow him to remain in his command, declaring, "My regiment has abandoned me, but I do not wish to abandon it." And so the emperor had left Colonel Roussille in command of the Fifth Ligne, and in the evening of Waterloo the colonel was mortally wounded while his troops successfully defended Plancenoit.

By an irony of fate, the other division of VI Corps, fighting tooth and nail to defend the high ground north of Plancenoit, included the Tenth Ligne, which until a few weeks previously had been fighting in the south of France under the Duc d'Angoulême, the Bourbon who had tried to incite the southern populations against Napoleon. As they entered Laon at the start of the Waterloo campaign, the soldiers of the Tenth Ligne had refused to shout, with the others, "*Vive l'Empereur,*" shouting instead "*Vive le roi de Rome.*" In the opinion of many, this slogan augured ill, being nothing more than an expedient way for the men to underline their loyalty to the king. And yet the monarchists of the Tenth Ligne fought as hard as the Bonapartists of the Fifth at Plancenoit.

In the end, the factor that probably explains the stubbornness of the French resistance better than any other is the presence of the Young Guard. These four regiments of light infantry had been constituted only after Napoleon's return from Elba by recalling veterans from leave, accepting a large number of volunteers in Paris and Lyon, and combining them into units of uneven experience that, while they were certainly not as solid as the Imperial Guard's grenadiers or *chasseurs à pied*, made up in enthusiasm what they lacked in homogeneity. Their commander, Duhesme, was exceptional. Although not at all exempt from criticism on a personal level—he was an old Jacobin fire-eater who, like many others, had grown rich in nebulous ways, and he had been involved in so many shady affairs, including accusations of murder, that in 1810 the emperor had dismissed him from his service and exiled him from Paris—Duhesme, having been restored to his rank, was an extraordinary battlefield commander, a specialist in precisely the sort of light infantry combat that led his troops to chase the Prussians out of the village a second time.

Their flight was so precipitous that the skirmishers of the Young Guard, pursuing the fugitives, left the village behind and moved forward through open country until they came within musket range of the hollow where the other Prussian battalions, which had taken many casualties in the previous fight, were still laboriously reordering themselves. The accurate and unexpected fire of the French caused a momentary panic in the ranks of the exhausted Prussian infantry, but then a squadron of the Sixth Hussars charged the *tirailleurs*, overwhelming some and compelling the others to return in haste to the village. Nevertheless, the progress made by the Prussians had once again been canceled out, and for the second time Blücher's attack was back where it started.

But reinforcements continued to arrive on the road from Wavre. The II Corps, commanded by General von Pirch, had started marching in the late morning, on the heels of Bülow's corps, and these men, likewise exhausted and covered up to their hats in mud, were starting to come into view. Thus assured that soon he would have new reserves at his disposition, Blücher ordered Bülow to attack again with what he had; this time, the worn-down battalions of the Fourteenth and Sixteenth Brigades penetrated past the village center and pushed all the way to the other end. Duhesme, who had spearheaded the resistance for so long, lay dying from a head wound; some of his men carried him to the rear, literally holding him in the saddle, and tried at first to bring him to safety; but that night they were obliged to abandon him, and the general was a prisoner of the Prussians when he died two days later. Around the cemetery, which had been fought over for so long, entire groups of the Young Guards were starting to raise their hands in surrender, although the Prussians, maddened by the stubborn defense the French had put up, were not always disposed to take prisoners.

As Napoleon was organizing his last reserves for the final attack against Wellington's wavering line, he trained his telescope on his right wing, and what he saw compelled him to take hasty countermeasures. All the troops left to him were the thirteen battalions of the Middle Guard and Old Guard.[31] All of which had already left their original positions on both sides of the main road just north of Rossomme and moved forward almost to La Belle Alliance, where they were waiting to advance against Wellington's center. Napoleon hurriedly ordered that those troops to the right of the main road should deploy into squares to form a last line of defense in case of a Prussian breakthrough; and two of those battalions, selected from among the most elite in the French army, the 1/2nd Grenadiers and the 1/2nd Chasseurs à pied of the Old Guard, were ordered to turn back, march to Plancenoit, and recapture it.

They were little more than a thousand bayonets, but all veterans with ten or twelve campaigns behind them; their skin was covered with tattoos, and large golden earrings hung from their ears, giving them the look of old-time pirates. An Englishman who saw them at Fontainebleau the previous year wrote: "More dreadful looking fellows than Napoleon's Guard I have never seen. They had the look of thoroughbred, veteran, disciplined banditti. Depravity, recklessness, and bloodthirstiness were burned into their faces. Black mustachios, gigantic bearskins, and a ferocious expression were their characteristics." The other soldiers in the French army had no great love for the men of the Imperial Guard, although everyone desired in his heart to be called one day to join its ranks. The severity and arrogance of the Imperial Guard's officers, the double pay and double rations that were the privilege of every one of its members down to the least drummer boy, and the precedence always given to the Guard's needs, whether of quarters or provisions, aroused all the more anger because it was clear to anyone who cared to look that the Guard was sent into combat much more rarely than the cannon fodder that constituted the line regiments. But at Plancenoit, these two Old Guard battalions showed that they were worth the privileges that Napoleon had always granted them. General Morand quickly deployed his men into columns and moved them out. Plancenoit was little more than half a mile from La Belle Alliance, and they had barely begun to descend the slope that led to the village when they encountered Young Guard fugitives, running away from the fight, some of them declaring that the Prussians were hot on their heels. The drums beat the *pas de charge*, and the men of the Old Guard advanced on Plancenoit with cadenced steps and fixed bayonets.

What happened next can be explained only by acknowledging the fatigue of the Prussian troops, the inexperience of the large number of them who were new recruits, and the terrible losses that they had already suffered. Morand's two battalions attacked and overwhelmed the first Prussian skirmishers, who had been cautiously peering out of the houses on the edge of the village. The French then fought their way through the rutted streets with bayonets and musket butts, amid burned houses and piles of dead and wounded, and the multitude of Prussians in front of them, a force many times their number, allowed itself to be driven back, first in disorder and then in a catastrophic rout. The Prussians were pitilessly massacred, trampled on by the triumphant French, and ejected from the village. It had taken the Old Guard twenty minutes to become masters of Plancenoit. They were so intoxicated with blood and victory that General Pelet, commander of the Second Chasseurs, found his men busy cutting prisoners' throats and had to resort to forceful measures before he could manage to save a few. Behind them, the battalions of the Young Guard, brought back into line by their officers and encouraged by the Old Guard's exploit, were returning to their earlier positions. At seven-thirty in the evening, Blücher's offensive was back at its starting point yet again.

FIFTY-SEVEN

---•◆•---

ZIETHEN AT SMOHAIN

Ironically, the attack on Plancenoit, delivered by Blücher with the bulk of his troops and at the cost of dreadful losses, was not what convinced Wellington that the Prussians were finally and unequivocally coming to his aid. The duke felt that conviction only when he saw other masses of Prussian troops pour onto the battlefield much closer to him than Plancenoit, in the area around Papelotte, and especially when he realized that this time they were not going to disappear into the woods to the south but were going into action against the French right wing. Finally accepting Bülow's suggestions, the Prussian command had ordered the last army corps to leave Wavre. Count von Ziethen's I Corps had marched along the more northerly road, following the course of the River Smohain and ending near the small group of houses that formed the village of the same name, right in the middle of the sector that Prince Bernhard's Nassauers had been defending against Durutte's men all day long. Lieutenant Colonel von Reiche, I Corps's chief of staff, had barely reached this spot, ahead of the column, when an extremely agitated Müffling approached and informed him, "The Duke was most desirous of our arrival and had repeatedly declared that this was the last moment, and if we did not arrive soon, he would be compelled to retreat." Together, the two went in search of General von Ziethen. Having found him, Müffling repeated that there wasn't a moment to lose. Ziethen, however, like Bülow before him, had little desire to send his men blindly forward along that little sunken lane, where they could suddenly find themselves in the path of the French offensive. An officer sent to assess the situation reported that there were signs of disintegration all along Wellington's line and that wounded soldiers and stragglers were thronging to the rear; the troops defending Papelotte and Smohain were also losing ground to the enemy. Should the Prussians continue to advance, they ran the risk of landing right in the middle of a defeat.

While Ziethen hesitated, another officer came galloping up from the south. Major von Scharnhorst, son of the famous reformer of the Prussian army, fallen two years previously in the wars of liberation, was an aide-de-camp on Bülow's staff. The major reported that the attack on Plancenoit was failing, that IV Corps needed help, and that by Blücher's orders Ziethen was to march his troops southwest and join the Prussian assault on the village. Reiche, who had just returned from a reconnaissance of his own, during the course of which he had formally promised immediate support to the officers of the Nassau forces engaged at Papelotte, tried to protest, but his commander signaled to the vanguard to turn for Plancenoit. Among the exhausted Allied troops deployed along the chemin d'Ohain, men who had withstood the bombardment of the Grande Batterie for hours and hours and were finding it increasingly difficult to stave off the infiltrations of enemy skirmishers, the sight of yet another Prussian column turning away from them and heading south as though withdrawing caused consternation.

Meanwhile, Müffling and Reiche continued the discussion with Ziethen, pleading with him to change his mind. Both of them were aware that Prussian reinforcements were indispensable to Wellington; moreover, Müffling knew that the duke was already on the verge of exasperation over the lack of Prussian support, that in general the British officers knew nothing about the action at Plancenoit, and that the Prussian army, despite all its efforts, was in danger of losing face before its ally. Faced with their insistence, Ziethen eventually assumed responsibility for ignoring the order to go to Bülow's aid and proceeding according to the original plan. His columns resumed their march toward Papelotte, and soon they began to engage the French skirmishers who were once again putting heavy pressure on the exhausted Nassauers: The *tirailleurs* had penetrated the perimeter of Papelotte and driven the defenders out of Smohain.

Ziethen's corps could not have started marching before two o'clock in the afternoon, and the column it formed on the narrow, muddy lane was so long, and so slowed down by sheer numbers and bad terrain, that in fact only its vanguard arrived in time to go into action before nightfall; only the three regiments of Steinmetz's First Brigade took part in the combat, and they had taken such losses at Ligny two days before that the three of them together could not field even four thousand muskets. But these newly arrived troops, supported by several artillery batteries, were nonetheless more than sufficient to stop Durutte's advance, all the more so because one of that general's two brigades had just been sent in the direction of La Haye Sainte to take part in the final offensive against the center of Wellington's line. Durutte was left with only four battalions, perhaps fifteen hundred muskets, and these had no chance of standing against the fresh forces deployed by the Prussians.

In the confusion of twilight, and in a part of the battlefield as thick with woods and hedges as the area around Papelotte, there was no lack of further incidents involving "friendly fire." As they were advancing toward Smohain in open order, the Prussians, suddenly seeing a mass of soldiers, apparently wearing French uniforms, running toward them, opened fire at once on their presumed assailants. In reality, these men were Nassauers fleeing from Smohain, and Prince Bernhard of Saxe-Weimar was in their midst, trying to bring some order among them. When he realized that the troops firing on him and his men were Prussians, the prince galloped off in search of their commander and was fortunate enough to come across General von Ziethen almost at once. Verbally assaulted by a foreign officer in excellent German, and unaware that he was speaking to a prince, Ziethen took offense and replied curtly, "My friend, it is not my fault if your men are dressed like Frenchmen."

On the high ground above Papelotte, the last regiment of Steinmetz's brigade, the First Westphalian *Landwehr*, was advancing with its skirmishers out ahead, moving toward the line held by Pack's men. The latter were so nervous that they too, seeing a large number of unknown troops bearing down upon them, opened fire without further ado. But the officer in command of the first patrol quickly managed to get himself recognized, and before long, the Prussians were shaking hands with Pack's Scotsmen and Best's Hanoverians. The junction of the two Allied armies had finally been accomplished. Without losing time, the guns of one of Ziethen's horse artillery batteries mounted the crest and took up positions alongside Wellington's battalions, while two other batteries deployed a few hundred yards from Smohain and began firing point-blank at the buildings that the *tirailleurs* had just occupied.

The French disbanded under this unexpected fire, but Durutte, a tough warrior, managed to get his men under control, and a new, bloody combat erupted amid the enclosures, hedges, and tree-shaded lanes around Smohain. The Brandenburgers of the Twelfth Regiment were resupplied with ammunition before going into action. Private Johann Karl Hechel later recalled, "Each of us received 80 cartridges, borrowed from another unit's munitions wagon, because ours had got bogged down far to the rear. We ate a few bites there, on our feet, and then we went forward to meet the enemy." While they proceeded along the road to Smohain, taking cover behind the row of poplars that bordered it, the regiment's skirmishers were targeted from behind by the men of the Westphalian *Landwehr*, who had mistaken them for French troops; advancing farther, the skirmishers found the enemy stationed along the final stretch of road—a sunken lane that descended toward the village—drove them off after a short, sharp clash, and burst in among the first houses of Smohain.

Hechel jumped a low hedge, looked around, and saw many wounded men lying on the ground. One was an enemy soldier, unable to move, who kept crying out a single word, "*Italiano! Italiano!*" Hechel, the son of a schoolteacher, spoke to the man in French and asked him if there were more of his comrades up ahead, to which the other replied, "*Oui, Monsieur.*" More Prussian soldiers arrived and wanted to finish off the poor fellow with their bayonets, but Hechel told them to leave him alone; the Frenchman clung to him and kissed his hand. Advancing among scattered corpses, Hechel saw a dead Prussian sergeant with a gold chain hanging from his breast pocket. He bent down to seize this prize, and at that moment a musket ball whizzed past his ear. *The hand of the Lord is upon me*, thought the devout Protestant, as a familiar Bible verse came into his mind almost immediately: "Whither shall I go from they spirit? Or whither shall I flee from they presence?"

Returning to the sunken lane, Hechel took up a position among the skirmishers, who were engaged in a lively firefight with a French unit stationed a stone's throw away. Hechel joined in until he felt a sudden pain in his lower abdomen; his eyes glazed over, and he staggered, crying out, "Comrades, I'm wounded!" Two men swiftly caught him under the arms and carried him to the rear; "a third picked up my knapsack and followed us. He didn't at all mind getting away from the firing." An officer ran over to them and asked where they were going. "It's not true that this man is wounded," he exclaimed, because no blood could be seen. The men lowered Hechel to a sitting position and unbuttoned his pants; blood and intestines came pouring out. With a horrified gesture, the officer ordered Hechel's two comrades to carry him to safety. "As for you," he said to the man holding Hechel's knapsack, "throw that thing down and get back to your post!" Hechel's account bears witness to the stubbornness with which Durutte's men (among them the ex-prisoners of the Eighty-fifth Ligne) continued to resist, even in that hour of extremity, still defending the ground that they and the enemy had fought over all day long; but the disproportion between the two forces was such that the inevitable outcome of the battle could be only a matter of time.

At Le Caillou farm, where Napoleon's imperial equipment and all his baggage had stopped, his worried valet, Marchand, was listening to the rumble of artillery and trying to deduce from it the progress of the battle when Ali the Mameluke, one of the emperor's most devoted servants, came galloping up, looking for something for his master to eat. Ali, who was in reality a quite normal Frenchman, a former employee in a notary's office, stopped briefly, barely long enough to tell Marchand "It looks bad" and declare that the Prussians were arriving on the battlefield, before putting spurs to his horse and galloping away. Seized by evil premonitions, Marchand sought out General Fouler, the director of the imperial stable. The general told Marchand not to repeat their conversation to anyone, but had it been up to him, the emperor's baggage and belongings would not have been allowed to remain so close to the battlefield. Only an order from the emperor could move them, however, and Marchand took solace in the thought that the emperor's personal carriage, filled with gold and diamonds, was even farther forward, near La Belle Alliance, and was someone else's responsibility.

FIFTY-EIGHT

─────◆◈◆─────

NAPOLEON'S LAST ATTACK

All the eyewitness accounts left by men who were in the Allied infantry squares between six and seven in the afternoon greatly resemble one another, and together they give the impression that Wellington's line would simply have collapsed, without the need of a French infantry attack, had the intense artillery bombardment gone on half an hour longer. In fact, however, the French batteries were using up their last rounds of canister, and they would not have been able to keep firing for another half hour. In the morning, no 6-pounder gun had been accompanied by more than three caissons of munitions, enough for a couple of hours of sustained fire. When La Haye Sainte fell and all available guns were hastily brought forward, most of the caissons were probably already empty. The enormous expenditure of ammunition on the part of the French artillery in the last moments was not made, and could not have been made, with a view to sweeping aside the British and German infantry; the aim was only to weaken the enemy as much as possible in anticipation of the final attack. The junior officers in the middle of the tumult may not have known this, but Napoleon knew it, and Wellington knew it equally well; otherwise, he would not have been able to remain so calm while the shattered bodies of his generals and aides-de-camp fell all about him in an unprecedented slaughter.

The emperor had to attack, and he decided to do so all along the line and with his entire infantry, including those troops who had fought all day and had now reached the limits of their endurance. On the left, Reille's corps was fully engaged in the siege of Hougoumont, and even though there was little hope of capturing the château, the *tirailleurs* ensconced in the park had to maintain pressure on the exhausted garrison. Farther to the right, d'Erlon's regiments, overwhelmed and routed by the British heavy cavalry, had had several hours in which to catch their breath and reorder their ranks, and a large number of stragglers had been rounded up and compelled to go back into line. On the main road, the French threw together a picket line made up of a few infantrymen and mounted lancers. Corporal Canler, one of the pickets, later recalled, "[My comrades and I were] ordered to allow only wounded men to pass through; all soldiers still able to bear arms were to be turned back. In less than an hour, we stopped more than 400 fugitives."

After the rout of d'Erlon's corps, the men in Kempt's and Pack's brigades had remained unoccupied for some time, and many of them left the line with impunity and busied themselves with "rifling the pockets of the dead, and perhaps the wounded," as a British officer remarked. At least one colonel, troubled by such a breakdown in discipline, had to resort to the flat of his sword to persuade his recalcitrant men to return to their posts. The same officers—at least those who knew French—began to read the letters they found in the knapsacks of their dead enemies. Contrary to their expectations, the British officers found that these letters "developed a great deal of proper and good feeling, and were, upon the whole, not only interesting, but argued an advanced state of morality and education which quite surprised us." A few officers even conversed with the French wounded who had been left lying on the ground in enemy territory; some of them "had just been liberated from our prison-ships by the closing of the war in 1814. They were exceedingly cautious in disclosing their sentiments on the state of affairs, not knowing how the day might end."

This interlude, however, did not last long, and soon Kempt's and Pack's troops were obliged to deal with the pressure exerted by a growing number of skirmishers advancing into no-man's-land, while on the low ground at the bottom of the slope the divisions of Quiot and Marcognet once more deployed into attack formation. Farther to the left, Donzelot's division, in spite of the losses it had suffered, still had enough *tirailleurs* inside the enclosure of La Haye Sainte to support the offensive with its fire. Finally, while one brigade of Durutte's division was engaged to the limit in the struggle for Papelotte, the other, commanded by Pégot, was almost intact, and the emperor ordered it to move up alongside La Haye Sainte in order to take part in the coming attack.

All along the front, from Hougoumont to Papelotte, swarms of *tirailleurs* went forward one more time, no longer bent only on engaging the enemy skirmishers and defending their own positions, but once again trying to drive off their adversaries and clear the way for the attack columns. All the artillery batteries that still had some ammunition in their caissons kept up their fire on the ridge as long as they could, and all the infantry battalions formed up shoulder to shoulder behind their officers and prepared to advance against the enemy positions. Given the situation, the number of men who participated in the final offensive is impossible to calculate, because virtually all the men in I and II Corps who were still capable of holding a musket were required to take part.

Yet no offensive could have succeeded with only such worn-down troops as these. After taking fire for several hours, even units that had suffered a limited number of casualties and continued to maintain a perfectly ordered appearance would have experienced a significant loss in morale. These troops had few cartridges remaining in their pouches, and little would have been required—a shell exploding in their midst, a cry of panic coming from who knew where, the impression that other units were retreating—to stop their reluctant advance in its tracks, despite all the exhortations of their officers, and to cause the men to start disbanding and turning back.

Only with fresh reserves, therefore, could an offensive be carried out successfully; for this reason, the last attack ordered by Napoleon in the evening of the Battle of Waterloo is known as the attack of the Imperial Guard. The emperor knew he could achieve the decisive breakthrough he had sought from the beginning only by sending in those Guard battalions that constituted the last fresh reserves available to him. With this in mind, clearly the Prussian advance on Plancenoit, despite being stalled, made a decisive contribution to reducing the probabilities of a Napoleonic victory. That morning, the emperor, envisioning a breakthrough, had kept at his disposal a strategic reserve of thirty-seven battalions; by evening, twenty-five of them were engaged in the combat with the Prussians and one was left behind at Le Caillou. Napoleon had eleven remaining battalions, and of these, six were Middle Guard and five Old Guard, a total of some six thousand men, all veterans. Half an hour earlier, a little more than a thousand of their comrades had driven the Prussians out of Plancenoit. Napoleon aimed his remaining forces at Wellington's center.

Not long before, the men of the Imperial Guard had remained at their leisure on both sides of the Brussels road, waiting for their moment to come, as it had in so many other battles, most recently the one at Ligny two days before. They had not been completely out of danger, because there was no place on the battlefield where a cannonball did not arrive from time to time, and a man could be cut down while peacefully sitting on his knapsack and smoking his pipe. In the early afternoon, shortly after the grenadiers of the Old Guard had taken up their positions, a ball had killed one of their *vivandières*, a woman from Elba named Maria, who had taken up with a Guard veteran on the island and wished to accompany him in his new adventure. Despite such risks, there had nevertheless been precious little for the men of the Guard to do all afternoon; they had even had time to dig a grave for Maria, bury her, and mark the spot with a wooden cross and a nailed-on epitaph. By evening, their hour had come.

FIFTY-NINE

"VOILÀ GROUCHY!"

Accompanied by Napoleon himself, and stepping to the exuberant beating of drums, the Imperial Guard marched up the cobblestone road almost as far as La Haye Sainte and then spread out to the left, moving across the plateau between La Haye Sainte and Hougoumont. To the right, d'Erlon's infantry also began to march, preceded by a long line of *tirailleurs*. The sound of musketry and cannon fire coming from the area around Papelotte had intensified in recent minutes, and d'Erlon's men looked nervously to their right, trying to understand what was happening over there. Discerning that the arrival of the Prussians might cause panic to spread among his troops, Napoleon made a deliberate decision to deceive them: His aides-de-camp were ordered to ride up and down the line, spreading the news that the infantry masses arriving on the battlefield were Grouchy's troops. One of these aides, General Dejean, galloped up to Marshal Ney, who was overseeing preparations for the attack, and shouted, "*Monsieur le Maréchal! Vive l'Empereur! Voilà Grouchy!*" Ney immediately commanded one of his adjutants, Colonel Levavasseur, to carry the good news to the troops; the colonel galloped along the line, holding his hat on the point of his saber and crying out, "*Vive l'Empereur! Soldats, voilà Grouchy!*" Thousands of voices took up his cry.

Carried along on a surge of enthusiasm, the advance of I Corps once again jolted the infantry of Picton's and Alten's decimated divisions. Up to that moment in the skirmishers' combat, the French had sent in their *tirailleurs* "in far greater numbers, and consequently doing more execution." But the Royal Scots officer who was responsible for this account added that the French were better armed and trained, and on the whole much more effective in this type of fighting. "The French soldiers, whipping in the cartridge, give the butt of the piece a jerk or two on the ground, which supersedes the use of the ramrod; and thus they fire twice for our once. I have occasionally seen some of our 'old hands' do the same. It was astonishing to find how galling the fire of the enemy proved to be, and how many men we lost." When the French made their final push, the line of British skirmishers was no longer capable of standing against them. "About this time our ball cartridge was all expended, and no supply being at hand the skirmishers were called in, seeing which, those of the enemy came on in the most daring manner step by step. The ammunition cart was brought as quickly as possible to the height, and the horses being withdrawn, it was left there for us." But every man sent to the cart for ammunition was killed or wounded; finally, a sergeant heaved a barrel full of cartridges onto his shoulder and ran back down the slope toward his comrades. Although he too was wounded and fell before reaching his goal, he managed to roll the barrel the rest of the way down the slope, and the men of his unit, their ammunition store thus replenished, were able to hold their ground.

Under fire from *tirailleurs* perched on the roofs of La Haye Sainte, the riflemen of the 1/95th were forced to take refuge in the sunken lane. D'Erlon's infantry, however, no longer had sufficient force to make a bayonet charge and settled down instead to a prolonged firefight. Captain Leach, who was commanding the Ninety-fifth's riflemen at this point, related that the entire French line, all along the front of Kempt's brigade, went down on one knee and kept up an uninterrupted fire. "The distance between the two hostile lines I imagine to have been rather more than one hundred yards," he wrote. "Several times the French officers made desperate attempts to induce their men to charge Kempt's line, and I saw more than once parties of the French in our front spring up from their *kneeling position* and advance some yards towards the thorn hedge, headed by their Officers with vehement gestures, but our fire was so very hot and deadly that they almost instantly ran back behind the crest of the hill, always leaving a great many killed or disabled behind them."

In the course of that firefight, the riflemen of the Ninety-fifth began to worry about being flanked on the right, as the advancing French were making steady progress along the cobblestones of the main road. These were the men of Pégot's brigade, probably the freshest troops in the entire sector; the German soldiers in front of them, the remaining infantrymen of Kielmansegge's and Ompteda's brigades, were compelled to give ground and began to disband. After the evacuation of La Haye Sainte, Major von Baring's men had taken refuge in the sunken lane a few hundred yards from the farm, and they were once again running short of ammunition. As the major rode back and forth behind his troops, trying to keep up their morale, his third horse was suddenly killed, and man and beast crashed to the ground. Baring was stunned by the fall and trapped under the animal's carcass. His men, believing him to be dead, left him there; sometime later one of them, perhaps with robbery on his mind, approached the major, discovered that he was still alive, and helped him get out from under his horse.

Still dazed and limping on a heavily bruised leg, Baring dragged himself to the rear, offering gold to anyone who would procure him another mount; but no one paid any attention to his pleas. Finally, a British soldier found a riderless horse and helped the major into the saddle. In great pain, Baring returned to the battle line, where he was informed that Sir Charles Alten had been gravely wounded. To his further consternation, the major noticed that there were but a few men in the positions formerly occupied by Ompteda's brigade, and when he reached the sunken lane, he found it empty: even his riflemen, having exhausted their ammunition, had fled to the rear. At this point, a solitary French dragoon appeared on the scene, and Baring, trembling with anger and humiliation, had to gallop away in order to avoid capture. One of the officers of the Ninety-fifth Rifles, whose position was in the sunken lane a few dozen yards to the east, suggested to Captain Leach that they should concentrate a part of their force on their extreme right, in order to keep the *chaussée* under fire. But the captain replied that the Twenty-seventh Regiment, formed up in square near the northeast corner of the crossroads, behind the 1/95th, would have to suffice for their defense on that side, "for the French are gathering so fast and thick in our *front* that we cannot spare a single man to detach to the right."

To support his wavering center, Wellington called back Vivian's and Vandeleur's cavalry from their rearward positions on his extreme left; together, the two brigades could still count nearly two thousand sabers. When they arrived behind La Haye Sainte, after having spent a great part of the day in relative calm, the brigades' officers were so shocked by what they saw that they became convinced that the battle was going very badly for the Allies. Sir Hussey Vivian declared that he had never seen such a sight: the ground literally covered with the dead and dying; cannonballs and shells flying around more thickly than musket balls; and the Allied forces, or at least part of them, in retreat. Colonel Murray, commander of the Eighteenth Hussars, confirmed Vivian's assessment: "The ground was strewed with wounded, over whom it was barely possible sometimes to avoid moving. Wounded or mutilated horses wandered or turned in circles. The noise was deafening, and the air of ruin and desolation that prevailed wherever the eye could reach gave no inspiration of victory."

Fragments from bursting shells and the fire from the *tirailleurs'* muskets came thick and fast, and Vivian later lamented, "No words can give any idea of it (how a man escaped is to me a miracle), we every instant expecting through the smoke to see the Enemy appearing under our noses, for the smoke was literally so thick that we could not see ten yards off." Major Luard of the Sixteenth Light Dragoons corroborated this description: "The fire became every moment hotter, and from the rapid way in which it approached us, appeared as if the Enemy was carrying the hill by which we were partially covered, and I confess I thought at that moment the day was going hard with us, that the Infantry were beaten, and that we (the Cavalry), by desperate charges, were to recover what they had lost."

That proved unnecessary, because Sir John Lambert brought the remaining two battalions of his brigade forward and aligned them with the Inniskillings on the other side of the *chaussée*. Deployed in a two-deep line, Lambert's men, 1,000–1,200 strong, covered a line more than three hundred yards wide, before which the French advance in the La Haye Sainte sector eventually stalled and turned into a confused, static firefight. Major Browne of the Fortieth saw the French advance as far as the farm and stop, but he was unable to tell whether the enemy troops were a disordered column or a multitude of skirmishers: "I think they had been driven back from their attempt to ascend the hill, partly by our fire, and partly by that of the troops on our right; but the cloud of smoke in which we were almost constantly enveloped prevented me from discovering their object in remaining there thus exposed, which they did in the most dauntless and daring manner; as fast as they fell their places were supplied with fresh troops." At one point in the fight, the *tirailleurs* occupying the knoll above the sandpit ("who whilst laying down, appeared to shoot their objects with great precision," as another officer of the Fortieth noted) tried to advance, but the fire from the British line quickly put an end to this attempt.

While d'Erlon's men, from Papelotte to La Haye Sainte, committed themselves to this persistent firefight, Reille's troops on the other side of the battleground had likewise obeyed orders and undertaken their last assault on Hougoumont. The skirmishers seized the orchard almost immediately, and once again the survivors of the garrison were obliged to barricade themselves inside the walled perimeter of the château. Adam's brigade, having moved down the slope all the way to the hedgerow enclosing the grounds of the château, came under fire from the *tirailleurs* in the orchard a short distance away and from artillery that had been brought up to within a few hundred yards. Colborne, the commander of the Fifty-second, saw some of the Hougoumont defenders take to their heels and thought that the château would not resist the French attack this time. Should Hougoumont have fallen, the already weakened position of Adam's brigade would have become untenable, and the British generals decided the brigade should fall back. Adam withdrew his men to a position behind the ridge, where most cannonballs would fly over their heads, and sent to the rear all the wounded who could walk. This withdrawal left several batteries exposed, which moreover were running short of ammunition, so the gunners spontaneously decided that there was no point in remaining there. They were in the act of abandoning the guns when Sir Augustus Frazer plunged into their midst and energetically persuaded them to return to their posts.

Shortly thereafter, a French deserter galloped up the slope to warn the British that the Imperial Guard was preparing to attack them. The narratives of this episode differ so widely in detail that they again serve to illustrate the difficulty in trusting eyewitness accounts. According to Colborne, the deserter was a colonel of cuirassiers who approached the ranks of the Fifty-second shouting, "*Vive le Roi!*" and then personally addressed to him these alarming words: "*Ce sacré Napoléon est là avec les Gardes. Voilà l'attaque qui se fait.*" According to Major Blair, General Adam's brigade major, the deserter was a Hussar officer who approached Blair while he was conversing with Frazer behind the Fifty-second's lines, and warned him that the Imperial Guard would attack within half an hour; Sir Augustus galloped away to notify the duke, and Blair stayed behind and guarded the prisoner for a while. Then, realizing that the Frenchman's warning was being verified before his eyes, Blair ordered a sergeant to escort him to the rear. In a letter to his wife, Frazer confirmed having spoken with the man and said he was an officer in the cuirassiers, but confessed that he did not understand whether the officer was a deserter or a prisoner. Frazer asserted that he handed the Frenchman over to Adam, charging him to transmit the information to the duke.[32]

Adam's infantry, deployed in four-deep lines thirty or forty yards behind the crest, could not see what was visible to Blair, who was on horseback at the farther edge, namely the Imperial Guard infantry, immediately recognizable by their enormous bearskins, as they occupied positions all along the relatively level ground between Hougoumont and La Haye Sainte. Young Ensign Leeke, who bore the colors of the Fifty-second, took advantage of this interval to look about him and analyze his own sensations. There was a strange smell in the air, the smell of ripe, trampled grain, mixed with the odor of gunpowder. All around him were dead or wounded horses, some of them—including the most horrifically mutilated—still trying to eat the crushed wheat and rye. A dead cat triggered a memory of home, and the boy became pensive for a while before he noticed that a cannonball was rolling down the slope, right at him. It reminded him of a cricket ball; "so slowly [did it move] that I was putting out my foot to stop it, when my coulour-sergeant quickly begged me not to do so, and told me it might have seriously injured my foot." In fact, the ball would probably have taken it off.

Soon enemy skirmishers returned to the attack, either troops from Bachelu's columns, which since Adam's withdrawal had enough space to deploy and advance, or the first squads of *tirailleurs* sent ahead as cover by the Imperial Guard. Adam tried to counter them by sending forward the skirmishers from his battalions, but almost immediately a few squadrons of French cuirassiers started moving up the slope, and the skirmishers had to make a hasty return to their ranks. Morale was already rather shaky in the batteries deployed behind Hougoumont, and when the French cavalry advanced yet again, panic spread among the gunners; following orders, many of them abandoned their pieces and ran to take refuge with the infantry, but in more than one case, officers and men did not have the heart to abandon the guns and hauled them away, retiring amid growing confusion all the way to the Nivelles road.

Amazingly, Kellermann's exhausted regiments were still capable of making an advance, which they did en masse in the Hougoumont sector, and to such effect that Frazer thought the final French attack was made by cavalry, with the infantry of the Imperial Guard playing only a supporting role. But the cuirassiers' strength had been too eroded for them to go far, and once again their charge dwindled into futility when they got among the abandoned British guns. Lord Saltoun saw a unit of cuirassiers hesitate before the square of the 3/1st Foot Guards: "Refusing us, [they] passed between us and the *inward rear angle* of the orchard, receiving our fire; did not charge between us and the 52nd, where the Rifles were, but rode along the front of the 52nd with a view of turning their right flank, and were completely destroyed by the fire of that Regiment." The Twenty-third Light Dragoons went forward to drive off the survivors, and General Adam, who had ridden forward to observe the enemy advance, was nearly swept along in the dragoons' charge, only just managing to return to his men. His servant brought him a fresh horse; immediately after mounting it, Adam was wounded in the leg by a musket ball, but he was able to stay in the saddle until the battle was over. This was not the moment to leave the field, because the Imperial Guard was moving forward to deal the decisive blow.

SIXTY

THE IMPERIAL
GUARD'S ADVANCE

I n spite of the thick smoke enveloping the battlefield, the Imperial Guard's aspect was so recognizable, and the advance of its columns across the plateau between Hougoumont and La Haye Sainte so solemn and imposing, amid the obsessive beating of drums and repeated cries of "*Vive l'Empereur!*" from thousands of hoarse throats, that at least the mounted Allied officers on the crest could tell what was about to happen. During the French cavalry charges, the Allied infantry, formed up in squares, had remained on the reverse slope of the ridge; now it was brought forward to prevent the enemy from reaching the guns, and to add its musketry to the fire of the Allied artillery. Maitland, who commanded one of the most exposed sectors of the front, received a visit from Wellington, who ordered him to deploy his men in line, but once again in the more robust four-deep formation instead of the customary two-deep line, because, according to Maitland, "His Grace expect[ed] that the French Cavalry would take part in the affair." Maitland obeyed, bringing his men forward all the way to the sunken lane and then ordering them to lie down in order to reduce the effects of the ongoing bombardment. "The formation of the Brigade was scarcely completed before the advance of the Enemy became apparent," Maitland noted.

Wellington galloped off in the direction of Hougoumont. Stopping at the first artillery battery he met on his way—a battery with only five guns left—he asked a young officer, Lieutenant Sharpin, the name of the battery commander. Sharpin replied that the commander was Captain Bolton, but he had just been killed, and the command had passed to Captain Napier. "His Grace then said," according to Sharpin, "'Tell him to keep a look to his left, for the French will soon be with him,' and then he rode off." Sharpin had just conveyed Wellington's warning to Captain Napier when, the lieutenant wrote, "we saw the French bonnets just above the high corn, and within forty or fifty yards of our Guns."

Even though they were deployed in a four-deep line, Wellington's infantry occupied a much greater space than when they were in square, which allowed him to leave the more shaken battalions in the rear and send forward only the most reliable units to meet the attack. Once the three brigades of Adam, Maitland, and Halkett, entirely composed of British infantry, were deployed in line, they covered almost the entire width of the front against which the Imperial Guard was advancing, and Wellington counted on their firepower to repulse the attack. Calculating how many men might have made up the three brigades at that moment is difficult, but at the end of the battle, Adam still had around two thousand in line, Maitland a little more than a thousand, and Halkett perhaps five or six hundred. This suggests that before their combat with the Imperial Guard, their ranks contained at least four thousand men. In turn, then, the three brigades, deployed in a four-deep line, would have presented to the enemy a front of a thousand men, which perfectly corresponds (taking into account the broad intervals between one battalion and another) to the width of the attack front, which was a thousand yards.

Behind this robust red line, Wellington still had considerable reserves available, although they were composed entirely of those foreign troops toward whom the British officers felt so ill-disposed. Behind Adam's brigade, the squares of Brunswick light infantry had suffered heavy casualties from the artillery bombardment and in addition had been obliged to detach several contingents to the defense of Hougoumont; nevertheless, the Brunswickers still had nearly two thousand muskets, and their officers' professionalism had demonstrated that the men, though inexperienced, would not run away. Behind Maitland's Foot Guards, Chassé's Third Netherlands Division had been in place for some time, after having spent the morning stationed well to the rear, near the little town of Braine-l'Alleud, barring the way to a possible attempt to outflank the Allies on the right. The fifty-year-old Chassé, a former Napoleonic officer, a veteran of Spain, and a baron of the empire, had been wounded the previous year while fighting for Napoleon against the Prussians; his division, 6,500 muskets strong, half of them troops of the line, formed the principal reserve at Wellington's disposal in the center of his deployment. Farther left, toward La Haye Sainte, stood the remaining men of the three Brunswick line infantry battalions, massed around their yellow-and-blue banners, and Kruse's three Nassau battalions.

In the rear of all this infantry, Wellington had also massed cavalry reserves superior in number to all those that Napoleon could still muster. Vivian's brigade, with more than a thousand sabers, was the only cavalry formation on the battlefield whose troops were still fresh. Vandeleur's brigade was in fair condition, and those of Grant, Dornberg, Trip, and Ghigny, although somewhat damaged, still included several combat-ready squadrons. The cavalry force, several thousand strong, was moved forward to just behind the Allied infantry with the purpose of compelling the foot soldiers, one way or another, to hold their positions. The adjutant of the Eighteenth Hussars, Duperier, an officer promoted from the ranks, had watched some Belgian officers beating their troops to hold them in line. During the attack of the Imperial Guard, Duperier's regiment was brought so far forward that the horses' muzzles were almost touching the backs of the infantry troops, and according to his memoirs, which make up in vivaciousness for what they lack in polished prose, he decided to emulate "the Belgum officers": "every one that faced about I laid my sword across his shoulders and told him that if he did not go back I would run him through, and that had the desired effect for they all stood it."

Many students of the battle maintain that the Imperial Guard's attack represented an almost desperate gamble on Napoleon's part, and from today's perspective this analysis is understandable. Yet, considering that the emperor was gambling on the relative moral capacity of the two armies necessarily changes that perspective. From a purely material point of view, the six thousand men of the Old Guard and Middle Guard would never have been able to prevail over the forces arrayed against them; in terms of morale, however, the balance was different. The British and German infantry had been tested almost to the limits of their endurance, they had taken frightful losses, and the fame of the Imperial Guard was rooted in the consciousness of every soldier, down to the least militiaman. When that mass of veterans attacked, the men deployed to face them might well have disbanded, and such disorder could have spread to Wellington's entire army.

This faith in the psychological effect also explains the caution with which Napoleon organized the final attack, as if he thought that the mere sight of the Imperial Guard would determine the collapse of its adversaries and that therefore it was unnecessary to engage the Guard in its entirety or to run useless risks. The two battalions of the oldest regiment, the First Grenadiers, remained in the vicinity of La Belle Alliance, as though to guarantee a last stand in case things should turn bad. Of the nine battalions ordered to attack, only five advanced in the first line until they reached La Haye Sainte. The other four battalions constituted a kind of second line, following the first five at a distance of two or three hundred yards. Finally—and most unusually—these battalions went forward neither in column nor in line, but in square.

In truth the accounts of the British officers who faced the Guard's advance invariably speak of columns, but from their viewpoint, and in the smoke that enveloped the entire battlefield, they could not distinguish one formation from another. French eyewitness accounts, on the other hand, spoke of squares, and these are the accounts we must trust. Despite its origins as a static formation, the square was capable of movement, and highly trained troops such as the Imperial Guard could certainly advance in square better and more quickly than any others. The decision to attack in this formation was made by the Guard's generals and, probably, Napoleon himself, as an immediate reaction to what had happened to d'Erlon's columns a few hours before; should the British cavalry try another sudden charge down the slope, they would find themselves confronting the Imperial Guard, already formed in square, and they would pay a heavy price.

And thus they advanced: the Middle Guard in front, five battalions, followed at some distance by another Middle Guard battalion and three battalions of the Old Guard, all with drummers beating out the charge. The men advanced in cadenced steps as officers checked the alignment of their ranks. They were accompanied by thirteen generals[33] and preceded by a multitude of *tirailleurs*. But in spite of the impressiveness of the French advance, we must not forget that, in this whole assault force, only the Old Guard battalions that formed the second line were really up to the old standards of the Imperial Guard. The battalions of the Middle Guard had been established only after Napoleon's return from Elba, when men were transferred from line regiments to form the new Guard units. Every regiment had been required to furnish thirty men, tall and robust, with good records and at least four years' service, not the most stringent requirements. The lack of a shared regimental experience was underlined even in the troops' appearance: Because of insufficient time and funds, the regiments of the Middle Guard had been provided only in part with regulation uniforms, so that many men did not wear the standard bearskin, covering their heads instead with shakos, two-cornered hats, and even woolen berets; their coats were of a variety of colors instead of the official dark blue. All things considered, these were good but not superb units, a fact that has not been stressed enough in accounts of this last offensive.

SIXTY-ONE

THE ATTACK OF THE IMPERIAL GUARD GRENADIERS

The first two battalions on the right were the 1/3rd Grenadiers and the Fourth Grenadiers, and they were also the first to come into contact with the defenders. In front of these thousand men, who tended to appear as a single column to the smoke-blinded observers, the remnants of Halkett's brigade were deployed; a little farther back stood the Brunswick line infantry brigade and Kruse's regiment, the only German units involved in defending the Imperial Guard's attack. Halkett's men were formed in lines four ranks deep, not only for fear of cavalry but also because this was the easiest formation to change into from square. ("In our condition at that time," Macready observed, "no power on earth could have formed a line of any kind out of us but that of a line four deep.") The German infantry, on the other hand, was probably still in square, the sole formation that could guarantee a minimum of solidity to the extremely young recruits that made up these battalions.

All day long, two batteries, those of Lloyd and Cleeve, had been stationed in front of Halkett's brigade, but by this time, out of twelve guns and more than six hundred gunners, not a single one remained in line. Cleeve's battery had run out of ammunition and cleared off to the rear sometime before; Lloyd's, which had stubbornly remained in position, occasionally sending an officer with an empty wagon to fetch a fresh supply of ammunition, was so badly shot up that the survivors could do nothing but run away when the first *tirailleurs* appeared in front of the guns. Major Lloyd, who had spent the entire day exposing himself to danger with a courage that verged on madness, remained a little too far behind his men; a French officer caught up with him and cut him down with his saber. After the battle, the major was found still alive and brought to a hospital, but he died a few weeks later.

When the defenders saw the French grenadiers bearing down on them, they opened fire; and, instead of continuing their advance with fixed bayonets, the masses of the attackers, who had just emerged from the smoke, stopped and began to fire back. There followed a confused combat, in which no one had any clear idea what was happening, and in which apparently more or less all the units involved, on one side as well as the other, sooner or later lost enthusiasm for the fight and fell back before their officers could regain control over them. The British and German infantry had moved forward in anticipation of the attack and occupied a very advanced position, well beyond the chemin d'Ohain; but it was not long before Kruse's men and then the Brunswickers, finding themselves exposed to enemy fire, fell back in search of some protection and perhaps would have retreated still farther had the cavalry deployed in their rear not compelled them to halt. Sir Colin Halkett's men, the majority of whom were recruits, had already looked death in the face two days previously at Quatre Bras and by this point had lost almost all of their officers; finding themselves alone, even though their well-aimed fire had brought the Imperial Guard's advance to a full stop, they too began to disband.

Wellington, who at the moment was a little farther down the line, behind Maitland's brigade, noticed the confusion and gave an order addressed to no one in particular: "See what's wrong there." Major Kelly, who had been detached to Halkett's brigade staff, galloped over in search of the general, found him, and was in the act of posing the duke's inquiry when, to his horror, he saw a musket ball strike Sir Colin in the face, passing through one cheek and exiting from the other side. In those days, bullets traveled at such low velocity that the general did not even fall from his horse, but Kelly nevertheless had to escort him to the rear; his brigade, or what remained of it, was left without a commander. Colonel Elphinstone, commander of the Thirty-third Foot and one of the least esteemed officers in the entire army, rode up to Kelly to ask him if he had any orders for him; none, Kelly replied, except "inquiring into the cause of the confusion." According to Kelly, the colonel answered that the situation could be explained by the fact that "they were much pressed, and the men exhausted."

Since Elphinstone was the most senior surviving officer, he had to take command of the brigade, a responsibility that he would have gladly done without. Bewildered, he asked Kelly, "What is to be done? What would you do?" The major, evidently exasperated, was suggesting that Elphinstone get his men under as much cover as possible, reorder their ranks, and have them lie on the ground, when two sergeants from the Seventy-third ran up to him and reported that all their officers had been killed or wounded, and they had no one to command them. Since this was Kelly's own regiment, he followed the men back to the position to survey the situation, and once he was among the men, he could not do otherwise than take command. The nearby regiments had already sent their colors to safety in the rear, and the major decided that the same should be done with the colors of the Seventy-third, "which had been completely riddled, and almost separated from the staff," Tom Morris noted. The two banners were removed from their standards and wrapped around the torso of a sergeant, who was ordered to leave at once for Brussels.

Although, for the moment, the Guard columns had halted their advance and were hidden in smoke, Major Kelly evidently had little hope that he and his men could hold out much longer. There was no remaining officer in the brigade superior in rank to the inept Elphinstone,[34] but Kelly probably ordered the surviving troops to take advantage of a moment when the enemy fire became less intense and fall back to the hedge bordering the sunken lane, where they could find some protection. Years later, Macready still shuddered at the thought that someone in command had been capable of giving such an order without taking into account its effect on morale. As soon as the Seventy-third began to retreat, the French redoubled their fire, accompanying it with roars of enthusiasm; the British wounded clung to their comrades, begging them not to abandon them; someone gave in to panic; and in a moment the withdrawal turned into a rout. Reduced to a crowd of runaways, Halkett's brigade fled well past the hedge, and it was only with difficulty that the surviving officers, by dint of a great deal of pulling and shouting, were able to bring their men to a halt. "I cannot conceive what the enemy was about during our confusion," Macready remarked acidly. "Fifty cuirassiers would have annihilated our brigade."

The reason why the Imperial Guard did not exploit the rout of the British is that the Prince of Orange, the only commander in the whole sector who was still in the saddle, realized that the prolonged firefight was likely to wear down the defenders and decided to put an end to it with a bayonet charge. With his saber unsheathed, afire with the ardor of his twenty-three years, the prince placed himself at the head of one of Kruse's battalions and led it in a charge; despite their fatigue and inexperience, the soldiers let themselves be swept away by his enthusiasm and followed him. The attack caught by surprise the square of the 1/3rd Grenadiers and caused a moment of confusion, but then the French opened fire with their customary, frightening effectiveness. The Prince of Orange was wounded in the shoulder almost at once, and his aides had a difficult time persuading him to retire; meanwhile, the battalion he had led to the attack was falling back in disorder. Colonel von Kruse was obliged to send his third battalion—a militia unit—into line as well, and under their protection managed to reorganize what was left of his regiment, but far enough to the rear not to be involved in any further combat.

In the meantime, the officers of Halkett's brigade had also succeeded in stemming the rout of their men; all remaining skirmishers were sent to the crest of the ridge with orders to hold the position at whatever cost, and the survivors of the several battalions were redeployed behind them. When they were finally in order, Major Kelly led them back into line, and barely in time, because the two Imperial Guard squares, having repulsed the Prince of Orange's attack, were advancing once again. As the major later described: "The *last attacking Column* made its appearance through the fog and smoke, which throughout the day lay thick on the ground. Their advance was as usual with the French, very noisy and evidently reluctant, the Officers being in advance some yards cheering their men on." As they advanced, the grenadiers kept up a confused and disordered fire, to which the British infantry did not reply until the enemy was at short range; there followed a brief firefight, at the end of which the French started to retreat. Soon they disappeared definitively into the smoke.

The unexpected conclusion of the French attack left the surviving officers of Halkett's brigade more perplexed than exultant. "Having expected great things from them, we were astonished at their conduct," wrote Ensign Macready. "We young soldiers almost fancied there was some 'ruse' in it." Major Kelly's hypothesis was that the units involved did not belong to the Imperial Guard, but rather were part of d'Erlon's corps, which was in action around La Haye Sainte, a few hundred yards away; but Macready went among the wounded French, questioning them, and found that they were all from the Middle Guard. Since the combat had taken place under conditions of zero visibility, Major Kelly wisely concluded that he should not endeavor to explain what really happened; because "the fog and smoke lay so heavy upon the ground," he recalled, "we could only ascertain the approach of the Enemy by the noise and clashing of arms which the French usually make in their advance to attack, and it has often occurred to me from the above circumstance that the accuracy and the particulars with which the *Crisis* has been so frequently and *so minutely* discussed, must have had a good deal of fancy in the narrative."

Actually, the failure of the French advance was not due to the few hundred muskets that Halkett's brigade had arrayed to defend against it but to the timely intervention of reserve troops from Chassé's Third Netherlands Division. Captain Krahmer's horse artillery battery took up a position alongside the British infantry and began firing its eight 6-pounder guns at point-blank range. These were the first cannon that the Imperial Guard had had to face in that sector, and it was under the unexpected hail of canister that the two grenadier squares began to waver. Macready remembered that battery well, even though he had no idea of its nationality. "Whosesoever they were," he later wrote, "they were served most gloriously, and their grand metallic bang, bang, bang, bang, with the rushing showers of grape that followed, were the most welcome sounds that ever struck my ears—until I married."

Meanwhile, Wellington had sent an aide-de-camp to Colonel Detmers, commander of the First Brigade of Chassé's division, with orders to bring three of his battalions into line at once. The colonel formed his men in columns and had them march parallel to the ridge and behind its crest, "in such a way," he reported, "that they were, up to a certain point, sheltered from the enemy musketry, and only our bayonets were struck by their bullets," underlining the intensity of the firing at this culminating moment of the battle. Finally, the colonel found a suitable place for his men to execute a right turn and deploy into line: "between the left flank of two battalions that were putting up a steady volleying fire, very furious and very well sustained, and a battalion formed in the shape of a triangle in a more rearward position"; that is, in all probability, between the battalions of Maitland's brigade and the remnants of Halkett's. As they took up this position, the Netherlanders found themselves on the flank of the grenadiers of the Guard, and just in time; at the moment they entered the line of battle, Detmers's troops saw the "triangle" start to break up, communicating its panic to units farther to its left.

Without losing time, except for a brief address to the troops, General Chassé ordered Detmer's entire brigade to charge—one battalion of Belgian *Jäger* and one Dutch line battalion, supported by a total of four Dutch militia battalions. For most of the morning, these troops had remained in position near the little town of Braine l'Alleud, where the men were well fed by the inhabitants and abundantly refreshed with beer and juniper brandy. Set in motion by Chassé, this multitude rushed forward in column, wildly enthusiastic, "drumming and shouting like mad, with their shakos on the top of their bayonets," according to Macready. Not all of the exhausted British soldiers understood who the strangers were, and while many greeted the Netherlanders with vigorous shouts and relieved laughter, others reacted quite differently; one officer reported that the Dutch-Belgians looked so much like French troops that he caught several of his men in the act of firing on them. As the grenadiers of the Guard watched these fresh troops cresting the ridge and bearing down on them, shouting "*Oranje boven!*" (the Dutch) and "*Vive le roi!*" (the Belgians), they could have had no doubts about which side their attackers were on; as a result, the grenadiers started falling back in growing disorder, and their panic spread to d'Erlon's troops, who had come up on their right. Throughout the sector, Napoleon's final attack had been brought to a halt.

SIXTY-TWO

"LA GARDE RECULE!"

While this confused fighting was taking place not far from La Haye Sainte, the two battalions of the Third Chasseurs à pied, also in square, were advancing up the slope toward the positions held by Maitland's brigade. This *chasseur* regiment, too, was newly formed; like other Middle Guard regiments, it had filled out its ranks by absorbing many men of the Young Guard, and its battle dress was rather irregular. The coming encounter—in which for the first time during the Napoleonic Wars the French Guards were about to confront the British Guards—could seem today to have been an equal contest a thousand muskets in the two French squares against a little more than a thousand in the two British battalions, although the formation used by the British allowed for much more effective fire. But before the infantry came within musket range, the artillery on both sides was unsparingly engaged in an attempt to weaken the enemy. Several artillery sections of two pieces each advanced together with the Guard squares, halted to fire a few shots, and then advanced even farther as soon as it was possible to do so. Maitland's men were all lying facedown among the remains of a wheat field, under cover of the sunken lane, which was particularly deep in this part of the field and bordered on one side by an embankment; a soldier who was there later remarked, "Without the protection of this bank every creature must have perished."

Only after the French guns, together with a number of *tirailleurs* advancing under their cover, drew to within relatively close range of Maitland's brigade did its losses begin to rise alarmingly; but by that point, the Third Chasseurs had already suffered even heavier casualties. The British artillery, which had several functioning batteries still in operation throughout this sector, rained canister on the French; one British officer compared the effect to that of a hailstorm battering down the standing grain. Another, who was farther away, viewed the squares as dark masses moving forward; every time the cannonballs struck down entire ranks of men, "long lanes of light are seen through the black body." When the *chasseurs* reached the top of the position, they did exactly what the grenadiers had done a little to their right: instead of continuing to advance with bayonets fixed, they stopped and started firing. Some British officers had the impression that only the first ranks fired, while the others tried to change from square to line.

It's difficult to say whether this refusal to drive the bayonet attack home reflected the already none-too-high morale of the Middle Guard or rather a conscious decision on the part of its generals, confident in the tremendous firepower they knew their men were capable of developing. At any rate, Maitland, who was with Wellington, did not consider the Guard's tactic a good idea: "With what view the Enemy halted in a situation so perilous, and in a position so comparatively helpless, he was not given time to evince." Maitland's men sprang to their feet in four-deep ranks—according to legend, the order to do so was given by Wellington himself ("Up, Guards, and at them!")—and opened fire at such short range, perhaps not more than fifty or sixty yards, that the effect was devastating. "Those who from a distance and more on the flank could see the affair, tell us that the effect of our fire seemed to force the head of the Columns bodily back," wrote an officer of the First Foot Guards.

Whether the cause was the sudden appearance of Maitland's men or the efficacy of their fire, the Third Chasseurs immediately began to crumble. General Michel, who commanded the division of *chasseurs à pied*, was killed in the midst of his men; the commander of the regiment, Colonel Malet (a veteran who had been a drummer boy at the time of the revolution and was among those who followed the emperor to Elba), was likewise killed, as was one of his two battalion commanders, while the other one, the "indestructible" Major Angelet, was wounded for the twelfth time in his career. Some of the surviving officers continued trying to change formation and deploy the regiment in line in order to respond to the enemy fire more effectively, but this attempt to maneuver ended by creating chaos among the ranks of the *chasseurs*. Seeing that their attackers were breaking up, Maitland's brigade advanced with fixed bayonets (according to legend, Wellington personally ordered this advance, too: "Now, Maitland, now is your time!"); to their great relief and no little amazement, the British realized that the Imperial Guard was not going to stand and wait for them to arrive. The French retreated, at first in disorder and then in a precipitous flight down the slope.

Maitland's men had already advanced some distance in pursuit of the routed enemy when the fifth and last battalion in the first line of attack, the Fourth Chasseurs, advanced and threatened their flank. Maitland's first idea was to have his entire line face right, but in the smoke, and with French artillery pounding the ridge, his order was not understood—nor, perhaps, could it have been.

Among the soldiers, who were expecting to be charged any minute by enemy cavalry, another order began to spread spontaneously, passed on from one man to the next: "Form square!" And as these contradictory orders followed one another, the brigade began to disband. Only with some effort did the officers got their men back in line and bring them rather hastily to their starting point, closely pursued by the French square as it mounted the slope, hard on their heels.

Two days earlier, at Ligny, the Fourth Chasseurs had suffered such heavy losses that its two battalions had been combined into one, albeit a very strong one with more than eight hundred muskets. All the Allied artillery posted in that sector was firing at them as their square came on, moving as though through a thunderstorm while their rolling drums obsessively beat the *pas de charge*. The officers of Bolton's battery watched the Fourth advance under fire, "the Column waving, at each successive discharge, like standing corn blown by the wind." When they reached the crest of the ridge, the French officers, like their colleagues, attempted to deploy their men into line, but by then Maitland's infantry had returned to their former position along the sunken lane, and their fire, combined with that of the Allied guns, was so destructive that the maneuver failed and the square was transformed into a disordered mass. Nevertheless, according to Lieutenant Sharpin, the French remained there for ten minutes, responding to the British fire as best they could, and making repeated efforts to advance.

While this combat was going on, General Adam, having ascertained that all the enemy columns were attacking the brigades to his left, decided that it was useless to remain where he was, and that, moreover, his troops had enough room to advance and counterattack. In the beginning, his advance was bitterly contested by the multitude of enemy skirmishers who had moved out ahead of their squares. The struggle was long and confused; Lord Hill, the II Corps commander, was in this sector of the field, observing the advance of Adam's brigade, when he was caught in crossfire by *tirailleurs*. His horse was killed under him, and Hill was so badly hurt in the fall that for half an hour his aides believed him dead. Adam's brigade was composed entirely of light infantry, including two battalions of the Ninety-fifth, armed with Baker rifles; under their pressure, the French skirmishers eventually were forced to abandon the field, leaving the flank of the advancing square exposed.

At this point, Sir John Colborne and his regiment, the Fifty-second, appeared. It was the strongest in the brigade, with around a thousand muskets, and it was also one of the best-trained light infantry regiments in the whole army. Colonel Colborne himself was an exceptional commander, adored by his men; according to Harry Smith, who had served under him in Spain, he inspired his men with "the most implicit confidence. He had more knowledge of ground, better understood the posting of picquets, consequently required fewer men on duty, knew better what the enemy were going to do, and more quickly anticipated his design than any officer; with that coolness and animation, under fire, no matter how hot, which marks a good huntsman when he finds his fox in his best country."[35]

Colborne's only defect was that sometimes, in battle, he tended to make excessively reckless decisions; his rashness had brought him grief once already, at La Albuera, in 1811. Provisionally in command of a brigade, he moved his troops forward during a thunderstorm that reduced visibility almost to zero; the Polish lancers made a flanking attack on the brigade and literally swept it away within a few minutes. After that, for understandable reasons, Colborne had never again been entrusted with a brigade, and so, more than four years after Albuera, and despite the fact that he enjoyed universal esteem, Sir John was still only a regimental commander. Nonetheless, when he saw the last French column advancing to his left, he once again made a sudden decision to trust to his instincts: He ordered his regiment to wheel to the left, thus forming a right angle with the rest of the brigade, and prepare to fall upon the flank of the enemy troops, who were moving past at that moment. It was a dangerous maneuver—it would have been sheer madness had any enemy cavalry still been in the area—but potentially decisive. Colborne's direct superior, General Adam, who was not fond of individual initiative, galloped up to Sir John and asked him what he planned to do. "Make that Column feel our fire," Colborne replied. The temptation was too great, and Adam yielded; he gave the colonel permission to advance, galloped over to the next regiment, and ordered its commander to follow the Fifty-second.

When the first skirmishers sent forward by Colborne got within range of the enemy and opened fire, the colonel had the impression that part of the French column halted and redeployed in line to face his troops; he was quite surprised by the rapidity of the maneuver and the intensity of the enemy fire. However, the *chasseurs* of the Imperial Guard were advancing in square, and therefore the entire flank of their formation was already prepared to open fire as soon as the enemy attacked on that side. "The Enemy was pressing on with shouts, which rose above the noise of the firing," remembered another British officer, likewise astounded, at a remove of so many years, by the unexpected effectiveness of the fire coming from that moving column. Colborne—who had become a colonel at thirty-six without ever buying a commission, having been promoted solely on the basis of merit—must have feared, for a moment, that he had once again thrown away his career.

In fact, as soon as the Fifty-second's whole line got within musket range, the volume of fire it developed was superior to anything the French were capable of; in addition, the square of the Fourth Chasseurs was receiving frontal fire from Maitland's brigade and the Allied artillery. More than two thousand muskets and at least fifteen guns were firing point-blank on the last Guard column in its densest formation. The square halted its advance and kept up an answering fire for a brief while, but the *chasseurs'* losses quickly became intolerable; the commander of the regiment fell wounded, and the battalion commander was killed. After only a few minutes, Colborne saw that the square was starting to break up, and once again seizing the decisive moment, he ordered a bayonet charge. The Fourth Chasseurs instantly collapsed, and the survivors fled down the slope in a rout.

When it was evident to all, in spite of the smoke obscuring the battlefield, that the attack of the Guard had failed, someone—at least according to legend—began to shout, *"La Garde recule!"* Despite the efforts of the French generals to keep their soldiers in formation, panic spread like lightning among them. Marshal Ney, who had already had four or five horses killed under him, shouted to d'Erlon that they must stand fast at all costs, "because if we don't die here, the émigrés will hang us."[36]

PART FOUR

"Victory! Victory!"

SIXTY-THREE

THE ALLIED ADVANCE

Napoleon had gambled for the last time and lost, and his army was suffering the moral collapse into which he had hoped to plunge the army of Wellington. The panic caused by the spectacle of the Imperial Guard in flight afflicted the entire left wing of the French, from Hougoumont to La Haye Sainte, and to this was added the equally disastrous panic produced on their right wing by the advance of Ziethen's Prussians from Smohain. The discovery that these troops were not, in fact, Grouchy's corps, whose arrival had been falsely proclaimed by the emperor's aides-de-camp, had the effect of a cold shower on the morale of the battle-weary French soldiers. Colonel Levavasseur had barely completed his gallop when the Prussian artillery opened fire with twenty-four guns, raking the flank and even the rear of the French infantry, which had advanced almost to the crest of the ridge. "The enthusiasm," Levavasseur reported, "gave way to a profound silence, to dismay, to anxiety." The colonel quickly galloped over to Marshal Ney, but the latter, who knew very well what was happening, forbade him to go and verify the facts. The incredulous Levavasseur applied to another general, whose name he later chose not to mention, and this man finally admitted the truth: "*Voyez! Ce sont les Prussiens!*"

After the battle, many witnesses linked the French army's collapse in morale to the uncertainty that had reigned among the soldiers ever since the beginning of the campaign. According to Captain Duthilt—who was thrown from his horse, wounded in the head by a saber blow, and taken prisoner during the great charge of the British heavy cavalry, then liberated by the countercharge of Jacquinot's lancers, and who later found himself, on foot and covered with blood, in the midst of a crowd of fugitives—the soldiers were upset at the excessive number of senior officers who had betrayed, or who were suspected of being ready to betray, the emperor. The troops had neither confidence in their commanders nor the ability to accept discipline. They were also terrorized by the proclamations of the Allied sovereigns, in which French soldiers taken prisoner were brutally threatened with "the deserts of Siberia or the English and Spanish prison-barges, where they would be lost forever," so that the dread of capture contributed to hastening their disbandment.

Even the Allied soldiers defending the ridge were astounded by the suddenness with which the French began to fall back before the Prussian advance. One of the Gordon Highlanders' skirmishers ran up to Sergeant Robertson and urged him to observe the enemy lines, because "something extraordinary" was going on. By that point, the Gordons had lost so many officers that Robertson, furnished with a telescope, was in command of two companies. Peering through the instrument, he saw what appeared to be men dressed in the same uniform firing on one another. Puzzled, the sergeant could not understand what was happening. Someone suggested that perhaps some sort of mutiny had broken out among the French soldiers; then an aide-de-camp arrived at a gallop, crying out, "The day is our own! The Prussians have arrived!" Robertson's sincere comment no doubt was widely echoed: "Never was reprieve more welcome to a death-doomed criminal."

On the opposite side of the battlefield, the Duke of Wellington and General Adam were discussing the merits of continuing to advance at once against the retreating enemy. Adam, concerned about the disorder in his ranks, requested permission to halt and redress the situation. Wellington reluctantly consented, but after observing the French for a few more seconds, he changed his mind and said, "They won't stand, better attack them!" Then he galloped over to Colborne's position to order him to advance as well. The men of the Fifty-second were in great disorder and also nervous because their flank was completely exposed. When a large and vociferous group of cavalry passed them at short range, the Fifty-second unhesitatingly fired on them, only to discover that they were part of the Twenty-third Light Dragoons sent in pursuit of the enemy. The dragoons' commander was bitterly protesting to Colborne, gesturing at the men and horses of his regiment struck down by the infantry fire ("It's always the case, we always lose more men by our own people than we do by the enemy"), when Wellington rode up and shouted to Colborne, "Never mind, go on, go on!" Colborne was on foot—his men had managed to kill his horse, too, with their disordered fire—but he did not need to be told twice; with bayonets fixed, the Fifty-second returned to the attack.

The duke had decided that the moment to play all or nothing had come, and he was galloping along the entire arc of his deployment, from Hougoumont to La Haye Sainte and beyond, giving his commanders the order for a general advance. The progress of his ride was marked by the cheers of triumph that rolled like a wave from one end of the front line to the other. Many memoirists assert that in those decisive moments, the duke galloped up to their regiments, sought out their commanders—in general, these were subalterns, the superior officers having been killed or wounded—and personally ordered the advance amid roars of enthusiasm from the troops. In the sunken lane behind La Haye Sante, Kincaid and his men were enveloped in smoke and dust, and he had not the least idea what was happening until "a cheer," which they knew to be British, "commenced far to the right, and made everyone prick up his ears—it was Lord Wellington's long-wished-for orders to advance; it gradually approached, growing louder as it grew near." Instinctively, Kincaid and his men began to move forward with fixed bayonets. When they reached the top of the knoll overlooking the sandpit, they broke through the smoke and were presented with the astonishing spectacle of the entire French army in full flight. Shortly thereafter, the duke appeared before Kincaid and his men; Wellington was greeted with cheers, to which he responded, cool as always, "No cheering, my lads, but forward, and complete your victory!"

Lord Uxbridge, alarmed by the risks inherent in such a disordered advance, advised that the troops should be halted upon reaching the crest of La Belle Alliance, but Wellington impatiently replied, "Oh, damn it! In for a penny, in for a pound is my maxim; and if the troops advance, they shall go as far as they can." In reality, most of the soldiers were so exhausted that they limited their advance to a few hundred yards, assuring themselves that the enemy was in flight before them, and then went into bivouac for the night. The only Allied units that continued to pursue were Adam's brigade, Du Plat's brigade, Detmers's Netherlands brigade, and one of the battalions of Hanoverian *Landwehr* commanded by Colonel Hew Halkett, which moved forward from its position near Hougoumont to cover the exposed left flank of Adam's line.

In the pursuit of the retreating enemy, Wellington also engaged his remaining cavalry, what was left of the brigades of Dornberg, Vandeleur, Trip, and Ghigny, along with Vivian's Hussar brigade, the only Allied cavalry force that had not yet exchanged so much as a saber-stroke with the enemy during the whole course of the day. Although in later years General Vivian yielded to the temptation to magnify his role in the battle,[37] there's no doubt that the intervention of his force—upward of a thousand fresh sabers—made a decisive contribution to accelerating the dissolution of the French army. Vivian was haunted by the memory of Marengo, where Napoleon's luck had transformed a battle already lost into a victory, and he was determined to avoid a repeat of history. Vivian proposed to lead his brigade into action with the set purpose of causing the enemy as much damage as possible, and he importuned Wellington to give him the order to charge without any further loss of time.

When the duke consented to the charge, Lord Uxbridge decided that he would lead it in person; but at that precise instant, a shell fragment shattered his right knee. Uxbridge exclaimed, "By God! I've lost my leg!" and Wellington coolly replied, "Have you, by God?" The anecdote may be apocryphal, but the code of honor to which these gentlemen adhered prized above all things composure and self-possession in the face of danger. This is confirmed by the observations of Duperier of the Eighteenth Hussars, who was watching the two commanders from not far away; all at once, he saw Lord Uxbridge shake Vivian's hand and guide his horse to the rear at a walk. Duperier suspected that Uxbridge had been wounded, "but he don it so well that nobody saw it." Shortly thereafter, in a house in Waterloo, surgeons amputated Lord Uxbridge's leg, and the earl had it buried with all honors in the garden.

Having taken his leave of the cavalry commanders, Wellington galloped over to Adam's brigade to encourage the foot soldiers to continue their pursuit; like them, the duke was filled with the excitement of victory. There was almost no one left of the numerous and gleaming staff that had accompanied him when the day began, and after Wellington reached the brigade, Major Blair was astonished to discover that there was only one other officer in the duke's retinue. Blair's amazement grew when he addressed this officer, only to hear him reply in French, "*Monsieur, je ne parle pas un seul mot d'Anglais.*"[38]

In the meantime, Sir Hussey Vivian led his squadrons down the slope at a trot and engaged the groups of French cavalry that were covering the infantry's retreat. Under normal conditions, the Hussars would have had some difficulty holding their own against cuirassiers and lancers, and here, too, Napoleon's cavalrymen, although weary and demoralized, seem to have shown enough fighting spirit to guarantee their retreat. In a letter to his wife, Captain Taylor of the Tenth Hussars reported, "A cuirassier made a good attack at me, which I caught on my sword, and gave him a back-hander, on which we parted, as I was, saving your presence, running away then, being alone amongst a whole lot of them, though they were so anxious about their own bacon, none but he thought of me." (The captain prudently added, "These anecdotes are only for private friends.") Shakespear, an officer in the same regiment, saw the lancers charge down the hill and, wielding their deadly weapons, force a way for themselves through the ranks of the British cavalry before being forced to fall back by sheer weight of numbers; he later remembered "seeing one of the lancers giving two or three pulls to get his lance out of one of our dragoons he had struck." Vivian himself found his way barred by a cuirassier who had no desire at all to surrender, and the general, with his right arm in a sling, still recovering from a wound received the previous year, was forced to swing his saber with his left hand. With great difficulty, Vivian managed to fend off his attacker until his German orderly arrived and "cut the fellow off his horse." Major Poten of the First KGL Hussars, who had lost his right arm in Spain, had the good luck to encounter an adversary who was a better sport. Despite his disability, the major was riding with his regiment, accompanied by an escort of two noncommissioned officers. In the confusion he got separated from them, and a cuirassier came galloping toward him with lifted saber. Poten showed his empty sleeve, whereupon the cuirassier stopped his whirling arm in midswing, transformed the saber-stroke into a salute, and spurred his horse away.

Pressed hard by Vivian's Hussars and by the other British and Netherlands cavalry brigades following on their heels, some of Napoleon's cavalry lost no time in abandoning the field; at one point, the pursuers found themselves literally riding amid cuirasses, which the cuirassiers had thrown away for the sake of a quicker escape. On the whole, however, the French cavalry retired in a comparatively ordered fashion. Colonel Hew Halkett later recalled, not without amusement, "[The retreating enemy] threatened us in a most *vociferous* manner." Captain Barton of the Twelfth Light Dragoons, at the head of his regiment, rode quite close to the Guard's *grenadiers à cheval*, who, according to Barton, were retreating in "a dense close column, and appeared to take but little notice of our advance, when opposite their flank they fired a few pistol or carbine shots. We were some distance in front of our Brigade, and being too weak to make an impression [on them], they literally walked from the field in a most majestic manner."[39]

SIXTY-FOUR

———◦•◦———

THE SQUARES OF
THE OLD GUARD

Amid the growing flood of fugitives, whom the retreat of the cavalry threatened to leave defenseless and exposed to the victors' pursuit, the only effective resistance was mounted by the four Guard infantry battalions, three Old Guard and one Middle Guard, which had constituted the French second line of attack. They were little more than two thousand muskets strong and therefore could have no conceivable hope of standing fast against the flood that was rushing toward them; but retiring step by step, without losing cohesion, and leaving behind them an unbroken trail of dead and wounded, they covered the retreat of the French army south along the main road to Charleroi. Their action was responsible for, among other things, the fact that the army managed to keep all its colors; incredibly, not a single Eagle was lost in the course of the retreat. The Prussian officers who were at that moment capturing Plancenoit were amazed to hear the French shouting not "*Sauve qui peut!*" but "*Sauvons nos aigles!*" even though they were withdrawing so hastily as to give very much the impression of a rout. On that June evening, the squares of the Old Guard wrote the last chapter in the Napoleonic epic and entered directly into legend.

The British cavalry tried repeatedly to break up the squares but discovered to its cost that their defensive capacity remained undiminished. When Major Howard of the Tenth Hussars received the order to charge a square, he asked the opinion of a colleague, who told him that it would be better to await the arrival of the infantry, because the square looked too solid to charge. Since he had been given an order to charge, the perplexed Howard declared, disobeying it seemed "a ticklish thing," and so he led his squadron forward; but another acquaintance of his, who nodded to him as he passed, observed that he "looked as if his time had come." As foreseen, the square stood fast, and the Hussars dispersed before coming into contact with it. Major Howard, galloping ahead of everybody else, took a ball in the face and fell from his horse right in front of the enemy bayonets; a French soldier stepped out from the ranks and bashed in the major's skull with the butt of his musket.

In other cases, attacks against the Guard squares miscarried before they began. Colonel Muter of the Inniskillings, with one arm in a sling and his helmet disfigured by saber blows, was in command of what was left of the Union Brigade when a young staff officer, the Honorable George Dawson, brother of the disgraced Lord Portarlington, came hurrying up, bearing orders for Muter and his men to join in the charge. Dawson later confessed that he would never forget the looks on their faces when he communicated these orders to them. The remaining dragoons, many of them battered and wounded, wearily hauled themselves back into their saddles and advanced at a walk until they came within musket range of a French square; one of the first balls struck Dawson in the knee and knocked him off his horse. "I think you ha' it nu', sir!" Colonel Muter growled in his broad Scots dialect, and that was the end of the charge.

In general, the accounts left by British officers leave the impression that the Allied pursuers learned almost immediately to stay away from the Guard squares, which were retiring in relatively good order, and turned instead to harrying the more exhausted line infantry units. Under the menace of cavalry, these also tried to form square, but they tended to disband, throw down their weapons, and surrender. Duperier, whose recollections are at least as colorful as his orthography, led his squadrons against "a regiment of infantry of the franch, nothing but 'vive le Roy,' but it was too late beside our men do not understand franch, so they cut a way all through till we came to the body of reserve when we was saluted with a voly at the length of two sords." At this point, the Hussars turned their horses and started chasing down runaways again; they offered much more *fun* (Duperier's word) and less resistance than the squares of the Imperial Guard.

Wherever the cavalry came, entire units threw down their weapons and clung to one another to avoid being trampled or flung themselves to the ground, out of reach of the sabers, and stayed there until someone took them prisoner. Colonel Murray, commander of the Eighteenth Hussars, described with some amazement the multitudes of surrendering French soldiers: "The sneaking prisoners we had taken holloaed, 'Vive le roi.' . . . On charging, not only did the infantry throw themselves down, but the cavalry also from off their horses, all roaring *'pardon,'* many of them on their knees." At this point, the fugitives were practically defenseless, and it was solely up to their pursuers whether to take them prisoner or to slaughter them. Murray found himself galloping into the midst of a crowd of French troops, one of whom aimed a bayonet thrust at him; his orderly "was compelled to cut down five or six in rapid succession for the security of his master." When Vandeleur's cavalrymen caught up with General Durutte, who had been cut off from his men in the French flight from Papelotte, one saber blow smashed his right hand, and another split his face open, leaving him disfigured and blind in one eye.[40]

Captain Tomkinson of the Sixteenth Light Dragoons also recalled "many of their infantry immediately throwing down their arms and crowding together for safety" when he and his men reached them; he saw others "lying together for safety, they were some yards in height, calling out, from the injury of one pressing upon another, and from the horses stamping upon them (on their legs)." Tomkinson pursued a man who had thrown away his musket, picked it up again, and fired it at the dragoons; the man flung himself atop his stacked comrades, and Tomkinson's horse, called "Cyclops" because it had but one eye, inadvertently trampled the pile, provoking howls of pain. Plunging among that terrorized and only partially disarmed throng, however, was a dangerous undertaking; at least one officer of the Sixteenth died in the midst of panic-stricken French troops. Eventually, the dragoons somehow managed to surround them and persuade them to surrender. Another officer, barely nineteen years old, disappeared in the pursuit and was never found again. Tomkinson concluded that the French had probably killed him, his body had lain hidden in a grain field, and the next day the peasants had stripped the corpse, rendering it unrecognizable.

The four Guard squares were able to hold out until nightfall, after which they dissolved into the crowd of fugitives filling the road to France; however, even they left a certain number of prisoners in the hands of their pursuers. A Hanoverian officer, Lieutenant Richers, wrote a graphic account of the attack of his militia battalion, commanded by Hew Halkett, which harried the squares, accelerating their retreat and, in some cases, their disintegration: "The battalion . . . advanced in silence, tense from the large number of both enemy and friendly cannon balls flying over our heads. . . . Once we had gone through the hollow and climbed the ridge on the other side, we saw an enemy column about 300 or 400 paces from us. It was either a regiment or battalion of the Old Guard. . . . Our skirmishers deployed against the Old Guard skirmishers and a firefight began. We were advancing, but the enemy stood where he was. The centre of our skirmish chain inadvertently closed together to allow the following column to pass as it was clear we were only a few moments away from a bayonet charge. Once the advancing battalion reached the skirmish line, its pace accelerated. We moved up, the enemy skirmishers disappeared and the front ranks of the columns fired a volley at us." French fire, even coming from so unfavorable a formation as a square, was always a fearful thing, especially for a unit composed of recruits; "I believe we all hesitated and stood where we were," Richers noted.   •

Colonel Halkett, who during the course of this brief combat had three horses killed under him, saved the situation by cheering his men and urging them on; the French lost heart when they saw the enemy advancing upon them with leveled bayonets. Richers continued: "They stood for a moment longer, then wavered, turned around and retired a short distance in relatively good order. Their formation then started to break up and finally they fled in total disorder. It seemed as if we were fresher than the tired-out Old Guard because we got closer and closer to them, taking many prisoners from those who could run no further. The wild chase continued forwards towards the enemy. Both sides fired only as much as they could when running. The enemy officers did attempt to rally their men, waving their swords and shouting 'en avant!' However, that was in vain for when an officer managed to gather a few men around him, our pursuit chased them away again."

The most famous of the prisoners captured on this occasion was General Cambronne, commander of the 2/1st Chasseurs, the same man who had disembarked near Antibes a little more than three months earlier at the head of the thousand grenadiers accompanying the emperor on his flight from Elba. According to the account that appeared in a Paris newspaper a few days after the battle, Cambronne was the French commander who declared, "The Old Guard dies, but it does not surrender!" when summoned to lay down his arms. Much more probably, as his troops were beginning to disband, the exclamation he uttered was "Merde!" The general and two of his aides had been riding back and forth outside their square, encouraging the troops; noticing this, Colonel Hew Halkett had called on him to surrender, thereby occasioning his gracious reply. The Hanoverian skirmishers quickly noticed the general's exposure and started firing at the three French officers. Soon Cambronne's horse was hit and fell, dragging down his rider. "I ordered the sharpshooters to dash on," Halkett wrote, "and I made a gallop for the General. When about cutting him down he called out he would surrender, upon which he preceded me to the rear, but I had not gone many paces before my horse got a shot through the body and fell to the ground. In a few seconds I got him on his legs again, and found my friend, Cambronne, had taken French leave in the direction from where he came. I instantly overtook him, laid hold of him by the aiguillette, and brought him in safety and gave him in charge to a sergeant to deliver to the Duke." The colonel did not yet know who his prisoner was and asked him his name in the midst of a crowd of German officers, who had gathered around out of curiosity. The prisoner was wounded, and his face was covered with blood; he wiped his mouth with the back of his hand and said, "Je suis le général Cambronne."

SIXTY-FIVE

THE MEETING AT
LA BELLE ALLIANCE

While the British advance was pushing the enemy back, the attacking Prussians finally got the better of the obstinate French defenders, both at Papelotte, where Durutte's men, reduced to a few hundred muskets, heard the musket fire coming closer on their flank and almost in their rear and yielded all at once to Ziethen's pressure, and at Plancenoit, where the fresh troops brought into line by Pirch at last overcame the resistance of the Imperial Guard. The attack was primarily led by the Twenty-fifth Infantry, which had been formed on the basis of the *Freikorps* led by the famous partisan commander, General von Lützow, and still wore its black uniform. Plancenoit church was burning and tongues of flame were darting out of almost all the houses in the village; yet a furious barrage of musketry was still coming from the walls of the cemetery, preventing the Prussians from advancing beyond the village square, which was already filled with heaps of corpses. The only way to dislodge the defenders was to outflank them, so Major von Witzleben led the Twenty-fifth's Fusilier battalion through the woods south of the village and burst in among the houses behind the French. The men of the Guard stubbornly defended every house, every hedge, every stone wall, but the Prussian skirmishers, vastly superior in numbers, continued to gain ground. Realizing that they were in danger of being caught in a pincer, the French abandoned the defense of the village and began an increasingly hasty retreat in the direction of Le Caillou, leaving behind the artillery's wagons and guns. Until they reached the main road, the French battalions maintained a certain order, repeatedly forming square to fight off Prussian cavalry; but once they were on the *pavé*, all semblance of order disappeared, and the stampede became general.

At La Belle Alliance, Marshal Soult met General Radet, commander of the military police, and ordered him to gather all the cavalry who were without mounts and arm them with muskets. Radet set about his appointed task, assisted by his aides-de-camp and a handful of gendarmes; they collected muskets from the battlefield, armed all the dismounted cuirassiers they could find, and combined them with infantry stragglers to form a unit. When the Prussians approached from Plancenoit, preceded by a chain of skirmishers, Radet deployed his heterogeneous forces and held off the enemy for a while to the sound of a drum that was beating the charge; meanwhile, he saw to securing the carriages belonging to the emperor and Marshal Soult, whose drivers had already started to unharness the horses and slink away. Then, as the dusk began to deepen, everyone's attention turned to escaping the present predicament: The inn from which Napoleon had directed the battle for a considerable part of the day was the point toward which Pirch's and Bülow's infantry from Plancenoit, Ziethen's from Papelotte, and Adam's and Hew Halkett's from Hougoumont were all converging.

By this point, it was nearly dark, and the only formation in all of Napoleon's army still capable of putting up a fight was the Old Guard's First Grenadiers à pied, commanded by General Petit. This regiment, the best of the best, comprised two battalions, about a thousand men in all, nearly half of them decorated with the Legion of Honor. Held in reserve near La Belle Alliance, these troops had not participated in the offensive and were retiring in good order, formed in square, and stopping every few paces to dress their ranks and fire a volley. Not only did their fire hold off their pursuers, it also kept at a distance the crowd of routed French soldiers who wanted to take refuge in the squares and who would certainly have determined their undoing. "We fired at all who presented themselves," General Petit confessed, "both friends and foes, for fear of letting in the ones with the others."

Not long before, Napoleon himself had been under the protection of one of these squares, but he was by then already galloping toward Le Caillou, from where he would depart immediately for France, escorted by a batalion of the Old Guard—the 1/1st Chasseurs—who had spent the entire day guarding the emperor's baggage and the imperial treasury.

Shortly after crossing the road near La Belle Alliance, Major Blair, Adam's brigade major, met the first Prussians. There were no more French in the area, and the British officers were busy chalking the numbers of their regiments on abandoned enemy guns so they could later claim them as their rightful booty. Hew Halkett maintained that he and his brigade had captured a dozen guns of the Imperial Guard but left them where they were in order to continue the pursuit of the enemy; the next day, to his great irritation, he found those guns marked with the numbers of the Fifty-second and Seventy-first Regiments. The Eighteeth Hussars, still led by Sir Hussey Vivian in person, also met the Prussians near the road. In their enthusiasm, Vivian's riders mistook the Prussians for French and cut down quite a few with their sabers. Night was falling fast, and in the thickening darkness British and Prussian troops fired on one another practically every time they met, causing a great many "friendly fire" casualties. Wellington himself noticed a Prussian battery that was firing on Adam's men and had to ask the Conte di Sales to gallop over to the battery and apprise the gunners of their mistake. Fortunately, when di Sales reached the guns, he found someone who spoke French, and he was able to have the bombardment stopped.

In some cases, the officers involved in such incidents adopted a philosophical attitude toward them. For example, Lieutenant Ingilby of the horse artillery, whose battery came under fire from the Prussians just when the lieutenant's men were harnessing the horses in order to join the pursuit, calmly suggested, "As the Prussians had never probably seen British troops before, it was not extraordinary that they should take us to be the Enemy in the *pêle-mêle* sort of confusion that was presented to their view at first coming up." Others, however, reacted less sportingly. When a Prussian battery took up a position a few hundred yards away and started firing on Captain Mercer's battery, he at once gave the order to return fire; soon a German officer came galloping up in great distress and remonstrated with the captain: "Dat is your friends de Proosians." Mercer replied that whoever fired on him was his enemy and continued to fire back, undeterred. The German officer took his leave after a cannonball nearly killed him, and the bombardment kept smashing up vehicles, men, and horses on both sides until a Belgian battery went into position nearby. Mercer managed to persuade them to fire on the Prussians rather than on him, and shortly thereafter the Belgians and Prussians ceased firing on one another and moved on.

After nine o'clock, not far from La Belle Alliance, the famous meeting between Wellington and Blücher took place. Probably influenced by the inn's prophetic name, the iconography of the battle has always represented this encounter as occurring right in front of the building itself. Although both men were on horseback, the Prussian commander managed to lean out of his saddle and embrace and kiss Wellington, to the latter's no little dismay, unaccustomed as he was to continental effusiveness. "*Mein lieber Kamerad! Quelle affaire!*" the old man stammered. Later, Wellington would maliciously comment on the scene: "That was about all the French he knew." The two commanders decided together that the Prussians alone would continue the pursuit. This decision is usually explained by citing the exhausted condition of Wellington's troops, but Blücher's were surely no less tired. More likely the choice reflected the plodding management and slowness of movement that characterized British troops, even when they were commanded by the best of their generals. The enormous number of friendly fire incidents that were occurring wherever the two Allied armies encountered each other also must have made separating them seem like a good idea.

Wellington's weary foot soldiers prepared to bivouac on the ground they had defended the whole day. But for hours fighting kept flaring up all along the front, so no one could really feel safe. Some officers of Halkett's brigade were gathered around their provisional commander, Colonel Elphinstone, talking about the course of the day; the happiest of the lot was Major Chambers, who had succeeded by seniority to command of the Thirtieth Regiment and declared that he expected to be promoted immediately to lieutenant colonel. While all the others were agreeing with him and offering their congratulations, a few shots sounded nearby and bullets whistled around them. Lieutenant Pattison said that he would go and see what was happening, saluted his friends, and advanced several paces before he spotted some isolated French soldiers who stubbornly kept firing at him and his comrades. When a ball hissed past him, Pattison instinctively turned around and saw Major Chambers put a hand to his chest and move away from the group in search of a clean place where he might lie down; "in five minutes he was a lifeless corpse."

Even in the rear, where small units of cavalry and militia were guarding large numbers of French prisoners, the tension of the battle was far from diminishing. The British or German cavalry troops could not afford to use good manners as they lined up the prisoners and drove them along the Brussels road, and more than one of the conquerors took advantage of the occasion to mistreat the French and mock their defeat. One or two writers remembered feeling nothing more than pity for those exhausted, ragged, sodden, mud-covered men, many of them disfigured by frightful wounds. But in some cases the prisoners, including those who were wounded, were so hostile and uncooperative that they could be made to march only under threat of arms. A British officer remarked that it would not have been wise to draw near to them without a loaded pistol or at least an unsheathed sword in one's hand. The next day, in the Brussels hospital, Captain Bridges of the Royal Engineers personally saw and heard wounded French soldiers crying out "Vive l'Empereur" as surgeons sawed off their arms and legs.

SIXTY-SIX

THE PRUSSIAN PURSUIT

At Le Caillou, a little more than a mile from La Belle Alliance, Marchand, Napoleon's valet, listened with mounting uneasiness as the musket fire drew closer. Acting on his own initiative, he had the emperor's camp bed packed up and loaded on a mule; then he locked the great imperial *nécessaire*—which contained, among other things, 100,000 francs in gold and 300,000 in banknotes—and loaded it on his own carriage. For the past few hours, a stream of wounded and fugitive soldiers had been steadily returning along the main road toward France; when this stream turned into a flood, Marchand, without asking for authorization from anyone, ordered the large convoy of vehicles that constituted the imperial baggage train to leave Le Caillou. But the road was thronged with wagons, and everything was moving at a slow walk. Before long, Napoleon himself, who was riding on the road accompanied by the 1/1st Chasseurs, caught up with the convoy. Overcome with weariness, he gave orders to keep heading for France and climbed into his campaign coach. A few minutes later, the Prussians reached Le Caillou, where they set fire to the farm and its adjacent barns, burning alive all the wounded French soldiers who had been brought into those buildings.

The Prussians carried out the pursuit of the defeated enemy in a paroxysm of ferocity, the result of the tension accumulated in the fighting without quarter that had raged in the streets of Plancenoit, but also of the fanatical anti-French propaganda that had been fed to Blücher's troops. Lieutenant Jackson of Wellington's staff found himself in the midst of the Prussians between La Belle Alliance and Rossomme and was genuinely afraid that they were going to fire on him, so great was their excitement; everywhere around him, they were bayoneting wounded French soldiers to death. Later, the lieutenant came across a group of Prussian infantry who were debating whether or not to kill a wounded cavalryman; drawing near, Jackson saw that the injured soldier was a British light dragoon and began shouting, "*Er ist ein Engländer!*" until the Prussians went away. By this point, Lieutenant Jackson had had enough of these loyal allies: "I got clear of the Prussians as soon as I could, and was glad to find myself with a whole skin among the 52nd."

Dr. Larrey, chief surgeon of the Imperial Guard and inventor of the ambulance, tried to escape amid throngs of Prussian cavalry; he had already suffered two saber wounds when an uhlan struck him down with his lance. Having dismounted to rob him, the uhlan realized that Larrey was not dead, whereupon he took everything of value that he could find on the doctor, tied his hands behind his back, and brought his bleeding prisoner to his general. According to Larrey, his squat frame and gray redingote deceived the uhlan, who was convinced that he had captured Napoleon himself. The Prussian general immediately saw the mistake and coldly gave orders for the prisoner to be shot. Larrey was standing in front of the firing squad when a Prussian surgeon who had worked with him in Berlin recognized him and managed to save his life.

The effectiveness of the Prussian pursuit, which enormously increased the victors' booty and contributed decisively to breaking the morale of Napoleon's army, is all the more noteworthy because the Prussians, no less exhausted than the British, had available very few troops still capable of marching. Gneisenau placed himself at the head of the vanguard and urged on his exhausted men all night long. According to Clausewitz, Gneisenau "had the drum beat incessantly, intending by this sign of his troops' approach to strike terror into the hearts of the fleeing enemy on all sides, to frighten him out of his resting places, and to keep him in continuous flight." With the Prussian drum hard on their heels, the French kept fleeing until dawn, abandoning guns and baggage every time the road became difficult. It was in the course of this pursuit and not in the battle proper that Napoleon's army was deprived of almost all its cannon, a loss that transformed the defeat into a disaster. "It was the finest night of my life," Gneisenau later wrote.

The majority of the booty was taken where the road went through inhabited centers and the inevitable traffic jams ensued. In Genappe, the road passed over the River Dyle on a single bridge, and there many artillerymen unharnessed their horses and cleared off, abandoning the guns to their pursuers. While houses were beginning to burn and Prussian fusiliers were clearing away a barricade constructed of wagons and cannon at the entrance to the village, Napoleon was obliged to leave his coach and get back in the saddle. A short time later, Major von Keller of the Fifteenth Infantry Regiment took possession of the emperor's sword, his medals, a purse of diamonds, and even his hat, which he had let fall to the ground in his panic.[41]

A little farther on, the uhlans reached the last carriages in the imperial train; they had been abandoned by Marchand and left in the middle of the road, each of them with a team of six or eight horses still in harness, but apart from the animals there was no living creature in sight. In these vehicles, too, were hidden bags of precious stones, which Napoleon always carried with him as a reserve of liquid assets in case of an emergency—a policy more befitting an adventurer than an emperor. As their officers were urging them forward, the uhlans hastily filled their pockets with whatever they found and rode on; the fusiliers of the Fifteenth arrived after them and seized the lion's share of the booty. The next day, one of their officers wrote, there were fusiliers selling diamonds as big as peas for a few francs. The rumor that Napoleon's carriages were full of precious gems spread like lightning. The next morning, a British officer passing by the remains of the carriages met several Prussian soldiers digging and sifting the earth around them, looking for fallen valuables.

At Genappe the retreat of the French army was definitively transformed into a rout. Colonel Brô, commander of one of the lancer regiments that had wreaked such a terrible revenge on the British cavalry, had suffered a wound in his right arm in the fighting and was so weak from loss of blood that he was obliged to lean on his servant for support. Having heard that all the wounded were to retire to Charleroi, Brô paid the driver of a cabriolet from the baggage train to take him there, but they were unable to get past Genappe, because the road was clogged with artillery wagons. Brô was still there when the fleeing soldiers started to pour into the road, announcing that the battle was lost and the army in retreat. Two riders, passing in great haste, shouted to him that Napoleon had been killed in one of the Guard's squares; the colonel needed some time to get over this tremendous news and start thinking about saving his own skin. Around him, the fugitives, maddened by fear, were killing one another in order to make way faster; General Radet, who was trying to maintain order, was pulled down from his horse and clubbed half to death with musket butts.

Major Trefcon, suffering from heavy bruises and a sprained wrist, had dragged himself toward the rear in search of an ambulance, and soon he too was on the road to Genappe, in the midst of a growing throng of fugitives. "I met an old cuirassier squadron commander, whom I had known in Spain in former days," Trefcon later wrote. "He, too, was wounded and looking for the ambulances. When he came up to me, he said, 'My poor colonel, we are most unfortunate. The battle is lost.' I was furious, and I believe I answered him rudely. The squadron commander said no more, but sadly hung his head, as though dazed. I felt sorry for him." Before long, however, Trefcon had to admit that his old comrade-in-arms was right; the fleeing soldiers were so numerous and so desperate that the day could not but be lost. Jostled about in the crowd and weakened by his injuries, the major decided to leave the road and seek a way to escape through the countryside; there, by good fortune, he was able to stop an abandoned horse, mount it, and head for the border.

In a house in Genappe, Chef de Bataillon Jolyet, who had suffered a stomach wound at Hougoumont, lay stretched out on a bed of straw after having comforted himself with a little bread and a glass of beer. He was thinking that perhaps the army would halt there and give battle again tomorrow, when he heard the bugles of the Prussian cavalry, which was galloping through the streets of the village. "*Pauvre France! Pauvre armée!*" he murmured, and so did the others there with him; however, they blew out the candle and locked the door, hoping they might be spared. The next morning, a Prussian officer knocked on the door and compelled them to open it; then he confiscated watches, money, and even the officers' epaulets, acting as if they were lucky he was not taking their lives. Jolyet, who had hidden part of his money in his socks, was searched by several soldiers, and one of them was on the point of stripping off his boots, but his own comrades made him desist. Nevertheless, Jolyet later recalled, "They took my braces, my cravat, my belt, and my shirt, but they magnanimously left me my overcoat and my trousers."

As soon as they got past Genappe, General von Gneisenau gathered the fusiliers around him and commanded them to sing the hymn "*Herr Gott, Dich loben wir*" ("Lord God, We Praise Thee"); then, in the thick darkness, he gave the order to continue the pursuit. Not far ahead of him, Marchand had almost reached Quatre Bras with his remaining carriages when he discovered that a cannon bogged down in the middle of the road made it impossible for him and his party to proceed. At that moment, Prussian cavalry caught up with the rearmost carriages and began to plunder them. Marchand opened the *nécessaire*, slipped the banknotes inside his shirt, and took to his heels, abandoning the rest. All the carriages fell into the hands of the Prussians, and thousands of louis d'or disappeared into the soldiers' pockets before the officers were able to establish a modicum of order and post sentinels. The vehicles belonging to the general staff and the marshals' personal carriages were also captured in that stretch of road, but Gneisenau kept pushing on with his remaining men, who were drunk with fatigue and weighed down by gold. "In the end," Clausewitz wrote, "the force accompanying General Gneisenau in his tireless advance was really nothing more than a fusilier battalion and its indefatigable drummer-boy, who by the general's order had been set upon one of Bonaparte's carriage-horses."

Napoleon himself continued his flight on horseback, the former colossus of Europe scampering away from the battlefield, in the midst of a crowd of his routed soldiers and accompanied by a few aides-de-camp. General Durutte met him at Gosselies, well past Quatre Bras, on the road to Charleroi. Despite his frightful wounds, Durutte was still alive. He had been assisted by a cavalry trooper, who had bound up his wounded arm with a handkerchief and stopped the loss of blood, and then he had come upon one of his staff officers and one of his servants, who had accompanied him as he fled through the fields. Whenever he felt himself fainting, the general summoned his servant, who held him up by his collar and revived him with a swallow of brandy. At Gosselies, Durutte recognized the emperor and tried to present himself to him, wishing to explain that in his present condition he was afraid he would be unable to continue fighting. But Napoleon, "irritated at having been recognized, or absorbed in his own reflections," did not even deign to respond to the general. It was left to one of his aides to exclaim, "Oh, General, look what they've done to you!"

In the last hours before dawn, the crowd of fugitives reached Charleroi, where a single bridge allowed them to cross the River Sambre and reenter France. The few remaining wagons were abandoned in the narrow streets that led down to this bridge. Sacks of flour and rice were scattered everywhere, along with bottles of wine and brandy and hundreds of loaves of bread, which the fleeing soldiers stopped to skewer on their bayonets before continuing on their way. Peyrusse, the official paymaster of the Armée du Nord, reached the banks of the Sambre with a wagon drawn by six horses and containing the emperor's personal treasury, a million francs in gold, only to discover that it was impossible for his vehicle to pass over the bridge. Peyrusse distributed bags of gold coins to the men of his escort, noting down all their names and making them swear to rejoin him on the other side of the river. As this process was going on, shots were fired a short distance away, and someone cried out, "The Prussians! Save yourselves!" In the general panic, Peyrusse's men were scattered, and all the gold was plundered. While the first Prussian uhlans were entering Charleroi, Napoleon's foreign minister, Maret, Duc de Bassano, who was in one of the carriages stuck in the bottleneck, ordered his men to shred all the official documents in his possession and throw the scraps on the muddy road.

In partial contrast to these images of disintegration stands the fact that most of the French combat units managed to maintain a modicum of cohesion and reach safety more or less intact. During the entire pursuit, the Prussians failed to capture even one Eagle, a sign that, at least as far as its regimental standards were concerned, Napoleon's army did not in fact disintegrate. Moreover, the French brought along on their retreat a large number of Allied prisoners, who were not set free until many days or even weeks later. One of them, Lieutenant Wheatley, had to traverse the battlefield at Quatre Bras on the arduous march to France. Naked, unburied corpses were lying everywhere, so thick on the ground that it was impossible not to tread on them in the dark. His boots having been stolen, Wheatley was barefoot, and he later confessed with some embarrassment that walking on dead flesh already trampled into pulp had been a pleasant sensation compared to the torture of the *pavé*.

SIXTY-SEVEN

NIGHT ON THE BATTLEFIELD

On the battlefield, officers and soldiers of the victorious army tried to cook themselves something to eat before they sank into sleep. Some lucky ones had enough alcohol left to celebrate their safe passage through great danger. When the survivors of the Seventy-third assembled for roll call, Private Morris found his old friend, Sergeant Burton, standing before him. Burton gave him a clap on the back and said, "Out with the grog, Tom. Didn't I tell you there was no shot made for you or me?" Captain Walcott of the horse artillery, charged with visiting all the batteries in order to draw up a list of the dead and wounded, spent a large part of the night roaming the battlefield on a weary horse requisitioned from a soldier; at two-thirty in the morning, when he made his report, Walcott was dead tired, but above all he was full of the brandy with which battery commanders and Prussian officers had abundantly refreshed him.

The distribution of any rations whatsoever was out of the question, and everyone had to make do as best he could. Sergeant Lawrence was given the task of turning up some forage for General Sir John Lambert's horse and eventually found a full feed sack that had been abandoned by the French. To his delight, he discovered that the sack contained, along with forage for the horse, a ham and two chickens. Sir John allowed him to keep the food for himself, but he warned Lawrence to keep it well away from the Prussians, "who were a slippery set of men and very likely to steal it if they saw it." Lawrence was in the act of cooking the ham when a crowd of these Prussians passed nearby, and two of them approached him to light their pipes at his fire. The two noticed the ham and casually observed that it looked good. Sergeant Lawrence immediately drew his sword and cut each of them a slice of ham, after which he had the satisfaction of seeing them take their leave without asking for any more. With a full stomach, Lawrence tried to sleep, but he was too worked up and in too much pain to succeed; a shell fragment had flayed his cheek, and the comrade standing directly behind him during the battle had handled his musket badly and scorched the sergeant's face.

Many others did not have enough strength left even to eat, to say nothing of cooking, as was the case with an officer in Picton's division, who fell asleep the very moment after the signal was given to break ranks. When he awoke in the middle of the night, his men were cooking cutlets, using the cuirass of a dead cuirassier as a skillet, and the officer realized he was hungry. He shared in the meal and later remarked that the French breastplates made excellent cooking utensils, but that it was necessary to use those without bullet holes; otherwise, the juices would leak out. Perhaps more wisely, the gunners in Mercer's battery preferred to use cuirasses to sit on. When they found, in a ditch, a piece of meat— tossed there who knew when—they trimmed it with their swords and fried it in a standard-issue frying pan, over a fire made of lance staffs and musket butts; then they gathered a large number of cuirasses around the fire and sat down to eat together.

In conditions such as these, no one felt fastidious. The Fifty-first bivouacked for the night in the orchard at Hougoumont. "This place was full of dead and wounded Frenchmen," Sergeant Wheeler remembered. "I went to the farm house, what a sight. Inside the yard the Guards lay in heaps, many who had been wounded inside or near the building were roasted, some who had endeavoured to crawl out from the fire lay dead with their legs burnt to a cinder." Amid all this horror, a lieutenant of the regiment found a loaf of black bread in the haversack of a dead French soldier; an officer of the Foot Guards, likewise dead, lay beside him, and brain matter had oozed from this man's head, soaking the Frenchman's haversack and, therefore, his loaf of bread as well. The lieutenant cleaned it carefully before consuming it. He had not had a bite to eat since the dawn of the previous day, and he was famished.

Ensign Keowan of the Fourteenth was unable to find his servant, who had gone off in search of plunder. Left alone and obliged to shift for himself, Keowan joined forces with another officer; together, they managed to get their hands on a piece of cooked meat, a former part of some unknown animal, and washed it down with a little bloodstained water: "Such was the wine we drank at our cannibal feast." Then the two prepared a bed of straw, in order that they "should not be taken for dead by plunderers," and lay down to sleep. Even so young an officer as Keowan knew that at that moment the battlefield was filled with soldiers rifling the pockets of the dead—and the wounded, too—and that such men would not hesitate to finish off their defenseless victims in the darkness to put a stop to their complaints. Covering himself with a bloody overcoat taken from the corpse of a French dragoon, Keowan found it hard to fall asleep, as did his comrade, because of "the shrieks of the dying and the agitation of our minds." When sleep finally came, it brought him nothing but visions of the most nerve-racking moments of the fighting.

Staff officers found better accommodation; Lieutenant Jackson, for example, went to dine in the Waterloo inn. The room was full of hungry foreign officers engaged in a lively discussion of the day's events. Fortunately for Jackson, a colleague had reserved a table, and the two sat down to a steaming ragout. "I had not tasted food since early morning," Jackson later recalled, "and before we sat down fancied myself hungry, but not a morsel could I swallow." His fellow officer was in the same condition, but a staff officer in the Netherlands army asked permission to sit at their table and devoured everything by himself, without interrupting for an instant the narrative of his personal impressions of the battle. Overcome by fatigue, Jackson asked for a room; the host offered him the one reserved for Sir William De Lancey, who was then in the hospital. Jackson wearily climbed the stairs, but upon entering the room he was greeted by a groan. Lifting the candle, he saw a French officer lying on the bed, his uniform and boots still on, his head split open by a saber blow, and blood everywhere.

The man told Jackson that he had been taken prisoner early in the battle and asked how it had ended; when he learned of the French defeat, he gnashed his teeth and said that death would be preferable. Then, thinking better of the matter, he went on to say that the French had had their moment of glory, and that it was useless to struggle against destiny. Jackson left him alone, went to the common room, wrapped himself in a blanket, and lay down on the floor. But it was very difficult for him to fall asleep, because the room was still full of foreign officers eating, drinking, and conducting loud discussions. Finally, the lieutenant dozed off and had a terrifying nightmare in which he and the entire British army were running away from the battlefield at breakneck speed, closely pursued by the Imperial Guard, and the wounded French officer threatened him with his saber, accusing Jackson of having lied to him.

Many soldiers had more pressing things to do than sleep. The search for plunder never justified absence without leave, but after such a day, officers were inclined to close one eye. Lieutenant Hay of the Twelfth Light Dragoons sent two of his troopers on patrol and was not surprised when they failed to return, for they were, he said, "two Irish lads, sharp, active, brave soldiers to a fault, but both great scamps and up to any lark, no such words as fear or danger were in their dictionary." When the two later reappeared, they brought with them three French prisoners, whom they had caught in the act of plundering a farm. A fourth Frenchman, a companion of the other three, had fallen to the dragoons' sabers. The indulgent Hay asked no further questions. Some scavengers felt more scruples than others, as is evidenced by the story of a group of troopers from the

Eleventh Light Dragoons. These men had dismounted from their horses in search of booty, and while they walked around among the corpses, their spurs kept catching in the clothing of the dead, sometimes becoming so entangled that they tripped and fell sprawling on the mangled bodies. Their corporal, Farmer, confessed that the experience was horrifying; but there was, he said, nothing to be done: "It would be ridiculous to conceal that when the bloody work of the day is over, the survivor's first wish is to secure, in the shape of plunder, some recompense for the risks which he has run and the exertions he has made."

Only rarely did the plunderers concern themselves with assisting the wounded; on the contrary, there was an excellent chance that these, too, would be robbed, if not worse. A wounded British officer regained consciousness in the dark and found himself unable to move; a dead French soldier was lying on top of him, his face disfigured by a dreadful saber wound. The officer held his breath and tried to make no sound while a Prussian soldier searched another British officer lying, still alive, a short distance away; when this other officer resisted the search, the Prussian stabbed him to death. As the villain was about to turn his attention to the first wounded officer, two British soldiers, a private and a sergeant, appeared on the scene. The wounded officer called to them, and the two helped get him out from under the corpse, stood him on his feet, and gave him a mouthful of brandy. When they started to take their leave, the officer told them that he was afraid the Prussian—who was hiding behind a dead horse—would kill him. The sergeant quickly flushed the Prussian out of his hiding place and cut him down, and the private gave the officer a loaded musket for his protection, saying they could not stay with him because they had left their regiment to do a little plundering and could not run the risk of being discovered. "We fought hard enough to allow us a right to share what no one claims, before the Flemish clowns come here by cock-crow."

The nightmare of scavengers also tormented Sir Frederick Ponsonby, who was still lying immobile in the same place he had been in all afternoon, miraculously alive after two squadrons of Prussian cavalry had passed over him at a trot. When he finally came to his senses during the night, a dying British dragoon, having dragged himself to where Ponsonby lay, was crushing him with his weight and clutching his legs. Seized by convulsions, the dying man held on tight, gasping for breath, and all the while air hissed atrociously through the open wound in his side. The night was clear, and Prussian soldiers, bent on looting, were circulating all around; more than one approached and took a look at Sir Frederick, but they let him alone. Finally, a British straggler passed that way and stopped to keep Ponsonby company, freeing him from the dying man and keeping scavengers at bay with a sword he had picked up off the ground, until morning came and the colonel could be loaded on a cart and carried to the surgeons.

Not even those officers who found plundering immoral risked making themselves unpopular by trying to forbid it; the most they could do was to refuse to buy. An officer in Picton's division wrote, "Plunder was for sale in great quantities, chiefly gold and silver watches, rings, etc., etc. Of the former, I might have bought a dozen for a dollar a piece but I do not think any officer bought . . . probably expecting (as I did) that in a few days our pockets would be rifled of them as quickly as those of the French had been." Like him, many were convinced that the battle they had just fought would be only the first in a long campaign. "About four o'clock, we sat up and conversed. Our minds more and more filled with *what they would say about us at home* than anything else. There was no exaltation! None! We had, many of us, when in the Peninsula, tried the mettle of French soldiers—we concluded the campaign *just begun*, and looked forward to have another desperate fight in a day or two, therefore we determined not to holloa until we got out of the wood."

In fact, the viewpoint of the great majority of combatants was limited; they were unable to appreciate the magnitude of the struggle, and that night hardly anyone had a clear idea of what had taken place. The morning after the battle, Kincaid came across an acquaintance and asked what had gone on with him and his unit the previous day. The man replied, "I'll be hanged if I know anything at all about the matter, for I was all day trodden in the mud and galloped over by every scoundrel who had a horse." He had no other story to tell. Macready, who was an inexperienced youth, actually wondered whether what he had seen could really be considered a battle, or whether it might not be classified by historians as a minor clash. After riding over most of the battlefield, Lieutenant Ingilby reported to his colleagues that he had seen so many dead and wounded, and so many abandoned French guns, that he thought the fight they had won must truly have been a great battle; but the other officers suggested that it would be better not to overstate the matter.

After a few hours of sleep, Sir Hussey Vivian presented himself to Wellington around four in the morning. When Vivian reported that the French had left abandoned guns all over the field, this news surprised the duke. "He told me no Returns he had received had at all amounted to what I had described, and I am quite certain he was not at that time aware of the full extent of his Victory."

SIXTY-EIGHT

——◆——

"A MASS OF DEAD BODIES"

In the first light of dawn, the battlefield at Waterloo presented a frightful spectacle, that could not be shut out by covering one's face or closing one's eyes, because the air was full of even more terrible sounds. Pistol shots of soldiers putting suffering horses out of their misery and hammer blows of blacksmiths removing the dead horses' shoes overlaid the cries of the wounded, who were dying of dehydration and crying out for water in many languages, their bodies already livid and swollen like so many corpses.

However horrid the scene, the first spectators soon began to arrive from Brussels, having come out expressly to see it, but perhaps without imagining what they would find. Captain Mercer saw an elegantly dressed gentleman, top hat and all, climb out of his carriage, pressing a perfumed white handkerchief to his nose. The captain watched this man approach: "[He stepped] carefully to avoid the bodies (at which he cast fearful glances *en passant*), to avoid polluting the glossy silken hose that clothed his nether limbs. Clean and spruce, as if from a bandbox, redolent of perfume, he stood ever and anon applying the 'kerchief to his nose."

Eager to impress this unrepeatable spectacle on their memories, many officers also turned into tourists. Lieutenant Pattison spent the morning wandering over the battlefield, filled with compassion for the fate of the men and especially the horses, both dead and wounded, that were lying everywhere. The body of an enemy artilleryman attracted his attention: "A French gunner, whose back had been placed in an erect position against the wheel of a broken gun-carriage, wore an expression so life-like it required almost minute examination to realize that the vital spark had fled. His shako, which lay at his right side, had fallen from his head, and completely exposed his face. His large blue eyes seemed fixed on *me*, and wore even in death a living expression. His right hand was raised as if under great excitement, and for a second I imagined him to be yet alive, and in the act of enthusiastically exclaiming: '*Vive l'Empereur!*'"

300

But not all the officers moving over the battlefield were impelled there by curiosity. Many regiments sent out patrols to collect their own wounded and bury their dead. Major Harry Smith, the commander of one such squad, had seen many battles, but none so devastating. "At Waterloo the *whole* field from left to right was a mass of dead bodies," Smith wrote. "In one spot, to the right of La Haye Sainte, the French cuirassiers were literally piled on each other." Recalling that the battle had been fought on a Sunday, the major silently recited the Ninety-first Psalm: "A thousand shall fall at thy side, and ten thousand at thy right hand; but it shall not come nigh thee." Not far from the main road, the officers of the Ninety-fifth Rifles had their men dig a common grave and bury their fallen comrades; the green uniforms of their regiment made them easy to identify. All around them were the echoes of isolated shots fired by Prussian patrols finishing off those too gravely wounded to be transported, including their own.

Both armies evacuated the area long before they had completed the task of burying the dead, which required some ten or twelve days in all; the gruesome work was left to the local peasants. The corpses were collected and transported in carts to common graves, great square holes in the earth six feet deep; thirty or forty corpses were haphazardly unloaded into each one. The bodies were completely naked; to the poorest peasants, even a pair of broken shoes or a torn coat seemed valuable. A witness recalled having watched the activity around one such grave: "The followers of the army were stripping the bodies before throwing them into it, whilst some Russian Jews were assisting in the spoliation of the dead by chiseling out their teeth, an operation which they performed with the most brutal indifference. The clinking hammers of these wretches jarred horribly upon my ears, and mingled strangely with the occasional reports of pistols [which] proceeded from the Belgians, who were killing the wounded horses." The carcasses of the horses were gathered and burned, and at least one eyewitness claimed to have seen the same procedure being applied to the bodies of French soldiers.[42]

Captain Mercer was in the courtyard at Hougoumont on the morning of June 19, and his account left no doubt about the treatment given to the bodies of the dead, and particularly to those of the defeated. In the midst of the swollen and blackened corpses of the men who had burned to death in the fire, local peasants and German soldiers were busying themselves, paying no attention at all to any survivors, although "amongst this heap of ruins and misery many poor devils yet remained alive, and were sitting up endeavouring to bandage their wounds." Mercer was speaking with a German dragoon when two of the local peasants, "after rifling the pockets, &c., of a dead Frenchman, seized his body by the shoulders, and, raising it from the ground, dashed it down again with all their force, uttering the grossest abuse, and kicking it about the head and face—

revolting spectacle!—doing this, no doubt, to court favor with us. It had a contrary effect, which they soon learned. I had scarcely uttered an exclamation of disgust, when the dragoon's sabre was flashing over the miscreants' heads, and in a moment descended on their backs and shoulders with such vigour that they roared again, and were but too happy to make their escape."

The wounded suffered tragically. During the night, many had been trampled by maddened horses running wildly over the battlefield, kicking out at whatever they encountered, or crushed by artillery wagons. Lieutenant Ingilby was certain that only the French artillery could be so inhuman as to pass over the bodies of the wounded, but his account nevertheless suggested that the danger was omnipresent: "In traversing the field, following the flight of the French, it was hardly possible to clear with the Guns the bodies of both Armies which strewed the ground, and afterwards late at night when dispatched to bring up some artillery wagons, it was with difficulty we could avoid crushing many of the wounded in the road near La Haye Sainte, that had crawled there in hopes of more ready assistance. There were some in whom life was not yet extinct that we supposed the French Artillery had crushed by passing over in their retreat." Even the next day, those who were incapable of moving were not safe; Tomkinson used the flat of his sword to drive off a Belgian peasant whom he surprised tugging off the boots of a still-living British soldier.

Even when the wounded were not abandoned on the battlefield, their fate was not to be envied. Private Hechel, wounded in the stomach during the fight for Smohain, was carried by his comrades to a medical station; but the surgeon, after barely looking at him, refused to take him under his care: "Drop him over there, he won't last two hours." Before his companions left him, Hechel gave them his watch, which had cost him thirty francs. "Had I thought about it," he later wrote, "I would also have given them the five thalers I had sown in the lining of my coat two years before, when I had to leave my dear homeland, and which I had not touched since." The room where Hechel was lying together with many other wounded men was next to a stable, where many full milk jugs were standing. The wounded men were suffering badly from thirst, but the peasant had no desire to waste his milk on them. At last, he carried in a big cooking pot filled with water and left it in the middle of the room. Hechel drank so much he made himself sick, and water began to flow from his wound. He remained there for three days, without care or nourishment, while most of the other sufferers around him died off, one by one. Finally, the few survivors called on God, praying that he would put an end to their torments. "But the Lord says, 'My thoughts are not your thoughts.'" At the end of the third day, the survivors were loaded onto a cart and taken to a hospital in Brussels, enduring terrible suffering as the cart jolted along the cobblestone road.

The hospital, where the wounded from the Battle of Quatre Bras had already been taken a few days previously, had by then become one of the circles of hell.

Sergeant Costello of the Ninety-fifth Rifles met a German boy there, a lad not yet twenty years old, who had been recruited as an artillery driver. He had lost both his legs to a cannonball; as he lay on the ground, a cuirassier had broken one of his arms with a saber blow, and a stray bullet had wounded him in the other arm. In the hospital, the surgeons had been forced to amputate both his arms, one above the elbow, and the other below. "The unfortunate youth," Costello wrote, "lay a branchless trunk, and up to the moment I left, though numbers died from lesser wounds, survived." Hospital admission did not do much to improve a wounded man's chances of survival; many died from peritonitis, gangrene, and loss of blood, aggravated by the bleedings which, together with amputations, formed the principal care the surgeons provided. Statistics show that the wounded kept on dying for months, right through the end of 1816, and that in the end the number of dead had risen by at least 50 percent over the number calculated the day after the battle.

SIXTY-NINE

---·◆·---

LETTERS HOME

The losses of the victorious army had been so fearful that, in those first hours of relative calm, many officers could think of nothing else. Kincaid remarked, "The usual salutation on meeting an acquaintance of another regiment after an action was to ask who had been hit, but on this occasion it was 'Who's alive?'" Shortly before midnight, Sir Augustus Frazer wrote his wife one of the long letters she had grown accustomed to receiving. "How shall I describe the scenes through which I have passed since morning? I am now so tired that I can hardly hold my pen. We have gained a glorious victory, and against Napoleon himself. Never was there a more bloody affair, never so hot a fire. . . . I have escaped very well. Maxwell's horse, on which I rode at first, received a ball in the neck, and I was afterwards rolled over by a round of case shot, which wounded my mare in several places, a ball grazing my right arm, just above the elbow, but without the slightest pain; and I now write without any inconvenience. I buried my friend Ramsay, from whose body I took the portrait of his wife, which he always carried next his heart. Not a man assisted at the funeral who did not shed tears. Hardly had I cut from his head the hair which I enclose, and laid his yet warm body in the grave, when our convulsive sobs were stifled by the necessity of returning to the struggle. . . . So many wounded, that I dare not enumerate their names. Bolton of ours is killed, so is young Spearman. What a strange letter is this, what a strange day has occasioned it! To-day is Sunday!"

Many other officers wrote home to give assurances that they were still alive, and to narrate what they had done. On the morning of the nineteenth, Captain Taylor of the Tenth Hussars led the regiment's horses to graze in a field of clover and then entered a nearby farmhouse, which he found "full of Officers writing to England." In many of these letters, even though they were meant to be reassuring, one finds the same anguished tone, the same distress over the army's terrible losses, that color Frazer's words to his wife. Wray of the Fortieth Regiment, unable to write an account of his experiences, could only give a casualty list: "Poor Major Heyland (who commanded) was shot through the heart, and poor Ford was shot through the spine of his back but did not die for a short time after he was carried away. Poor Clarke lost his left arm, and I am much afraid Browne will lose his leg, he is shot through the upper part of the thigh and the bone terribly shattered. There are eight more of our officers wounded, but all doing well except little Thornhill, who was wounded through the head. Anthony got his eighth wound and is doing well." Kelly, of the First Life Guards, wrote to his wife, addressing her as "My dearest dear love," to inform her that he was alive, though wounded, but there was nothing triumphant about the tone of his letter: "All my fine Troopers knocked to pieces . . ."

Other letters were written in a much different tone. Before finally going to sleep, Blücher wrote to his wife: "Together with my friend Wellington, I have brought Napoleon's dance to an end. His army is completely routed, and the entirety of his artillery, caissons, baggage, and equipage is in my hands. I have just been brought the insignia of all the different decorations he had won, found in a box in his carriage. Yesterday I had two horses killed under me. Soon it will be all over with Bonaparte." At two o'clock in the morning, the Prince of Orange wrote a letter in French to his parents, the king and queen of the Netherlands: "*Victoire! Victoire! Mes très chers parents*, we have had a magnificent affair against Napoleon today. It was my corps which principally gave battle and to which we owe the victory, but the affair was entirely decided by the attack which the Prussians made on the enemy's right. I am wounded by a ball in the left shoulder, but only slightly. *À vie et à mort tout à vous, Guillaume.*"

Among the British officers, paradoxically, the youngest and most frivolous, those least inclined to reflect upon the tragedy of their losses, seem to have first grasped the full significance of the events they had just lived through. Thirty-year-old Sir William Gomm, a lieutenant colonel in the Coldstream Guards and assistant quartermaster to Picton's division, wrote a letter to reassure his sister. He told her of the two bruises he had suffered, which were of little importance, and of his two wounded horses, which were very important indeed. He went on: "I am so hoarse at hurrahing all yesterday, that I can scarcely articulate. I have been four days without washing face or hands, but am in hourly expectation of my lavender water." But underneath his dandy's pose is his certainty of having witnessed a historic day, comparable only to Marlborough's great victories against the armies of Louis XIV: "We have done nothing like it since Blenheim."

Ensign Howard of the Thirty-third was also aware of the importance of what had happened, but the memory of the dangers he had passed dampened his enthusiasm. "Thank God I am safe," he wrote to his brother. "I had a very narrow escape that day, a bullet passed through my cap and must have been within the eighth of an inch of my head. I intend bringing the cap to England. I can scarcely fancy myself alive and writing to you after what I have seen. We may almost say England conquered France in one battle."

SEVENTY

"I NEVER WISH TO SEE ANOTHER BATTLE"

After the battle, Wellington returned to the village of Waterloo, to the same inn where he had passed the preceding night. When the duke dismounted and gave his faithful charger, Copenhagen, a firm pat on the croup, the horse kicked out, almost scoring a direct hit on his master. As had happened to Wellington on other occasions, the excitement of the battle suddenly drained away and left him in a state of exhaustion so profound as to border on depression, intensified this time by the terrible losses he knew his army had suffered, including men from among the circle of his closest collaborators.[43] Before sitting down to eat, Wellington went to see Sir Alexander Gordon, perhaps the most intimate of the friends who had accompanied him to Belgium, and whose leg had been amputated a few hours before. The duke told him the news of the victory and assured him that he was going to be all right, but Gordon did not reply. Since there were no free beds in the inn, Wellington gave orders to carry Sir Alexander up to his bed and then went down to dine.

The table was set exactly as it had been the previous evening, with a place for each of his aides; but there was only one who was able to sit down with him. This was General Don Miguel de Alava, the envoy of the king of Spain, who had been attached to Wellington's staff for years and was a perfectly integrated part of it. The duke ate little and in silence. Whenever someone entered, Wellington turned toward the door, hoping to be able to add a name to the list of those who were still alive. He drank one toast during the entire dinner, lifting a glass with Alava to the memory of the war in Spain. This behavior was in stark contrast to the numerous, enthusiastic toasts that always concluded a British dinner, particularly in such triumphant circumstances as these appeared to be. Before going to bed,

307

the duke spread out his arms and spoke a sentence that was destined to be repeated ad infinitum, by others as well as himself: "The hand of Almighty God has been upon me this day." Then he wrapped himself in his coat and lay down on a camp bed that had been hastily prepared for him.

After sleeping for perhaps two hours, he was awakened because the quartermaster general, the officer responsible for the provisioning and lodging of the troops, needed orders; since the duke was already awake, his personal physician, Dr. Hume, gave him the news that Sir Alexander Gordon had died. Hume next read aloud the casualty list that he had managed to put together thus far, and at a certain point in his reading, he realized that the duke, incredibly, was weeping. Wellington brusquely dried his tears with his hand, and the doctor saw that his face was soiled with sweat and dust; he had not yet had time to wash. Then the duke uttered another of the statements that would become part of his lasting fame: "Well, thank God, I don't know what it is to lose a battle; but certainly nothing can be more painful than to gain one with the loss of so many of one's friends."

There was too much work for Wellington to go back to sleep. Having washed and shaved, he sat down to write the official dispatch in which he announced his victory to the government. In the June 22 issue of the *London Times*, this dispatch occupied four columns, and it certainly must have taken him several hours to write, especially considering the continual interruptions. It is a precise, dispassionate account, in the duke's style, which some found admirable for its understatement and others judged unbearably cold. As was necessary in a document of this kind, Wellington made sure to mention all those officers who had distinguished themselves in combat. The duke was a politician, and he may have gone too far in parceling out his citations, reserving perhaps too respectful an eye for influential generals well introduced at court and important foreign representatives, while forgetting to mention, for example, Sir John Colborne; in any case, the publication of the official dispatch aroused, in some quarters, long-lasting resentment. (The duke himself, many years later, when asked if there were anything in his life which he regretted and could have done better, replied, "Yes, I should have given more praise.")

At dawn, carrying the dispatch he intended to post, the duke got back on his horse and left for Brussels, from where he could communicate more rapidly with England. After having sealed the official dispatch—which was immediately sent to London, together with the two Eagles captured during the battle—Wellington spent a large part of the day writing private letters, which give clear evidence of the emotional shock that had been so carefully masked in the dispatch for the government. One of the first letters, dated at eight-thirty in the morning, was for Lady Frances Webster. "My loss is immense. Lord Uxbridge, Lord FitzRoy

Somerset, General Cooke, General Barnes, and Colonel Berkeley are wounded: Colonel De Lancey, Canning, Gordon, General Picton killed. The finger of Providence was upon me, and I escaped unhurt." The deaths of his friends removed all triumphalism from his feeling of having been protected by Providence; on the contrary, they transformed that feeling into something resembling a sense of guilt. He wrote to Viscount Gordon of Aberdeen to inform him of the death of his brother, Sir Alexander Gordon: "I cannot express to you the regret and sorrow with which I look round me, and contemplate the loss which I have sustained, particularly in your brother. The glory resulting from such actions, so dearly bought, is no consolation to me." To the Duke of Beaufort, informing him that his brother, Lord Fitzroy Somerset, had lost an arm, Wellington wrote, "The losses I have sustained, have quite broken me down; and I have no feeling for the advantages we have acquired."

A certain rhetoric of grief informs these sorrowful letters, and not everything Wellington wrote can be taken literally; but there can be no doubt that he was in a state of deep distress. In the most sincere letter of all, written to his brother William, another theme emerged, one destined to surface again and again: the awareness that his great victory had been within a hair of turning into a catastrophe. "It was the most desperate business I ever was in. I never took so much trouble about any Battle, & never was so near being beat. Our loss is immense particularly in that best of all Instruments, British Infantry, I never saw the Infantry behave so well."[44] Recognizing the English member of Parliament, Mr. Creevey, among the crowd gathered under the windows of his inn, the duke invited him upstairs and said the same things to him, although this time colored by a tinge of personal satisfaction. "It has been a damned serious business," the duke declared. "It has been a damned nice thing—the nearest run thing you ever saw in your life. By God! I don't think it would have done if I had not been there."

The knowledge that he had been extremely close to losing the battle remained alive in the duke for some time, before the triumphant welcome he received in England began to blur that aspect of his memory. One month after the battle, one of his trusted retainers, Thomas Sydenham, who had not been at Waterloo but joined the duke in Paris a short time afterward, wrote a letter to his brother, recounting his long talks with the "Padrone," as they called him, about that memorable day. The duke continued to hold a low opinion of Bonaparte as a general and persisted in describing him by means of unflattering pugilistic metaphors: "He said that he always thought him a great glutton, fighting very hard to carry a particular point, but showing no recourse if his main attack failed." And nevertheless, Sydenham continued, "I observed that in talking about the Battle of Waterloo he invariable [sic] mentioned it with some expression of horror, such as, 'it was a tremendous affair,' 'it was a terrible battle,' or, 'it was a dreadful day,' holding up his arms above his head and shaking his hands. He repeatedly said he never had taken so much pains about a battle, that no battle had ever cost him so much terrible anxiety." Among the young officers of Wellington's staff, whose admiration for the great man was tempered by a touch of irreverence, it was no secret that the Padrone had come close to defeat in the Battle of Waterloo. After talking with some of them, Captain Jackson reported them "all agreeing that the Duke had never before been so severely pressed; or had so much difficulty to maintain his position."

By the time Wellington had a conversation with Lady Shelley a few weeks later, the horror of warfare had taken on a new form in his mind: "I hope to God that I have fought my last battle. It is a bad thing to be always fighting." Even on that first night, at the bedside of Sir William De Lancey—who seemed likely to survive his injuries but instead died a few days later—the duke had said that "he never wished to see another battle; this had been so shocking. It had been too much to see such brave men, so equally matched, cutting each other to pieces as they did." Lord Fitzroy Somerset, who was present, repeated to others what the duke had said, and Wellington's words circulated among the officers, winning the approval of many. Some reported the remarks to Sir Augustus Frazer; the duke, they told him, had declared that he had never seen such a battle and hoped never to see another one. Frazer thought there was only one fitting comment: "To this hope we will all say: Amen."

EPILOGUE

On Waterloo Day, nearly 200,000 men confronted one another on a scrap of land barely four kilometers (2.5 miles) square; never, either before or after, have such a great number of soldiers been massed on so circumscribed a battlefield. (By way of comparison: More than 250,000 men of Paulus's Sixth Army were surrounded and trapped by the Soviets at Stalingrad at the end of 1942, but the trap had a diameter more than thirty-five miles long.) It is natural to ask how many of the men gathered to fight at Waterloo died there, but limited statistics prevent a certain answer to that question. The most reliable data for Wellington's army list its losses as 3,500 dead, 3,300 missing, and 10,200 wounded, a shocking one-quarter of his troops. Of the missing British soldiers, a good half of them later returned to their regiments, while the others were officially declared dead. But until someone examines, regiment by regiment, all the data preserved in the Public Record Office, it will be impossible to establish the number of wounded soldiers who did not survive their injuries, although by comparing existing samples we can propose an estimate of between 1,000 and 2,000.

The Prussian losses, according to the available statistics, amounted to 1,200 dead, 1,400 missing, and 4,400 wounded, but no data have been published concerning the number of missing who returned or the number of wounded who died of their wounds, and no such data will likely be published in the future, given the destruction of the Prussian military archives during the bombardments of the Second World War. As for the French, their losses are impossible to calculate, because no one thought about bringing the regimental rolls up to date in the days immediately following the catastrophe. On June 22, at Laon, when the great flight of the French army finally came to an end, Soult, d'Erlon, and Reille succeeded in gathering 30,000 troops who were still disciplined and capable of combat, together with around fifty guns. Some 40,000 men, therefore, were missing, but how many of them had died in battle, how many had been wounded or taken prisoner, and how many had simply gone home is unknowable. Nevertheless, in the years immediately following Waterloo, the French press estimated the emperor's losses at 24,000–26,000 men, including 6,000–7,000 prisoners, and these figures seem not at all unlikely—in addition to which another 15,000 men, a third of the survivors, deserted the ranks at the end of the battle and in the following days, broken by their army's defeat and the pitiless Prussian pursuit.

Many historians propose a higher number for the French dead and wounded, arguing that the losses suffered by the defeated army at Waterloo must have been decisively superior to those of its adversaries; however, the only available data, which relate to the officers, would lead one to question this argument. During the Battle of Waterloo, a total of 207 French officers died or went missing, and another 66 died later as a consequence of their wounds. The statistics for the Allied armies are more numerous and sometimes contradictory, partly because they cover several armies that were, administratively speaking, completely distinct from one another; collating them, we find that a minimum of 218 officers were dead or missing from Wellington's army and 61 from that of the Prussians. With rare exceptions, the wounded men who died after the battle do not seem to have been included in these totals, nor have any reliable data on the subject been published, except in regard to the British army. Consequently, if these are excluded, at Waterloo on June 18, during the day, statistics suggest that 207 French officers died or went missing, as opposed to a total of 279 for their adversaries. Therefore, based on traditional ratios of officers to enlisted men, it seems legitimate to wonder whether the losses suffered by Napoleon's army in the course of the battle might even have been inferior to those of his enemy.

In short, contrary to general belief, the Armée du Nord was not entirely destroyed at Waterloo; but its will to resist had been broken forever. "The men are disappearing in all directions at the first opportunity," Soult wrote to the emperor four days after the battle. "The cavalry show more discipline and is in better shape. The infantry is totally demoralized, and the men are saying the most incredible things." By that time, the emperor was no longer with the army.

Three days after the battle, Napoleon was back in Paris, trying to galvanize the country and put together a parliamentary majority in order to continue the fight. His army, or what was left of it, retreated for some days to the interior of France, where its generals discovered that fewer than half of those who had been mustered at Waterloo were still in the ranks. The Prussians were hard on their heels, while Wellington's army followed in a much more leisurely way. On June 22 Napoleon, finding himself politically isolated and facing a rebellious Chamber and despondent Marshals, abdicated; on June 29 he left Paris, after a provisional government had refused his offer to take command of the army and to lead the war against the invaders as General Bonaparte. He planned to sail to America, but British ships blocked the French ports, and on July 15, after some days of frantic negotiations, he embarked on HMS *Bellerophon*, believing she would take him to an honorable retirement in England. Instead he was taken to his life confinement on the tiny volcanic island of St. Helena, lost in the southern Atlantic some 1,250 miles from the coast of Africa, and more than 600 miles from the nearest island: the place farthest from any other place on Earth. Here he would die, probably of cancer, six years later.

As Napoleon left Paris, some units of the French army, resenting the brutality of the Prussian invasion, had put up a stiff resistance on the outskirts of Paris and Versailles; but theirs was a lost cause. On July 3, the French provisional government capitulated, and the following day the Allies entered Paris. On July 8, King Louis XVIII returned to his palace at the Tuileries, less than four months after he had hurriedly left it.

Although everyone recognized its momentous importance, determining how to designate the battle that had taken place on June 18 took a little time. Tradition has it that Blücher, struck by the prophetic nature of the name La Belle Alliance, proposed it that very evening as the name of the battle. The Prussians tried hard for a long time to accredit this appellation: One of the most important public squares in Berlin was rechristened "Belle-Alliance-Platz" (now Mehringplatz), and until the First World War German historians usually invoked the "*Schlacht bei Belle-Alliance.*" The French, at least in the beginning, were uncertain. During the battle, Marshal Soult dated his one o'clock dispatch to Grouchy "*Du champ de bataille de Waterloo,*" but sometime afterward, Colonel Combes-Brassard was still calling it the "*bataille de Soignies,*" and the publications that appeared in Paris in the years immediately following the great event mostly referred to it as "*la journée de Mont-Saint-Jean.*" But Wellington preferred to use the name of the village of Waterloo, from which he dated his victory dispatch, and which had the advantage of being decidedly more pronounceable for an English tongue. British hegemony in Europe and in the world, which Waterloo itself had confirmed, caused this to become in the end the accepted name for the battle.

And thus the Battle of Waterloo entered into history, and into legend. For every generation in Europe from 1815 to the First World War, the struggle at Waterloo was the decisive turning point that had changed world history. For many, the battle marked the opening of a period of astonishing peace, prosperity, and progress; Lieutenant Pattison, for example, writing his memoirs in 1868 as a souvenir for his grandchildren, spoke of the Waterloo campaign as having "dethroned Napoleon, and secured an uninterrupted peace for more than forty years. During all the interval we have been reaping the fruits of it." For others, less satisfied to live in a world dominated by British commerce and guarded by

His Majesty's gunboats, the name Waterloo had a sinister ring; to Victor Hugo, it was the "*morne plaine*," the "dismal plain," where the Eagle had wound up in the mud and the generous dream of the greatest man who ever lived had been shattered. Most, however, would have agreed with the French writer's statement: "On that day, the perspective of the human race was altered. Waterloo is the hinge of the Nineteenth Century."

Later, the twentieth century swept away the illusions of unlimited progress and perpetual peace that had become widespread after Waterloo. The great celebrations planned for the hundredth anniversary of the battle in 1915 had to be canceled with Europe inflamed by the First World War. Since then, other men have stepped before the footlights of history, men capable of climbing up out of nothing and plunging back into it headlong, spilling much more blood along the way than Napoleon ever did. At the same time, modern historical scholarship, with its ever-increasing attention to the workings of underlying causes, to economic conditions, to structural factors, and to the long term, has accustomed us to the belief that no single event, no matter how memorable, can reverse the evolution of human history.

If I had to write one of those amusements called "What-ifs" and imagine what would have happened had Napoleon won the Battle of Waterloo, I would be tempted to propose a different history only for the years immediately following 1815. Liberal ideas would have been less marginalized and persecuted than was actually the case during the time of the Holy Alliance (1815–23), and there probably would have been no revolution in France in 1830. But after this date, the differences reduce themselves to simple details, such as a different political career for the Duke of Wellington. The economic, and therefore political, hegemony of Great Britain would have been imposed on the world all the same; a half century after the battle, Prussia would still have pushed its candidacy for the leadership of a united Germany; and in France, sooner or later, no matter what, Napoleon III would have mounted the throne. One might further suppose that the history of the world after approximately 1850 would have been perfectly identical with the one we know today.

But these are the musings of a historian, who has the luxury of the long view and can make decades fly past his fingertips. For the men who fought on the battlefield at Waterloo, and for the majority of their contemporaries, life would have been altered had the battle ended differently. At the time, everyone in western Europe who heard the news and comprehended its significance felt intense emotion, which they were not long in attributing to a powerful symbolic force. Once great events are incised so deeply in the collective memory, they take on a life of their own, despite the changes wrought by time; this is the reason that today, nearly two centuries later, and without even knowing exactly why, we all continue to be fascinated by the name Waterloo.

NOTES

1 Apparently, conversations between Prussian officers and British officers were held in French, the international language of the time, even though it was the enemy's language, too.

2 This observation should put an end once and for all to debates about the importance of the Prussian contribution to Napoleon's defeat. (As for the emperor himself, he never had the least doubt in the matter. "Ah! He ought to light a fine candle to old Blücher," he said, speaking of Wellington one day on St. Helena. "Without him, I don't know where *His Grace*, as they call him, would be; but as for me, I certainly wouldn't be here."

3 They were not mistaken: A few weeks later, the regimental commander and one of his captains were killed at Waterloo, and shortly thereafter, four of the junior officers had their promotions.

4 Lady Frances's father.

5 French infantry regiments were known as *Régiments d'infanterie de ligne* (often shortened to *Régiments de ligne*), or "line regiments." The regiment in question, for example, was the *85ème de ligne*.

6 Sir Andrew was a man who liked to live well. He went to war accompanied by his French chef, a prisoner taken at Salamanca, and was capable of downing three bottles of wine at dinner. He was, moreover, one of the most popular officers in the army.

7 The regiments of the Prussian *Landwehr* were designated by an ordinal number and the name of the province where the unit was recruited—in this case, the electorate (*Kurmark*) of Brandenburg.

8 In fact, not even Waterloo served to change the emperor's opinion of his adversary, though the defeat made it rather awkward for Napoleon to express that opinion aloud, and he preferred to speak of Wellington as little as possible. As Las Cases noted on St. Helena, "I've noticed that the emperor is generally loath to mention Lord W . . ." But when coaxed into discussing the duke, Napoleon abused him mightily.

9 By a dynastic fluke the army of the Netherlands comprised—in addition to around 4,000 Belgians and 9,000 Dutch—a little more than 4,000 men recruited inside Nassau, so that Wellington's army contained, all told, some 30,000 Germans.

10 This, at least, was Napoleon's assertion; according to Carl von Clausewitz, however, the division "was unequivocally forgotten."

11 The British manual included instructions for the skirmisher, should he find himself in such a situation, but they weren't very reassuring; the principal piece of advice was to play dead.

12 Twenty-nine years old, he would be condemned by a Bourbon tribunal for high treason and shot by a firing squad outside of Paris exactly two months later.

13 As noted, Gneisenau had little faith in Wellington, and the Prussian chief of staff had written to Müffling again that morning: "I beg you to discover with the utmost certainty whether the Duke really intends to give battle in his present position or whether he is simply making a demonstration, which could cause our army great harm."

14 All three of these officers were British, which was the case with more than a few of the KGL's junior officers after the heavy losses it suffered in Spain.

15 But Captain Blaze, a French veteran who had seen it all, assures us that in Napoleon's army, "When it's time for troops to advance, everyone from the commander in chief to the corporal uses the same formula: '*Sacré nom de Dieu, en avant, en avant sacré nom de Dieu!*' They never say anything more eloquent than that.")

16 This is one of the possible versions; according to another, Napoleon said, "Stop all that bowing, we're not at the Tuileries!"

17 In an attempt to regain his lost honor, the ex-colonel purchased a commission as an ensign in an infantry regiment, restarting his career from scratch and rising to the rank of captain. But good society never forgave him, and Portarlington sank into alcoholism, dissipated his entire inheritance, and died penniless in a London slum.

18 This was the episode that Victor Hugo was later to interpret in his own fashion in a famous passage of *Les Misérables*.

19 The news of his death cast the British sporting world into mourning. Sir Walter Scott, who was one of Shaw's fans, had his body transferred to England; a plaster cast of Shaw's skull was displayed in the Windsor Museum.

20 In this case, too, the nature of the ground rendered impossible the headlong gallop dear to printmakers.

21 The only Italian officer in Wellington's army, Prince Ruffo di Castelcicala, fought with the Inniskillings and many years later became the ambassador of the Kingdom of the Two Sicilies in London.

22 And perhaps also by memories of the dead boys; there were three very young officers with the rank of cornet in the Grays, and all three were killed at Waterloo.

23 Not coincidentally, the number of lance-armed regiments increased in all armies during the course of the nineteenth century; by the eve of the First World War, all European cavalry, including cuirassiers, were issued lances.

24 Sporting slang for a boxer not afraid of a slugfest and willing to take a beating rather than give up.

25 A short time later, the boy took a ball in the throat and lay unconscious until night, when the stretcher bearers gathered him up and brought him to a hospital; against all expectations, he survived, and some years later the Prince of Saxe-Weimar encountered him, recognized him, and gave him a decoration.

26 All eyewitness statements regarding the time of day are unreliable, and it was surely much later.

27 In this description, the ensign finds no fault with the sergeant's behavior, but he nonetheless feels the need to justify it. Later, when the men were on their feet again, a shell passed close above their heads, and many instinctively ducked. The regimental commander, Sir John Colborne, cried out, "For shame! For shame! That must be the Second Battalion, I am sure." This Battalion was made up of recruits.

28 On the march from Wavre, the men had torn off their collars because of the heat, an episode that earned the regiment the privilege of wearing pink collars after the Battle of Waterloo.

29 This dialect name for the steel-producing city of Birmingham was slang for *bayonet*.

30 Curiously, Ryssel himself was a native of Saxony, and he had made his career in the Saxon army, an ally of Napoleon; in 1813, before suddenly finding himself a Prussian subject, he had received the Legion of Honor.

31 There should have been fourteen, but one of them, the 1/1st Chasseurs, had been left behind at Le Caillou farm with the imperial baggage and treasury.

32 In 1844, Sergeant Cotton, who made his living as a tourist guide to the Waterloo battlefield, met this French officer, who confirmed that he had indeed deserted, because he was a thorough monarchist; according to Cotton, he belonged to the Second Carabiniers à Cheval. Although speaking from hearsay, Captain Duthilt also states that "this infamous criminal" was a captain in the mounted carabineers.

33 In the Imperial Guard every battalion was commanded by a brigadier general.

34 In spite of everything he would have a long career in military service and lead an entire English army to annihilation in Afghanistan thirty years later.

35 Only once had his courage found a limit: At the assault on the fortress of Ciudad Rodrigo in 1812, a ball entered his right shoulder and lodged in the bone, in a spot that the surgeons were apparently unable to reach; some months later, when the wound began to suppurate, an operation nevertheless became imperative. "The pain he suffered in the extraction of the ball was more even than his iron heart could bear," Smith recalled. "He used to lay his watch on the table and allow the surgeons five minutes' exertions at a time, and they were three or four days before they wrenched the ball from its ossified bed."

36 Ney was mistaken in only one particular: Six months later, a Bourbon tribunal had him shot. D'Erlon, too, was condemned to death, but he escaped abroad and lived long enough to become governor of Algeria and a marshal of France under Louis-Philippe.

37 So much so that there was a great deal of ironic waggery in military circles about how Sir Hussey Vivian won the Battle of Waterloo.

38 For many years, Blair remained persuaded that this man was a French officer in the service of Louis XVIII and never got over his amazement at recalling that in such an hour Wellington's only companion had been a Frenchman; but in fact he was the Conte di Sales, an envoy of the king of Sardinia.

39 In later years, Barton, somewhat embarrassed, let a voluble French officer convince him that the grenadiers à cheval had not been engaged at any point in the battle and that therefore it had been a good idea not to come to blows with them; but it's instructive to compare Barton's account with Captain Mercer's, which gives the impression that the grenadiers had been practically annihilated while charging his battery.

40 Amazingly, the general escaped capture, reached Paris alive—after undergoing the amputation of his right hand along the way—and lived for another twelve years.

41 Shortly after the battle, the splendid blue-and-gold imperial coach, with its bright red wheels and bulletproof glass, was acquired by a British entrepreneur, and soon it was being exhibited to the public in London, where for the price of a few shillings any curious person could experience the emotion of sitting inside it.

42 A print published in London in 1817 shows peasants engaged in stacking wood under a heap of naked bodies in the courtyard at Hougoumont.

43 A month later, he explained to Lady Shelley, "While in the thick of it, I am too occupied to feel anything; but it is wretched just after. It is impossible to think of glory. Both mind and feelings are exhausted."

44 Later, on St. Helena, Napoleon remarked, "I certainly made him spend un mauvais quart d'heure [a bad quarter of an hour]."

BIBLIOGRAPHY

The bibliography for the Napoleonic period is notoriously immense and practically impossible to master. For general orientation, one can begin with D. D. Horward, *Napoleonic Military History: A Bibliography* (New York and London, 1986) and J. Tulard, *Nouvelle bibliographie critique des mémoires sur l'époque napoléonienne* (Geneva, 1991); but now works of this type have been conveniently replaced by references found on the Internet (see Web sites below). The primary and secondary sources hereinafter cited are only those that are most useful for reconstructing the Battle of Waterloo, with particular emphasis on those that have been chiefly utilized in the present book.

PRIMARY SOURCES

British Sources

By far the most valuable collection of British eyewitness accounts of the battle is H. T. Siborne, ed., *Waterloo Letters* (London, 1891), to which should be added the letters originally excluded by Siborne and recently published by G. Glover, ed., *Letters from the Battle of Waterloo* (London and Mechanicsburg, Penn., 2004).

Wellington's official correspondence is published in *The Despatches of Field Marshal the Duke of Wellington*, ed. J. Gurwood, 13 vols. (London, 1837–39) and *Supplementary Despatches and Memoranda of Field Marshal Arthur Duke of Wellington*, ed. A. R. Wellesley, 15 vols. (London, 1858–72).

Enormous numbers of memoirs, letters, and combat diaries were published in the course of the nineteenth century. Many of these works have recently been reprinted, especially by Ken Trotman at Cambridge, even though they are indicated in the following list with their original publication date. Most of these accounts were written by officers; the most important of these are the following, listed in alphabetical order by author:

Letters of Colonel Sir Augustus Frazer. Ed. E. Sabine. London, 1859.
Letters and Journals of Field-Marshal Sir William Maynard Gomm, GCB. London, 1881.
The Reminiscences and Recollections of Captain Gronow. London, 1862.
Hay, W. *Reminiscences under Wellington, 1808-1815.* London, 1901.
Hope Pattison, F. *Personal Recollections of the Waterloo Campaign.* Glasgow, 1870.

BIBLIOGRAPHY

Jackson, B. *Notes and Reminiscences of a Staff Officer.* London, 1903.
Kincaid, J. *Adventures in the Rifle Brigade.* London, 1830.
Leach, J. *Rough Sketches of the Life of an Old Soldier.* London, 1831.
Leeke, W. *History of Lord Seaton's Regiment at the Battle of Waterloo.* London, 1866.
Macready, E. N. In *Colburn's United Service Magazine*, vol.1 (1845),
    pp. 388–404, and vol.2 (1852), pp. 518–30.
Mercer, A. C. *Journal of the Waterloo Campaign.* London, 1870.
The Autobiography of Sir Harry Smith, 1787-1819. London, 1910.
Letters of Captain Thomas William Taylor. Tetbury, 1895.
Tomkinson, W. *The Diary of a Cavalry Officer.* London, 1895.
The Reminiscences of William Verner. (1782–1871), Ed. R. W. Verner. London, 1965.
The Wheatley Diary, Ed. C. Hibbert. London, 1964.

Another fundamental source is the anonymous account titled "Operation of the Fifth or Picton's Division in the Campaign of Waterloo," published in the *United Service Journal*, June 1841; the author, usually referred to simply as an officer in Picton's division, belonged to Pack's brigade, and internal analysis makes it a certainty that he was a junior officer in the 3/1st (Royals).

Eyewitness accounts written by enlisted men are rarer and therefore particularly interesting. For Waterloo, the most relevant of these are the following:

Anton, J. *Retrospect of a Military Life.* Edinburgh, 1841.
Clay, M. In *The Household Brigade Magazine*, 1958.
Costello, E. *Adventures of a Soldier.* London, 1841.
Farmer G. and Gleig G. *The Light Dragoon.* London, 1844.
The Autobiography of Sergeant William Lawrence. London, 1886.
Morris, T. *Recollections of Military Service.* London, 1845.
Journal of Sergeant D. Robertson, Late 92nd Foot. Perth, 1842.
The Letters of Private Wheeler, Ed. B. H. Liddell Hart. London, 1951.

Similarly irreplaceable are accounts that have come down to us from civilians who were closely acquainted with the Duke of Wellington; of particular use are *The Creevey Papers*, ed. L. Gore (London, 1963) and the letters of Thomas Sydenham to his brother Ben in *The Waterloo Papers: 1815 and Beyond*, ed. E. Owen (Tavistock, 1997).

Allied Sources
Waterloo memoirs written by German, Dutch, and Belgian authors were not as numerous as those produced by their British allies, and the same can be said of letters and official reports. The destruction of archives during the Second World

319

War further diminished the available material. Much of it has been published only in part, generally in historical studies specifically dedicated to the contribution of the Allied armies. From this point of view, the following works are particularly valuable: N. L. Beamish, *History of the King's German Legion* (London, 1837); D. C. Boulger, *The Belgians at Waterloo, with Translations of the Reports of the Dutch and Belgian Commanders* (London, 1900); J. von Pflugk-Harttung, *Belle-Alliance* (Berlin, 1915); and F. Schirmer, *Nec aspera terrent. Geschichte der Hannoverschen Armee 1617–1866* (Leipzig, 1937).

Equally rich in firsthand sources, some of them never previously used, are two works by P. Hofschröer—*1815, the Waterloo Campaign: Wellington, His German Allies and the Battle of Quatre Bras* (London, 1998) and *1815, the Waterloo Campaign: The German Victory: From Waterloo to the Fall of Napoleon* (London, 1999)—as well as the series, still in progress, edited by B. Coppens and P. Courcelle, *Waterloo 1815. Les Carnets de la Campagne* (Brussels, 1999–).

Among the individually published eyewitness accounts, I found the following especially useful:

Baring, G. von. In the *Hannoversches militärisches Journal*, 1831. English translation in Beamish, N. L., *History of the King's German Legion*, Vol. 2, Appendix 21. London, 1837.

Müffling, F. C. von. *Aus meinem Leben*. Berlin, 1851, translated into English as *Memoirs of Baron von Müffling*. London, 1997.

Reiche, L. von. *Memoiren*, ed. L. von Weltzien. Leipzig, 1857.

Scheltens, C. *Souvenirs d'un vieux soldat belge*. Brussels, 1880.

Scriba, von. *Das leichte Bataillon der Bremen-Verdenschen Legion in den Jahren 1813–20*. Hameln, 1849.

Thurn und Taxis, A. von. *Aus drei Feldzügen, 1812 bis 1815*. Leipzig, 1912.

French Sources

The official documentation on Napoleon at Waterloo is available in *La Correspondance de l'Empereur Napoléon 1er*, vols. 28–31 (Paris, 1868-70); orders and official dispatches can be found in (G. Le Doulcet de Pontécoulant), *Napoléon à Waterloo, ou Précis rectifié de la campagne de 1815* (Paris, 1866). Napoleon's own, highly subjective view emerges in his *Mémoires pour servir à l'histoire de France en 1815* (Paris, 1820), as well as in the transcriptions of his conversations that were made while he was in exile on the island of St. Helena: E. de Las Cases, *Mémorial de Sainte-Hélène* (Paris, 1823), and G. Gourgaud, *Sainte-Hélène. Journal inédit de 1815 à 1818* (Paris, 1899).

Many of the best French memoirs were written by military men who were not present at the Battle of Waterloo. We nevertheless cite these texts, as they are invaluable for their insiders' portrayal of Napoleon's army: E. Blaze, *La Vie militaire sous le premier empire* (Paris, 1837), translated into English as *Military Life under Napoleon: The Memoirs of Captain Elzéar Blaze* (Chicago, 1995); *Les Cahiers du capitaine Cognet* (Auxerre 1851–53), translated into English as *The Note-Books of Captain Cognet* (London, 1897); and *Souvenirs du Capitaine Parquin, 1803-1814* (Paris, 1892).

Some interesting texts come from the pens of soldiers who participated in the Waterloo campaign and in the battles of Ligny and Wavre but were not at Waterloo itself: E. F. Berthezène, *Souvenirs militaires* (Paris, 1855); *Journal du général Fantin des Odoards. Etapes d'un officier de la Grande Armée, 1800-1830* (Paris, 1895); and *Journal du Capitaine François, 1792-1830*, ed. C. Groleau (Paris, 1903-4). Naturally, this category also includes the *Mémoires du Maréchal Grouchy* (Paris, 1873).

Although not as abundant as British sources, French eyewitness accounts of the Battle of Waterloo are nonetheless fairly numerous, but it should be pointed out that these texts are rarely as detailed and impassioned as those of their adversaries. We can cite at least the following, in alphabetical order:

Mémoires du général Bro, 1796–1844. Paris, 2001.

Drouet, Le Maréchal, comte d'Erlon. *Vie militaire écrite par lui-même*. Paris, 1844.

Mémoires du capitaine Duthilt. Ed. C. Levi. Lille, 1909.

Fleury de Chaboulon. *Les Cent Jours*. London, 1820.

Larréguy de Civrieux. *Souvenirs d'un cadet*. Paris, 1912.

Lemonnier-Delafosse. *Souvenirs historiques*. Le Havre, 1849.

Levavasseur, O. *Souvenirs militaires*. Paris, 1914.

Marbot, M. de. *Mémoires*. Ed. Koch. Paris, 1891.

Mémoires de Marchand. Ed. J. Bourguignon. Paris, 1952.

H. de Mauduit, *Les Derniers Jours de la Grande Armée*. Paris, 1847.

Petiet, A. *Souvenirs militaires*. Paris, 1844.

Mémoires du Général Radet. Ed. A. Combier. Paris, 1892.

Trefcon. *Carnet de campagne*. Paris, 1914.

Certain accounts of particular importance, published in the nineteenth century in various places and difficult to track down, have recently appeared in two small volumes published by Teissèdre. These accounts are those of Colonels Brack and Heymès in *Waterloo, Récits de combatants* (Paris, 1999), and, especially, those of General Desales, Colonel Combes-Brassard, and Chef de bataillon Jolyet in *Souvenirs et correspondance sur la bataille de Waterloo* (Paris, 2000).

SECONDARY SOURCES

The Waterloo historiographical industry went into operation the day after the battle. Among the very earliest works, those that are still of some interest today include C. Kelly, *A Full and Circumstantial Account of the Memorable Battle of Waterloo* (London, 1817); J. Booth, *The Battle of Waterloo, also of Ligny and Quatre-Bras* (London, 1817); A. Gore, *An Historical Account of the Battle of Waterloo* (Brussels, 1817); C. von Plotho, *Der Krieg des verbündeten Europa gegen Frankreich im Jahre 1815* (Berlin, 1818); G. Gourgaud, *Campagne de 1815* (Paris, 1818); J. Berton, *Précis historique* (Paris, 1818); Fayolle, *Journée de Mont-Saint-Jean* (Paris, 1818); R. Batty, *An Historical Sketch of the Campaign of 1815* (London, 1820).

Certain works published somewhat later—posthumously, in a few cases—and based on eyewitness accounts reworked and reconsidered in tranquillity are deserving of even greater interest: C. von Clausewitz, *Der Feldzug von 1815 in Frankreich* (Berlin, 1835); C. von Damitz, *Geschichte des Feldzuges von 1815 in den Niederlanden und Frankreich* (Berlin, 1837–38); H. de Mauduit, *Les Derniers Jours de la Grande Armée* (Paris, 1847); E. Cotton, *A Voice from Waterloo: A History of the Battle Fought on the 18th June 1815, with a Selection from the Wellington Dispatches, General Orders and Letters Relating to the Battle* (Mont-St.-Jean, 1852); and (G. Le Doulcet de Pontecoulant), *Napoléon à Waterloo, ou Précis rectifié de la campagne de 1815* (Paris, 1866).

In the course of the nineteenth century, the major national historiographical communities produced elaborate versions of the story of Waterloo that were meant to be considered definitive, and in some sense all of them actually were; monumental and meticulously detailed, these works remain indispensable today. For British historiography, the fundamental reference point is the work of W. Siborne, first published as *History of the War in France and Belgium in 1815* (London, 1844) and then in definitive form as *History of the Waterloo Campaign* (London, 1848). Siborne dominated the field for well over half a century, and his primacy of place continued even after the publication of the important works of C. Chesney (*Waterloo Lectures*, London, 1907) and A. F. Becke (*Napoleon and Waterloo*, London, 1914).

Among French studies, the work of J. B. A. Charras, *Histoire de la Campagne de 1815* (Brussels, 1858), was later superseded by that of H. Houssaye, *1815. Waterloo* (Paris, 1903), which is still of seminal importance today. German historiography, which was then in the period of its greatest flourishing, produced three fundamental works: K. von Ollech, *Geschichte des Feldzuges von 1815 nach archivalischen Quellen* (Berlin, 1876); O. von Lettow-Vorbeck, *Napoleons Untergang 1815* (Berlin, 1904); and J. von Pflugk-Harttung, *Belle-Alliance* (Berlin, 1915). Two equally fundamental studies of the campaign from the perspective of the Netherlands are D. C. Boulger, *The Belgians at Waterloo* (London, 1901) and F. de Bas and J. de T'Serclaes de Wommersson, *La Campagne de 1815 aux Pays-Bas* (Brussels, 1908).

For a long time, these masterworks overshadowed twentieth-century scholarship on the Battle of Waterloo. After an interval extending from World War I through World War II, a period when interest in the battle was at a low point, the production of books on Waterloo increased steadily; but these were, for the most part, syntheses tailored for a popular audience, often heavily illustrated, excellently legible, but not particularly innovative in structure or interpretation. The best-known titles are J. Weller, *Wellington at Waterloo* (London, 1967); D. Howarth, *Waterloo: A Near Run Thing* (London, 1968); H. Lachouque, *Waterloo 1815* (Paris, 1972); N. Vels Heijn, *Glorie zonder helden. De slag bij Waterloo, waarheid en legende* (Amsterdam, 1974); *Waterloo—Battle of Three Armies*, edited by Lord Chalfont (London, 1979); D. Chandler, *Waterloo: The Hundred Days* (London, 1980); J. Logie, *Waterloo, l'évitable défaite* (Paris, 1989): and A. A. Nofi, *The Waterloo Campaign: June 1815* (London, 1993).

For easily conceivable reasons, Waterloo generally occupies a greater space in biographies of Wellington than it is granted in biographies of Napoleon. One biography of the duke includes a reconstruction of the Battle of Waterloo that makes it particularly worthy of mention: E. Longford, *Wellington: The Years of the Sword* (London, 1971).

For an analysis of the forces in the field, see S. Bowden, *Armies at Waterloo: A Detailed Analysis of the Armies that Fought History's Greatest Battle* (Arlington, Tex., 1983), to which should be added the small monographs issued by Osprey Publishing in its Men-at Arms series and especially valuable for the smaller armies. See, in particular, O. von Pivka and B. Fosten, *Brunswick Troops, 1809–1815* (Men-at-Arms, 167, Botley, 1985); M. Chappell, *The King's German Legion, (2) 1812–1816* (Men-at-Arms, 339, Botley, 2000); R. Pawly and P. Courcelle, *Wellington's Belgian Allies, 1815* (Men-at-Arms, 355, Botley, 2000); and R. Pawly and P. Courcelle, *Wellington's Dutch Allies, 1815* (Men-at-Arms, 371, Botley, 2000).

The most important innovation in the historiography of the second half of the twentieth century was the growing attention paid to history as seen from below, the effort to produce a narrative of the battle entirely based on eyewitness accounts of men in the front lines and focused on their experiences. The most spectacular results in this area are certainly those of J. Keegan, *The Face of Battle: A Study of Agincourt, Waterloo and the Somme* (London, 1976) and P. J. Haythornthwaite, *Waterloo Men: The Experience of Battle, 16–18 June 1815* (Marlborough, 1999). A further similarity of these two studies is their limitation to exclusively British sources.

In recent years, historical works on the Battle of Waterloo have taken a significant turn. This can be seen primarily in the publication of some deliberately polemical studies. Designed to overturn the orthodox interpretation of the battle, they have given rise to a heated debate. This is the case with D. Hamilton-Williams, *Waterloo: New Perspectives* (London, 1993), which is perhaps too drastic in denouncing the "politically correct" vision imposed on the battle by Siborne in the nineteenth century; although often unreliable in detail, Hamilton-Williams's study is nevertheless important and refreshing. This category also includes two works by P. Hofschröer, studies that emphasize the role of the German armies at Waterloo with ample recourse to sources hitherto little used: *1815, the Waterloo Campaign: Wellington, His German Allies and the Battle of Quatre Bras* (London, 1998) and *1815, the Waterloo Campaign: The German Victory: From Waterloo to the Fall of Napoleon* (London, 1999).

Among French historical studies, special mention must go to the heavily illustrated volumes, or rather albums, by B. Coppens and P. Courcelle (who have now been joined by other collaborators) in the series titled *Waterloo 1815. Les Carnets de la Campagne* (Brussels, 1999–). Six of these albums have appeared so far, each with its own title but related to the others by a shared, innovative formula that offers abundant, uniformly presented tables, a vast collection of eyewitness statements, rare images from the period, and original points of view concerning individual aspects of the battle.

In recent years, two works have appeared that, though differing in dimensions, must be considered fundamental for reference and statistical data; one is M. Adkin, *The Waterloo Companion* (London, 2001), with an excellent series of maps, and, in French, a treatment that is not limited only to the Waterloo campaign, namely A. Pigeard, *Les Campagnes napoléoniennes* (Entremont-le-Vieux, 1998). But in regard to the British army, the information contained in C. Dalton, *The Waterloo Roll Call* (London, 1890), remains indispensable.

Web Sites

When I typed the word *Waterloo* into the Google search engine on September 5, 2004, I was offered a total of around 3.65 million choices. The referenced sites included Waterloo University in Ontario, the town of Waterloo, Illinois, the Waterloo/Cedar Falls (Iowa) *Courier*, and so forth. More prudently, I typed in the combination *Waterloo Napoleon Wellington*, which reduced the total to 31,500 sites, of which 26,200 were in English. Still too many. Whatever your reason for seeking information about Waterloo, the best idea is to go through one of the big portals: www.napoleonseries.org, www.napoleonguide.com, www.napoleonic-literature.com, and www.napoleonicsociety.com. If you're not looking for anything specific, a pleasant way of spending your time is the Waterloo game at www.pbs.org/empires/napoleon.

INDEX

Acte additionel, 96
Adam, General, 213, 258, 259, 272, 273;
  his brigade, 184, 196, 214, 219, 258,
  262, 272, 279, 280, 287, 288; final
  defense of Hougoumont, 227, 228, 229;
  wounded, 260
aftermath of battle, 296–303; burials, 301;
  casualty figures, 311–12; plunder,
  296–9; political, 312–14; treatment of
  wounded, 302–3
Afghanistan, 317
Agincourt, Battle of, 37
Alava, don Miguel de, 307
Albuera, Battle of, 273
Algeria, 317
Ali the Mameluke, 250
Alten, Karl von (Sir Charles Alten), 33,
  63, 64, 114, 172, 233, 253; wounded,
  240, 257
ambulances, 291
America, 24, 172, 313; Revolutionary War,
  135, 158; see also North America
amputations, 303
Ancona, 96
Anderson, Sergeant, 158
Angelet, Major, 271
Angluches, 23
Angoulême, Duc d', 243–4
Antibes, 1, 285
Antwerp, 41, 43, 44
Arentschildt, General, 64, 191
Armée du Nord, 3, 101, 294, 312;
  ideological purity, 96
artillery, 60–1, 74, 85, 90; accuracy, 100–1,
  128; ammunition, 90, 99–100; batteries,
  99–100; duels, 92, 97, 103, 128, 172;
  howitzers, 90; "le brutal", 101;

psychology, 101–2; rates of fire, 102,
  128; see also Grande Batterie
August, Prince, of Thurn and Taxis, 199,
  201
Aulard, Baron, 119, 131; his brigade, 117,
  118, 122, 125, 126, 134, 148, 149;
  death, 132
Austerlitz, Battle of, 20, 60, 62
Austria, 2

Bachelu, General, 38, 227, 259
baggage, 41, 291; Napoleon's, 250, 287
bagpipers, 151
Baker rifles, 131, 179, 189, 227, 236, 272;
  accuracy and rate of fire, 81, 115, 117;
  ammunition, 230–1
Balaklava, Battle of, 164
Ballam, Sergeant Major, 237
Baring, Major von, 115, 122, 179, 183;
  horse wounded, 118; his troops, 115,
  117, 120, 179–80, 182; comments on
  French cavalry, 187; final defense of La
  Haye Sainte and retreat, 230–1, 232,
  256; falls from horse, 256–7
Barnard, Sir Andrew, 54, 116, 126, 131
Barnes, General, 309
Barnes, Sir Edward, 174–5
Barton, Captain, 281, 317
Bauduin, General, 86, 89, 91, 95
Bayonne, 232
Beaufort, Duke of, 309
Belcher, Lieutenant, 132
Belgian army, see Dutch–Belgian army
Belgian–French border, 3, 7, 12, 152
Belgium, 2, 3, 9, 12, 32, 43, 142
Beresford, Lord, 189
Berezina, Battle of, 168